Editor
DIANA SCHUTZ

Designer
AMY ARENDTS

DH Maverick Art Director
CARY GRAZZINI

Publisher
MIKE RICHARDSON

This volume collects issues 39-45
of the Dark Horse comic-book series *Usagi Yojimbo Volume Three*.

Visit the Usagi Dojo web site
www.usagiyojimbo.com

Published by
Dark Horse Comics, Inc.
10956 SE Main Street
Milwaukie, Oregon 97222

First edition: February 2002
ISBN 1-56971-660-9

Limited hardcover edition: February 2002
ISBN 1-56971-661-7

1 3 5 7 9 10 8 6 4 2
Printed in Canada

USAGI YOJIMBO™

─ GRASSCUTTER II ─
JOURNEY TO ATSUTA SHRINE

Created, Written, and Illustrated by
STAN SAKAI

Introduction by
GREG RUCKA

Usagi Yojimbo

Introduction

THERE'S A MARK TWAIN LINE that I'm fond of paraphrasing, one of those well-burnished pearls o' wisdom that I drop whenever someone comes to me and asks for advice in writing.

"I never use 'policeman' for a dime when I can get 'cop' for a nickel."

When pressed, I explain that — at least to me — Twain's talking about efficiency and economy, talking about the need of the artist to get out of the way of his or her work. He's cautioning against self-indulgence, something that every artist in every medium must guard against. The worst thing a storyteller can do is believe that he is more important than the story being told.

But I've said it so often, it's starting to sound a little hollow, even to me.

Then I pick up some of Stan Sakai's work, I read a tale of Usagi and Gen, and the truth of it comes back — the essence of storytelling, and perhaps even the essence of capital-A Art, is honesty. The resonance of the image, the power of the story, the emotional connection the audience makes with the work, all of it lives or dies on the basis of its honesty. Set your story in the far-flung reaches of the universe with great quantum-drive battle cruisers, set it in a superheroic nihilistic future, hell, set it in feudal Japan with your cast portrayed as anthropomorphized rhinos and rabbits — it doesn't matter as long as the story is fundamentally *honest*.

Because there are things we all share. We've all been cold, we've all been hungry. We've all been betrayed, if not all of us on a grand scale. We've all loved.

We've all lost.

The best storyteller can hold those truths in one hand, and conjure the tale in the other. The best storyteller can mesh them seamlessly, creating a connection with his audience that at once is both fantastic and absolutely real. In the ideal, a tale is told that resonates long after the last word is read, the last image viewed.

Stan Sakai ... Stan Sakai not only does this, but he does it consistently, issue after issue, executing with elegance and economy the epic of *Usagi Yojimbo*. This collection is Sakai at his best — not a word out of place, not a brush stroke laid in error.

Disguised as an adventure story of the most elementary kind — what can be more basic than a chase, after all? — *Grasscutter II* is so much more. From the foreshadowing prologue to the haunting first epilogue, Sakai teases out themes in word and image that first propel the narrative, then move the heart. His language, both in text and image, is succinct, deft, and ever-precise.

Nothing in these pages is wasted.

In an age of self-indulgence, where more and more comics and their creators are enamored of flash and image, Stan Sakai never stands in the way of his own work. When we as a profession seem to be moving both forward and back all at the same time, that may be the highest praise anyone can offer.

Enjoy your journey to Atsuta.

Abayo!

GREG RUCKA
PORTLAND, OREGON
DECEMBER, 2001

Contents

FOR MY GOOD FRIENDS LINDA AND JACK BELL
AND MY "OTHER SON" MICHAEL TAYLOR.

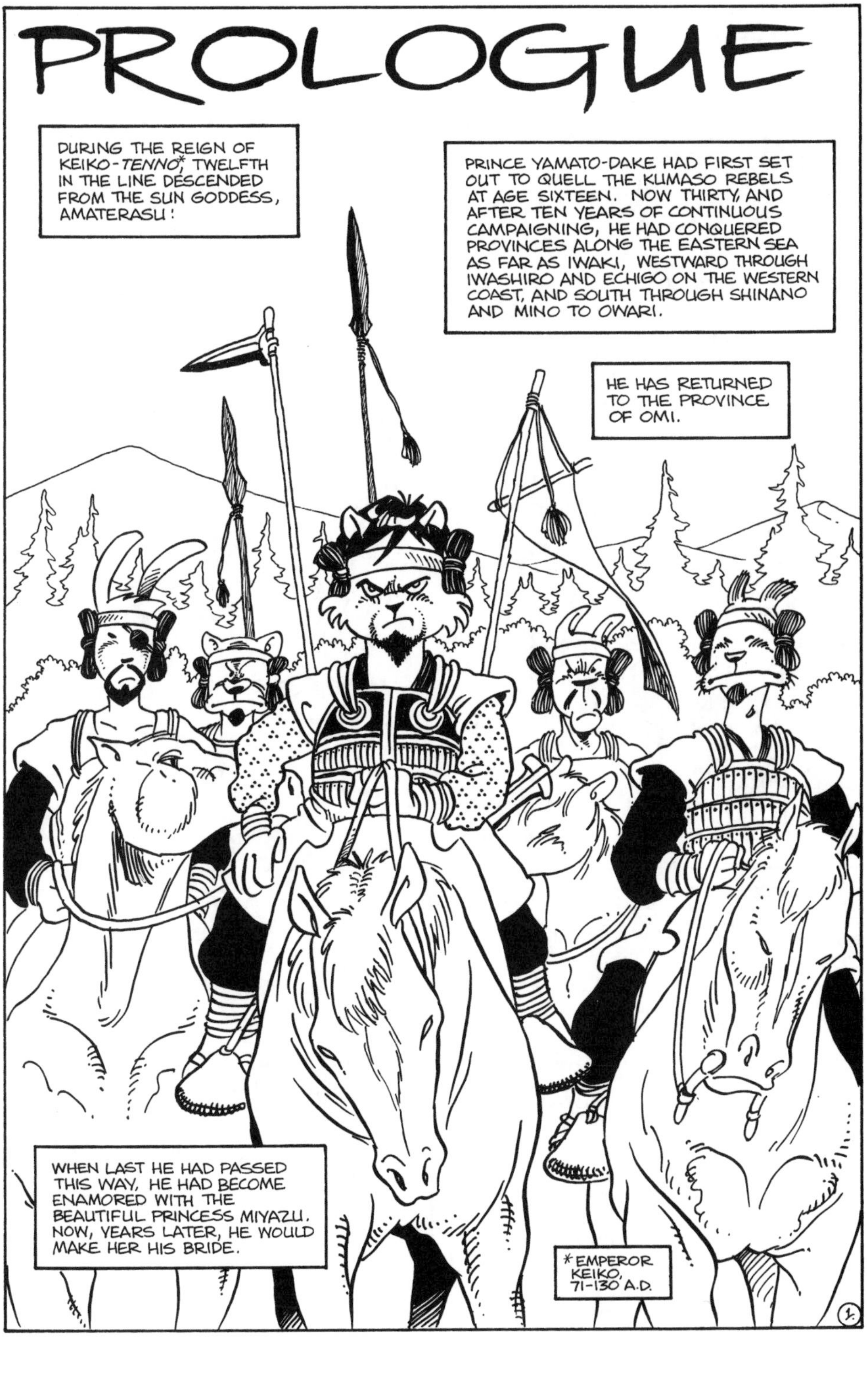
PROLOGUE
DURING THE REIGN OF KEIKO-*TENNO*,* TWELFTH IN THE LINE DESCENDED FROM THE SUN GODDESS, AMATERASU:
PRINCE YAMATO-DAKE HAD FIRST SET OUT TO QUELL THE KUMASO REBELS AT AGE SIXTEEN. NOW THIRTY, AND AFTER TEN YEARS OF CONTINUOUS CAMPAIGNING, HE HAD CONQUERED PROVINCES ALONG THE EASTERN SEA AS FAR AS IWAKI, WESTWARD THROUGH IWASHIRO AND ECHIGO ON THE WESTERN COAST, AND SOUTH THROUGH SHINANO AND MINO TO OWARI.
HE HAS RETURNED TO THE PROVINCE OF OMI.
WHEN LAST HE HAD PASSED THIS WAY, HE HAD BECOME ENAMORED WITH THE BEAUTIFUL PRINCESS MIYAZU. NOW, YEARS LATER, HE WOULD MAKE HER HIS BRIDE.
*EMPEROR KEIKO, 71-130 A.D.
1

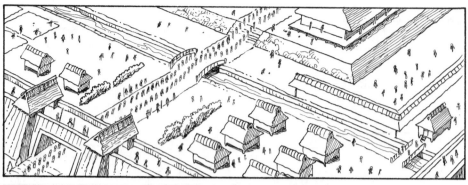

HA HA HA HA!

AND THE BRIDE SAID, "NO, NOT ON MY WEDDING NIGHT!"

HA HA!

THE GROOM ASKED, "WHEN?"

"THE TIME IS NEVER RIGHT!"

YOU HAVE MADE ME THE HAPPIEST OF WOMEN, MY LORD. I PLEDGE TO YOU MY FATHER'S KINGDOM.

THANK YOU, MY LOVE. I MUST GIVE YOU A WEDDING GIFT AS WELL.

IT IS UNNECESSARY TO FAVOR ME OVER YOUR OTHER CONSORTS, MY LORD.

8

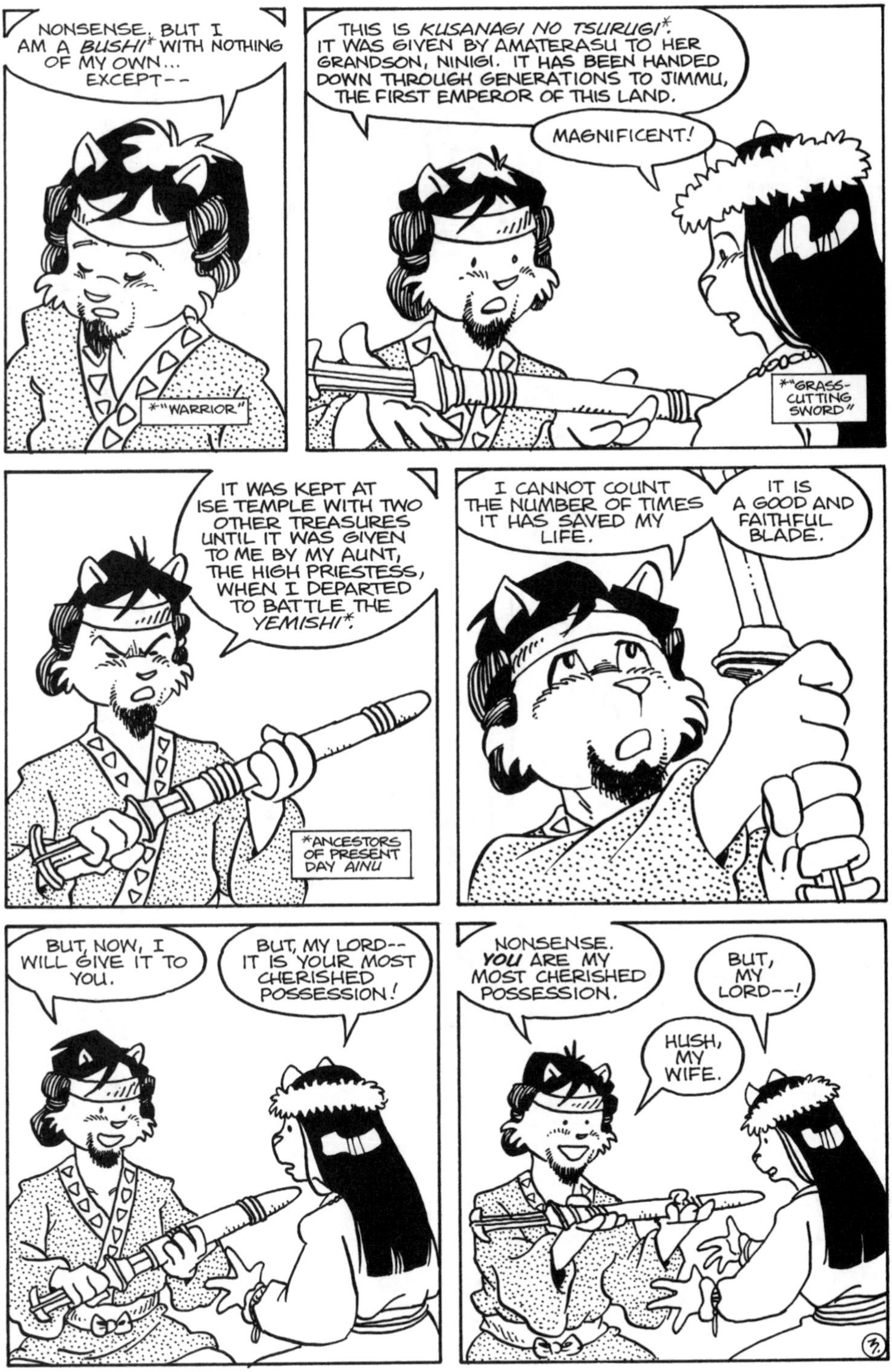
NONSENSE. BUT I AM A *BUSHI** WITH NOTHING OF MY OWN... EXCEPT--
*"WARRIOR"
THIS IS *KUSANAGI NO TSURUGI**. IT WAS GIVEN BY AMATERASU TO HER GRANDSON, NINIGI. IT HAS BEEN HANDED DOWN THROUGH GENERATIONS TO JIMMU, THE FIRST EMPEROR OF THIS LAND.
MAGNIFICENT!
*"GRASS-CUTTING SWORD"
IT WAS KEPT AT ISE TEMPLE WITH TWO OTHER TREASURES UNTIL IT WAS GIVEN TO ME BY MY AUNT, THE HIGH PRIESTESS, WHEN I DEPARTED TO BATTLE THE *YEMISHI**.
*ANCESTORS OF PRESENT DAY *AINU*
I CANNOT COUNT THE NUMBER OF TIMES IT HAS SAVED MY LIFE.
IT IS A GOOD AND FAITHFUL BLADE.
BUT, NOW, I WILL GIVE IT TO YOU.
BUT, MY LORD-- IT IS YOUR MOST CHERISHED POSSESSION!
NONSENSE. ***YOU*** ARE MY MOST CHERISHED POSSESSION.
BUT, MY LORD--!
HUSH, MY WIFE.
3.

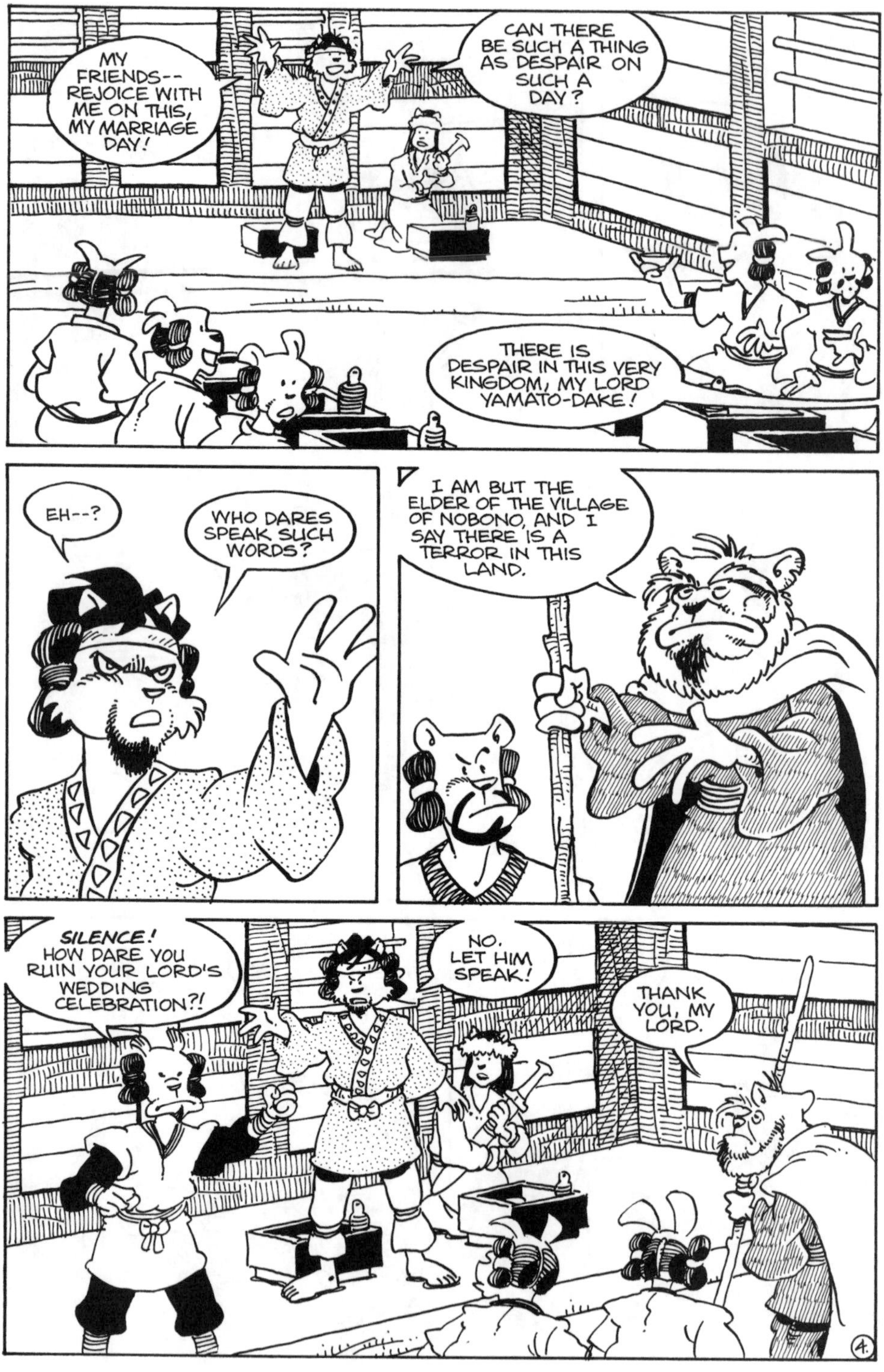
MY FRIENDS-- REJOICE WITH ME ON THIS, MY MARRIAGE DAY!
CAN THERE BE SUCH A THING AS DESPAIR ON SUCH A DAY?
THERE IS DESPAIR IN THIS VERY KINGDOM, MY LORD YAMATO-DAKE!
EH--?
WHO DARES SPEAK SUCH WORDS?
I AM BUT THE ELDER OF THE VILLAGE OF NOBONO, AND I SAY THERE IS A TERROR IN THIS LAND.
SILENCE! HOW DARE YOU RUIN YOUR LORD'S WEDDING CELEBRATION?!
NO. LET HIM SPEAK!
THANK YOU, MY LORD.
4.

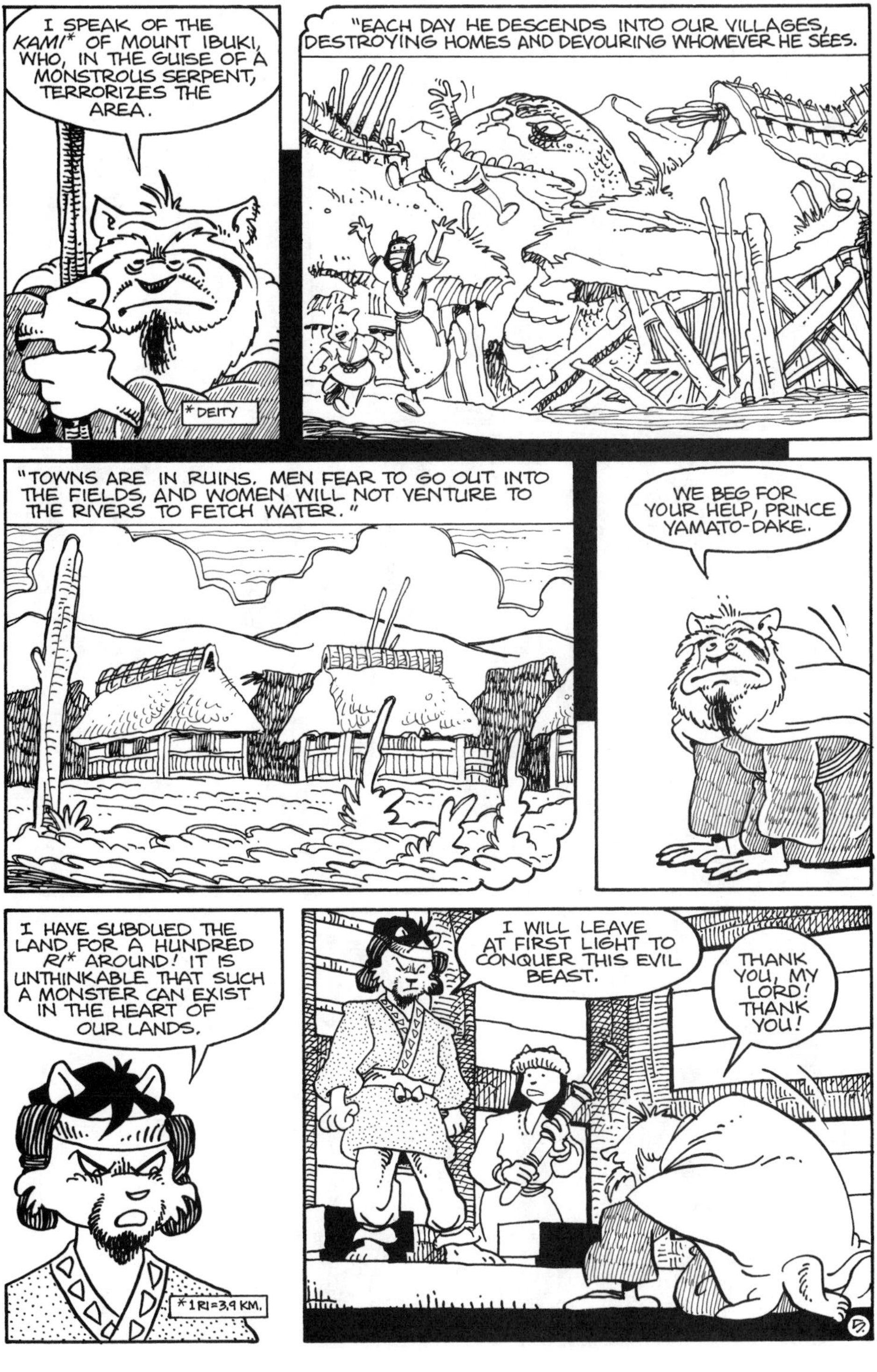
I SPEAK OF THE KAMI* OF MOUNT IBUKI, WHO, IN THE GUISE OF A MONSTROUS SERPENT, TERRORIZES THE AREA.
*DEITY
"EACH DAY HE DESCENDS INTO OUR VILLAGES, DESTROYING HOMES AND DEVOURING WHOMEVER HE SEES.
"TOWNS ARE IN RUINS. MEN FEAR TO GO OUT INTO THE FIELDS, AND WOMEN WILL NOT VENTURE TO THE RIVERS TO FETCH WATER."
WE BEG FOR YOUR HELP, PRINCE YAMATO-DAKE.
I HAVE SUBDUED THE LAND FOR A HUNDRED RI* AROUND! IT IS UNTHINKABLE THAT SUCH A MONSTER CAN EXIST IN THE HEART OF OUR LANDS.
*1 RI=3,9 KM.
I WILL LEAVE AT FIRST LIGHT TO CONQUER THIS EVIL BEAST.
THANK YOU, MY LORD! THANK YOU!

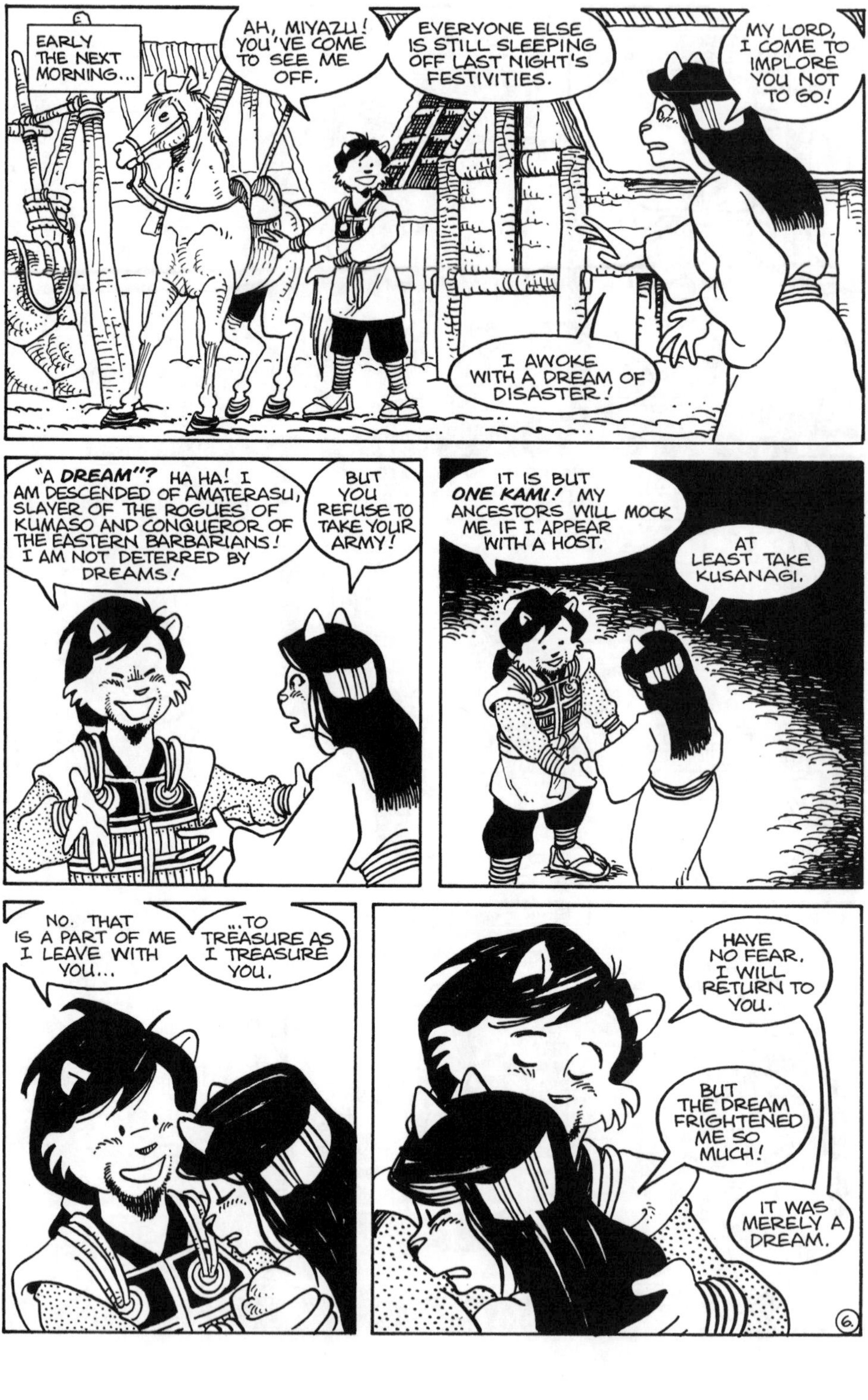
EARLY THE NEXT MORNING...
AH, MIYAZU! YOU'VE COME TO SEE ME OFF.
EVERYONE ELSE IS STILL SLEEPING OFF LAST NIGHT'S FESTIVITIES.
MY LORD, I COME TO IMPLORE YOU NOT TO GO!
I AWOKE WITH A DREAM OF DISASTER!
"A DREAM"? HA HA! I AM DESCENDED OF AMATERASU, SLAYER OF THE ROGUES OF KUMASO AND CONQUEROR OF THE EASTERN BARBARIANS! I AM NOT DETERRED BY DREAMS!
BUT YOU REFUSE TO TAKE YOUR ARMY!
IT IS BUT ONE KAMI! MY ANCESTORS WILL MOCK ME IF I APPEAR WITH A HOST.
AT LEAST TAKE KUSANAGI.
NO. THAT IS A PART OF ME I LEAVE WITH YOU...
...TO TREASURE AS I TREASURE YOU.
HAVE NO FEAR. I WILL RETURN TO YOU.
BUT THE DREAM FRIGHTENED ME SO MUCH!
IT WAS MERELY A DREAM.
6.

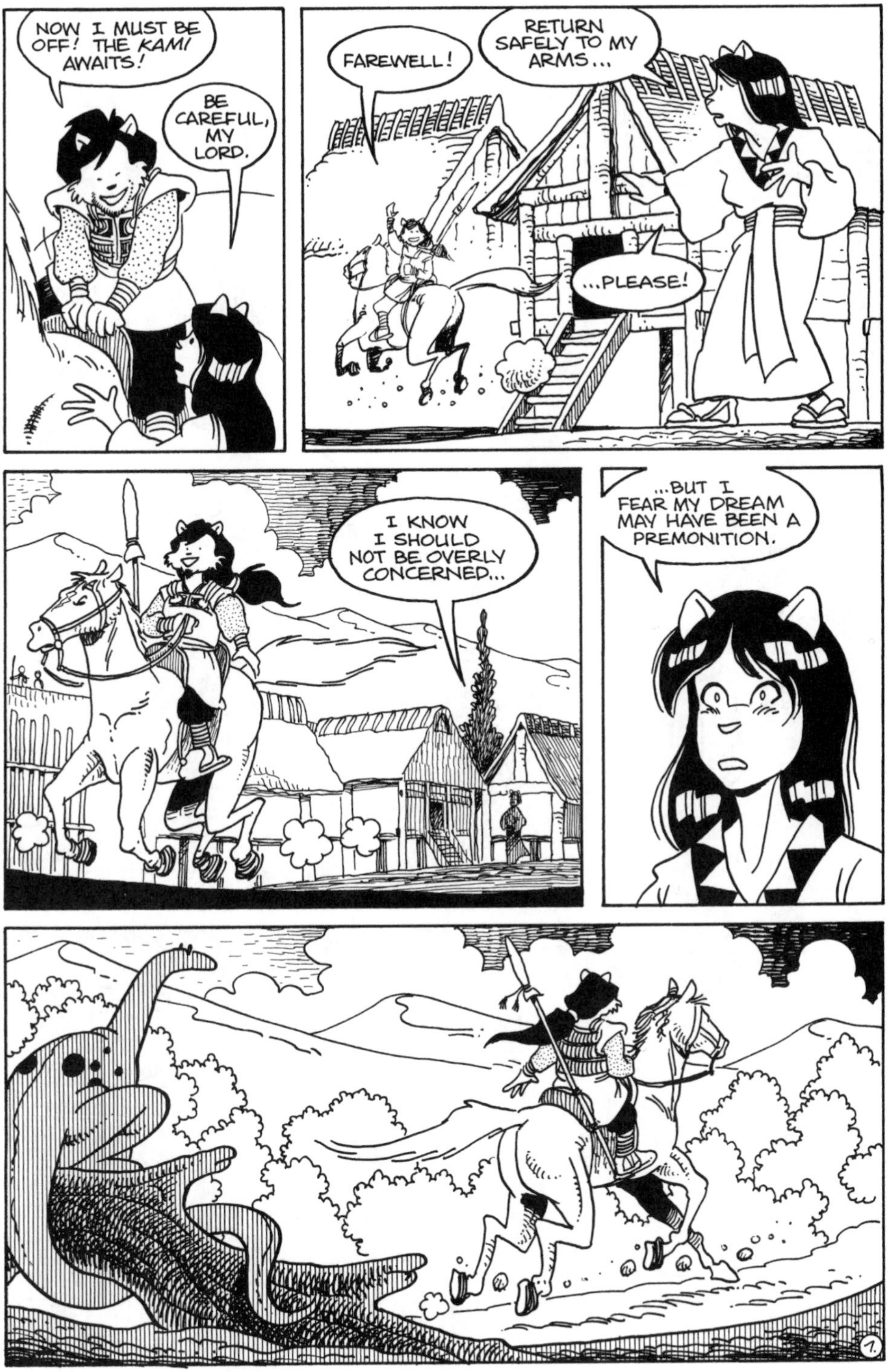
NOW I MUST BE OFF! THE KAMI AWAITS!
BE CAREFUL, MY LORD.
FAREWELL!
RETURN SAFELY TO MY ARMS...
...PLEASE!
I KNOW I SHOULD NOT BE OVERLY CONCERNED...
...BUT I FEAR MY DREAM MAY HAVE BEEN A PREMONITION.
1.

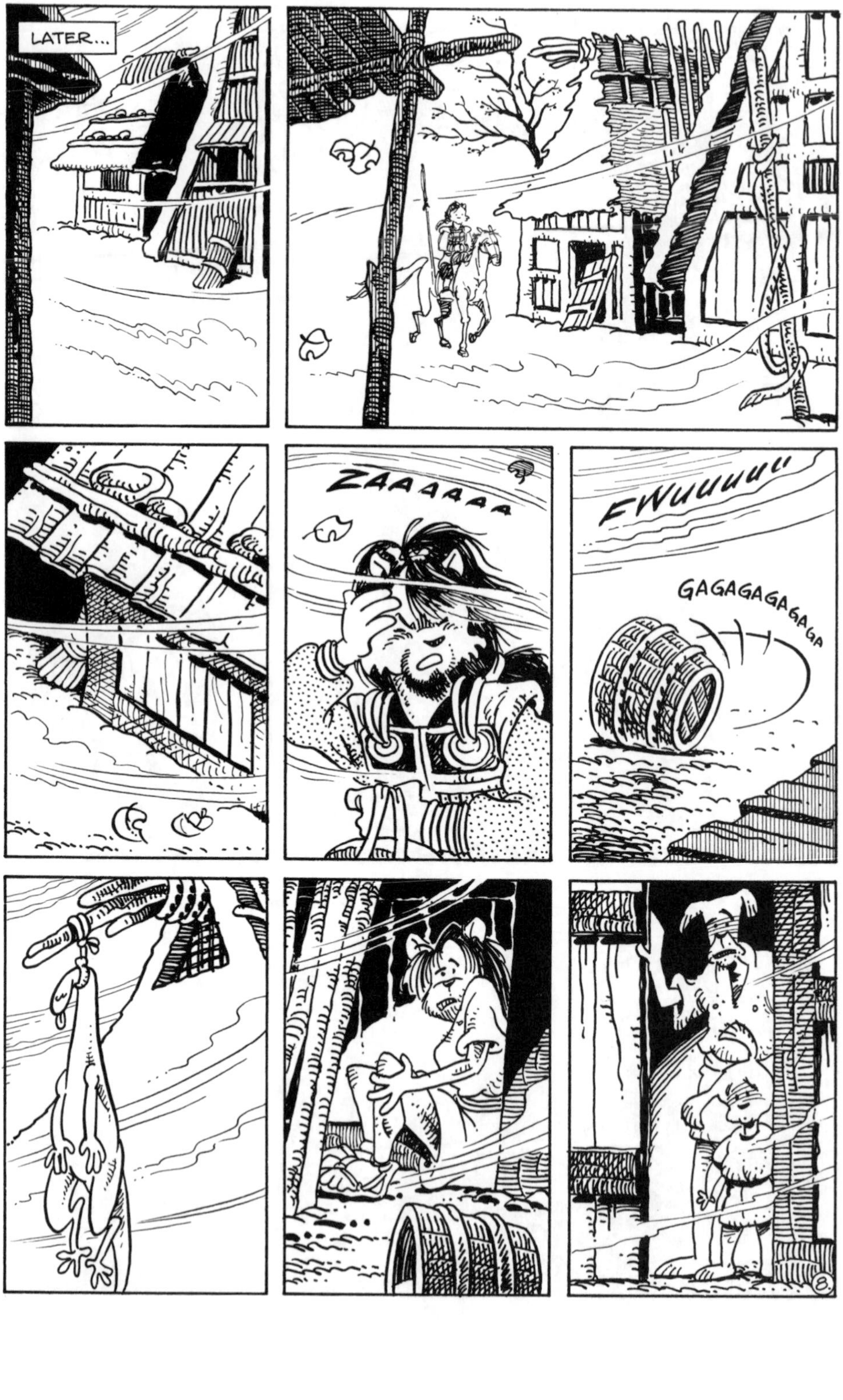
LATER...
ZAAAAAA
FWUUUUUU
GAGAGAGAGAGAGA
8.

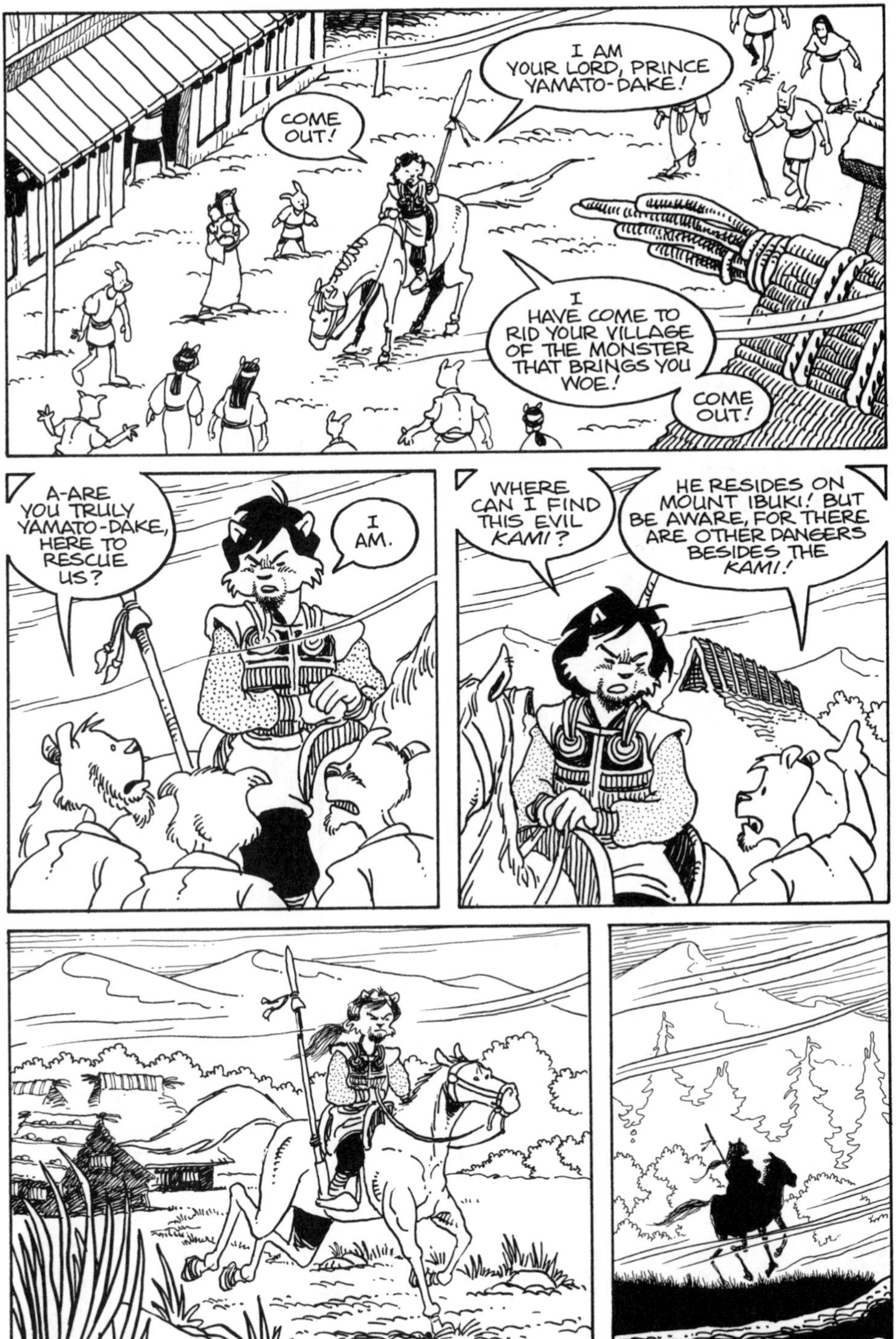
COME OUT!
I AM YOUR LORD, PRINCE YAMATO-DAKE!
I HAVE COME TO RID YOUR VILLAGE OF THE MONSTER THAT BRINGS YOU WOE!
COME OUT!
A-ARE YOU TRULY YAMATO-DAKE, HERE TO RESCUE US?
I AM.
WHERE CAN I FIND THIS EVIL *KAMI*?
HE RESIDES ON MOUNT IBUKI! BUT BE AWARE, FOR THERE ARE OTHER DANGERS BESIDES THE *KAMI*!
9.

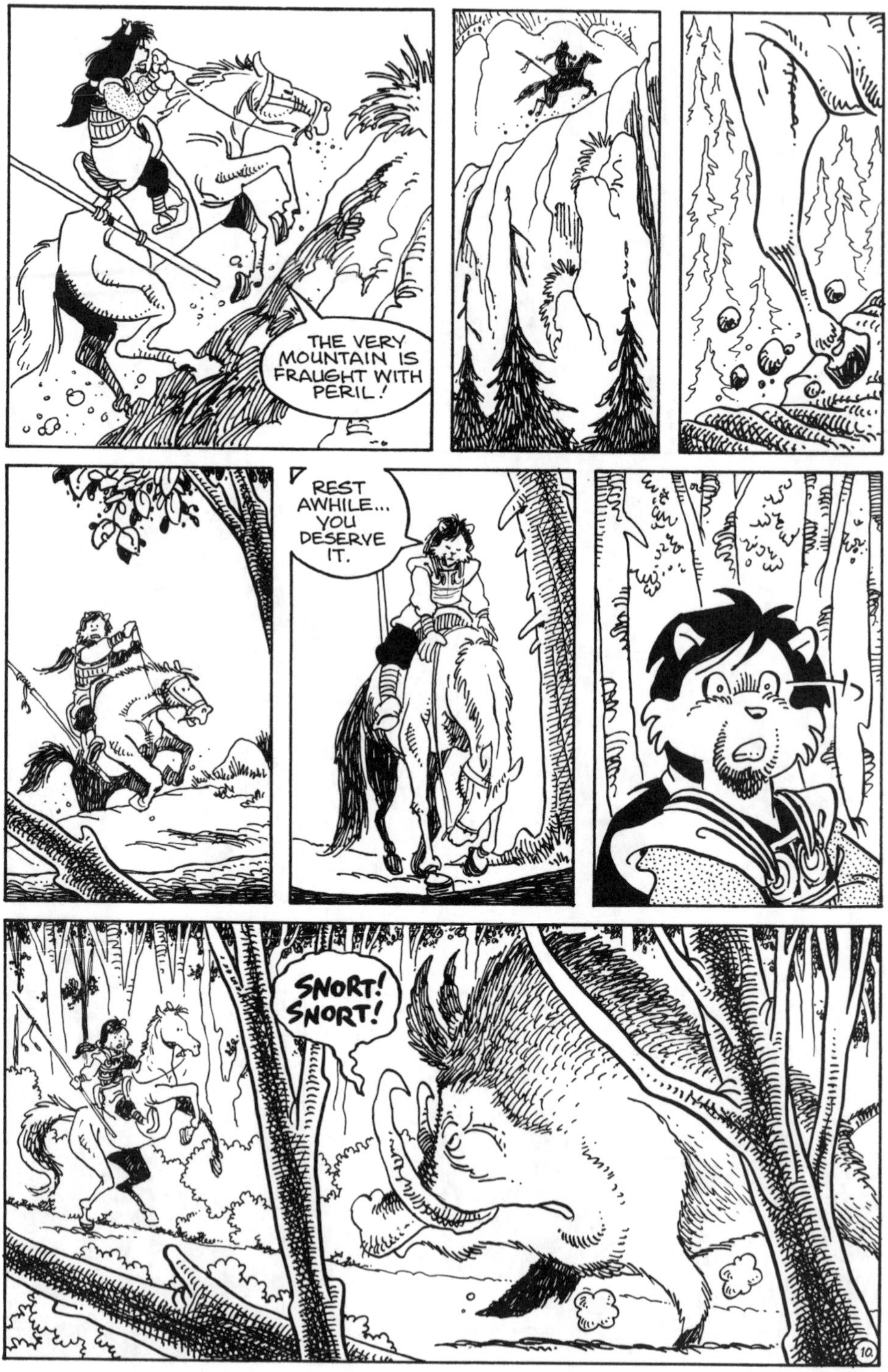
THE VERY MOUNTAIN IS FRAUGHT WITH PERIL!
REST AWHILE... YOU DESERVE IT.
SNORT! SNORT!
10.

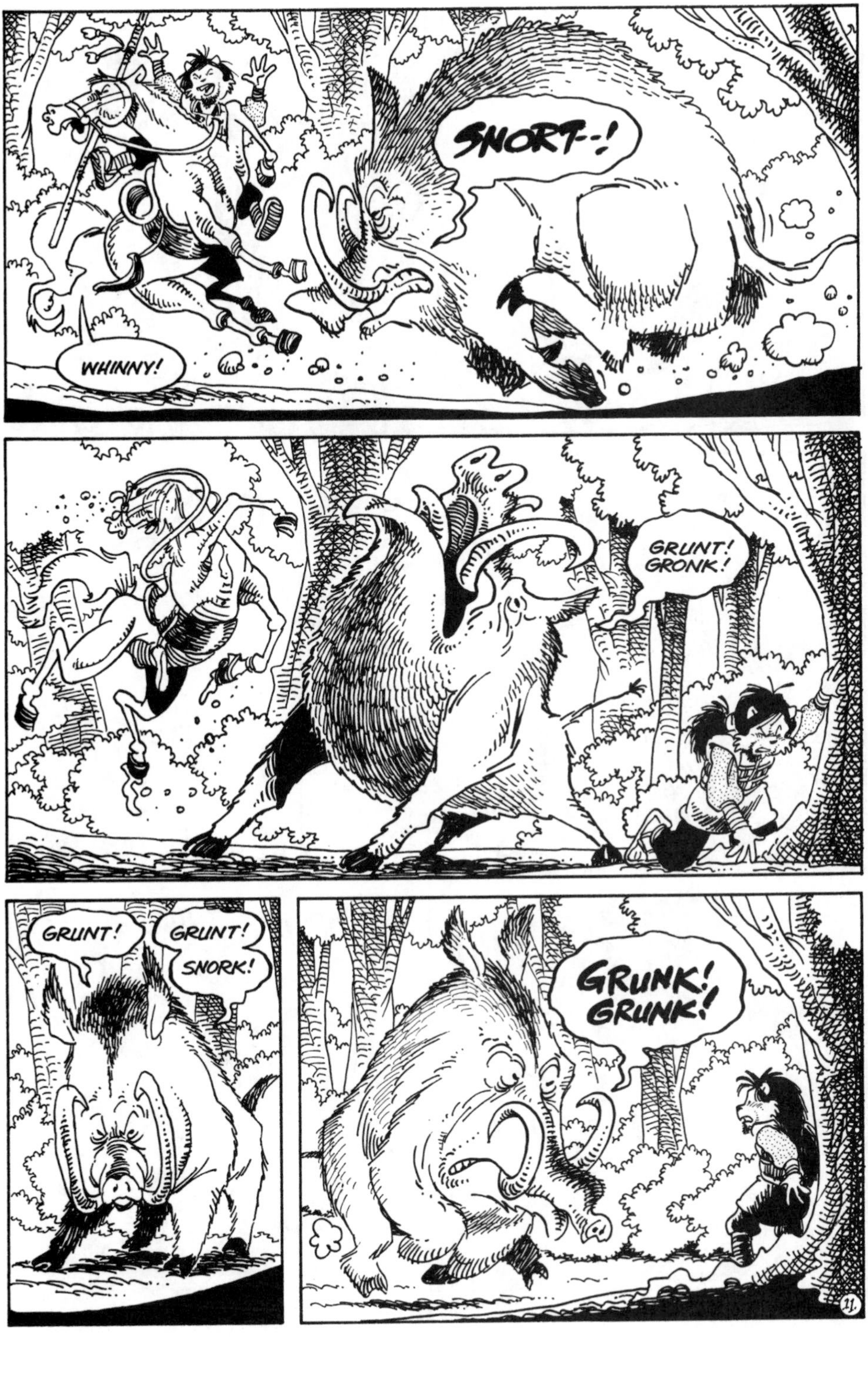
SNORT-!
WHINNY!
GRUNT! GRONK!
GRUNT!
GRUNT! SNORK!
GRUNK! GRUNK!
11.

CRASH!

GRONK!

HIYAHH!

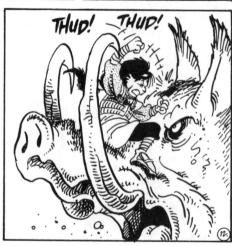

THUD! THUD!

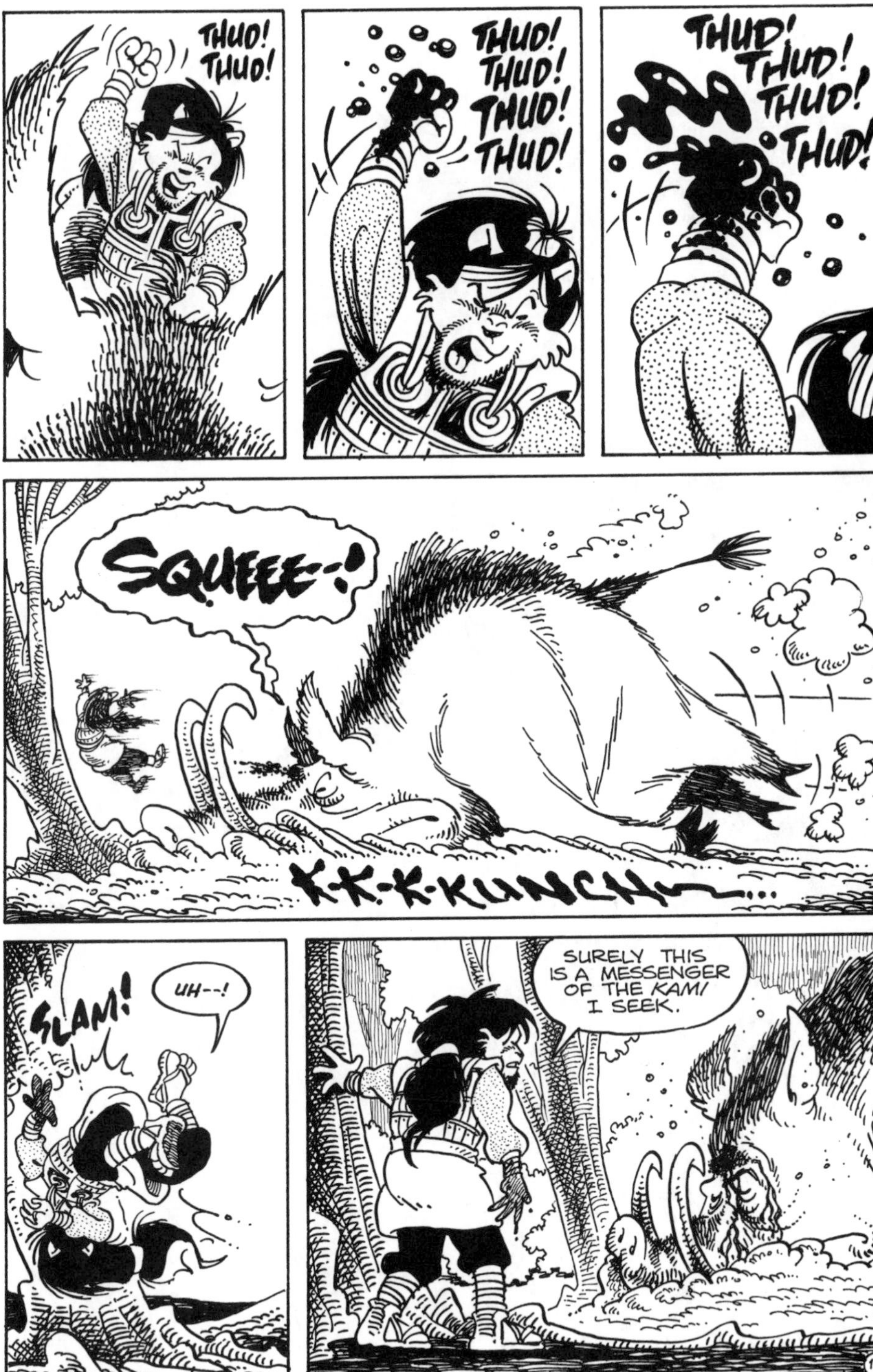
THUD! THUD!
THUD! THUD! THUD! THUD!
THUD! THUD! THUD! THUD!
SQUEEE-!
K-K-K-KUNCH...
SLAM!
UH--!
SURELY THIS IS A MESSENGER OF THE *KAMI* I SEEK.
13

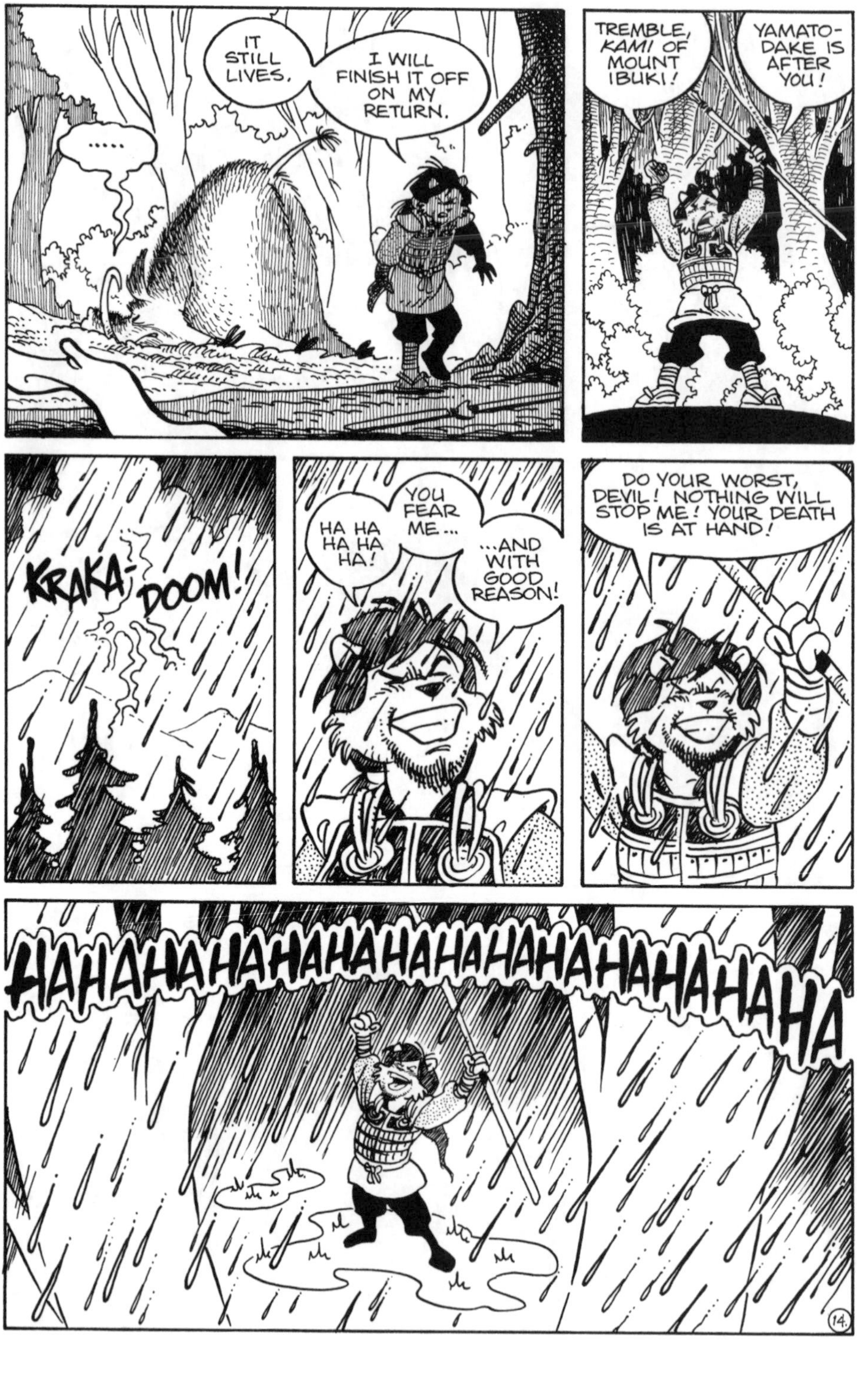
......
IT STILL LIVES.
I WILL FINISH IT OFF ON MY RETURN.
TREMBLE, KAMI OF MOUNT IBUKI!
YAMATO-DAKE IS AFTER YOU!
KRAKA-DOOM!
HA HA HA HA HA!
YOU FEAR ME...
...AND WITH GOOD REASON!
DO YOUR WORST, DEVIL! NOTHING WILL STOP ME! YOUR DEATH IS AT HAND!
HAHAHAHAHAHAHAHAHAHAHAHAHAHAHAHAHA
14.

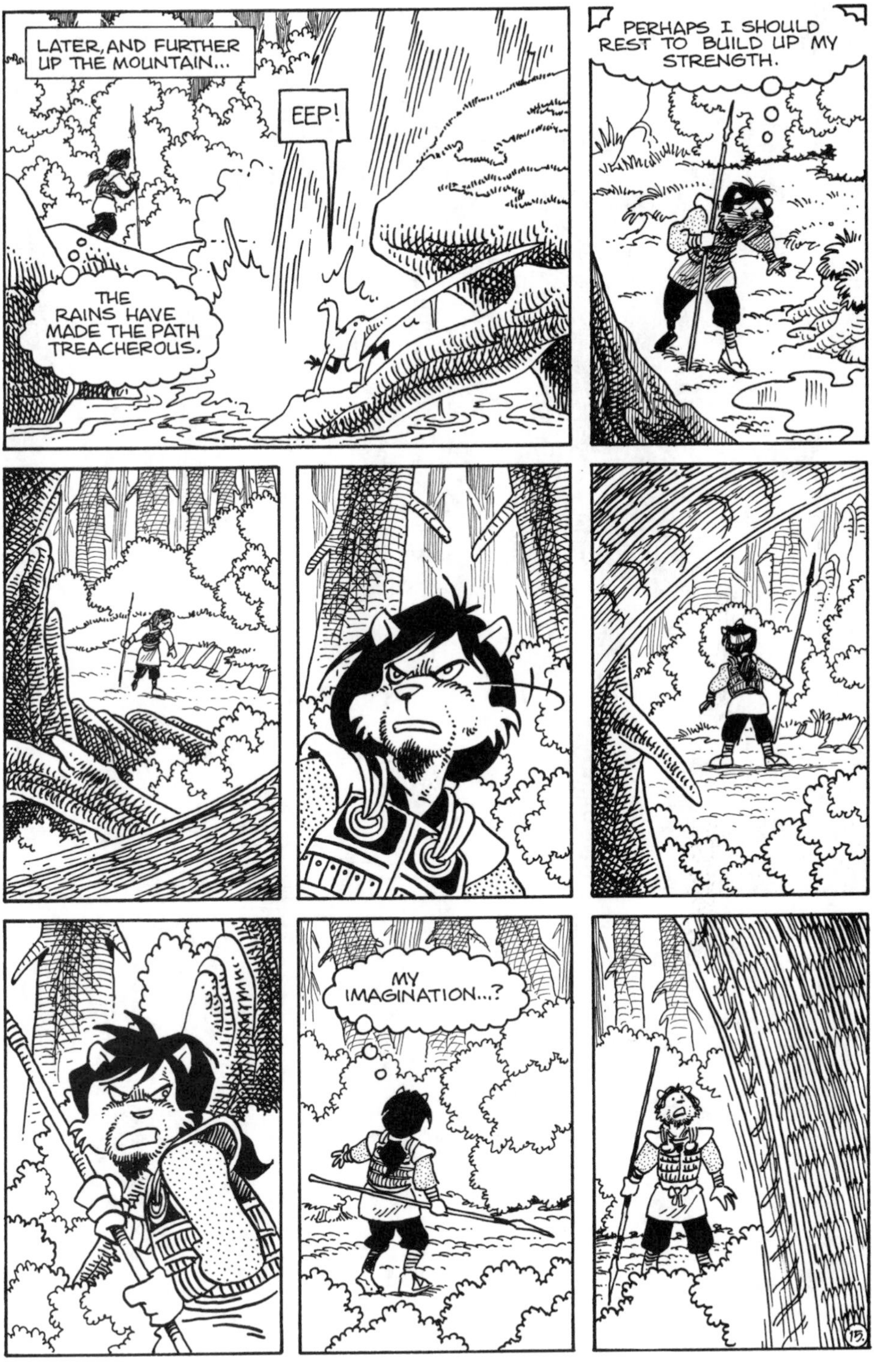
LATER, AND FURTHER UP THE MOUNTAIN...
EEP!
THE RAINS HAVE MADE THE PATH TREACHEROUS.
PERHAPS I SHOULD REST TO BUILD UP MY STRENGTH.
MY IMAGINATION...?
15.

KAMI!

I DEFEATED YOUR EMISSARY. NOW I WILL SLAY YOU!

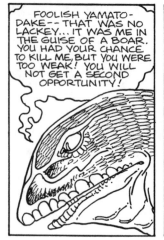

FOOLISH YAMATO-DAKE-- THAT WAS NO LACKEY... IT WAS ME IN THE GUISE OF A BOAR. YOU HAD YOUR CHANCE TO KILL ME, BUT YOU WERE TOO WEAK! YOU WILL NOT GET A SECOND OPPORTUNITY!

I VANQUISHED YOU ONCE, AND I WILL DO SO AGAIN!

#RAAAAAAA!

16

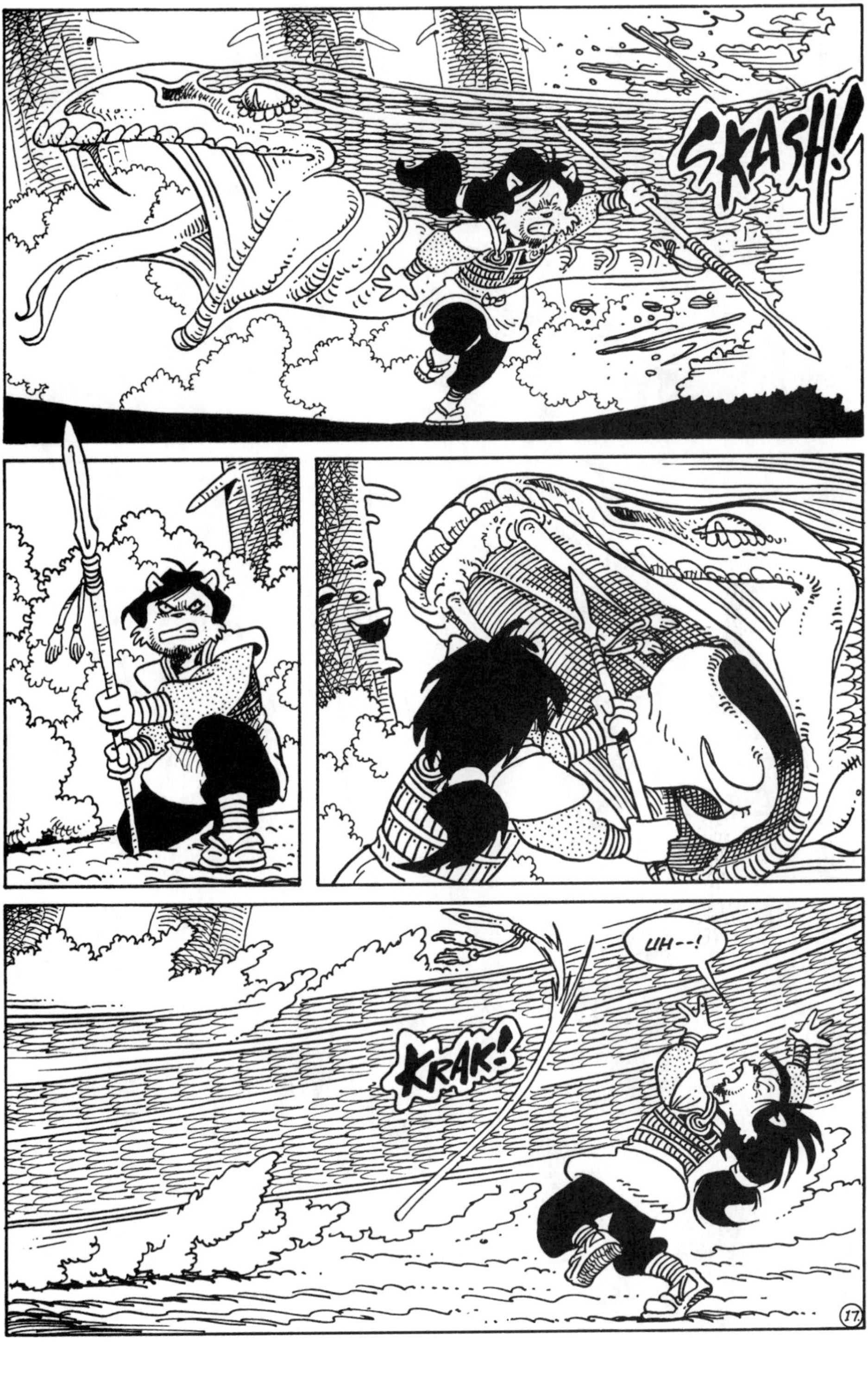
SKASH!
UH--!
KRAK!
17

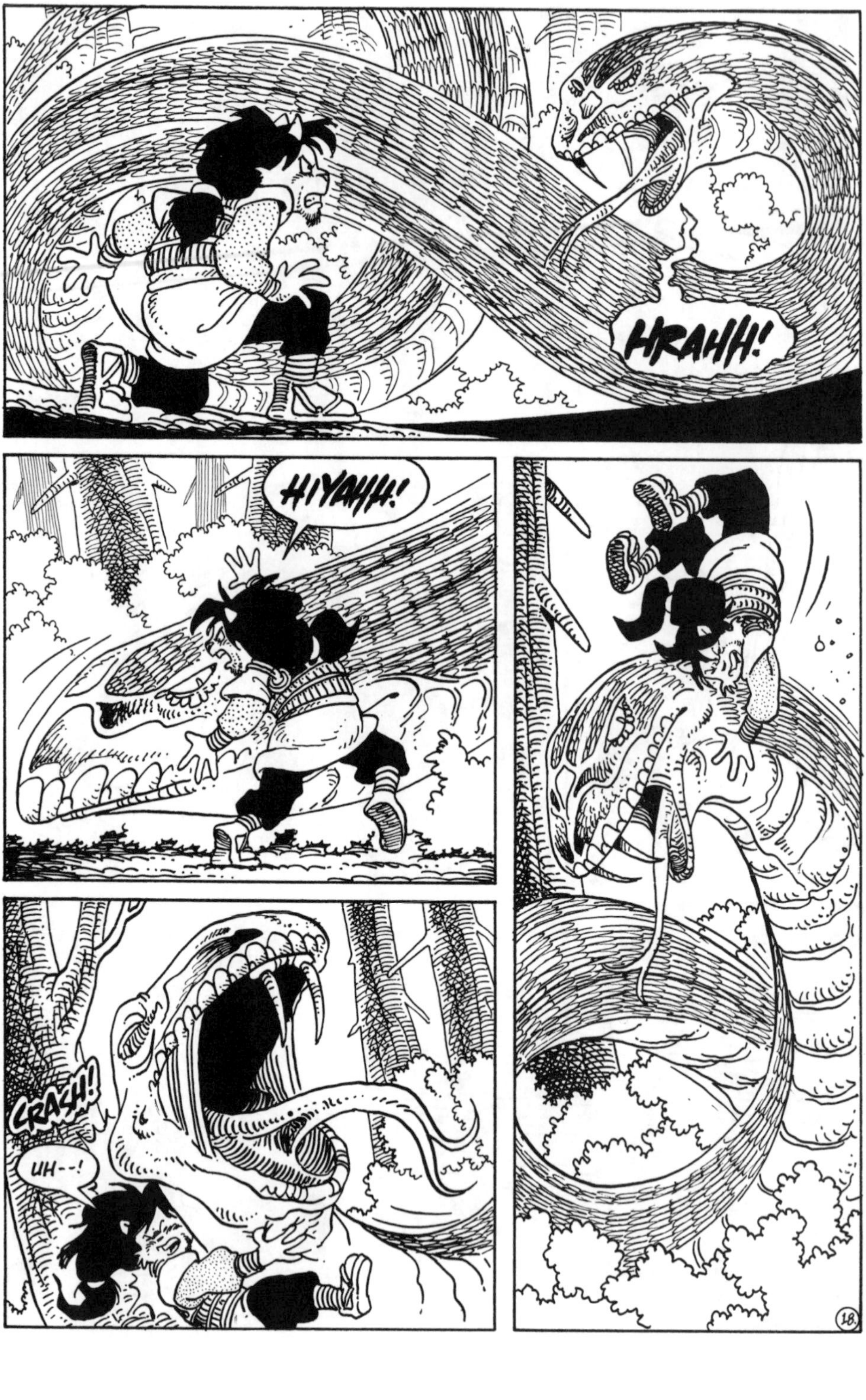
HRAHH!
HIYAHH!
CRASH!
UH--!
18

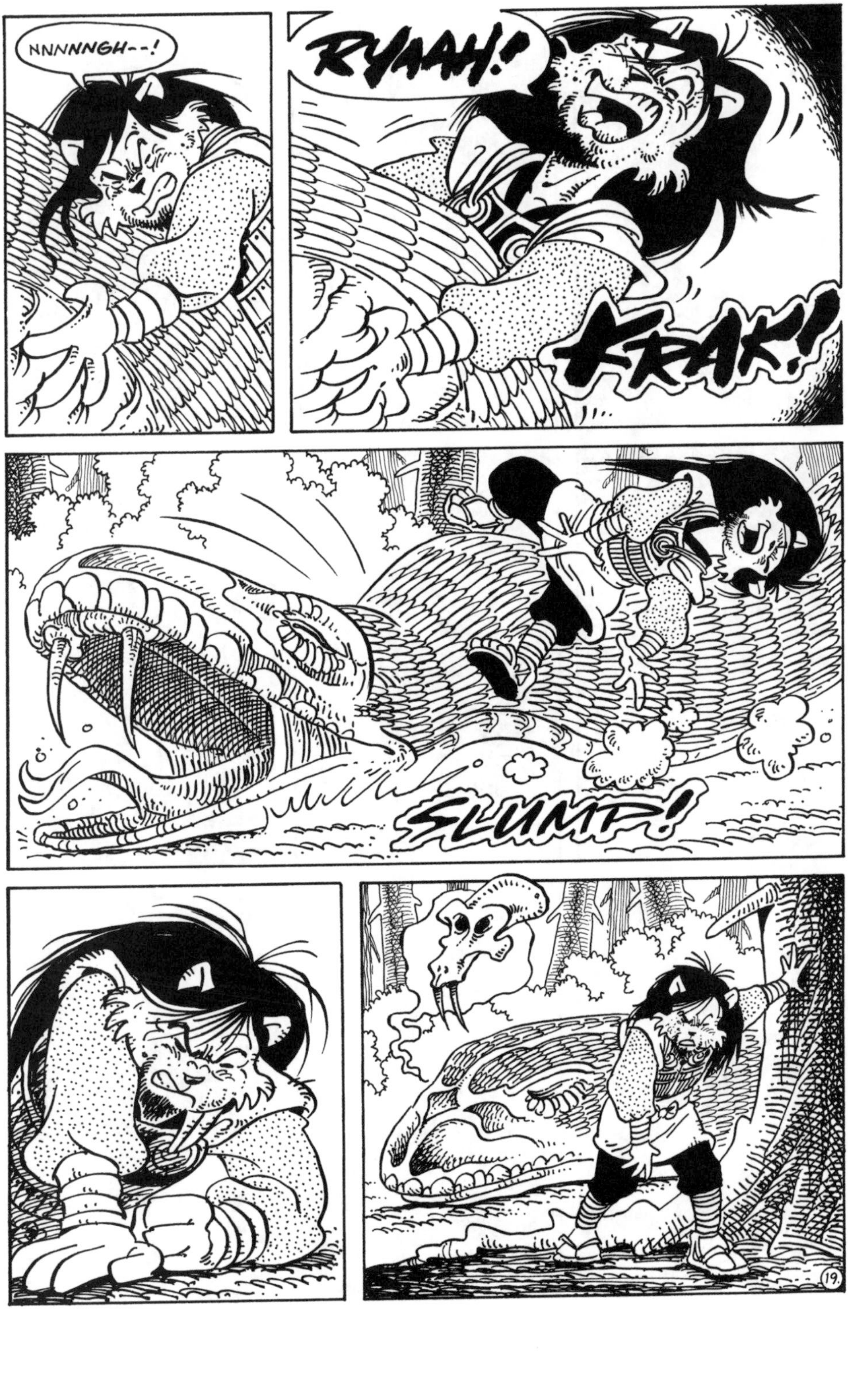
NNNNNGH--!
RYAAH!
KRAK!
SLUMP!
19.

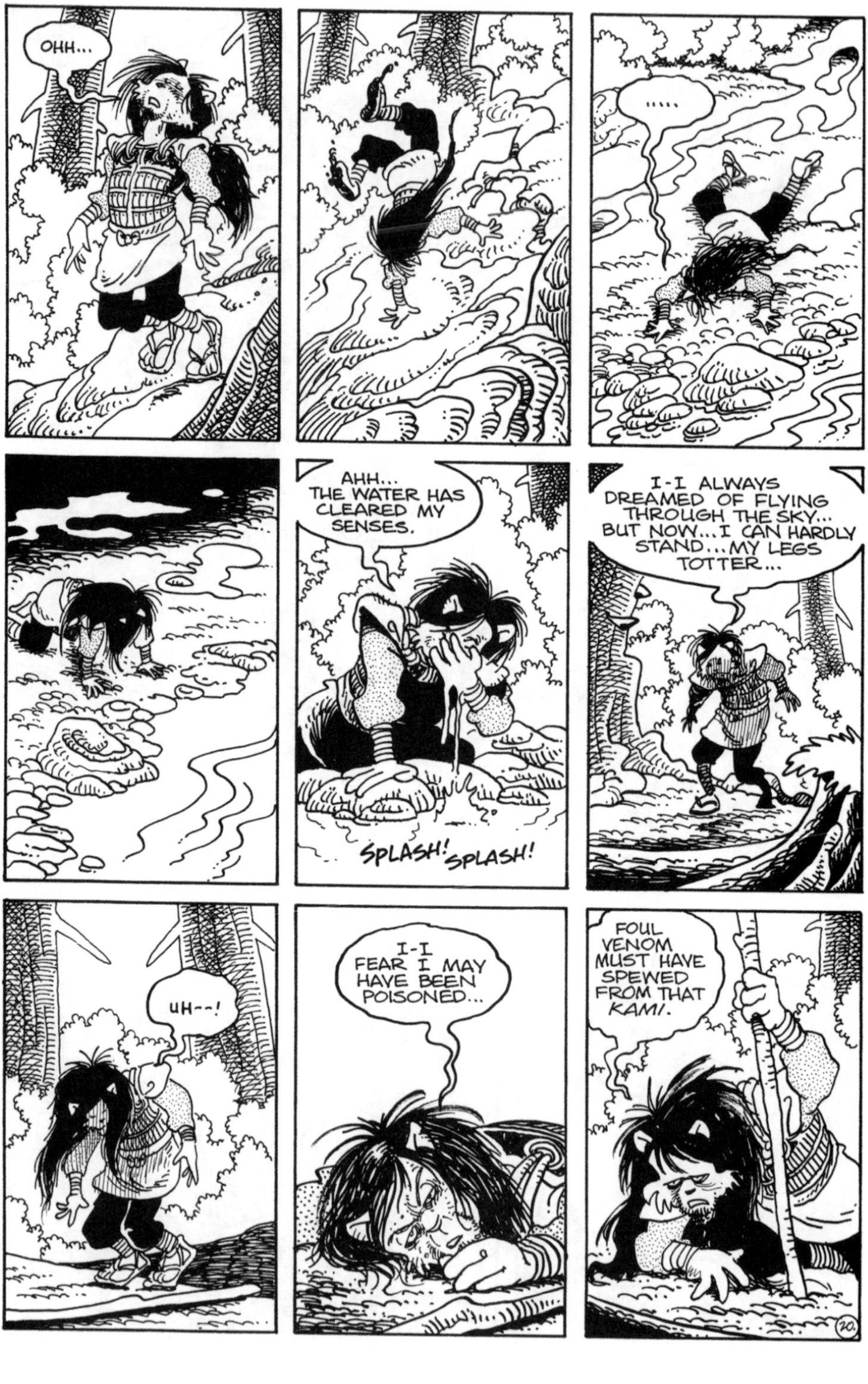
OHH...
.....
AHH... THE WATER HAS CLEARED MY SENSES.
SPLASH! SPLASH!
I-I ALWAYS DREAMED OF FLYING THROUGH THE SKY... BUT NOW... I CAN HARDLY STAND... MY LEGS TOTTER...
UH--!
I-I FEAR I MAY HAVE BEEN POISONED...
FOUL VENOM MUST HAVE SPEWED FROM THAT *KAMI*.
20.

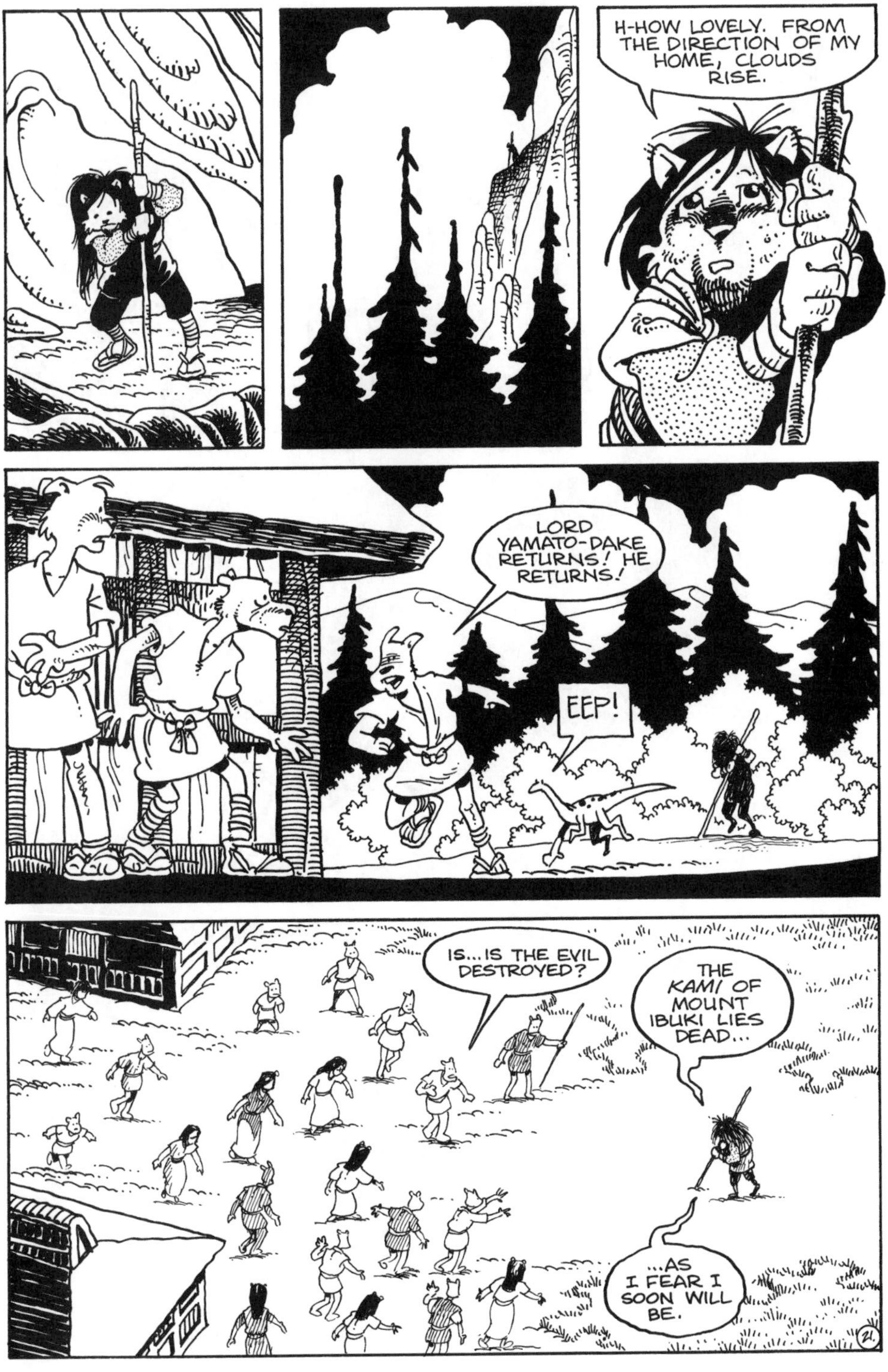
H-HOW LOVELY. FROM THE DIRECTION OF MY HOME, CLOUDS RISE.
LORD YAMATO-DAKE RETURNS! HE RETURNS!
EEP!
IS... IS THE EVIL DESTROYED?
THE KAMI OF MOUNT IBUKI LIES DEAD...
...AS I FEAR I SOON WILL BE.
21.

SUMMON A HEALER! THE LORD IS INJURED!
A HEALER WOULD BE USELESS.
OH, IF ONLY I HAD BROUGHT...
...GRASS-Cutter.....
SEND COURIERS TO SPREAD THE NEWS...
PRINCE YAMATO-DAKE IS DEAD.

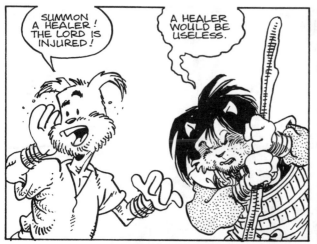

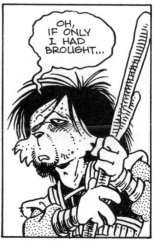

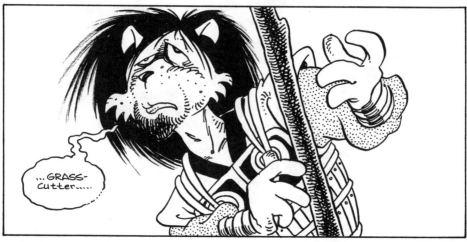

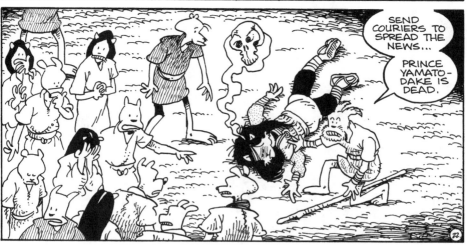

YAMATO-DAKE'S WIVES AND CHILDREN ARRIVED IN VARIOUS GROUPS AND BUILT A TOMB. WHEN IT WAS COMPLETED, THEY SANG.

HERE AND THERE ALONGSIDE THE RICE STALKS OF ADJOINING RICE FIELDS...

THERE AND HERE ALONGSIDE THE RICE STALKS GROW THE VINES OF WILD YAMS.

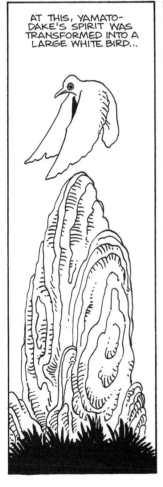

AT THIS, YAMATO-DAKE'S SPIRIT WAS TRANSFORMED INTO A LARGE WHITE BIRD...

...AND FLEW TOWARD THE BEACH, FOLLOWED BY HIS FAMILY.

THE FIELD OF OVERGROWN BAMBOO GRASS TEARS AT OUR WAISTS...

WE DO NOT FLY THROUGH THE SKY. WE MUST RUN WITH OUR FEET.

THEY WADED INTO THE SURF AFTER THE BIRD...

THE WATERS ENCUMBER US. WE WAVER AS THE GRASS ON A RIVERBED.

23

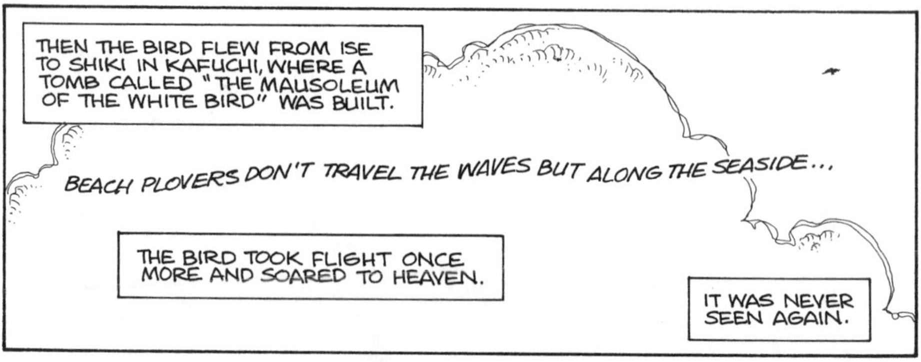
THEN THE BIRD FLEW FROM ISE TO SHIKI IN KAFUCHI, WHERE A TOMB CALLED "THE MAUSOLEUM OF THE WHITE BIRD" WAS BUILT.
BEACH PLOVERS DON'T TRAVEL THE WAVES BUT ALONG THE SEASIDE...
THE BIRD TOOK FLIGHT ONCE MORE AND SOARED TO HEAVEN.
IT WAS NEVER SEEN AGAIN.

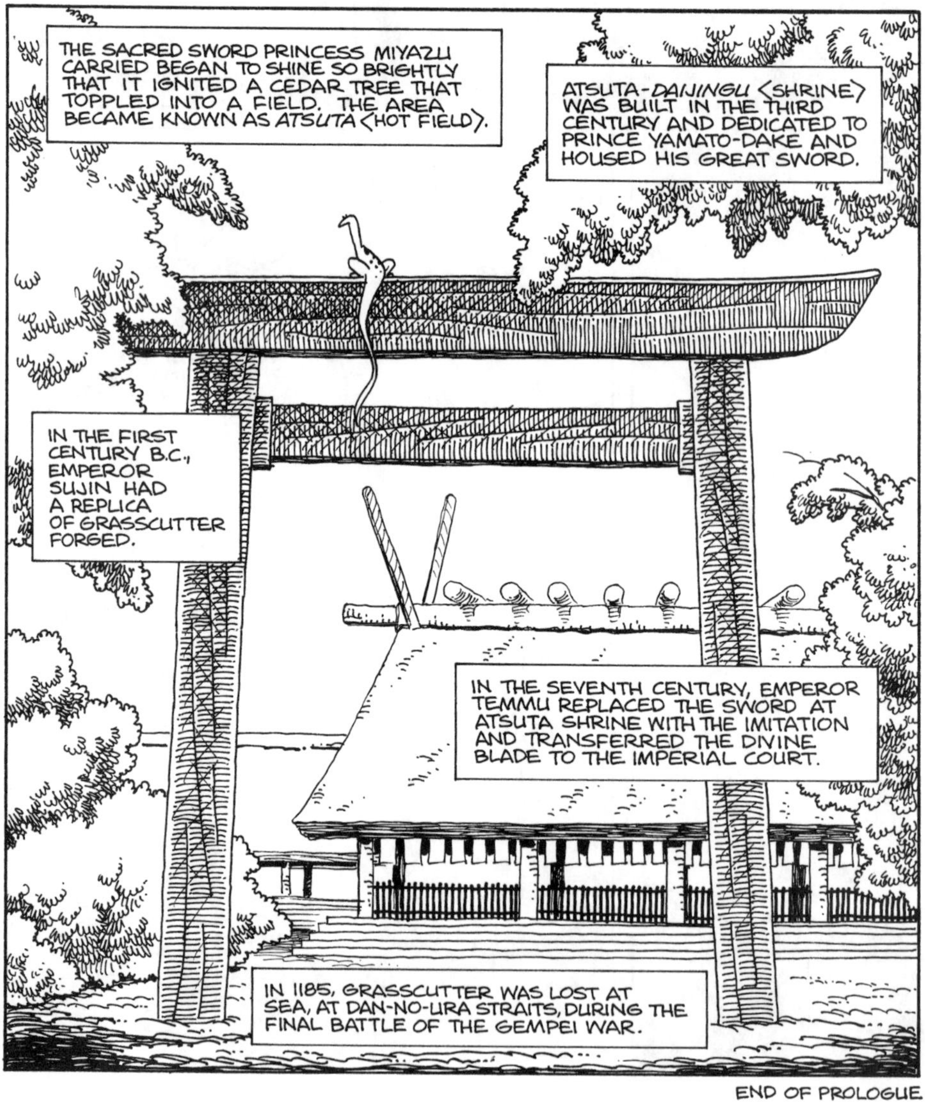
THE SACRED SWORD PRINCESS MIYAZU CARRIED BEGAN TO SHINE SO BRIGHTLY THAT IT IGNITED A CEDAR TREE THAT TOPPLED INTO A FIELD. THE AREA BECAME KNOWN AS ATSUTA <HOT FIELD>.
ATSUTA-DAIJINGU <SHRINE> WAS BUILT IN THE THIRD CENTURY AND DEDICATED TO PRINCE YAMATO-DAKE AND HOUSED HIS GREAT SWORD.
IN THE FIRST CENTURY B.C., EMPEROR SUJIN HAD A REPLICA OF GRASSCUTTER FORGED.
IN THE SEVENTH CENTURY, EMPEROR TEMMU REPLACED THE SWORD AT ATSUTA SHRINE WITH THE IMITATION AND TRANSFERRED THE DIVINE BLADE TO THE IMPERIAL COURT.
IN 1185, GRASSCUTTER WAS LOST AT SEA, AT DAN-NO-URA STRAITS, DURING THE FINAL BATTLE OF THE GEMPEI WAR.

END OF PROLOGUE

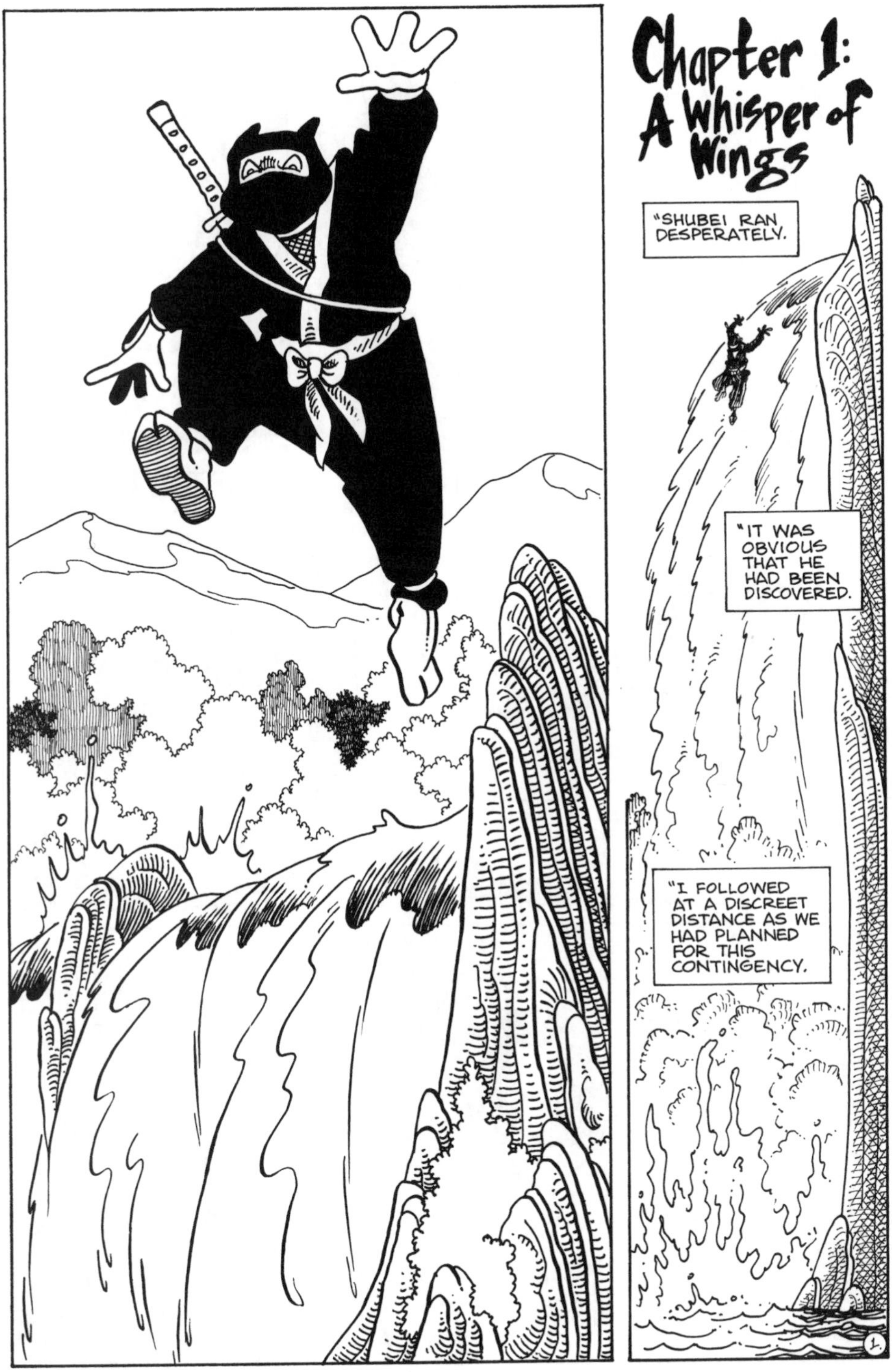
Chapter 1:
A Whisper of Wings
"SHUBEI RAN DESPERATELY.
"IT WAS OBVIOUS THAT HE HAD BEEN DISCOVERED.
"I FOLLOWED AT A DISCREET DISTANCE AS WE HAD PLANNED FOR THIS CONTINGENCY.
1.

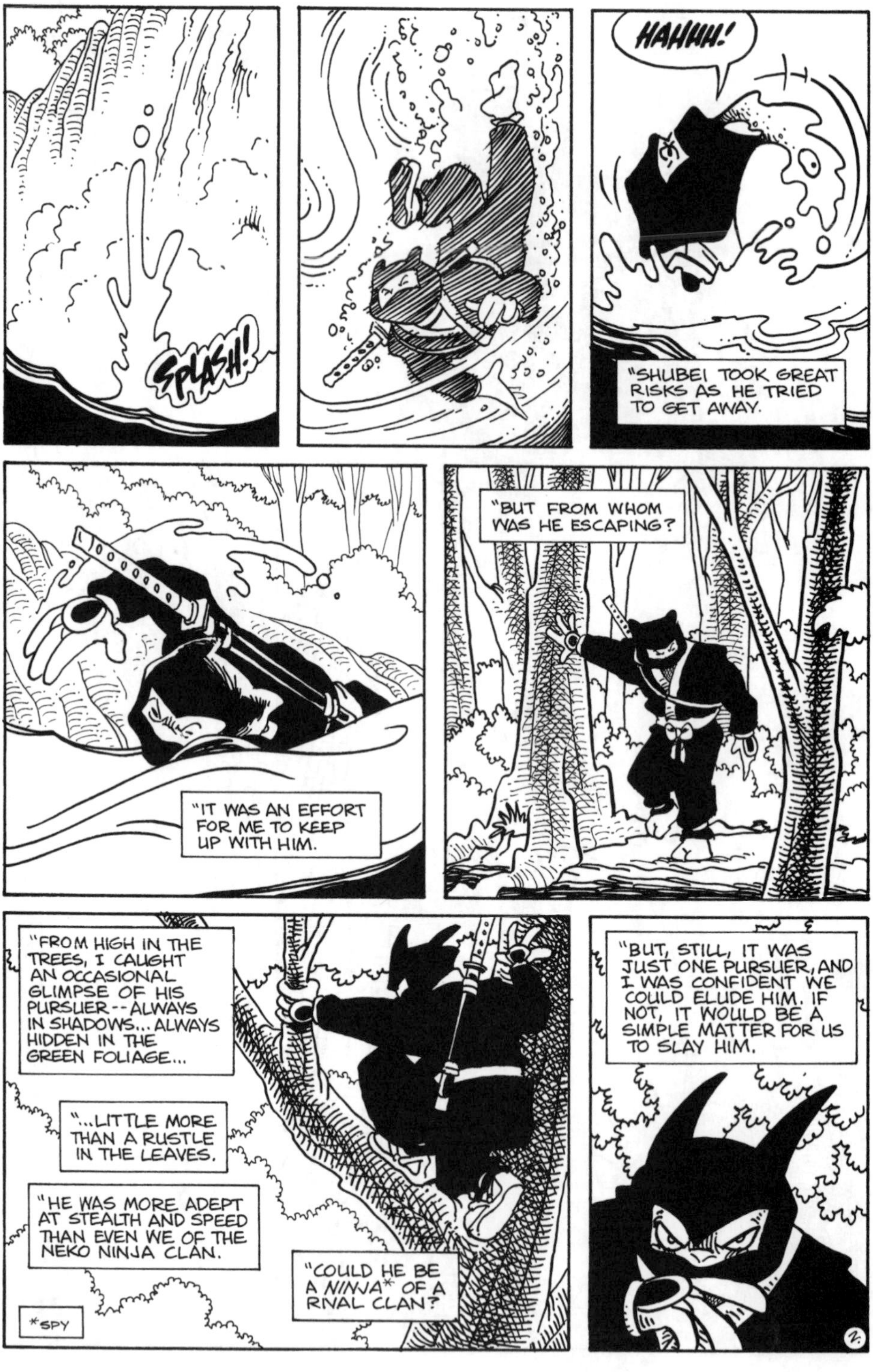
SPLASH!
HAHHH!
"SHUBEI TOOK GREAT RISKS AS HE TRIED TO GET AWAY.
"IT WAS AN EFFORT FOR ME TO KEEP UP WITH HIM.
"BUT FROM WHOM WAS HE ESCAPING?
"FROM HIGH IN THE TREES, I CAUGHT AN OCCASIONAL GLIMPSE OF HIS PURSUER--ALWAYS IN SHADOWS...ALWAYS HIDDEN IN THE GREEN FOLIAGE...
"...LITTLE MORE THAN A RUSTLE IN THE LEAVES.
"HE WAS MORE ADEPT AT STEALTH AND SPEED THAN EVEN WE OF THE NEKO NINJA CLAN.
"COULD HE BE A NINJA* OF A RIVAL CLAN?
*SPY
"BUT, STILL, IT WAS JUST ONE PURSUER, AND I WAS CONFIDENT WE COULD ELUDE HIM. IF NOT, IT WOULD BE A SIMPLE MATTER FOR US TO SLAY HIM.
2.

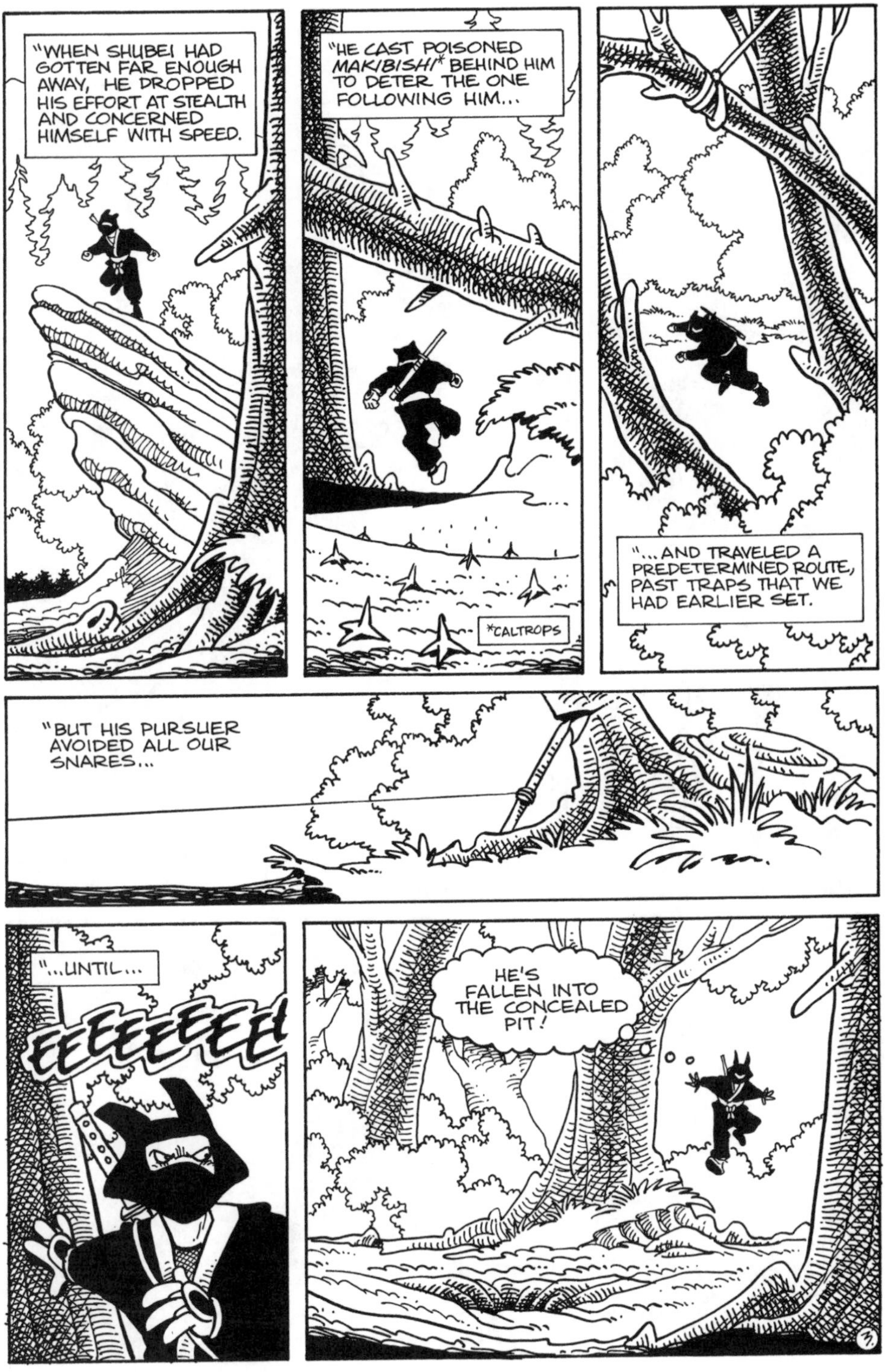
"WHEN SHUBEI HAD GOTTEN FAR ENOUGH AWAY, HE DROPPED HIS EFFORT AT STEALTH AND CONCERNED HIMSELF WITH SPEED.
"HE CAST POISONED MAKIBISHI* BEHIND HIM TO DETER THE ONE FOLLOWING HIM...
*CALTROPS
"...AND TRAVELED A PREDETERMINED ROUTE, PAST TRAPS THAT WE HAD EARLIER SET.
"BUT HIS PURSUER AVOIDED ALL OUR SNARES...
"...UNTIL...
EEEEEEEEE
HE'S FALLEN INTO THE CONCEALED PIT!
3

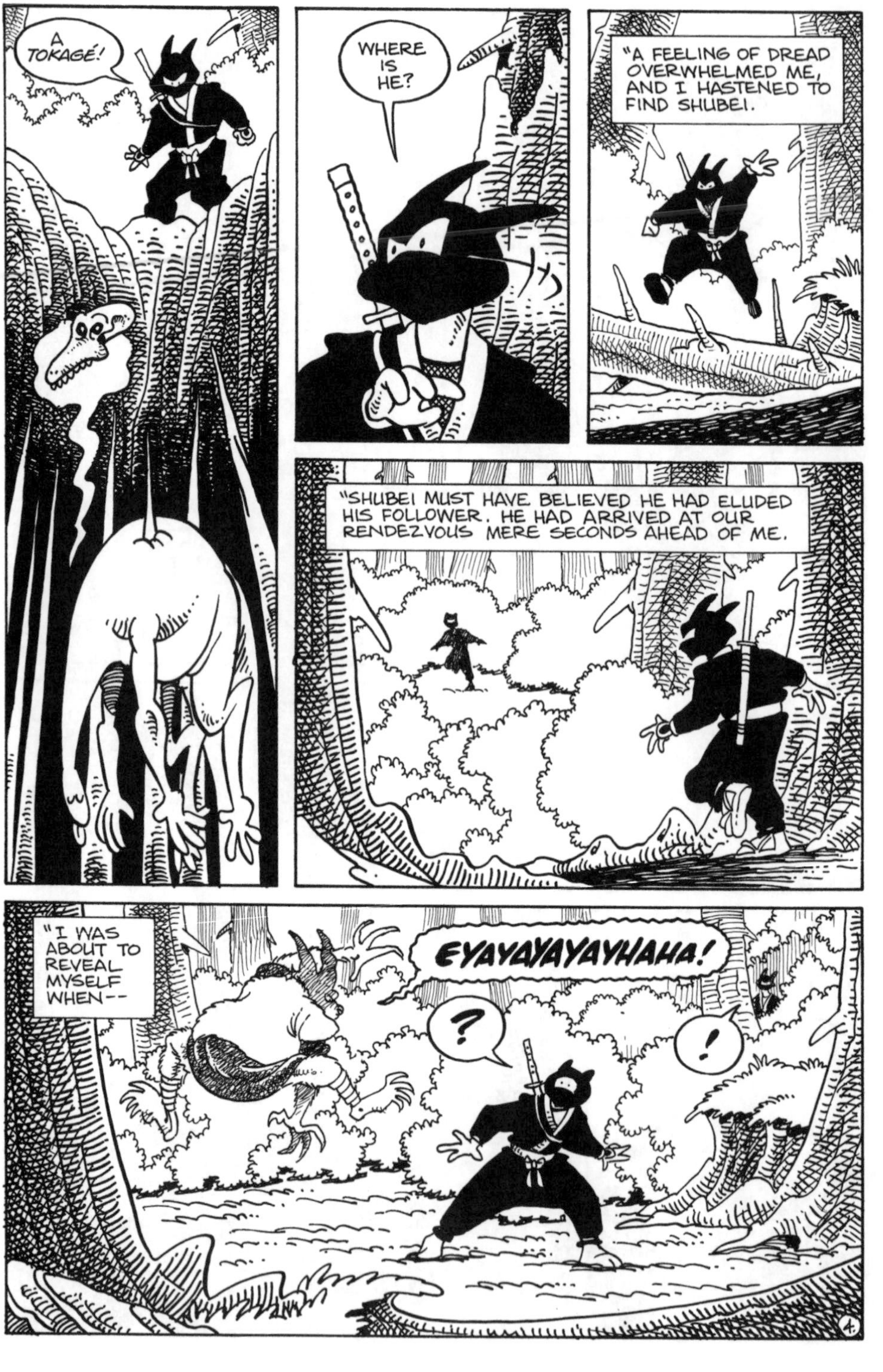
A TOKAGÉ!
WHERE IS HE?
"A FEELING OF DREAD OVERWHELMED ME, AND I HASTENED TO FIND SHUBEI.
"SHUBEI MUST HAVE BELIEVED HE HAD ELUDED HIS FOLLOWER. HE HAD ARRIVED AT OUR RENDEZVOUS MERE SECONDS AHEAD OF ME.
"I WAS ABOUT TO REVEAL MYSELF WHEN--
EYAYAYAYAYHAHA!
?
!

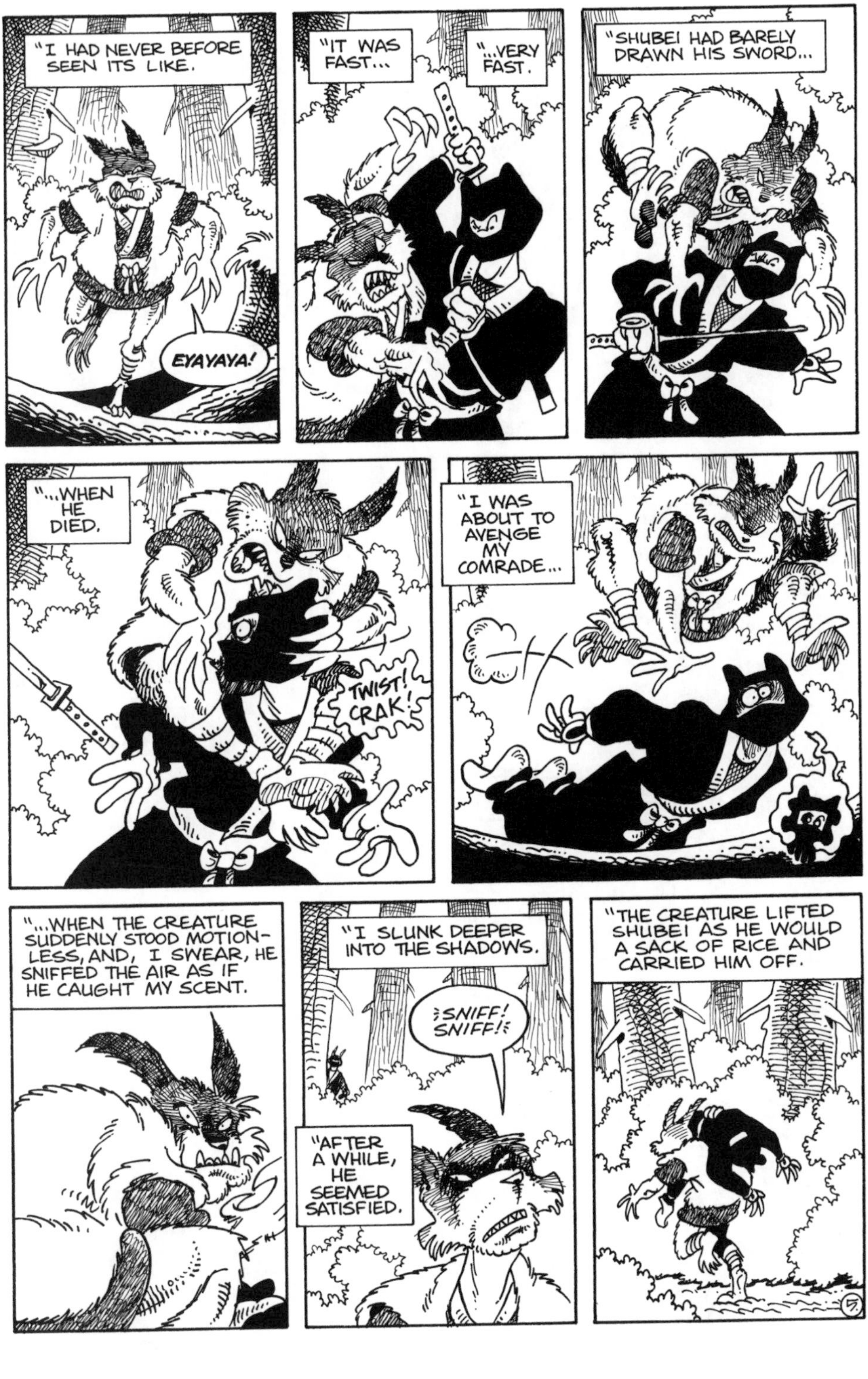
"I HAD NEVER BEFORE SEEN ITS LIKE.
EYAYAYA!
"IT WAS FAST...
"...VERY FAST.
"SHUBEI HAD BARELY DRAWN HIS SWORD...
"...WHEN HE DIED.
TWIST! CRAK!
"I WAS ABOUT TO AVENGE MY COMRADE...
"...WHEN THE CREATURE SUDDENLY STOOD MOTIONLESS, AND, I SWEAR, HE SNIFFED THE AIR AS IF HE CAUGHT MY SCENT.
"I SLUNK DEEPER INTO THE SHADOWS.
SNIFF! SNIFF!
"AFTER A WHILE, HE SEEMED SATISFIED.
"THE CREATURE LIFTED SHUBEI AS HE WOULD A SACK OF RICE AND CARRIED HIM OFF.

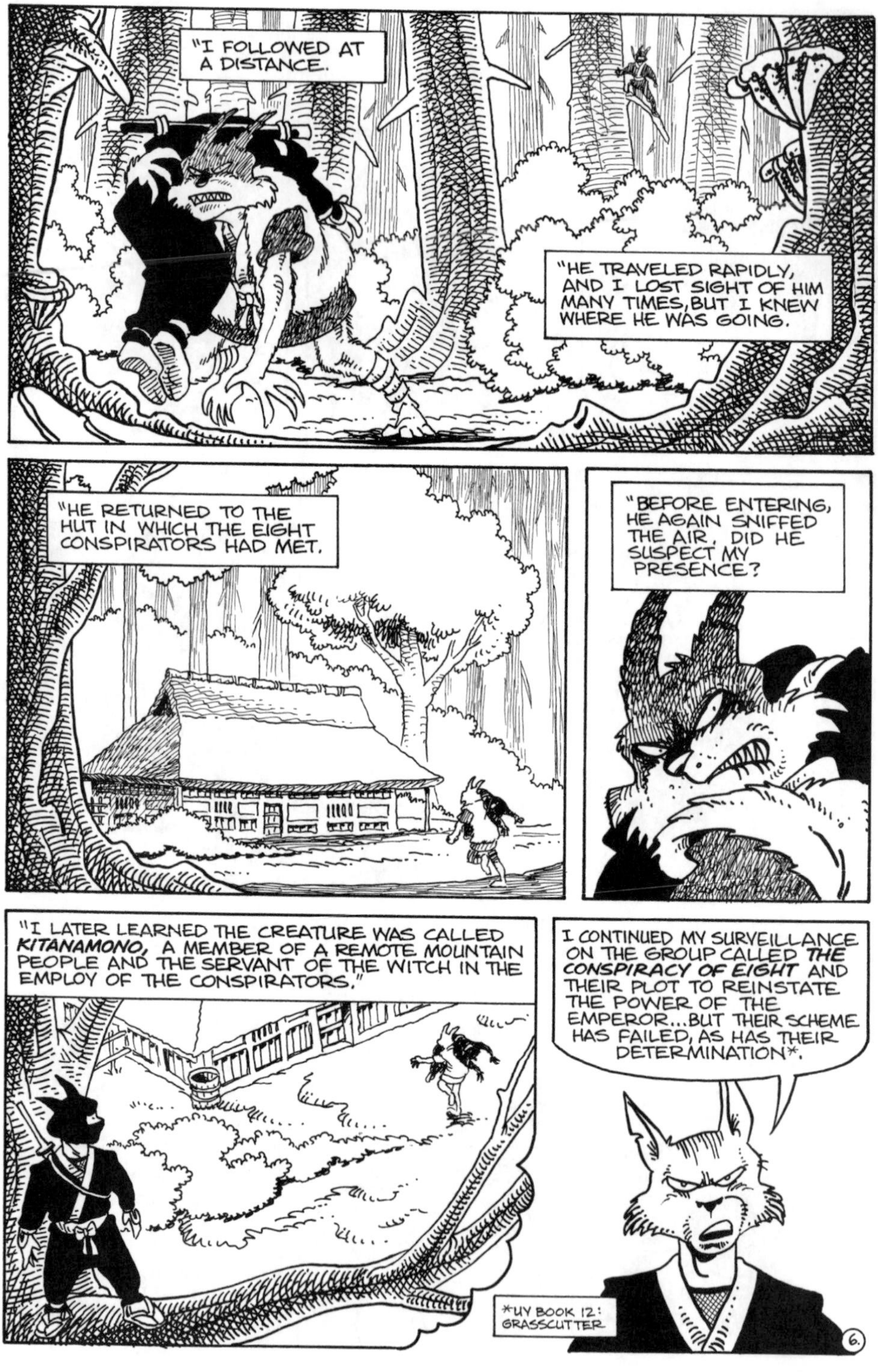
"I FOLLOWED AT A DISTANCE.
"HE TRAVELED RAPIDLY, AND I LOST SIGHT OF HIM MANY TIMES, BUT I KNEW WHERE HE WAS GOING.
"HE RETURNED TO THE HUT IN WHICH THE EIGHT CONSPIRATORS HAD MET.
"BEFORE ENTERING, HE AGAIN SNIFFED THE AIR. DID HE SUSPECT MY PRESENCE?
"I LATER LEARNED THE CREATURE WAS CALLED KITANAMONO, A MEMBER OF A REMOTE MOUNTAIN PEOPLE AND THE SERVANT OF THE WITCH IN THE EMPLOY OF THE CONSPIRATORS."
I CONTINUED MY SURVEILLANCE ON THE GROUP CALLED THE CONSPIRACY OF EIGHT AND THEIR PLOT TO REINSTATE THE POWER OF THE EMPEROR...BUT THEIR SCHEME HAS FAILED, AS HAS THEIR DETERMINATION*.
*UY BOOK 12: GRASSCUTTER
6.

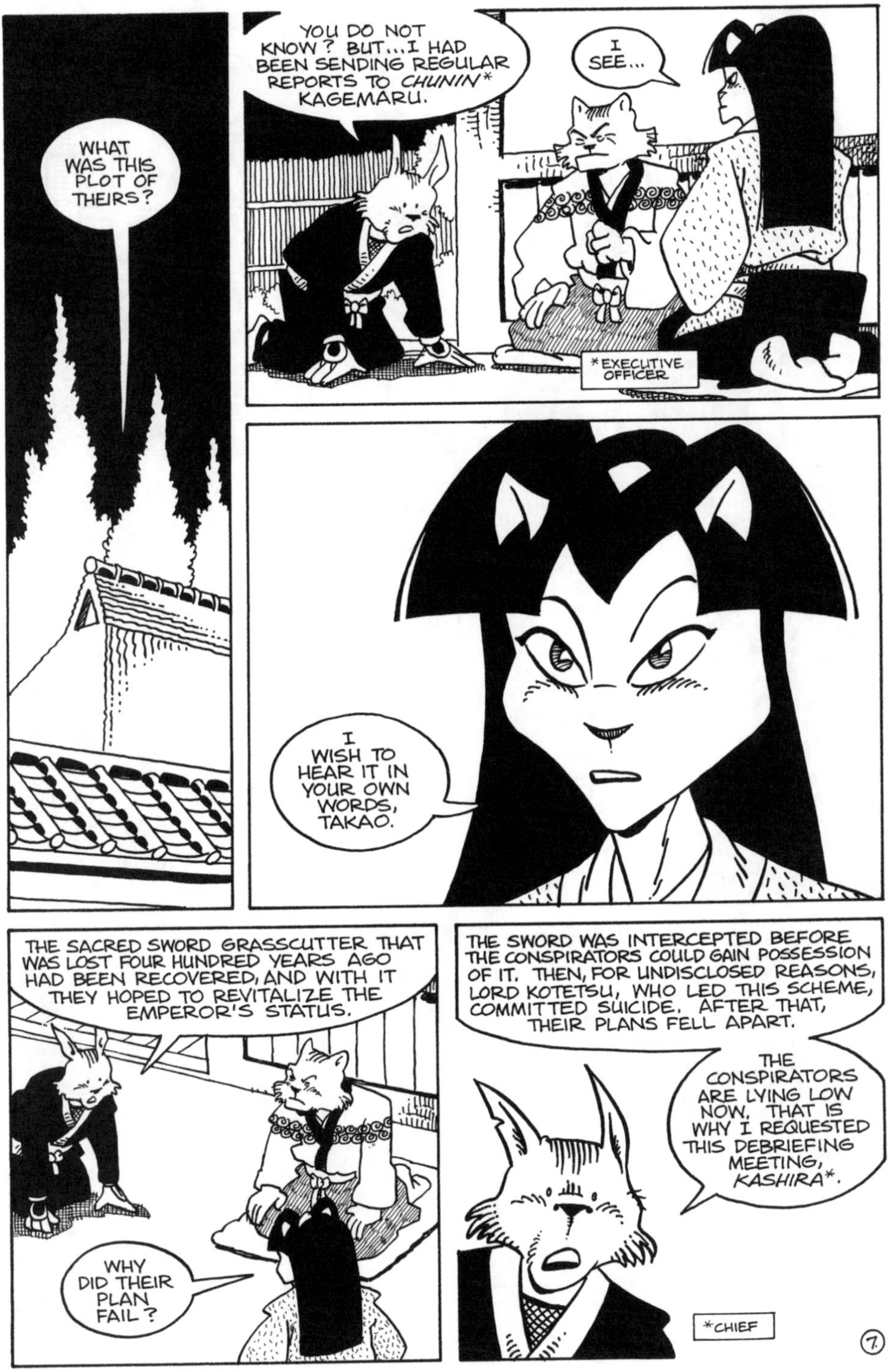
WHAT WAS THIS PLOT OF THEIRS?
YOU DO NOT KNOW? BUT...I HAD BEEN SENDING REGULAR REPORTS TO CHUNIN* KAGEMARU.
I SEE...
*EXECUTIVE OFFICER
I WISH TO HEAR IT IN YOUR OWN WORDS, TAKAO.
THE SACRED SWORD GRASSCUTTER THAT WAS LOST FOUR HUNDRED YEARS AGO HAD BEEN RECOVERED, AND WITH IT THEY HOPED TO REVITALIZE THE EMPEROR'S STATUS.
WHY DID THEIR PLAN FAIL?
THE SWORD WAS INTERCEPTED BEFORE THE CONSPIRATORS COULD GAIN POSSESSION OF IT. THEN, FOR UNDISCLOSED REASONS, LORD KOTETSU, WHO LED THIS SCHEME, COMMITTED SUICIDE. AFTER THAT, THEIR PLANS FELL APART.
THE CONSPIRATORS ARE LYING LOW NOW. THAT IS WHY I REQUESTED THIS DEBRIEFING MEETING, KASHIRA*.
*CHIEF
7

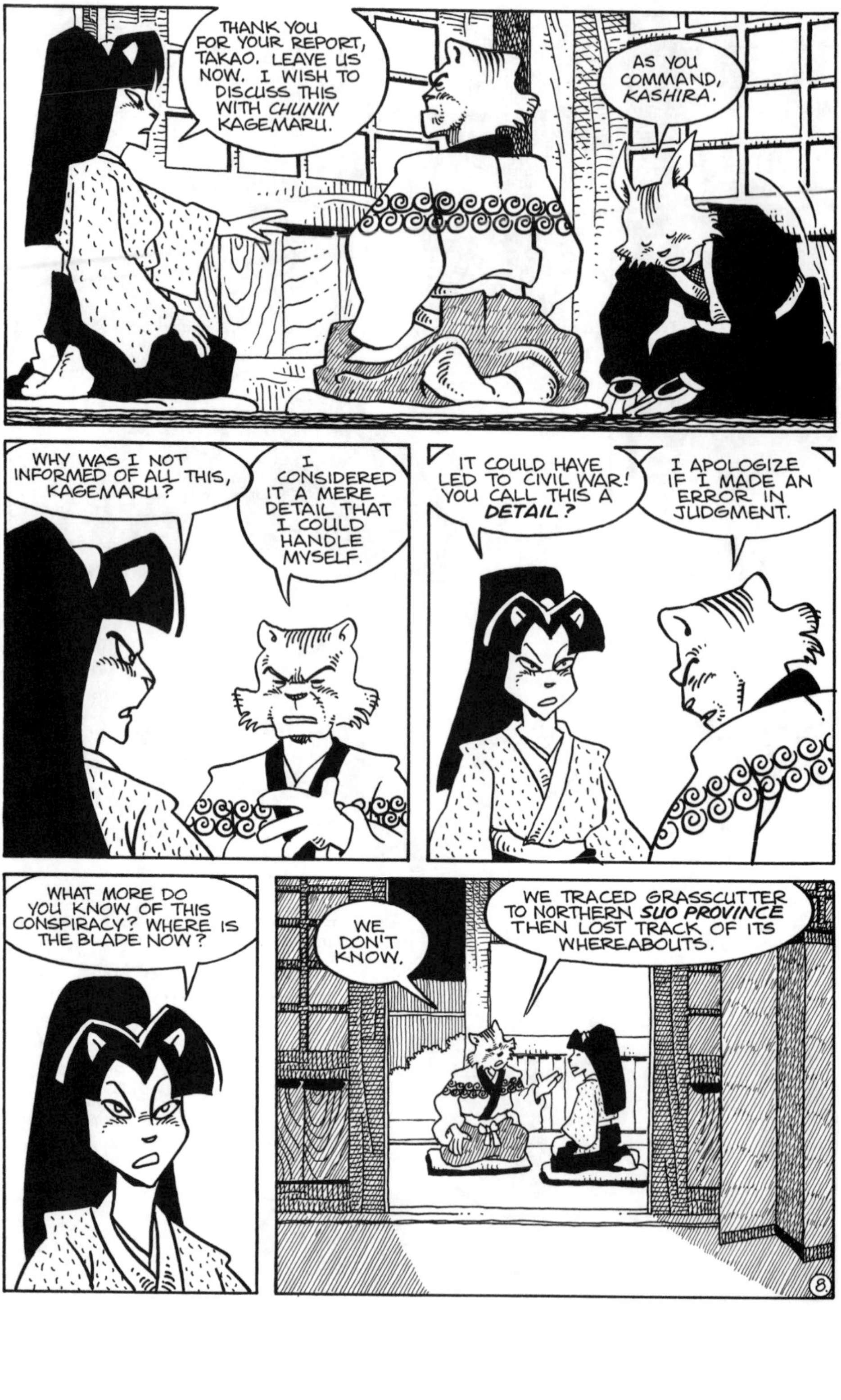
THANK YOU FOR YOUR REPORT, TAKAO. LEAVE US NOW. I WISH TO DISCUSS THIS WITH *CHUNIN* KAGEMARU.
AS YOU COMMAND, *KASHIRA.*
WHY WAS I NOT INFORMED OF ALL THIS, KAGEMARU?
I CONSIDERED IT A MERE DETAIL THAT I COULD HANDLE MYSELF.
IT COULD HAVE LED TO CIVIL WAR! YOU CALL THIS A *DETAIL?*
I APOLOGIZE IF I MADE AN ERROR IN JUDGMENT.
WHAT MORE DO YOU KNOW OF THIS CONSPIRACY? WHERE IS THE BLADE NOW?
WE DON'T KNOW.
WE TRACED GRASSCUTTER TO NORTHERN *SUO PROVINCE* THEN LOST TRACK OF ITS WHEREABOUTS.
8

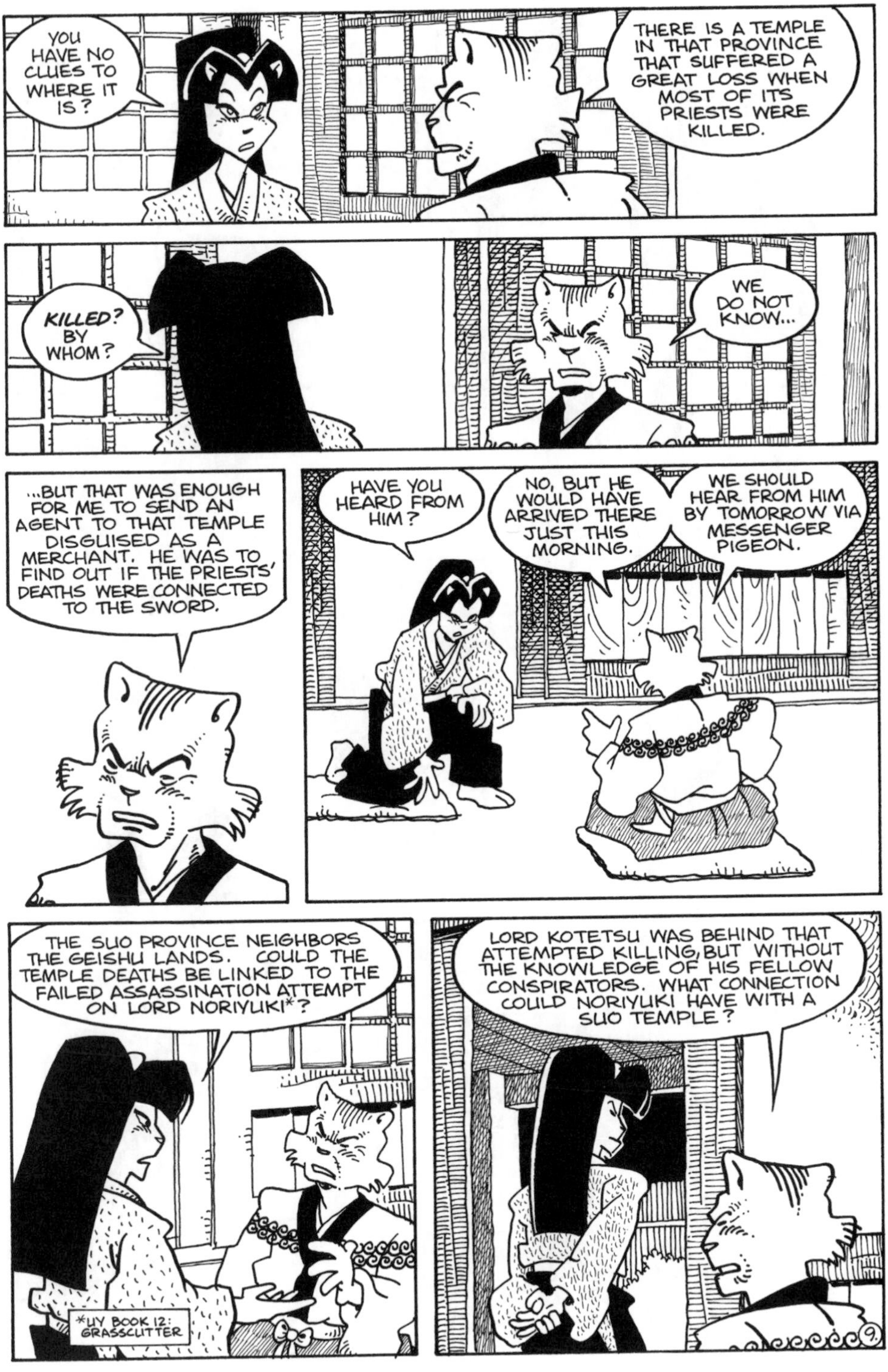
YOU HAVE NO CLUES TO WHERE IT IS?
THERE IS A TEMPLE IN THAT PROVINCE THAT SUFFERED A GREAT LOSS WHEN MOST OF ITS PRIESTS WERE KILLED.
KILLED? BY WHOM?
WE DO NOT KNOW...
...BUT THAT WAS ENOUGH FOR ME TO SEND AN AGENT TO THAT TEMPLE DISGUISED AS A MERCHANT. HE WAS TO FIND OUT IF THE PRIESTS' DEATHS WERE CONNECTED TO THE SWORD.
HAVE YOU HEARD FROM HIM?
NO, BUT HE WOULD HAVE ARRIVED THERE JUST THIS MORNING.
WE SHOULD HEAR FROM HIM BY TOMORROW VIA MESSENGER PIGEON.
THE SUO PROVINCE NEIGHBORS THE GEISHU LANDS. COULD THE TEMPLE DEATHS BE LINKED TO THE FAILED ASSASSINATION ATTEMPT ON LORD NORIYUKI*?
*UY BOOK 12: GRASSCUTTER
LORD KOTETSU WAS BEHIND THAT ATTEMPTED KILLING, BUT WITHOUT THE KNOWLEDGE OF HIS FELLOW CONSPIRATORS. WHAT CONNECTION COULD NORIYUKI HAVE WITH A SUO TEMPLE?
9.

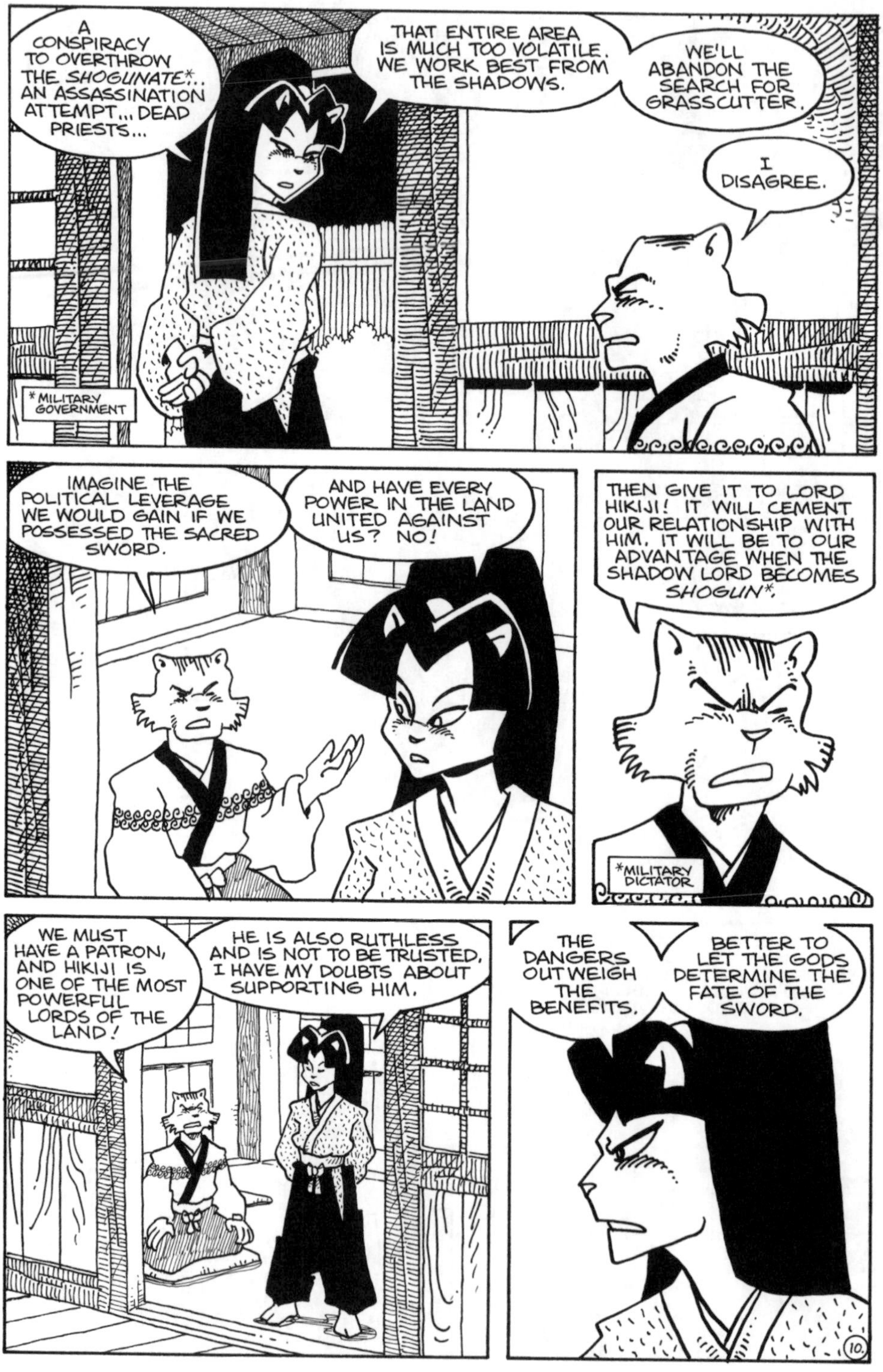
A CONSPIRACY TO OVERTHROW THE *SHOGUNATE**... AN ASSASSINATION ATTEMPT... DEAD PRIESTS...
THAT ENTIRE AREA IS MUCH TOO VOLATILE. WE WORK BEST FROM THE SHADOWS.
WE'LL ABANDON THE SEARCH FOR GRASSCUTTER.
I DISAGREE.
*MILITARY GOVERNMENT
IMAGINE THE POLITICAL LEVERAGE WE WOULD GAIN IF WE POSSESSED THE SACRED SWORD.
AND HAVE EVERY POWER IN THE LAND UNITED AGAINST US? NO!
THEN GIVE IT TO LORD HIKIJI! IT WILL CEMENT OUR RELATIONSHIP WITH HIM. IT WILL BE TO OUR ADVANTAGE WHEN THE SHADOW LORD BECOMES *SHOGUN**.
*MILITARY DICTATOR
WE MUST HAVE A PATRON, AND HIKIJI IS ONE OF THE MOST POWERFUL LORDS OF THE LAND!
HE IS ALSO RUTHLESS AND IS NOT TO BE TRUSTED. I HAVE MY DOUBTS ABOUT SUPPORTING HIM.
THE DANGERS OUTWEIGH THE BENEFITS.
BETTER TO LET THE GODS DETERMINE THE FATE OF THE SWORD.
10.

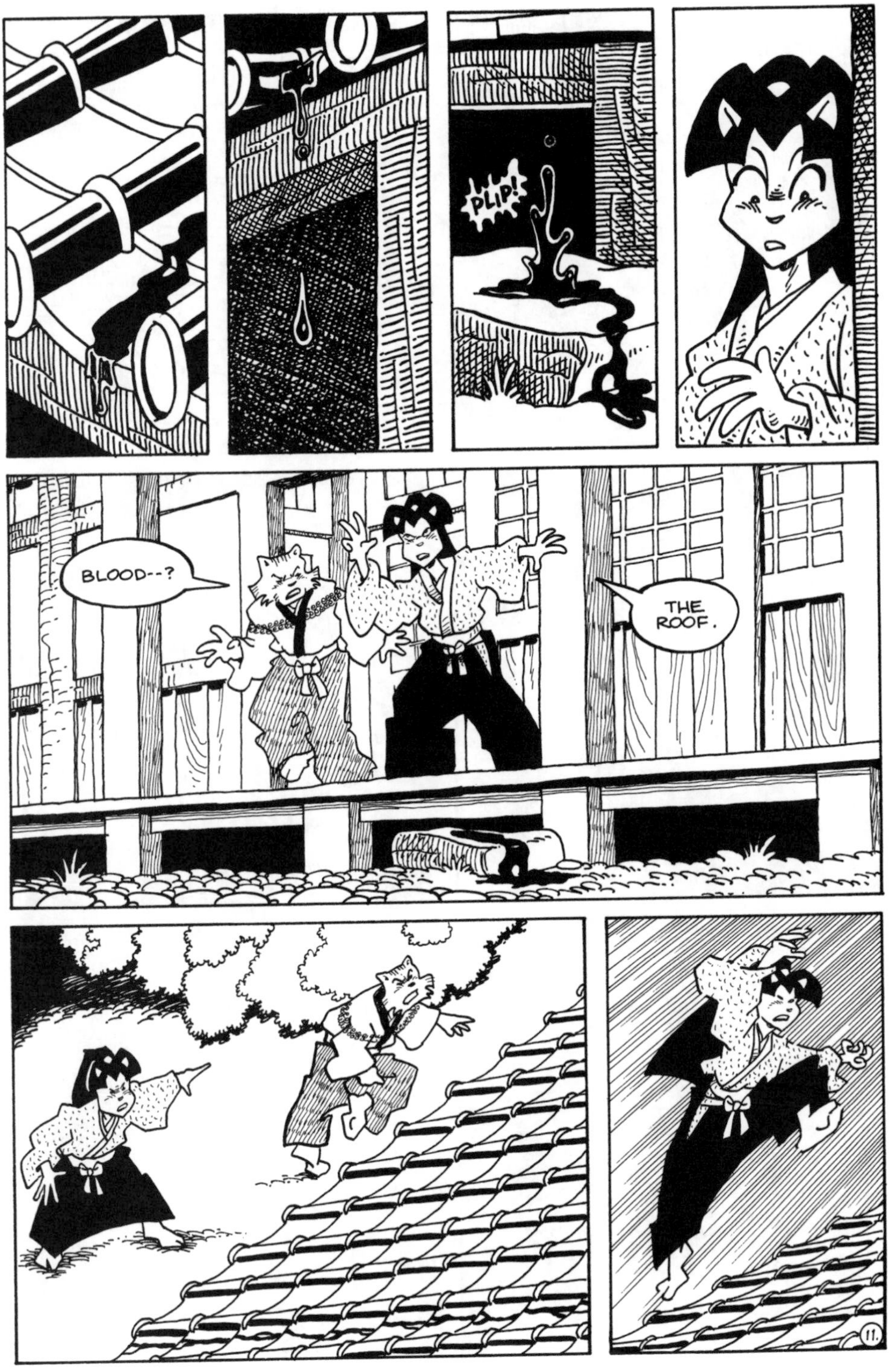
PLIP!
BLOOD--?
THE ROOF.
11.

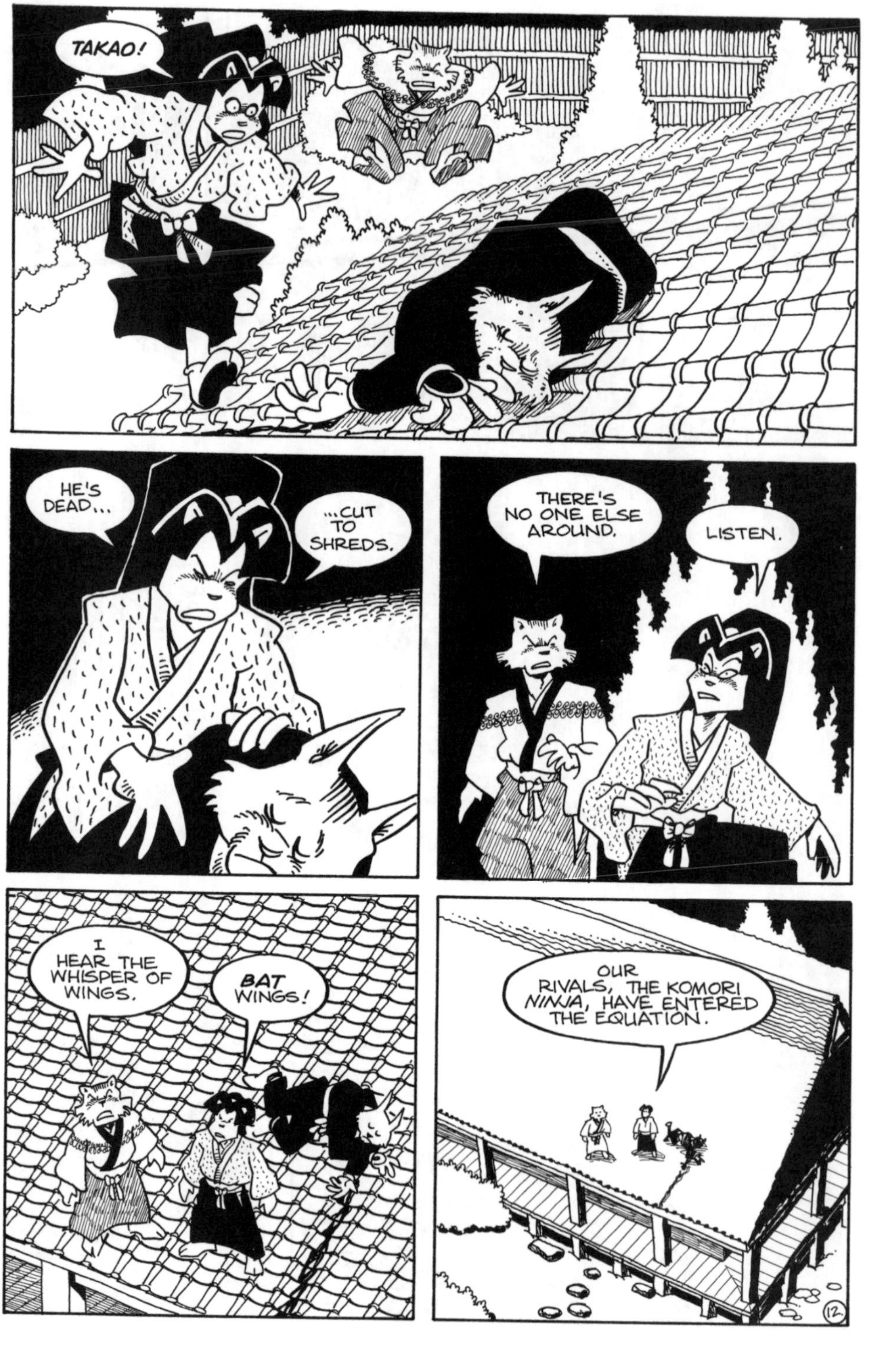
TAKAO!
HE'S DEAD...
...CUT TO SHREDS.
THERE'S NO ONE ELSE AROUND.
LISTEN.
I HEAR THE WHISPER OF WINGS.
BAT WINGS!
OUR RIVALS, THE KOMORI NINJA, HAVE ENTERED THE EQUATION.
12

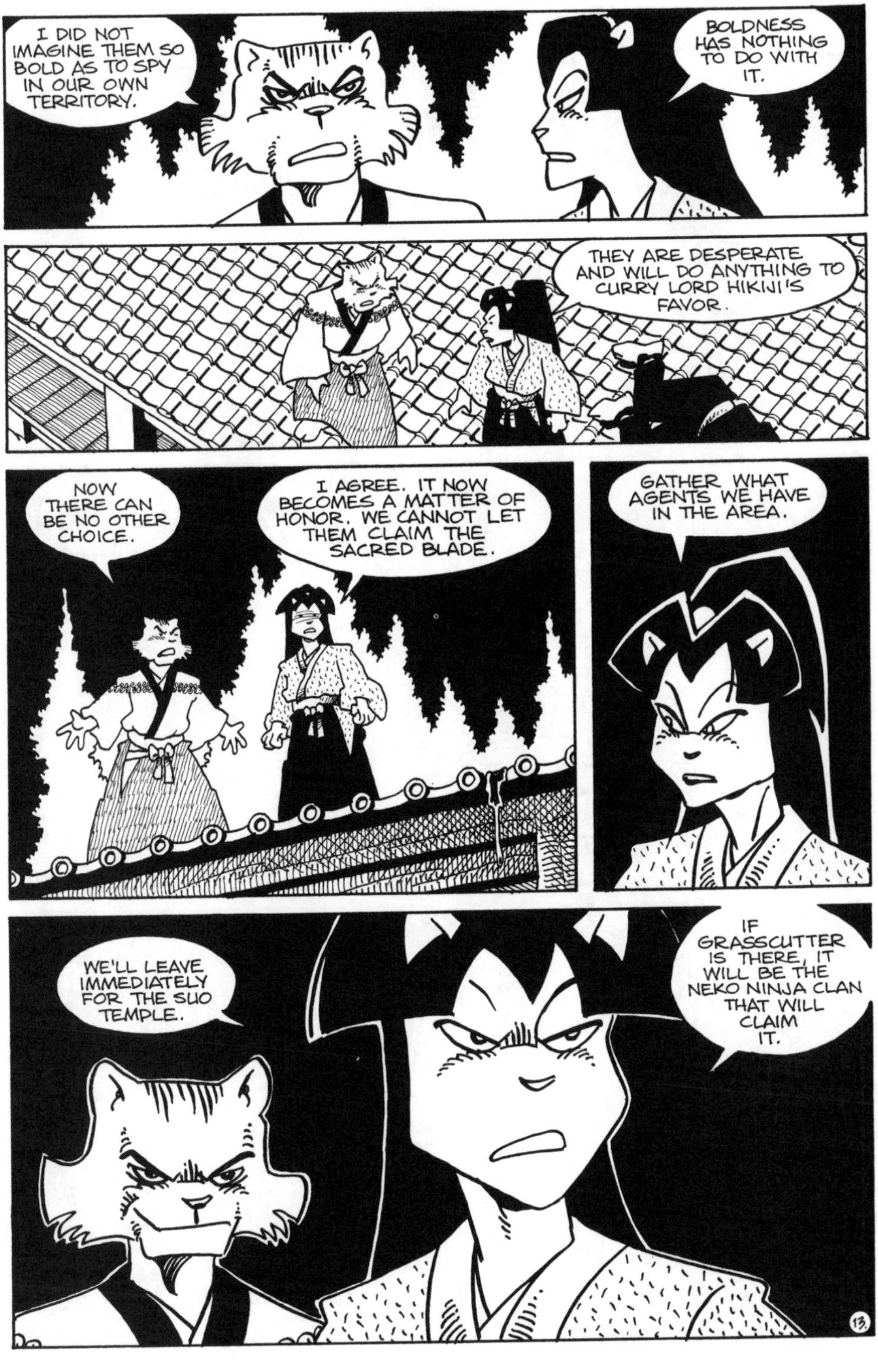
I DID NOT IMAGINE THEM SO BOLD AS TO SPY IN OUR OWN TERRITORY.
BOLDNESS HAS NOTHING TO DO WITH IT.
THEY ARE DESPERATE AND WILL DO ANYTHING TO CURRY LORD HIKIJI'S FAVOR.
NOW THERE CAN BE NO OTHER CHOICE.
I AGREE. IT NOW BECOMES A MATTER OF HONOR. WE CANNOT LET THEM CLAIM THE SACRED BLADE.
GATHER WHAT AGENTS WE HAVE IN THE AREA.
WE'LL LEAVE IMMEDIATELY FOR THE SUO TEMPLE.
IF GRASSCUTTER IS THERE, IT WILL BE THE NEKO NINJA CLAN THAT WILL CLAIM IT.
13

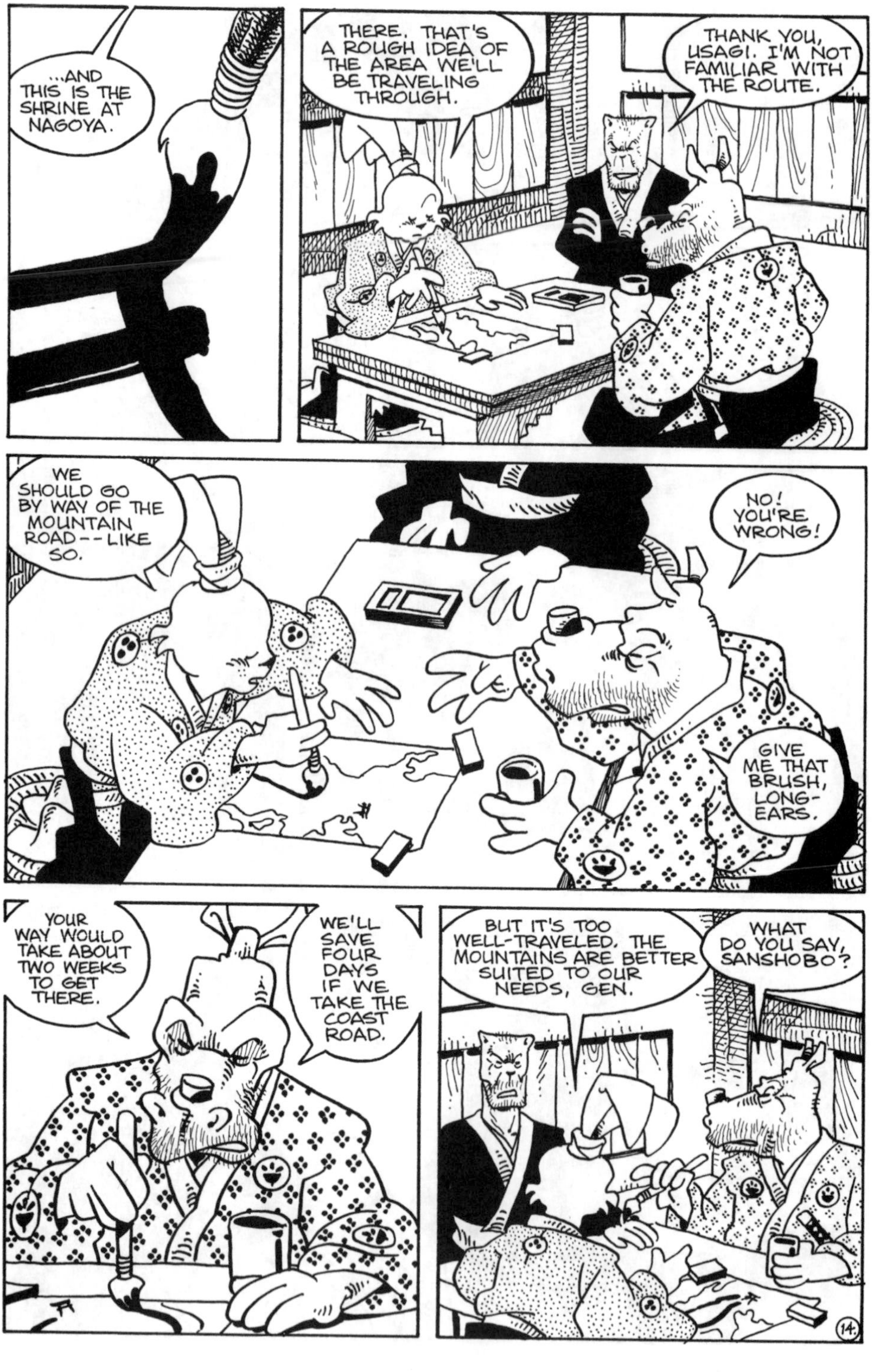
...AND THIS IS THE SHRINE AT NAGOYA.
THERE. THAT'S A ROUGH IDEA OF THE AREA WE'LL BE TRAVELING THROUGH.
THANK YOU, USAGI. I'M NOT FAMILIAR WITH THE ROUTE.
WE SHOULD GO BY WAY OF THE MOUNTAIN ROAD--LIKE SO.
NO! YOU'RE WRONG!
GIVE ME THAT BRUSH, LONG-EARS.
YOUR WAY WOULD TAKE ABOUT TWO WEEKS TO GET THERE.
WE'LL SAVE FOUR DAYS IF WE TAKE THE COAST ROAD.
BUT IT'S TOO WELL-TRAVELED. THE MOUNTAINS ARE BETTER SUITED TO OUR NEEDS, GEN.
WHAT DO YOU SAY, SANSHOBO?
14.

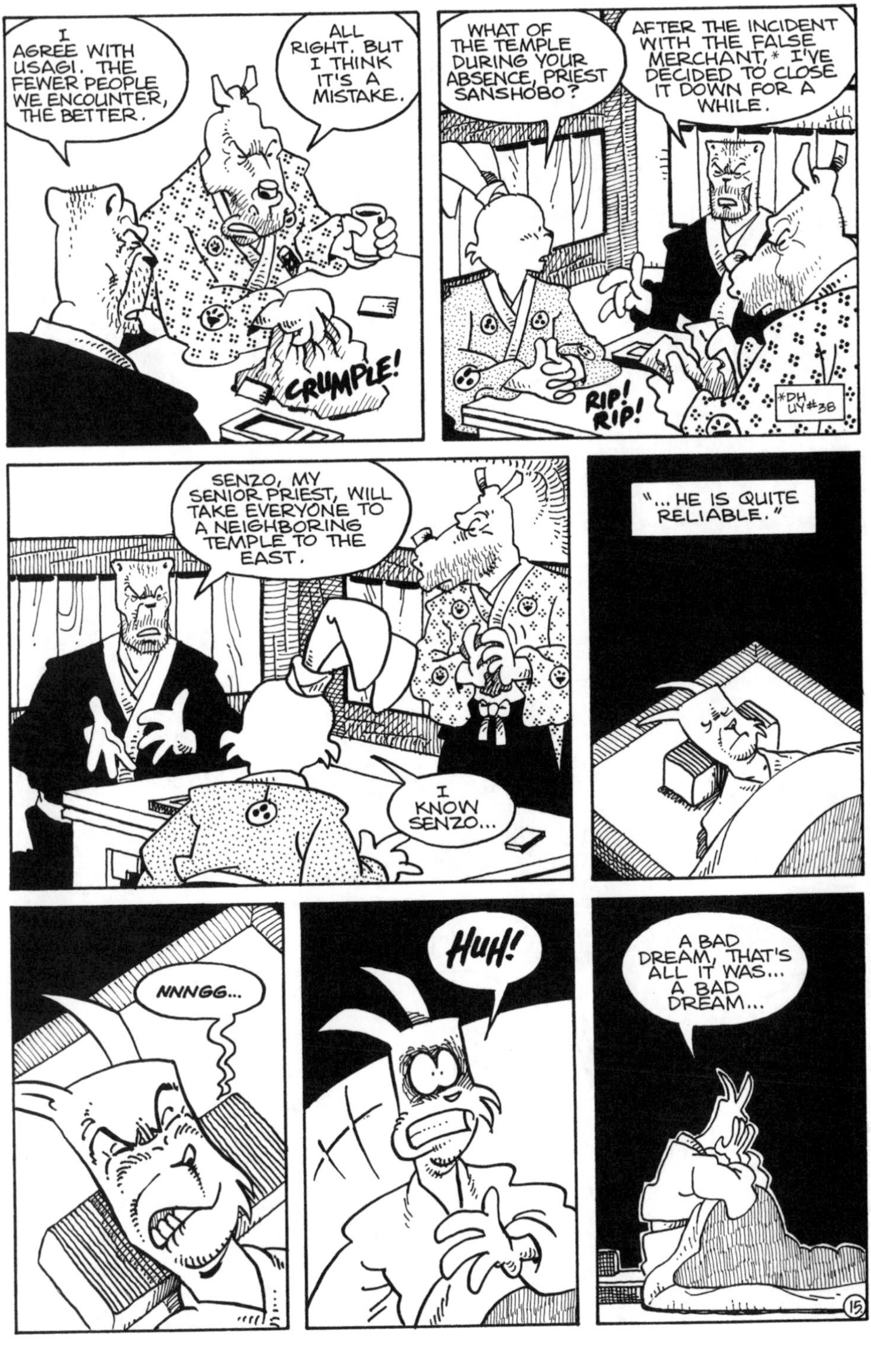

I AGREE WITH USAGI. THE FEWER PEOPLE WE ENCOUNTER, THE BETTER.
ALL RIGHT. BUT I THINK IT'S A MISTAKE.
CRUMPLE!
WHAT OF THE TEMPLE DURING YOUR ABSENCE, PRIEST SANSHOBO?
AFTER THE INCIDENT WITH THE FALSE MERCHANT,* I'VE DECIDED TO CLOSE IT DOWN FOR A WHILE.
RIP! RIP!
*DH UY #38
SENZO, MY SENIOR PRIEST, WILL TAKE EVERYONE TO A NEIGHBORING TEMPLE TO THE EAST.
I KNOW SENZO...
"...HE IS QUITE RELIABLE."
NNNGG...
HUH!
A BAD DREAM, THAT'S ALL IT WAS... A BAD DREAM...
15

WE HAD BETTER GET THE SWORD IF WE'RE SERIOUS ABOUT GOING TO ATSUTA DAIJINGU*.

WHERE DID YOU HIDE THAT THING, ANYWAY?

* "GREAT SHRINE."

IT'S IN HERE.

THE WELL?

THIS WELL IS OUT OF THE WAY--HARDLY USED.

GRASSCUTTER LAY ON THE SEA BED FOR MORE THAN FOUR HUNDRED YEARS...

...A FEW MORE WEEKS UNDERWATER SHOULDN'T HAVE HURT IT.

THE SWORD OF THE SUN GODDESS... INSPIRING, ISN'T IT?

I WONDER HOW MUCH WE COULD SELL IT FOR.

WHAT?

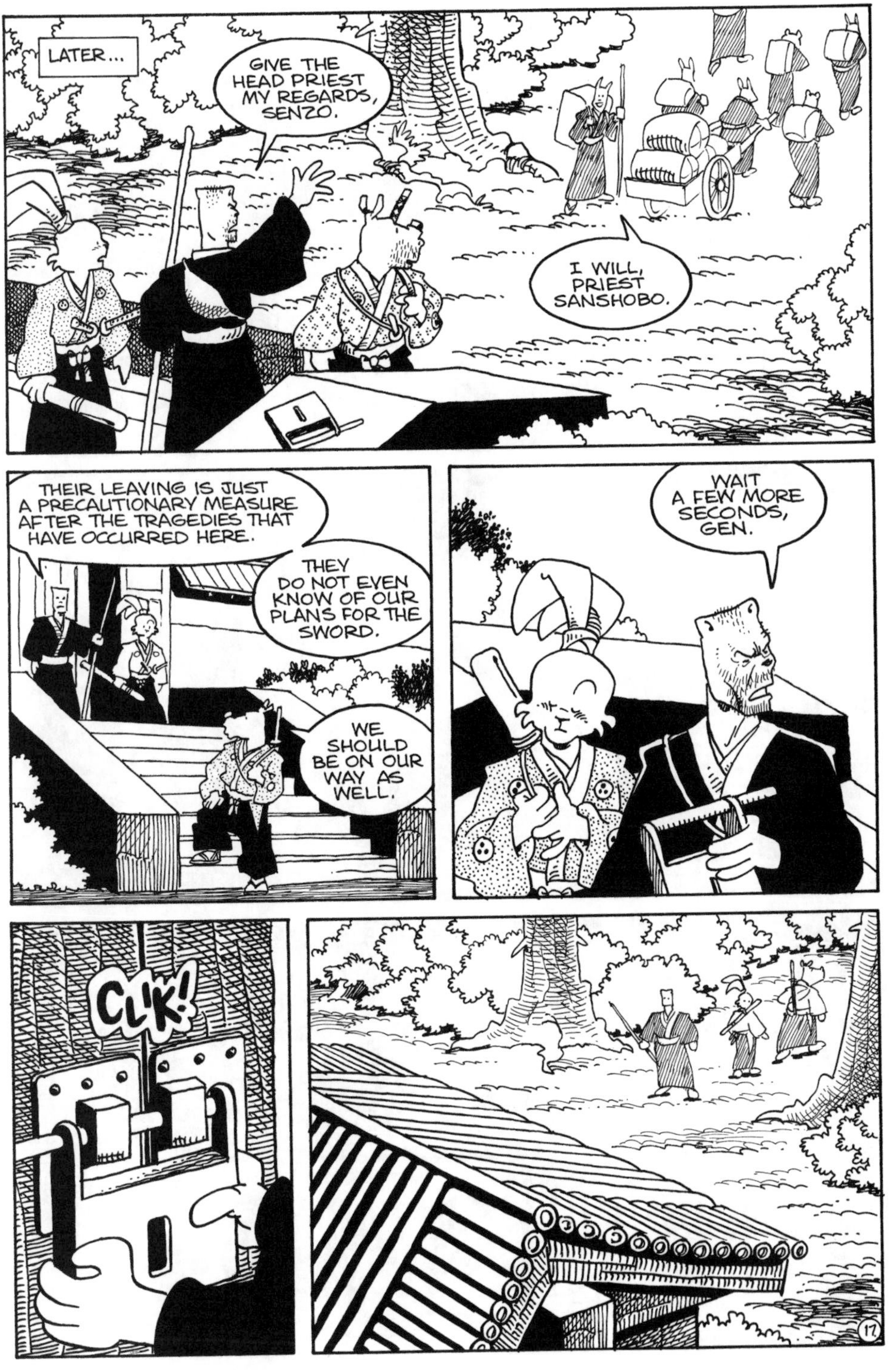
LATER...
GIVE THE HEAD PRIEST MY REGARDS, SENZO.
I WILL, PRIEST SANSHOBO.
THEIR LEAVING IS JUST A PRECAUTIONARY MEASURE AFTER THE TRAGEDIES THAT HAVE OCCURRED HERE.
THEY DO NOT EVEN KNOW OF OUR PLANS FOR THE SWORD.
WE SHOULD BE ON OUR WAY AS WELL.
WAIT A FEW MORE SECONDS, GEN.
CLIK!
17

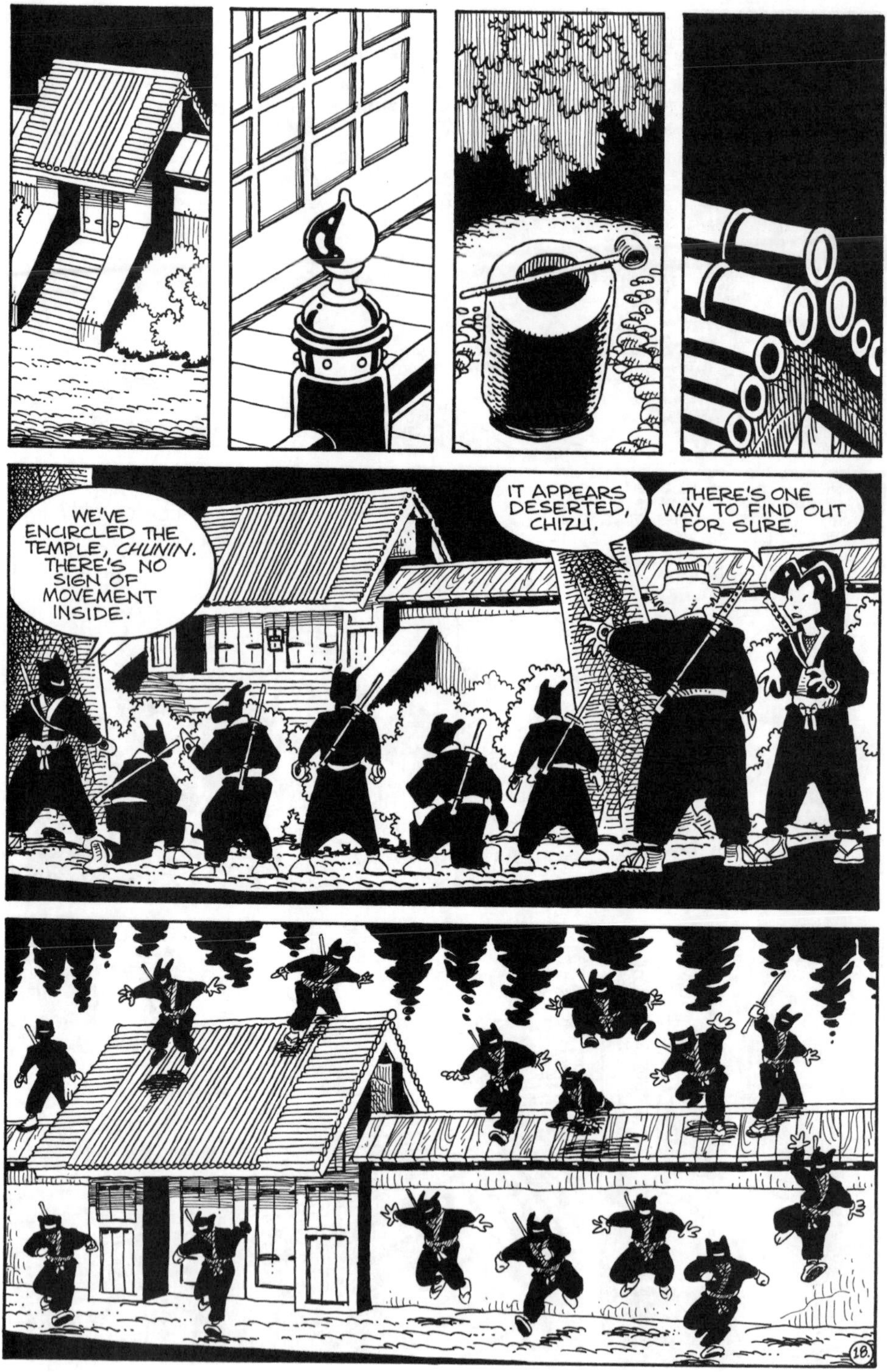
WE'VE ENCIRCLED THE TEMPLE, *CHUNIN*. THERE'S NO SIGN OF MOVEMENT INSIDE.
IT APPEARS DESERTED, CHIZU.
THERE'S ONE WAY TO FIND OUT FOR SURE.
18.

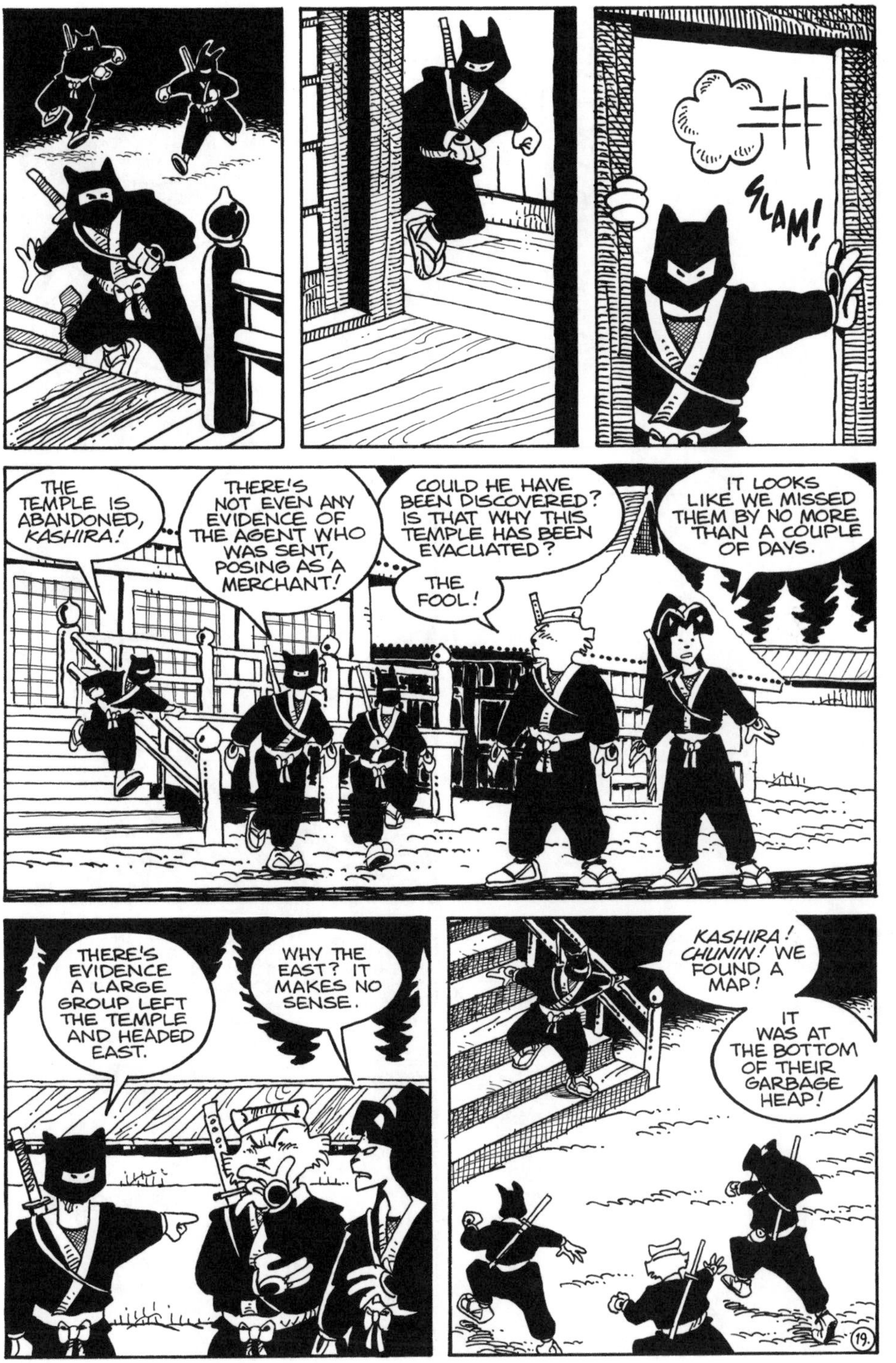
SLAM!
THE TEMPLE IS ABANDONED, KASHIRA!
THERE'S NOT EVEN ANY EVIDENCE OF THE AGENT WHO WAS SENT, POSING AS A MERCHANT!
COULD HE HAVE BEEN DISCOVERED? IS THAT WHY THIS TEMPLE HAS BEEN EVACUATED?
THE FOOL!
IT LOOKS LIKE WE MISSED THEM BY NO MORE THAN A COUPLE OF DAYS.
THERE'S EVIDENCE A LARGE GROUP LEFT THE TEMPLE AND HEADED EAST.
WHY THE EAST? IT MAKES NO SENSE.
KASHIRA! CHUNIN! WE FOUND A MAP!
IT WAS AT THE BOTTOM OF THEIR GARBAGE HEAP!
19.

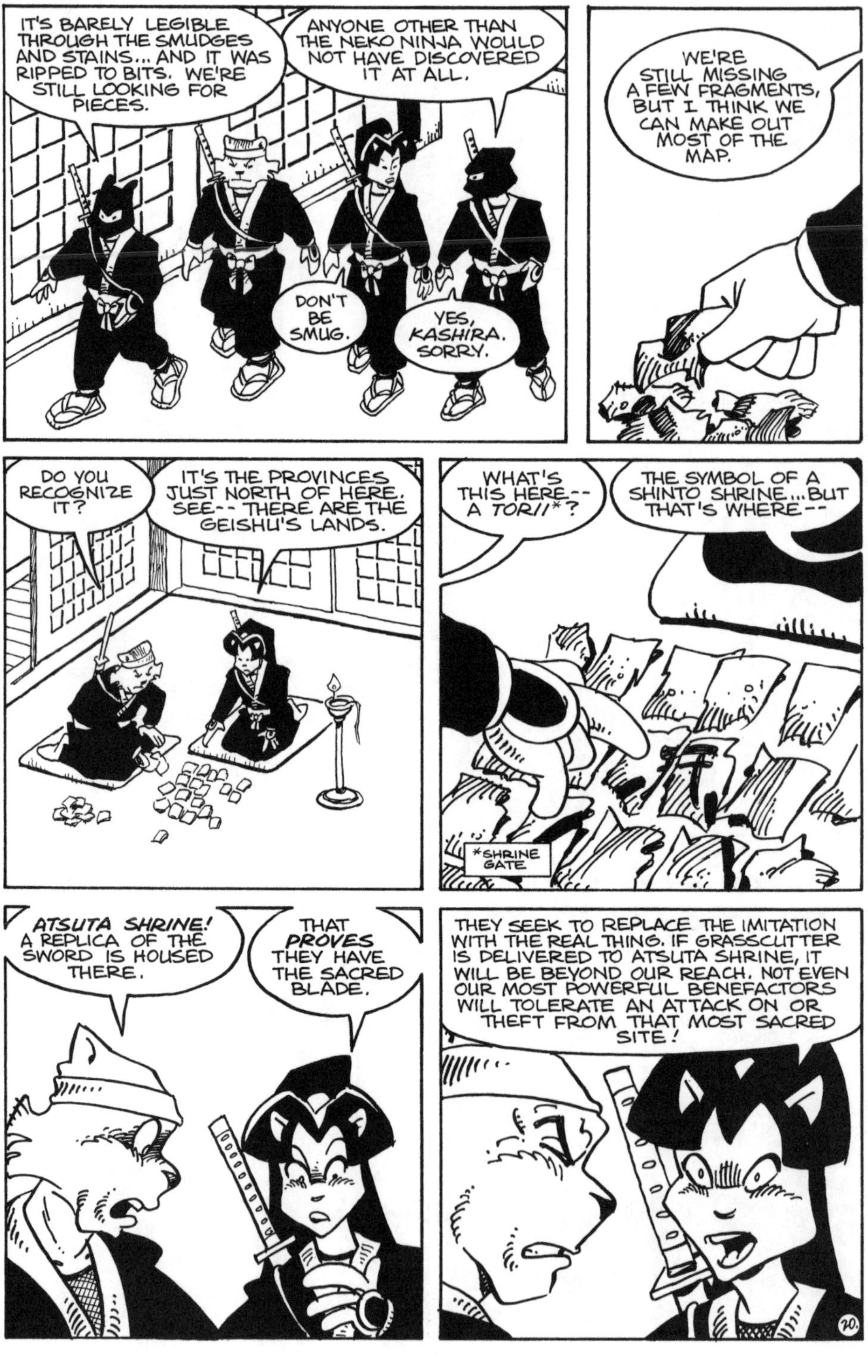
IT'S BARELY LEGIBLE THROUGH THE SMUDGES AND STAINS... AND IT WAS RIPPED TO BITS. WE'RE STILL LOOKING FOR PIECES.
ANYONE OTHER THAN THE NEKO NINJA WOULD NOT HAVE DISCOVERED IT AT ALL.
DON'T BE SMUG.
YES, *KASHIRA*. SORRY.
WE'RE STILL MISSING A FEW FRAGMENTS, BUT I THINK WE CAN MAKE OUT MOST OF THE MAP.
DO YOU RECOGNIZE IT?
IT'S THE PROVINCES JUST NORTH OF HERE. SEE-- THERE ARE THE GEISHU'S LANDS.
WHAT'S THIS HERE-- A *TORII**?
THE SYMBOL OF A SHINTO SHRINE...BUT THAT'S WHERE--
*SHRINE GATE
ATSUTA SHRINE! A REPLICA OF THE SWORD IS HOUSED THERE.
THAT *PROVES* THEY HAVE THE SACRED BLADE.
THEY SEEK TO REPLACE THE IMITATION WITH THE REAL THING. IF GRASSCUTTER IS DELIVERED TO ATSUTA SHRINE, IT WILL BE BEYOND OUR REACH. NOT EVEN OUR MOST POWERFUL BENEFACTORS WILL TOLERATE AN ATTACK ON OR THEFT FROM THAT MOST SACRED SITE!
20.

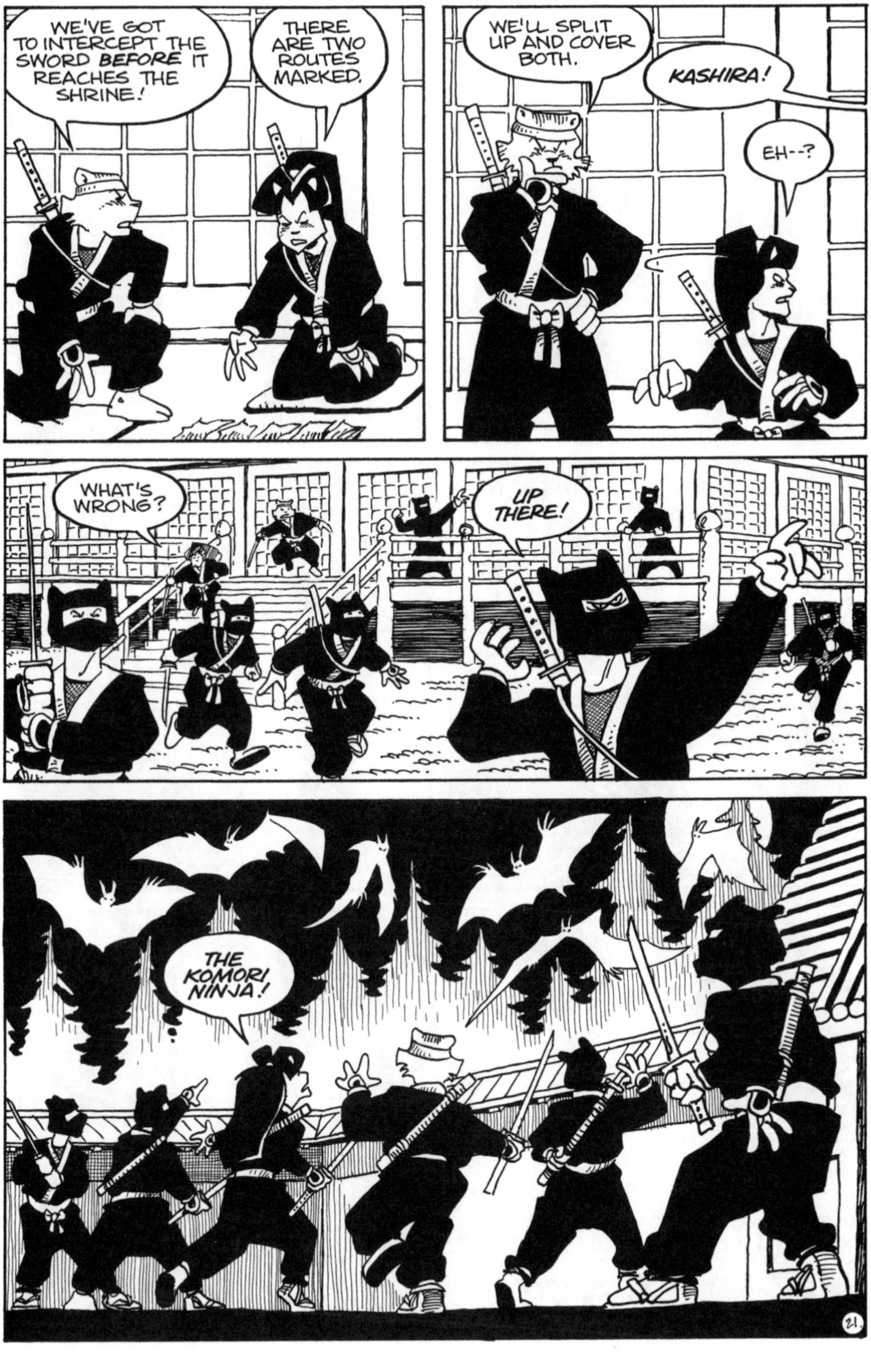
WE'VE GOT TO INTERCEPT THE SWORD BEFORE IT REACHES THE SHRINE!
THERE ARE TWO ROUTES MARKED.
WE'LL SPLIT UP AND COVER BOTH.
KASHIRA!
EH--?
WHAT'S WRONG?
UP THERE!
THE KOMORI NINJA!
21.

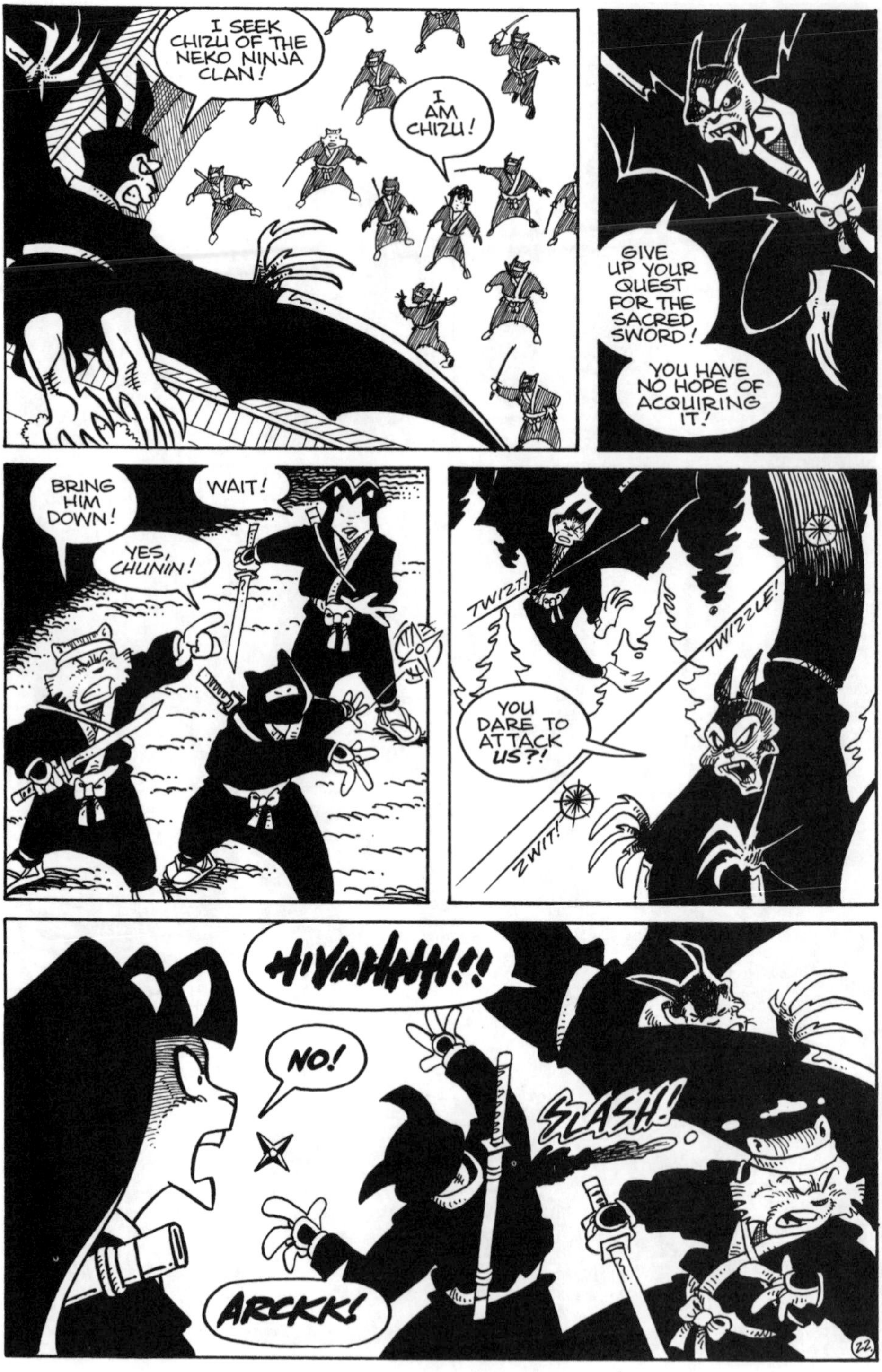
I SEEK CHIZU OF THE NEKO NINJA CLAN!
I AM CHIZU!
GIVE UP YOUR QUEST FOR THE SACRED SWORD!
YOU HAVE NO HOPE OF ACQUIRING IT!
BRING HIM DOWN!
WAIT!
YES, CHUNIN!
TWIZT!
TWIZZLE!
ZWIT!
YOU DARE TO ATTACK US?!
HI-YAHHHH!!
NO!
SLASH!
ARCKK!
22

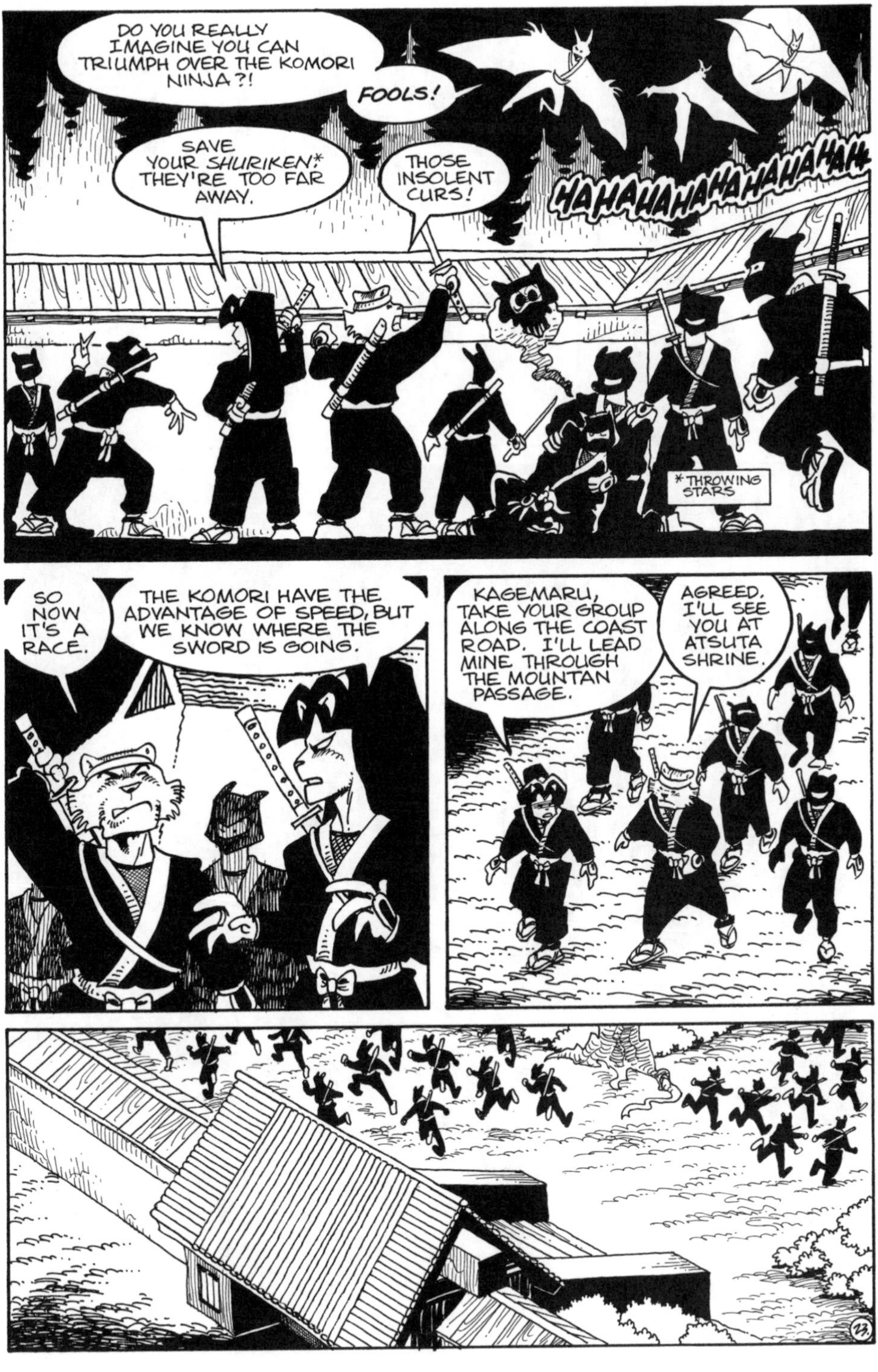
DO YOU REALLY IMAGINE YOU CAN TRIUMPH OVER THE KOMORI NINJA?!
FOOLS!
SAVE YOUR SHURIKEN!* THEY'RE TOO FAR AWAY.
THOSE INSOLENT CURS!
HAHAHAHAHAHAHAHAHAH
*THROWING STARS
SO NOW IT'S A RACE.
THE KOMORI HAVE THE ADVANTAGE OF SPEED, BUT WE KNOW WHERE THE SWORD IS GOING.
KAGEMARU, TAKE YOUR GROUP ALONG THE COAST ROAD. I'LL LEAD MINE THROUGH THE MOUNTAN PASSAGE.
AGREED. I'LL SEE YOU AT ATSUTA SHRINE.
23.

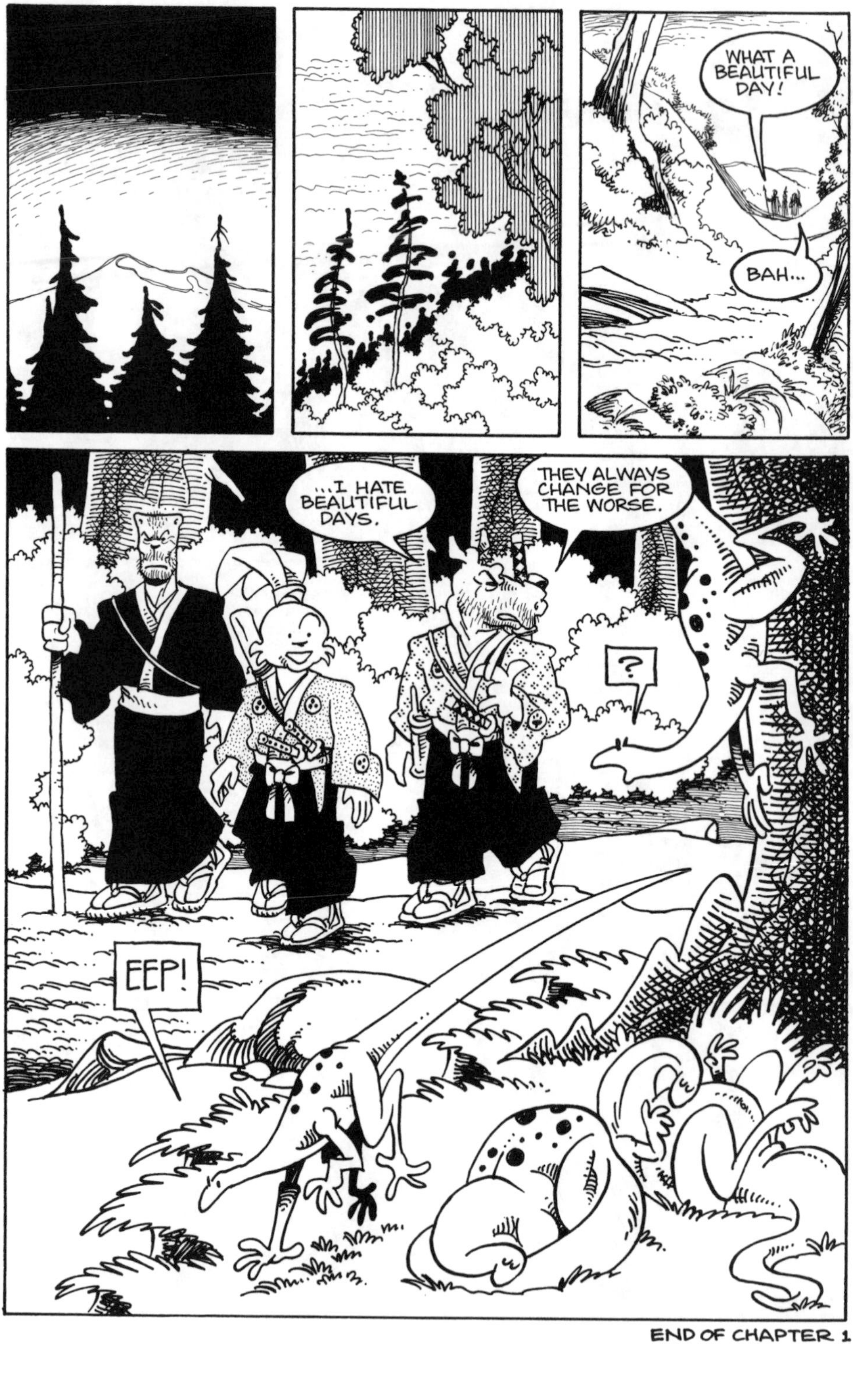
WHAT A BEAUTIFUL DAY!
BAH...
...I HATE BEAUTIFUL DAYS.
THEY ALWAYS CHANGE FOR THE WORSE.
?
EEP!

END OF CHAPTER 1

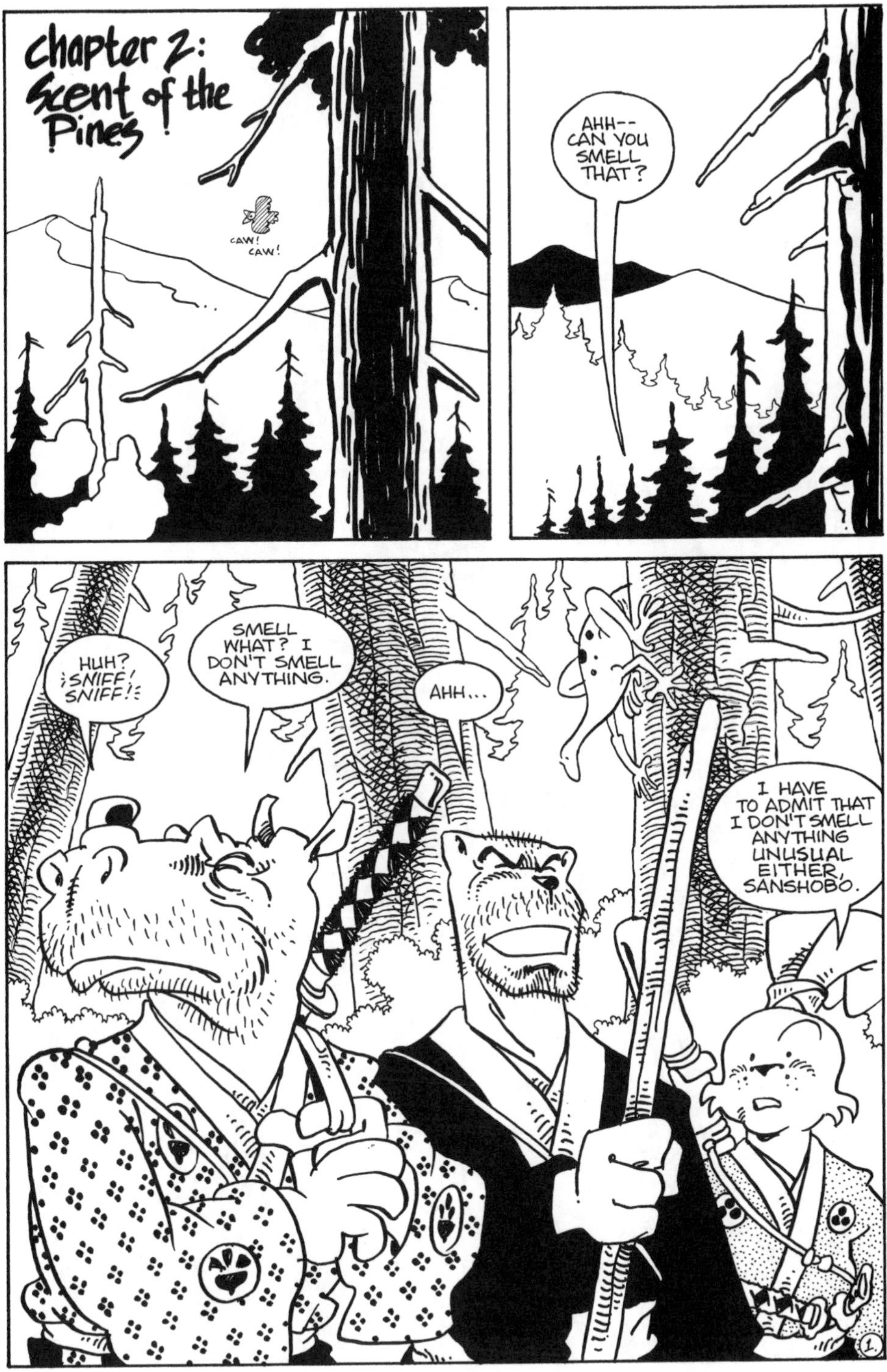
Chapter 2: Scent of the Pines
CAW! CAW!
AHH-- CAN YOU SMELL THAT?
HUH? SNIFF! SNIFF!
SMELL WHAT? I DON'T SMELL ANYTHING.
AHH...
I HAVE TO ADMIT THAT I DON'T SMELL ANYTHING UNUSUAL EITHER, SANSHOBO.
1.

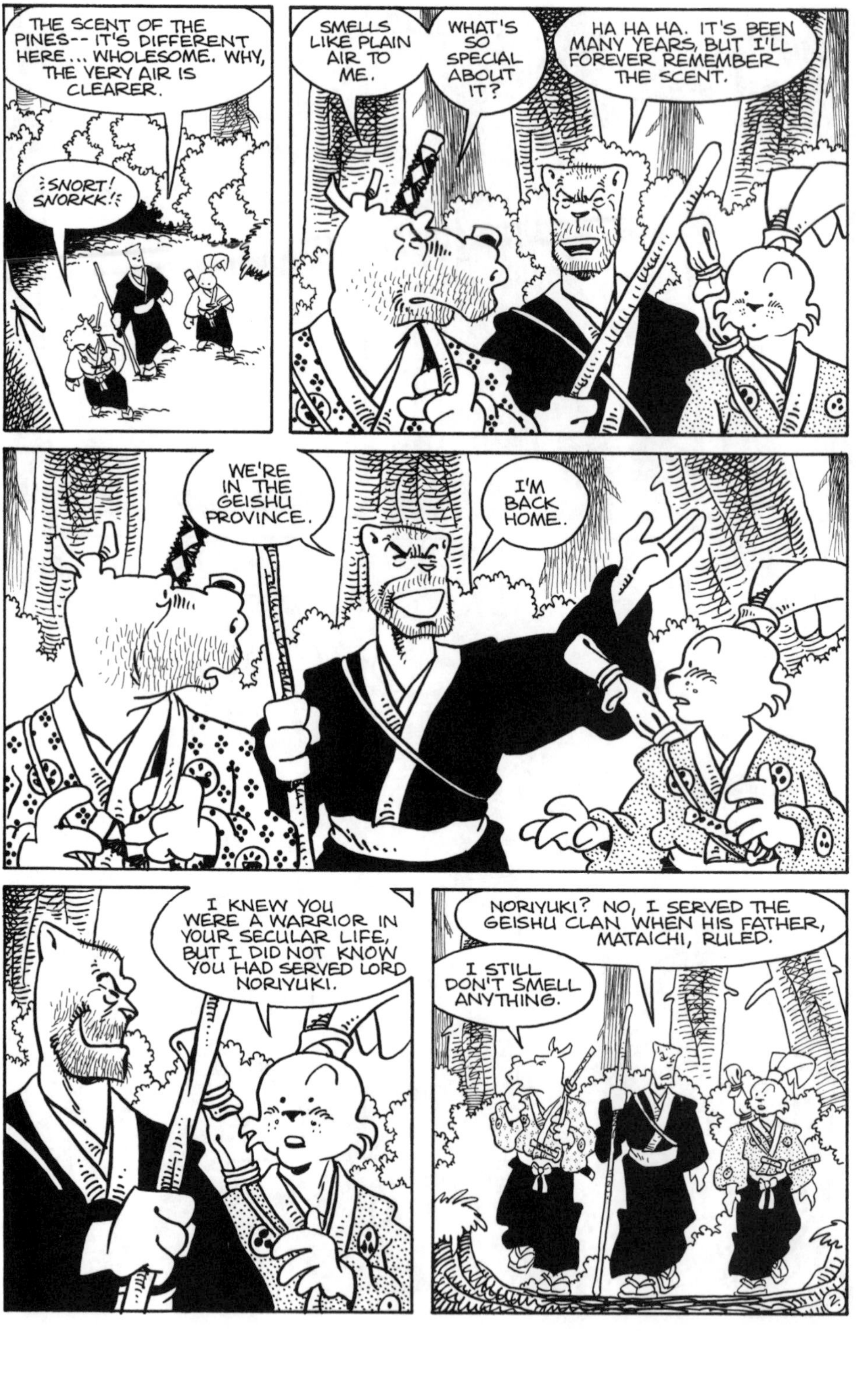

THE SCENT OF THE PINES-- IT'S DIFFERENT HERE... WHOLESOME. WHY, THE VERY AIR IS CLEARER.
SNORT! SNORKK!
SMELLS LIKE PLAIN AIR TO ME.
WHAT'S SO SPECIAL ABOUT IT?
HA HA HA. IT'S BEEN MANY YEARS, BUT I'LL FOREVER REMEMBER THE SCENT.
WE'RE IN THE GEISHU PROVINCE.
I'M BACK HOME.
I KNEW YOU WERE A WARRIOR IN YOUR SECULAR LIFE, BUT I DID NOT KNOW YOU HAD SERVED LORD NORIYUKI.
NORIYUKI? NO, I SERVED THE GEISHU CLAN WHEN HIS FATHER, MATAICHI, RULED.
I STILL DON'T SMELL ANYTHING.
2

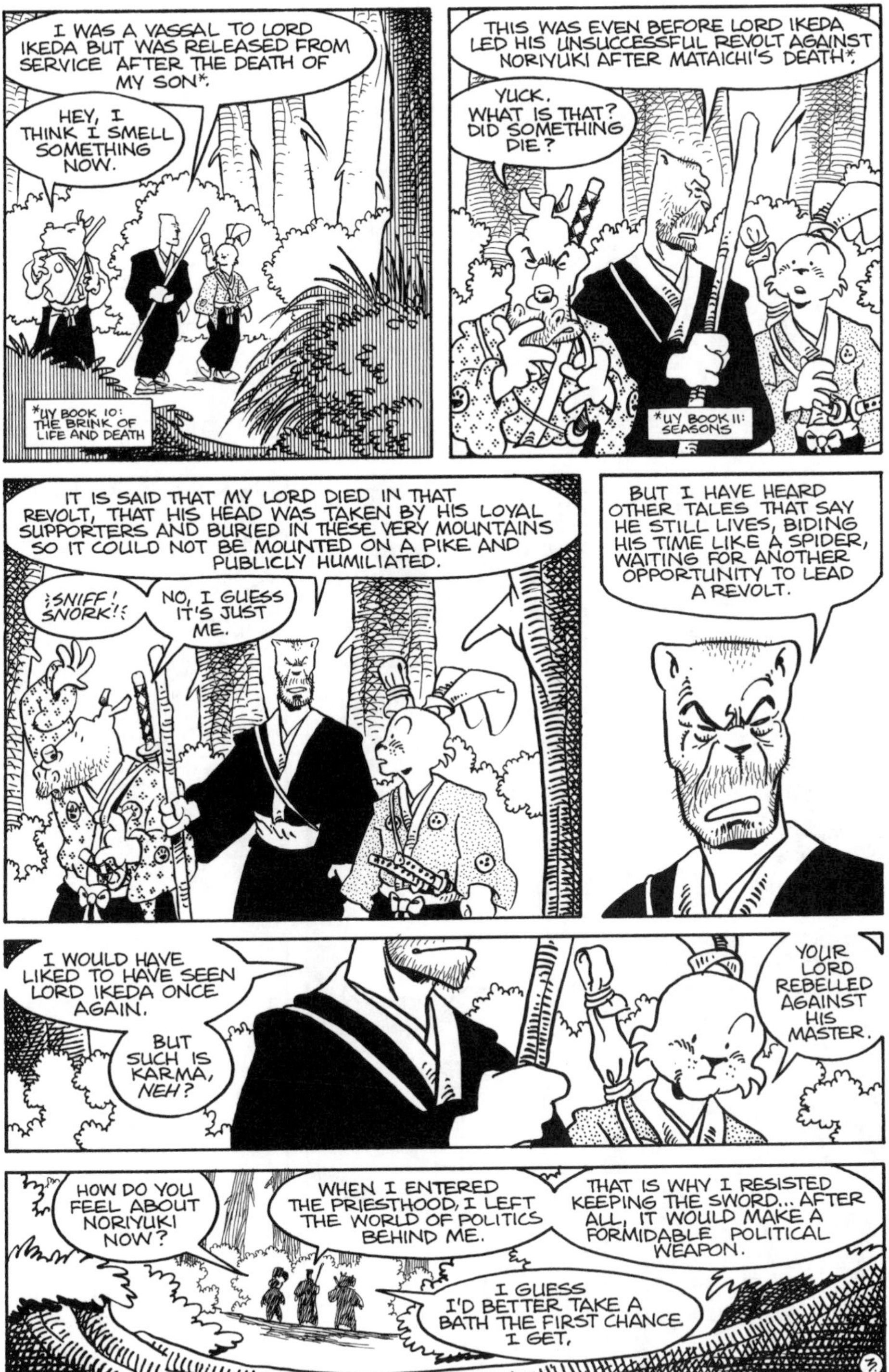

I WAS A VASSAL TO LORD IKEDA BUT WAS RELEASED FROM SERVICE AFTER THE DEATH OF MY SON*.
HEY, I THINK I SMELL SOMETHING NOW.
*UY BOOK 10: THE BRINK OF LIFE AND DEATH
THIS WAS EVEN BEFORE LORD IKEDA LED HIS UNSUCCESSFUL REVOLT AGAINST NORIYUKI AFTER MATAICHI'S DEATH*.
YUCK. WHAT IS THAT? DID SOMETHING DIE?
*UY BOOK 11: SEASONS
IT IS SAID THAT MY LORD DIED IN THAT REVOLT, THAT HIS HEAD WAS TAKEN BY HIS LOYAL SUPPORTERS AND BURIED IN THESE VERY MOUNTAINS SO IT COULD NOT BE MOUNTED ON A PIKE AND PUBLICLY HUMILIATED.
SNIFF! SNORK!
NO, I GUESS IT'S JUST ME.
BUT I HAVE HEARD OTHER TALES THAT SAY HE STILL LIVES, BIDING HIS TIME LIKE A SPIDER, WAITING FOR ANOTHER OPPORTUNITY TO LEAD A REVOLT.
I WOULD HAVE LIKED TO HAVE SEEN LORD IKEDA ONCE AGAIN.
BUT SUCH IS KARMA, *NEH*?
YOUR LORD REBELLED AGAINST HIS MASTER.
HOW DO YOU FEEL ABOUT NORIYUKI NOW?
WHEN I ENTERED THE PRIESTHOOD, I LEFT THE WORLD OF POLITICS BEHIND ME.
THAT IS WHY I RESISTED KEEPING THE SWORD... AFTER ALL, IT WOULD MAKE A FORMIDABLE POLITICAL WEAPON.
I GUESS I'D BETTER TAKE A BATH THE FIRST CHANCE I GET.
3

WHAT ARE WE TALKING ABOUT-- THE SMELL?

THAT WAS HALF AN HOUR AGO.

LORD IKEDA MUST HAVE BEEN A GREAT LEADER TO HAVE INSPIRED SUCH DEVOTION FROM YOU.

HE WAS A WISE LEADER... A BRILLIANT STRATEGIST. I REMEMBER A TIME LONG AGO-- BEFORE I BECAME A PRIEST-- WHEN I WAS STILL KNOWN AS KONUMA INUSHIRO...

" THIS WAS DURING THE YEARS OF WARS, BEFORE THE *SHOGUN'S** PEACE WAS ESTABLISHED.

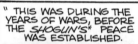

*MILITARY RULER

"A *NINJA* FROM THE NOTORIOUS NEKO CLAN HAD INFILTRATED OUR CASTLE."

④

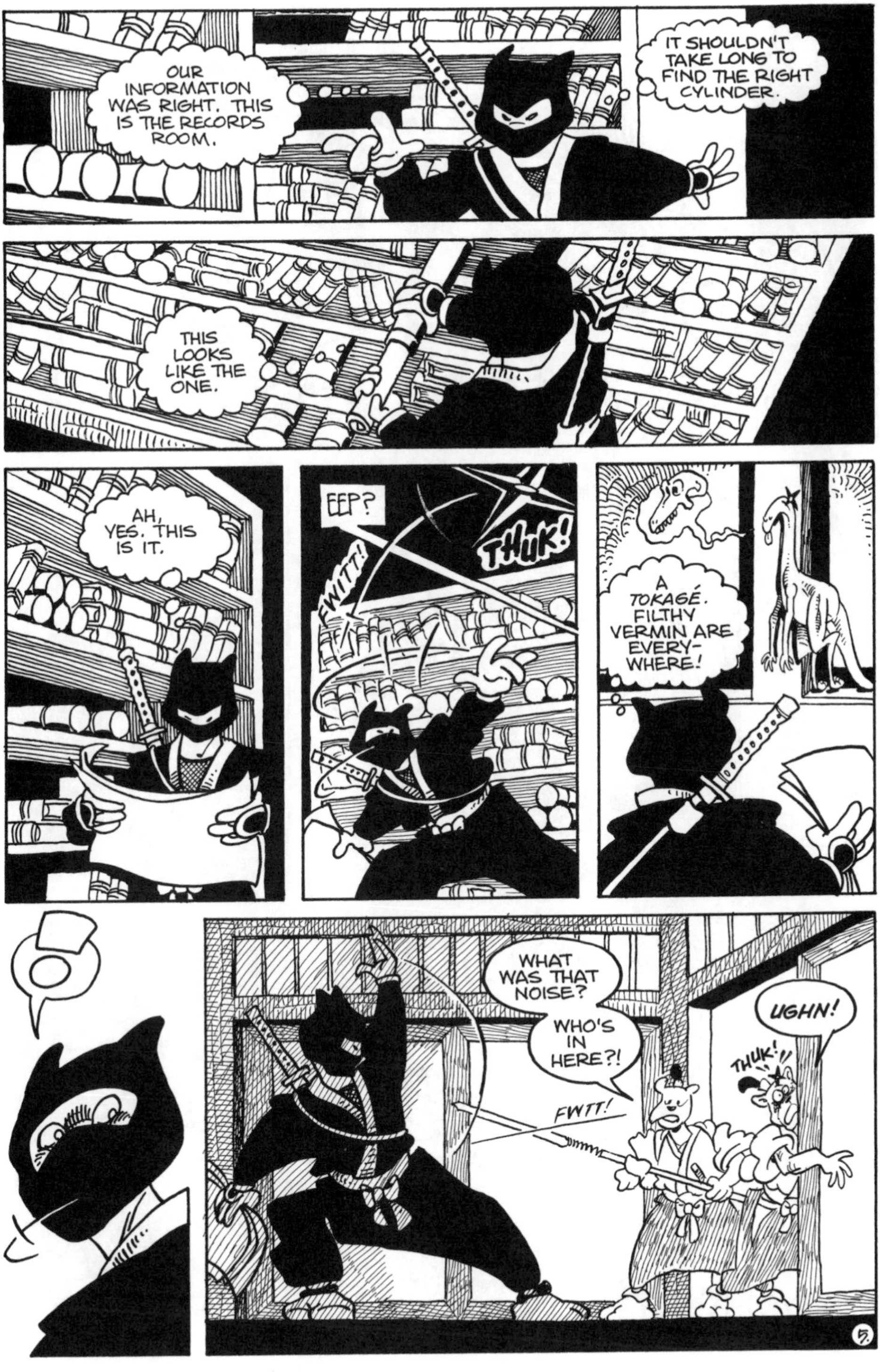
OUR INFORMATION WAS RIGHT. THIS IS THE RECORDS ROOM.
IT SHOULDN'T TAKE LONG TO FIND THE RIGHT CYLINDER.
THIS LOOKS LIKE THE ONE.
AH, YES. THIS IS IT.
EEP?
FWITT!
THUK!
A TOKAGÉ. FILTHY VERMIN ARE EVERYWHERE!
WHAT WAS THAT NOISE?
WHO'S IN HERE?!
FWTT!
THUK!
UGHN!
5

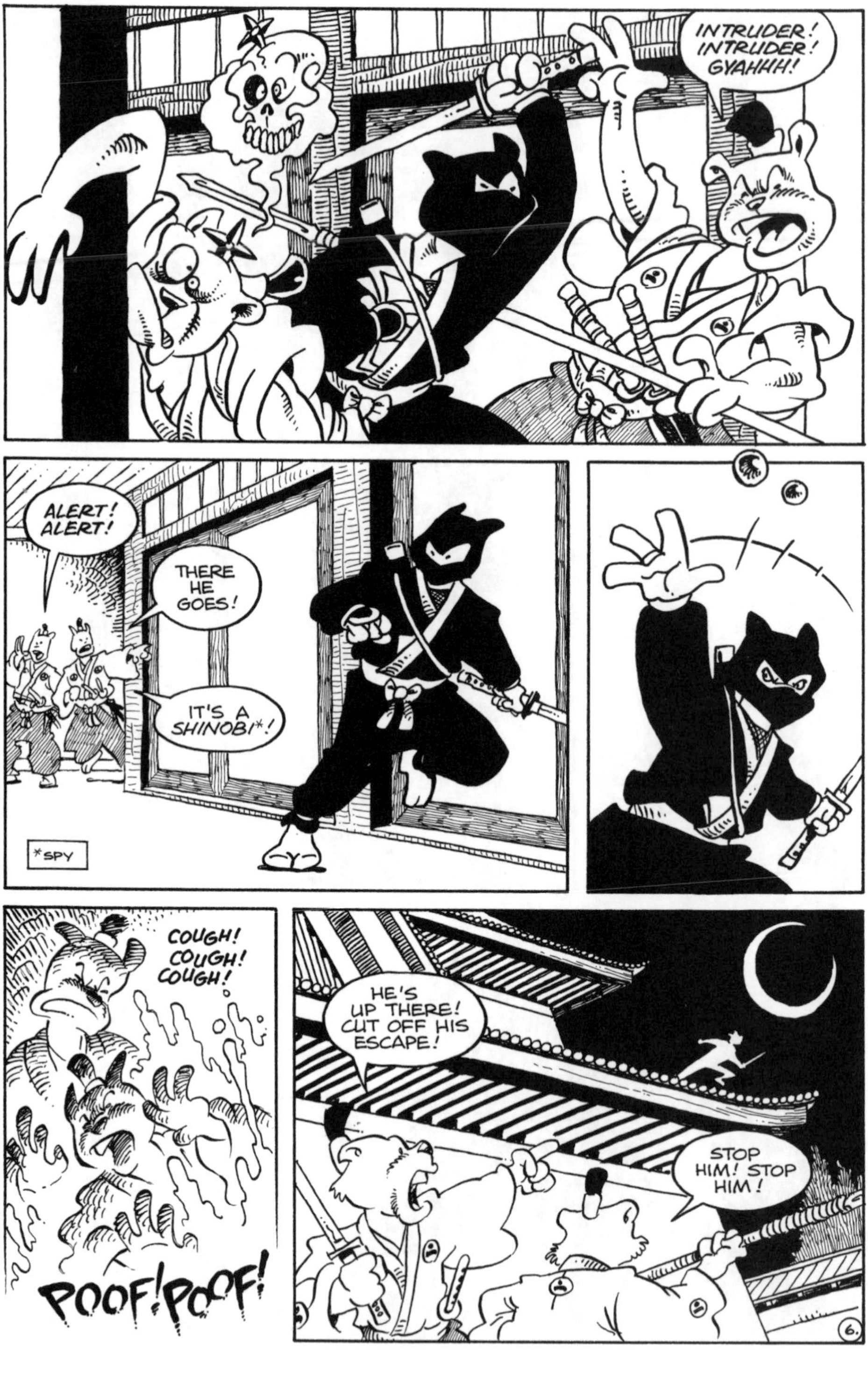
INTRUDER! INTRUDER! GYAHHH!
ALERT! ALERT!
THERE HE GOES!
IT'S A SHINOBI*!
*SPY
COUGH! COUGH! COUGH!
POOF! POOF!
HE'S UP THERE! CUT OFF HIS ESCAPE!
STOP HIM! STOP HIM!
6.

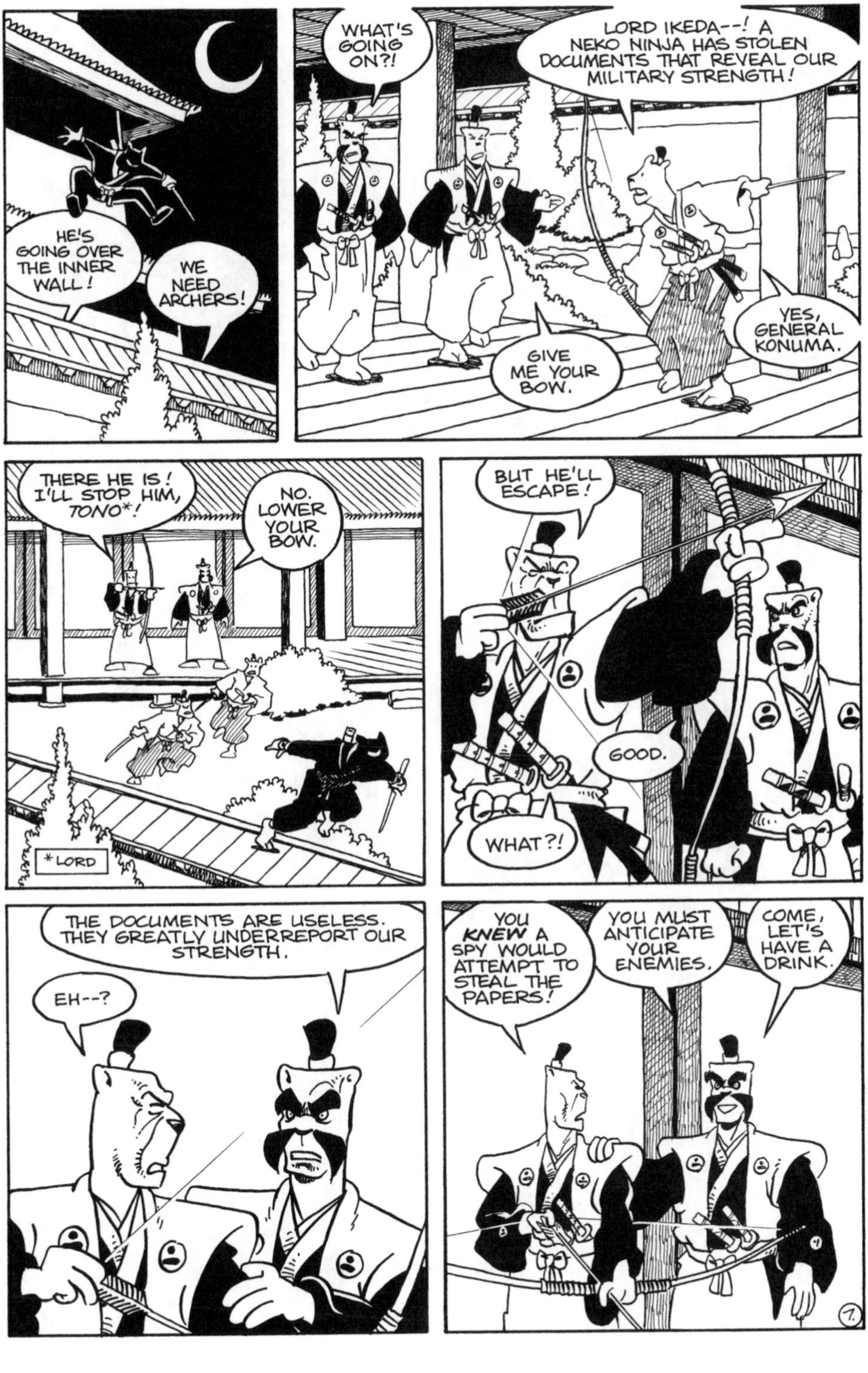
HE'S GOING OVER THE INNER WALL!
WE NEED ARCHERS!
WHAT'S GOING ON?!
LORD IKEDA--! A NEKO NINJA HAS STOLEN DOCUMENTS THAT REVEAL OUR MILITARY STRENGTH!
GIVE ME YOUR BOW.
YES, GENERAL KONUMA.
THERE HE IS! I'LL STOP HIM, TONO*!
NO. LOWER YOUR BOW.
*LORD
BUT HE'LL ESCAPE!
GOOD.
WHAT?!
THE DOCUMENTS ARE USELESS. THEY GREATLY UNDERREPORT OUR STRENGTH.
EH--?
YOU KNEW A SPY WOULD ATTEMPT TO STEAL THE PAPERS!
YOU MUST ANTICIPATE YOUR ENEMIES.
COME, LET'S HAVE A DRINK.
7.

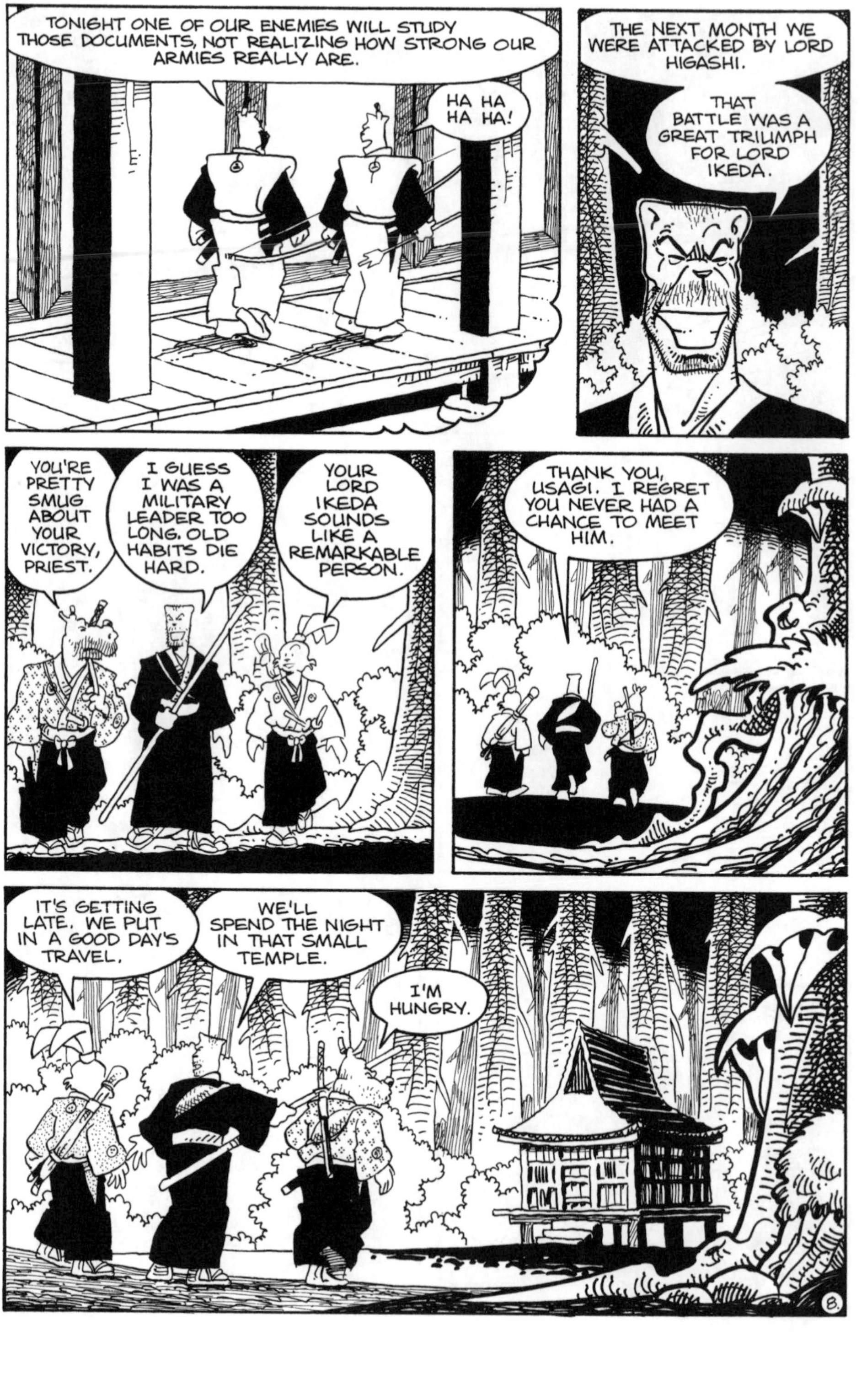
TONIGHT ONE OF OUR ENEMIES WILL STUDY THOSE DOCUMENTS, NOT REALIZING HOW STRONG OUR ARMIES REALLY ARE.
HA HA HA HA!
THE NEXT MONTH WE WERE ATTACKED BY LORD HIGASHI.
THAT BATTLE WAS A GREAT TRIUMPH FOR LORD IKEDA.
YOU'RE PRETTY SMUG ABOUT YOUR VICTORY, PRIEST.
I GUESS I WAS A MILITARY LEADER TOO LONG. OLD HABITS DIE HARD.
YOUR LORD IKEDA SOUNDS LIKE A REMARKABLE PERSON.
THANK YOU, USAGI. I REGRET YOU NEVER HAD A CHANCE TO MEET HIM.
IT'S GETTING LATE. WE PUT IN A GOOD DAY'S TRAVEL.
WE'LL SPEND THE NIGHT IN THAT SMALL TEMPLE.
I'M HUNGRY.
8.

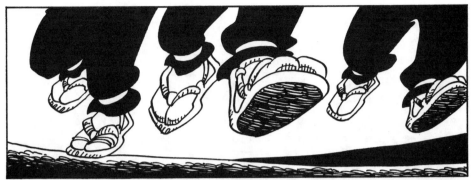

HERE ARE THE THREE SETS OF FOOTPRINTS AGAIN. THEY'RE ONLY A FEW HOURS AHEAD OF US NOW, KASHIRA*.

THEY ARE TRAVELING QUICKLY BUT NOT BOTHERING TO COVER THEIR TRACKS. I DON'T THINK THEY SUSPECT WE'RE ON THEIR HEELS.

EXCELLENT.

*CHIEF

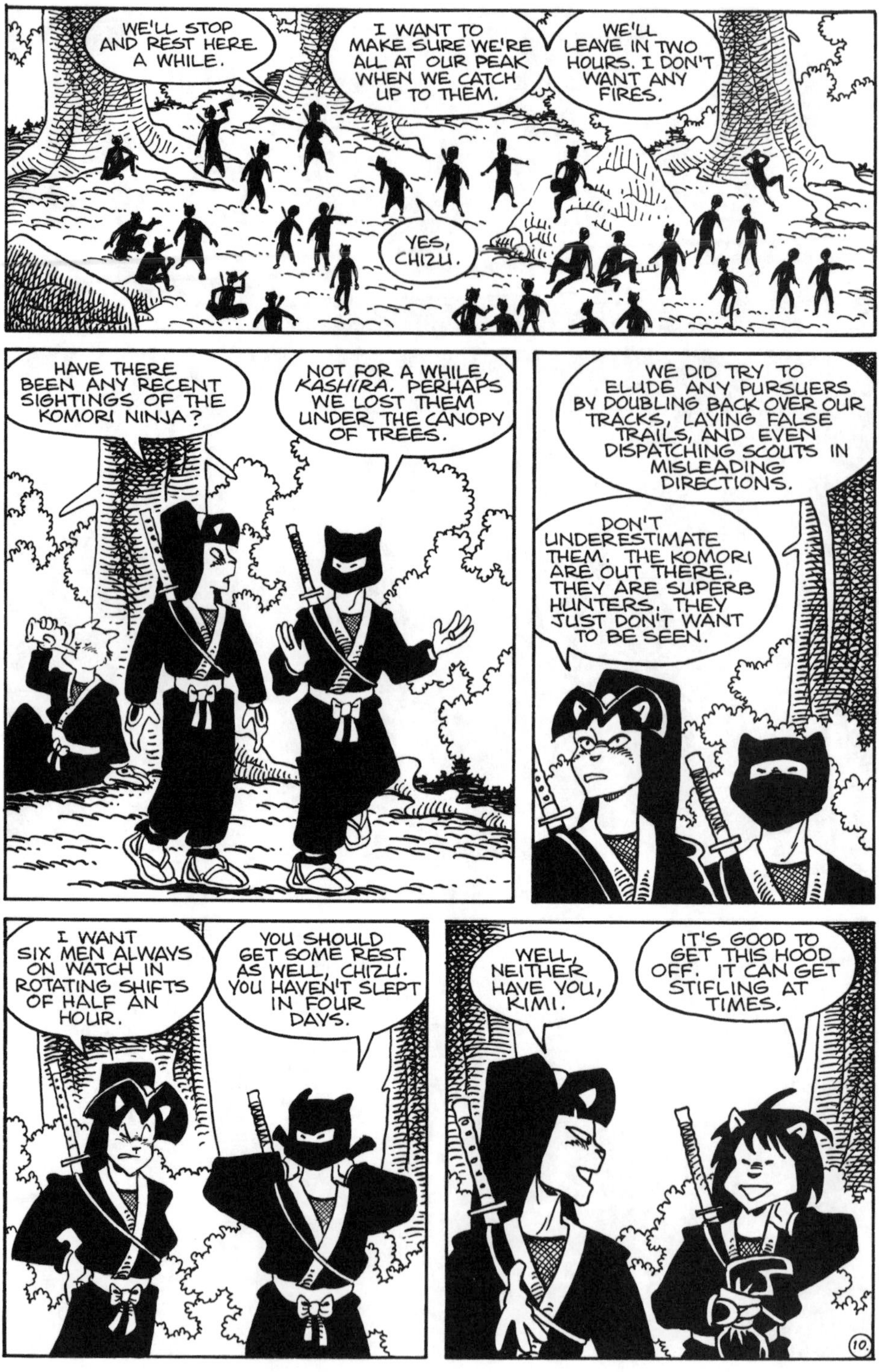
WE'LL STOP AND REST HERE A WHILE.
I WANT TO MAKE SURE WE'RE ALL AT OUR PEAK WHEN WE CATCH UP TO THEM.
WE'LL LEAVE IN TWO HOURS. I DON'T WANT ANY FIRES.
YES, CHIZU.
HAVE THERE BEEN ANY RECENT SIGHTINGS OF THE KOMORI NINJA?
NOT FOR A WHILE, *KASHIRA*. PERHAPS WE LOST THEM UNDER THE CANOPY OF TREES.
WE DID TRY TO ELUDE ANY PURSUERS BY DOUBLING BACK OVER OUR TRACKS, LAYING FALSE TRAILS, AND EVEN DISPATCHING SCOUTS IN MISLEADING DIRECTIONS.
DON'T UNDERESTIMATE THEM. THE KOMORI ARE OUT THERE. THEY ARE SUPERB HUNTERS. THEY JUST DON'T WANT TO BE SEEN.
I WANT SIX MEN ALWAYS ON WATCH IN ROTATING SHIFTS OF HALF AN HOUR.
YOU SHOULD GET SOME REST AS WELL, CHIZU. YOU HAVEN'T SLEPT IN FOUR DAYS.
WELL, NEITHER HAVE YOU, KIMI.
IT'S GOOD TO GET THIS HOOD OFF. IT CAN GET STIFLING AT TIMES.
10.

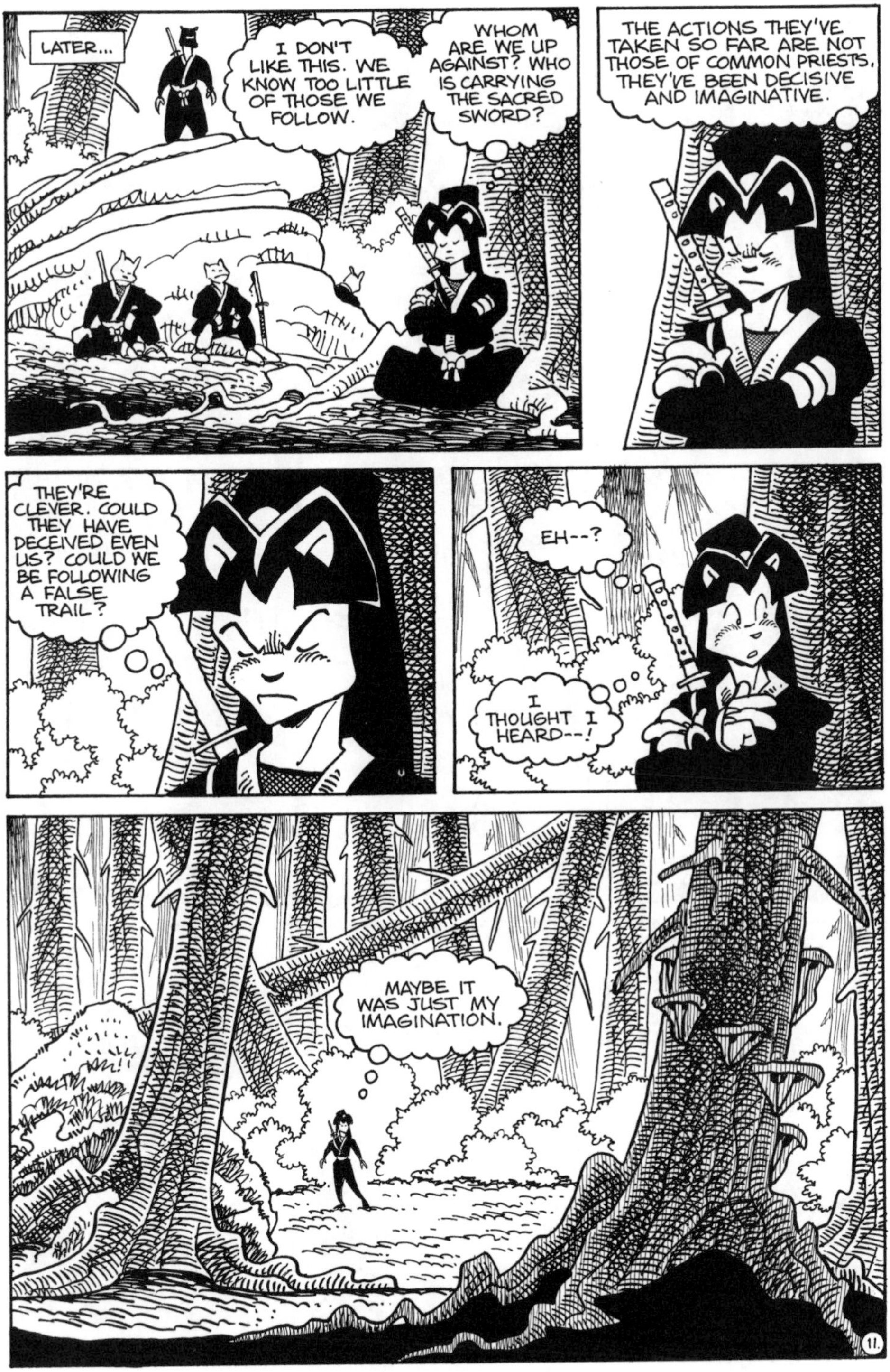
LATER...
I DON'T LIKE THIS. WE KNOW TOO LITTLE OF THOSE WE FOLLOW.
WHOM ARE WE UP AGAINST? WHO IS CARRYING THE SACRED SWORD?
THE ACTIONS THEY'VE TAKEN SO FAR ARE NOT THOSE OF COMMON PRIESTS. THEY'VE BEEN DECISIVE AND IMAGINATIVE.
THEY'RE CLEVER. COULD THEY HAVE DECEIVED EVEN US? COULD WE BE FOLLOWING A FALSE TRAIL?
EH--?
I THOUGHT I HEARD--!
MAYBE IT WAS JUST MY IMAGINATION.
11.

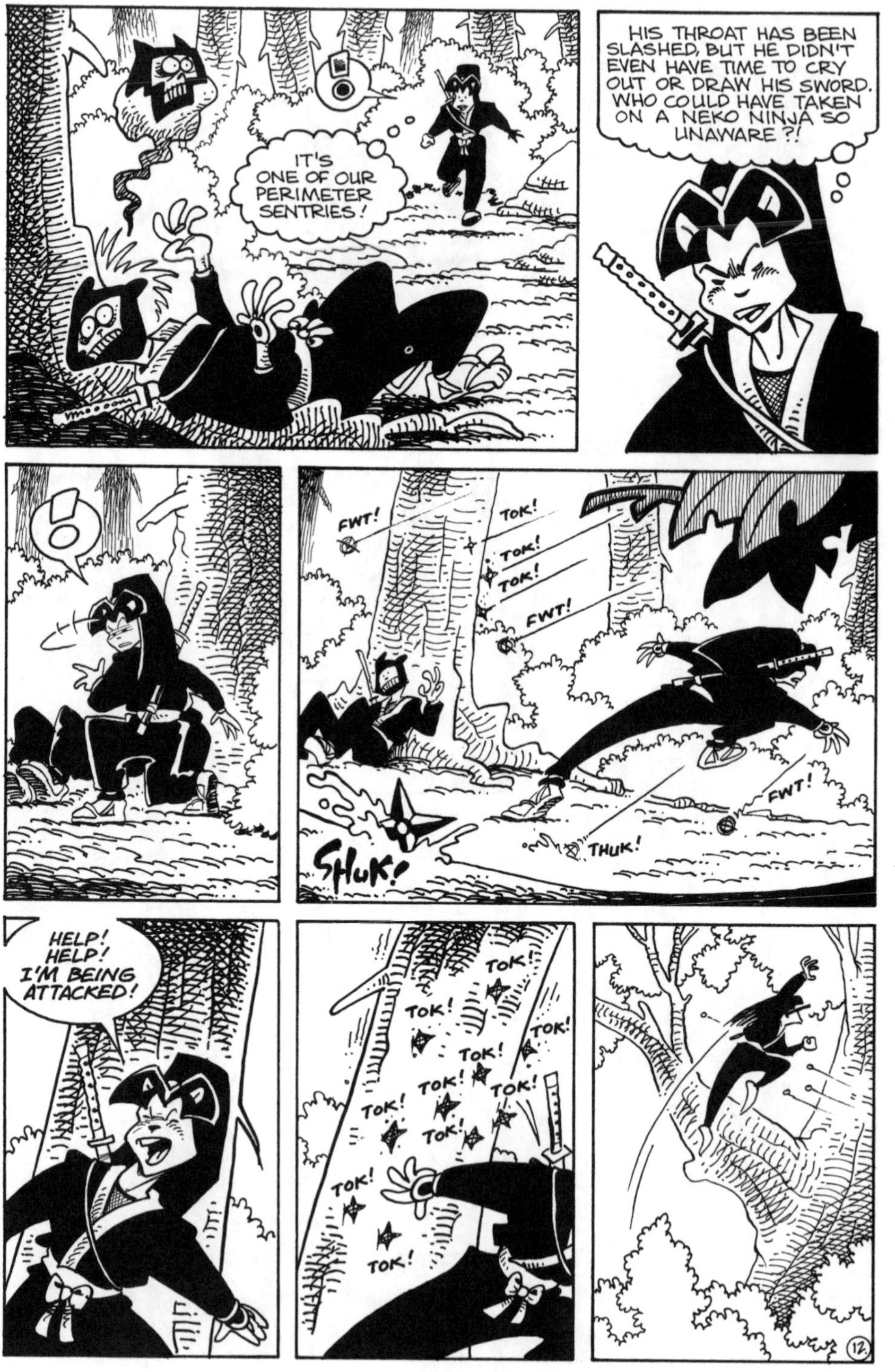
IT'S ONE OF OUR PERIMETER SENTRIES!
HIS THROAT HAS BEEN SLASHED, BUT HE DIDN'T EVEN HAVE TIME TO CRY OUT OR DRAW HIS SWORD. WHO COULD HAVE TAKEN ON A NEKO NINJA SO UNAWARE?!
FWT!
TOK!
TOK!
TOK!
FWT!
SHUK!
THUK!
FWT!
HELP! HELP! I'M BEING ATTACKED!
TOK!
TOK!
TOK!
TOK!
TOK!
TOK!
TOK!
TOK!
TOK!
TOK!
12

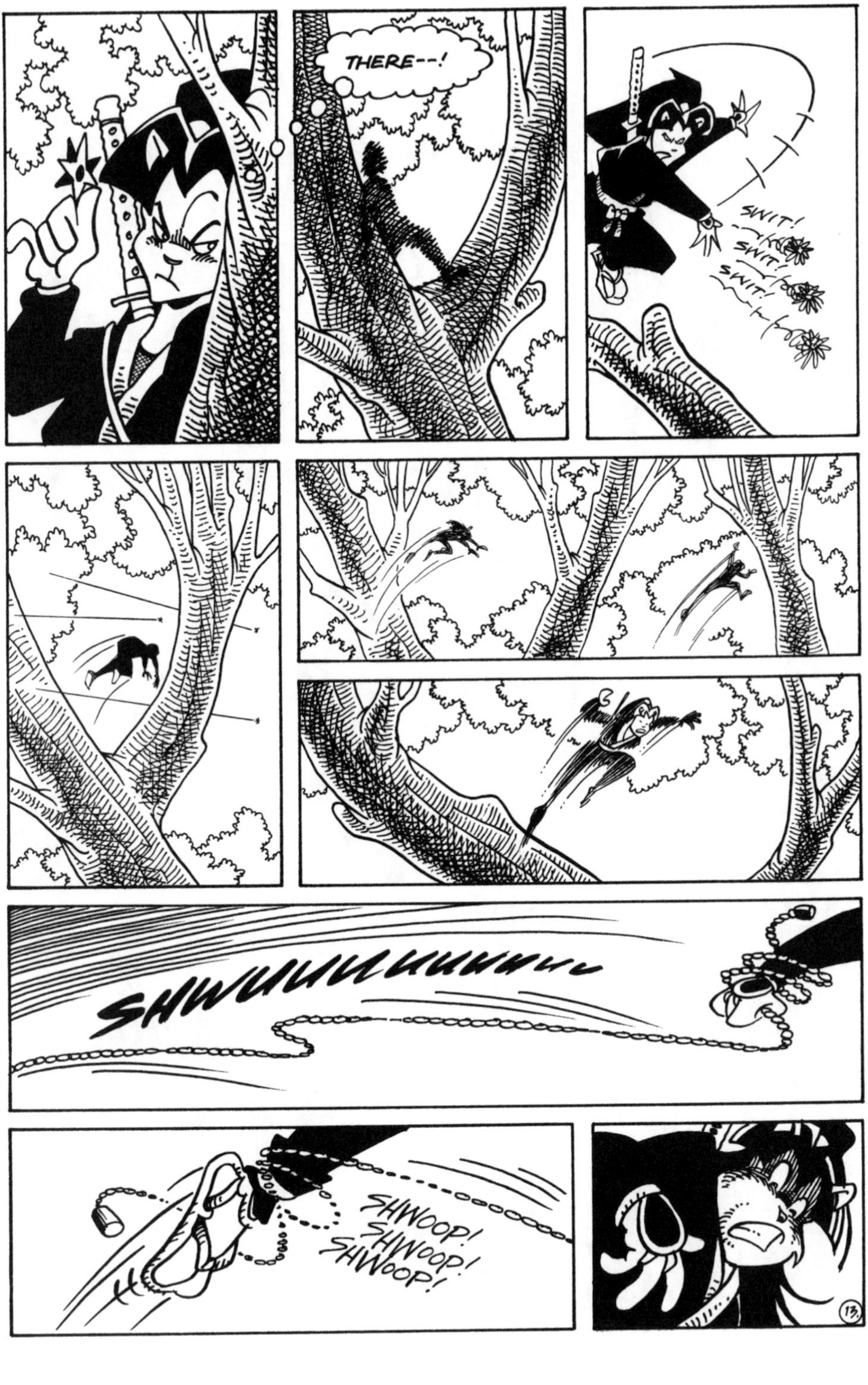
THERE--!
SWIT!
SWIT!
SWIT!
SHWUUUUUUUUUUUU
SHWOOP!
SHWOOP!
SHWOOP!
13

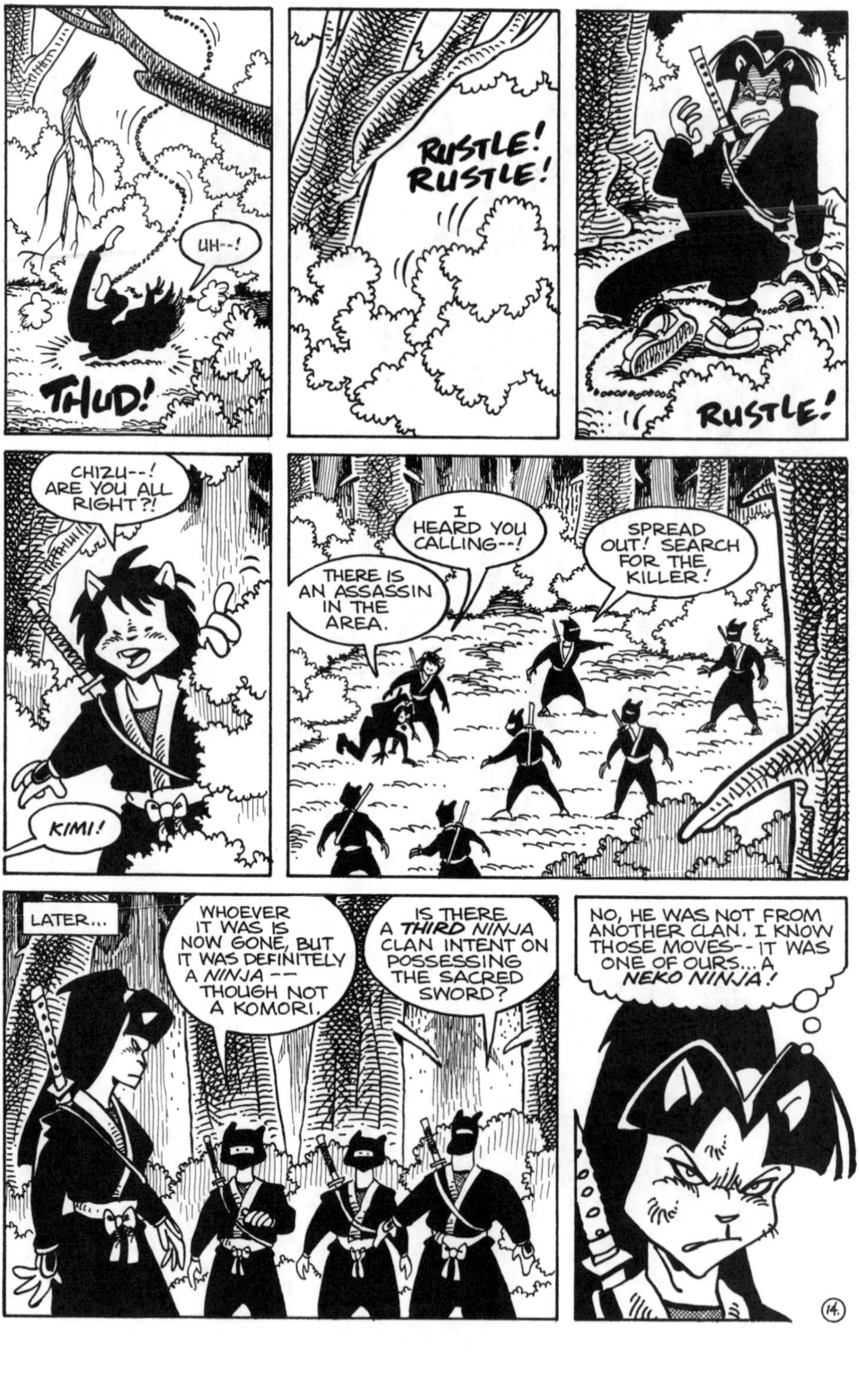
UH--!
THUD!
RUSTLE! RUSTLE!
RUSTLE!
CHIZU--! ARE YOU ALL RIGHT?!
KIMI!
I HEARD YOU CALLING--!
THERE IS AN ASSASSIN IN THE AREA.
SPREAD OUT! SEARCH FOR THE KILLER!
LATER...
WHOEVER IT WAS IS NOW GONE, BUT IT WAS DEFINITELY A NINJA -- THOUGH NOT A KOMORI.
IS THERE A THIRD NINJA CLAN INTENT ON POSSESSING THE SACRED SWORD?
NO, HE WAS NOT FROM ANOTHER CLAN. I KNOW THOSE MOVES-- IT WAS ONE OF OURS... A NEKO NINJA!
14.

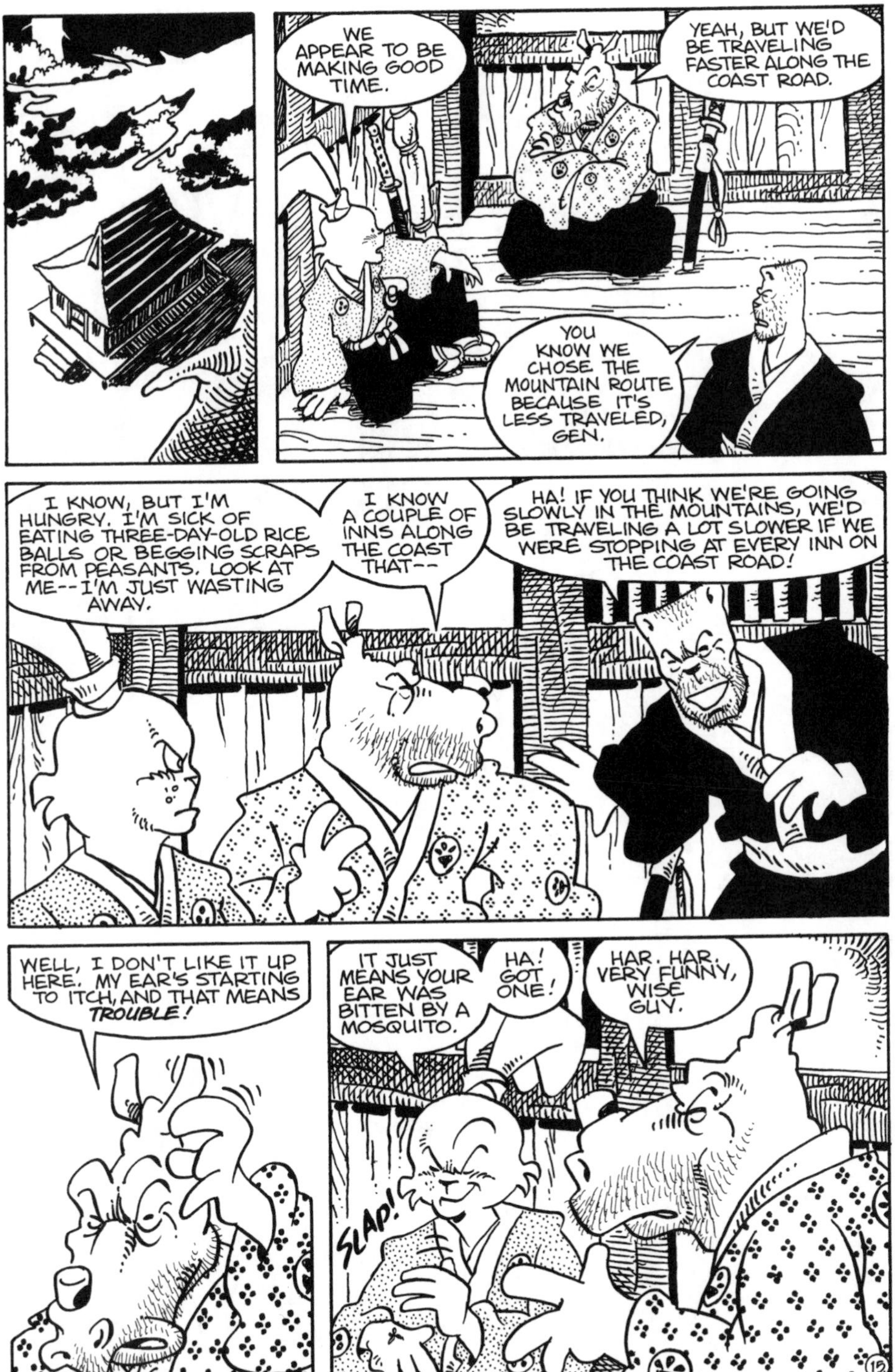
WE APPEAR TO BE MAKING GOOD TIME.
YEAH, BUT WE'D BE TRAVELING FASTER ALONG THE COAST ROAD.
YOU KNOW WE CHOSE THE MOUNTAIN ROUTE BECAUSE IT'S LESS TRAVELED, GEN.
I KNOW, BUT I'M HUNGRY. I'M SICK OF EATING THREE-DAY-OLD RICE BALLS OR BEGGING SCRAPS FROM PEASANTS. LOOK AT ME--I'M JUST WASTING AWAY.
I KNOW A COUPLE OF INNS ALONG THE COAST THAT--
HA! IF YOU THINK WE'RE GOING SLOWLY IN THE MOUNTAINS, WE'D BE TRAVELING A LOT SLOWER IF WE WERE STOPPING AT EVERY INN ON THE COAST ROAD!
WELL, I DON'T LIKE IT UP HERE. MY EAR'S STARTING TO ITCH, AND THAT MEANS ***TROUBLE!***
IT JUST MEANS YOUR EAR WAS BITTEN BY A MOSQUITO.
HA! GOT ONE!
HAR. HAR. VERY FUNNY, WISE GUY.
SLAP!
15

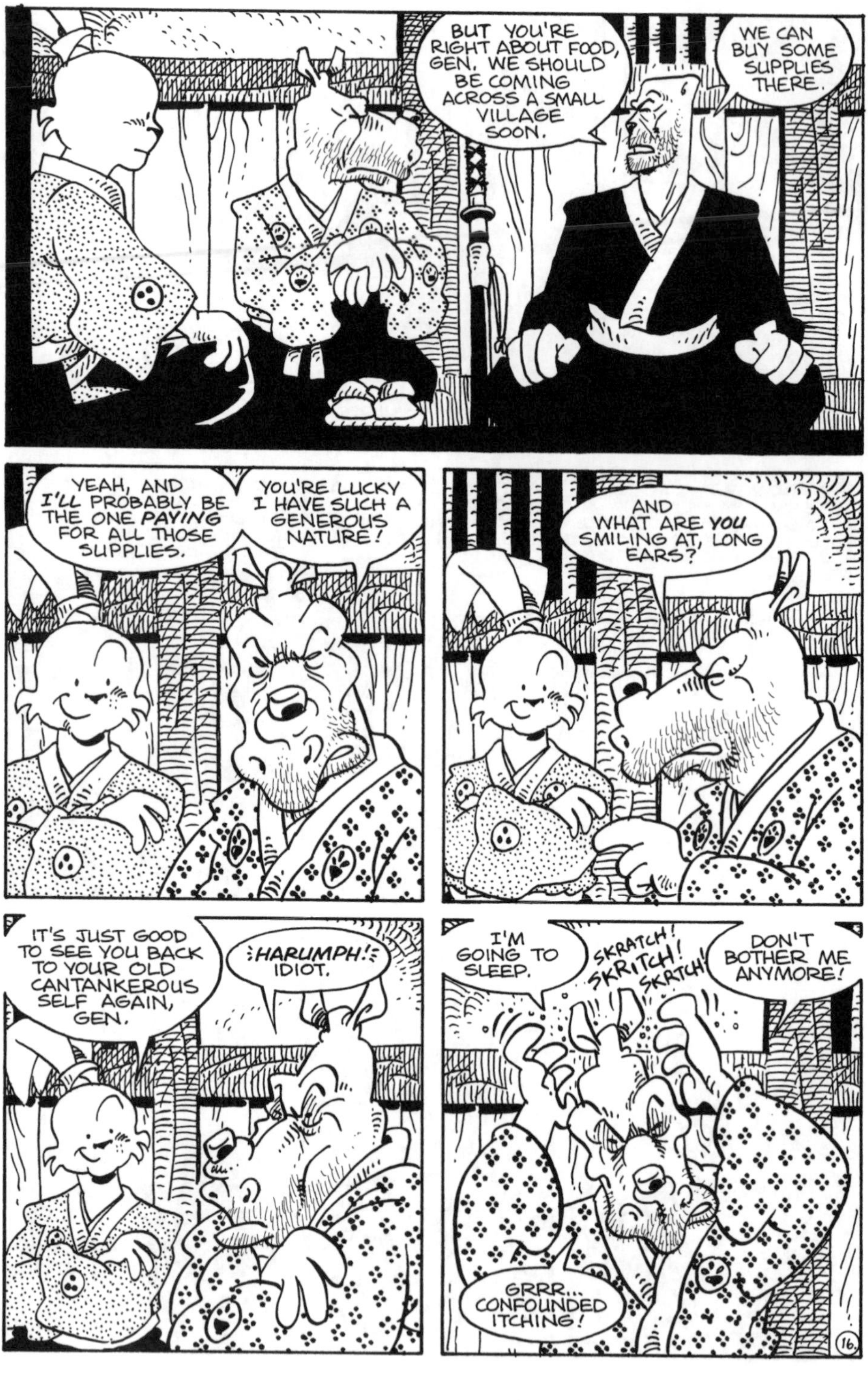
BUT YOU'RE RIGHT ABOUT FOOD, GEN. WE SHOULD BE COMING ACROSS A SMALL VILLAGE SOON.
WE CAN BUY SOME SUPPLIES THERE.
YEAH, AND I'LL PROBABLY BE THE ONE PAYING FOR ALL THOSE SUPPLIES.
YOU'RE LUCKY I HAVE SUCH A GENEROUS NATURE!
AND WHAT ARE YOU SMILING AT, LONG EARS?
IT'S JUST GOOD TO SEE YOU BACK TO YOUR OLD CANTANKEROUS SELF AGAIN, GEN.
HARUMPH! IDIOT.
I'M GOING TO SLEEP.
SKRATCH! SKRITCH! SKRTCH!
DON'T BOTHER ME ANYMORE!
GRRR... CONFOUNDED ITCHING!
16.

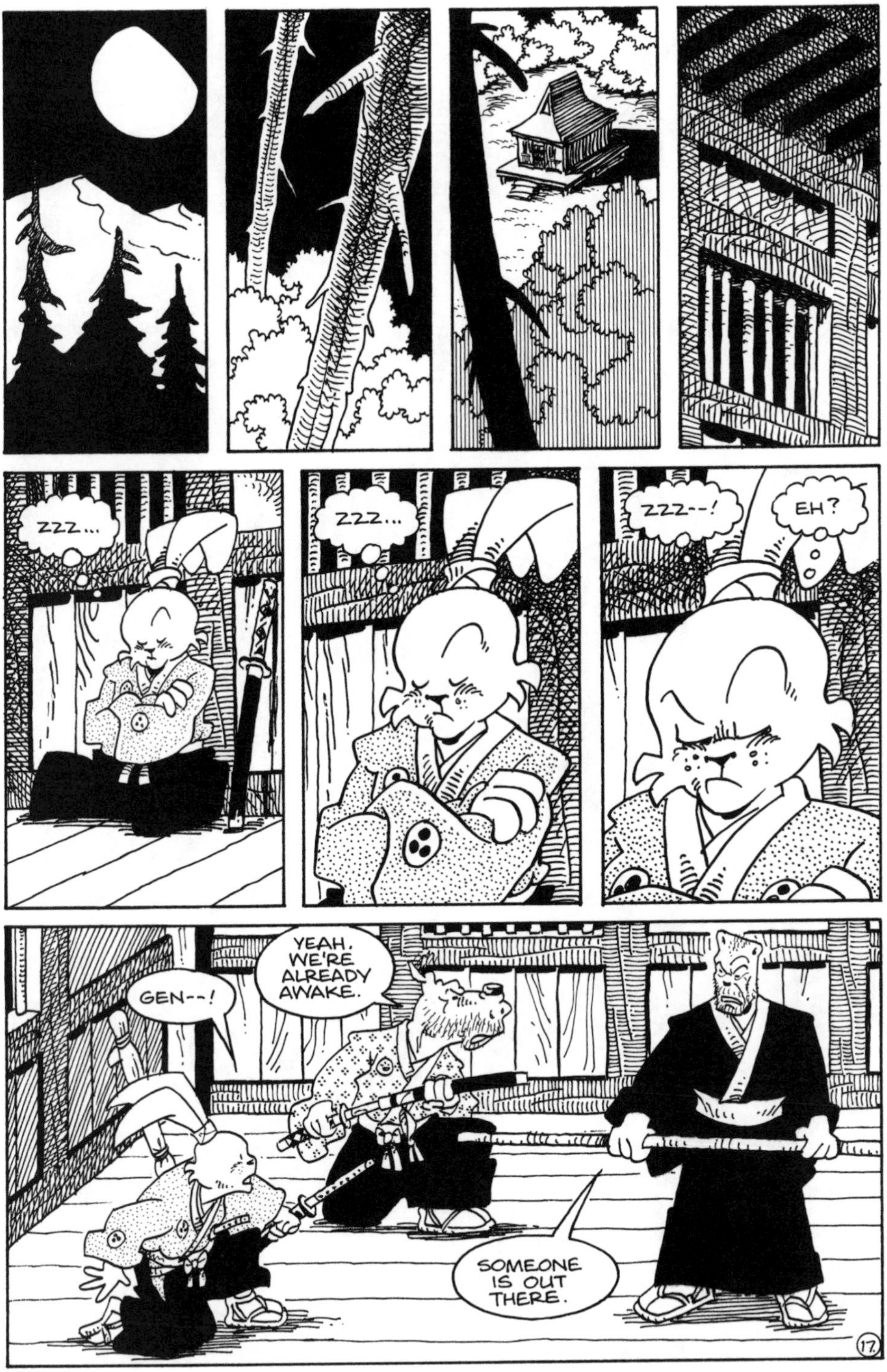
ZZZ...
ZZZ...
ZZZ--!
EH?
GEN--!
YEAH. WE'RE ALREADY AWAKE.
SOMEONE IS OUT THERE.
17

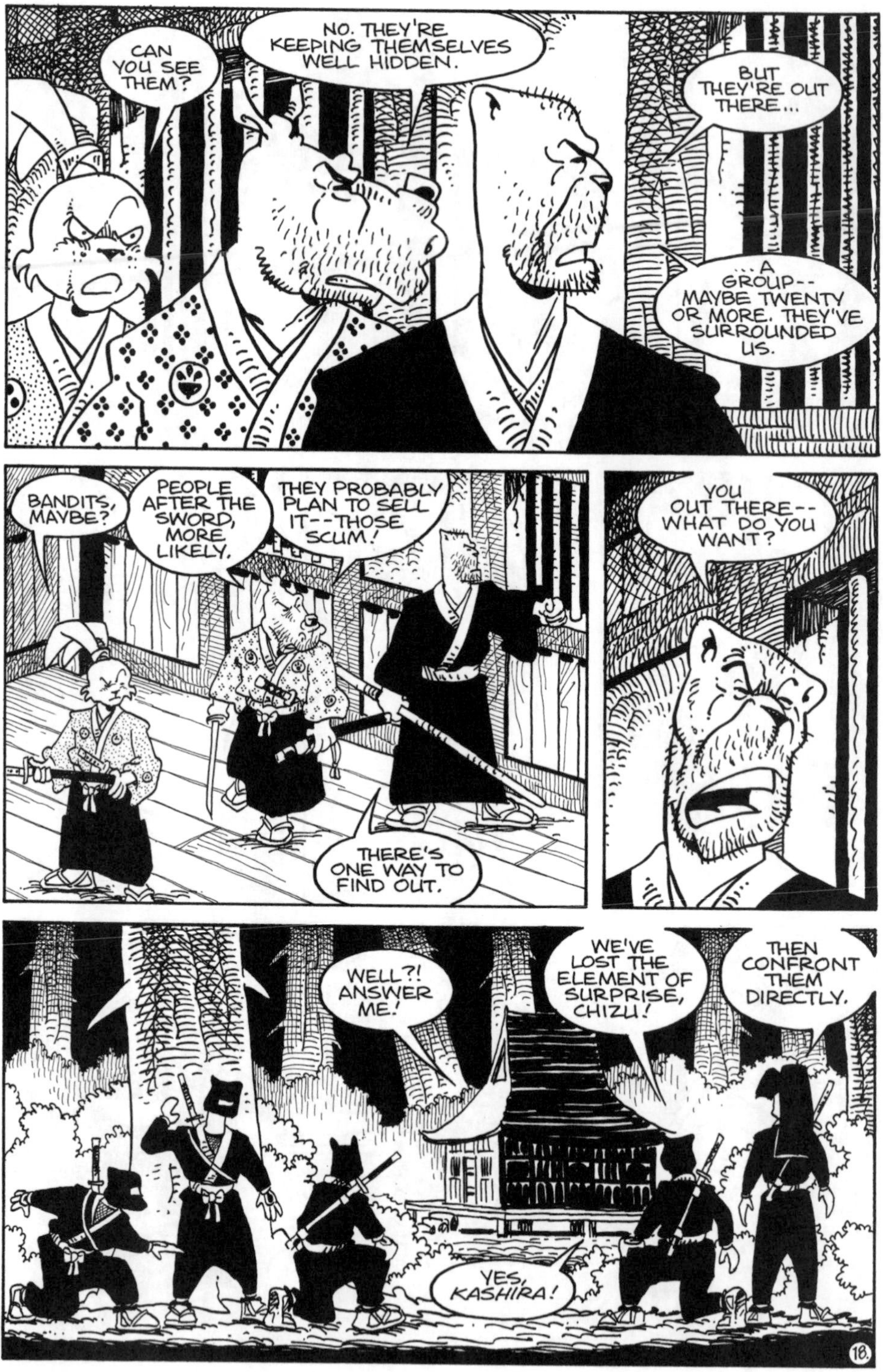
CAN YOU SEE THEM?
NO. THEY'RE KEEPING THEMSELVES WELL HIDDEN.
BUT THEY'RE OUT THERE...
...A GROUP-- MAYBE TWENTY OR MORE. THEY'VE SURROUNDED US.
BANDITS, MAYBE?
PEOPLE AFTER THE SWORD, MORE LIKELY.
THEY PROBABLY PLAN TO SELL IT--THOSE SCUM!
THERE'S ONE WAY TO FIND OUT.
YOU OUT THERE-- WHAT DO YOU WANT?
WELL?! ANSWER ME!
WE'VE LOST THE ELEMENT OF SURPRISE, CHIZU!
THEN CONFRONT THEM DIRECTLY.
YES, KASHIRA!
18.

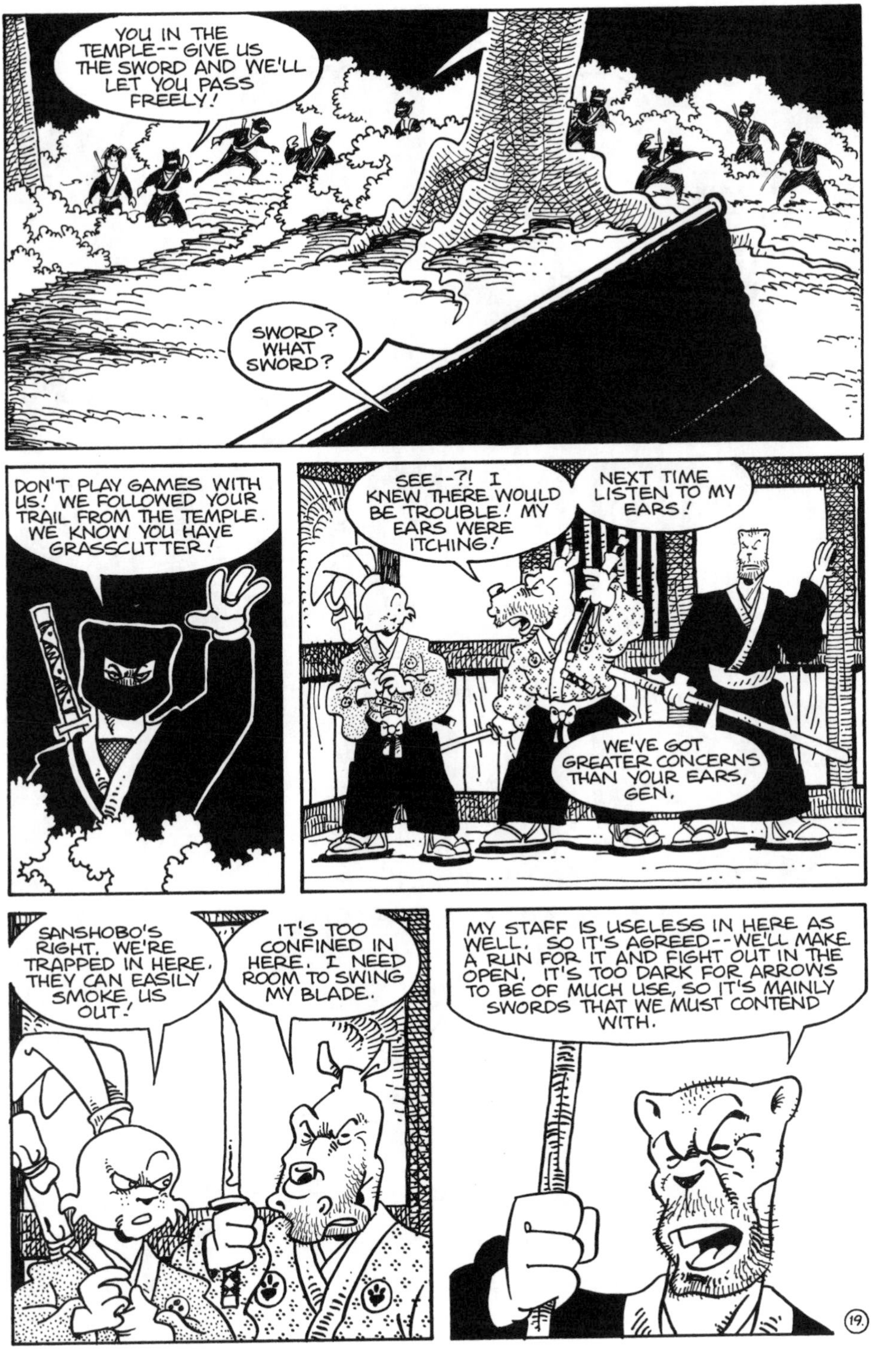
YOU IN THE TEMPLE-- GIVE US THE SWORD AND WE'LL LET YOU PASS FREELY!
SWORD? WHAT SWORD?
DON'T PLAY GAMES WITH US! WE FOLLOWED YOUR TRAIL FROM THE TEMPLE. WE KNOW YOU HAVE GRASSCUTTER!
SEE--?! I KNEW THERE WOULD BE TROUBLE! MY EARS WERE ITCHING!
NEXT TIME LISTEN TO MY EARS!
WE'VE GOT GREATER CONCERNS THAN YOUR EARS, GEN.
SANSHOBO'S RIGHT. WE'RE TRAPPED IN HERE. THEY CAN EASILY SMOKE US OUT!
IT'S TOO CONFINED IN HERE. I NEED ROOM TO SWING MY BLADE.
MY STAFF IS USELESS IN HERE AS WELL. SO IT'S AGREED--WE'LL MAKE A RUN FOR IT AND FIGHT OUT IN THE OPEN. IT'S TOO DARK FOR ARROWS TO BE OF MUCH USE, SO IT'S MAINLY SWORDS THAT WE MUST CONTEND WITH.
19.

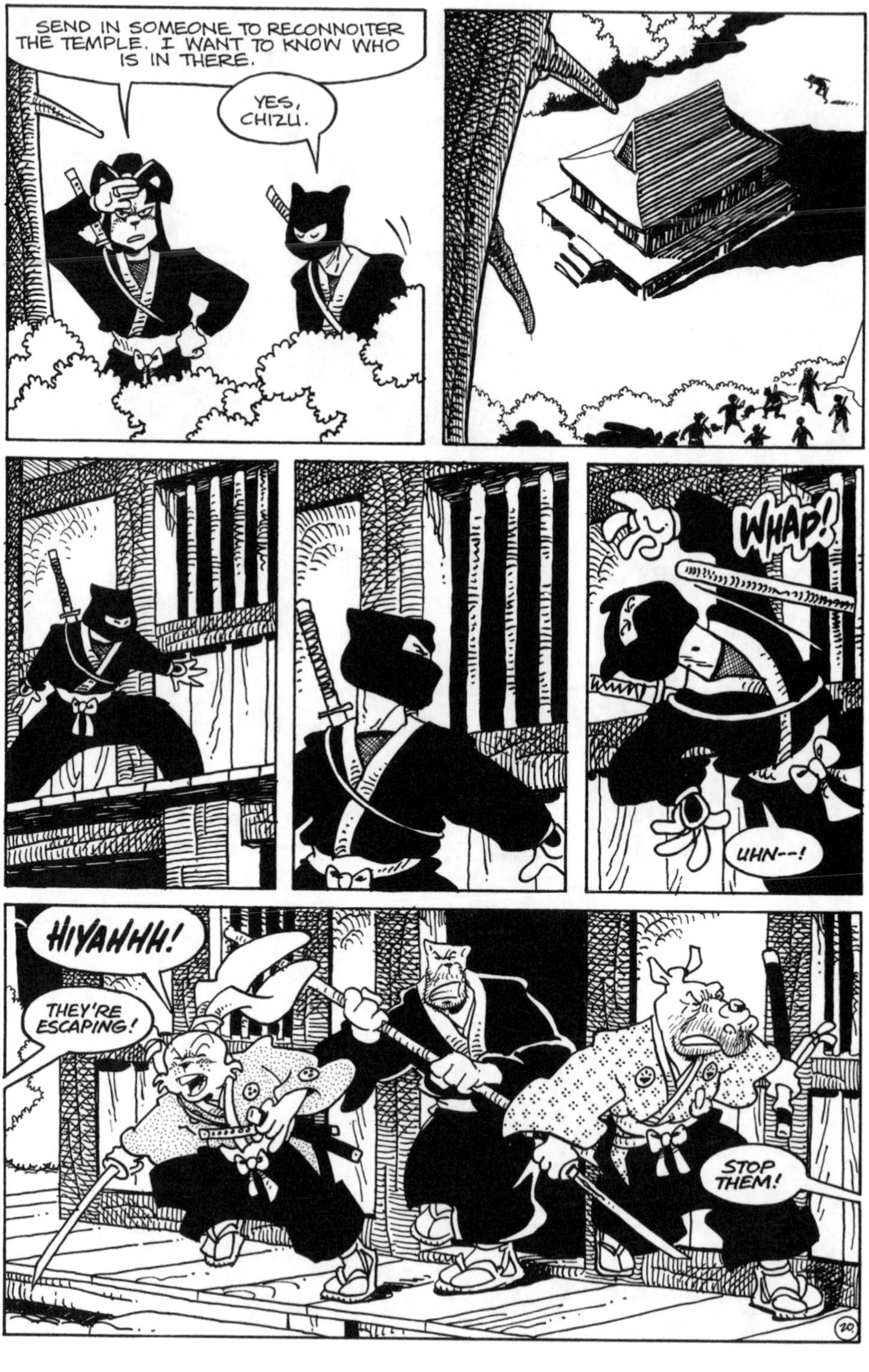
SEND IN SOMEONE TO RECONNOITER THE TEMPLE. I WANT TO KNOW WHO IS IN THERE.
YES, CHIZU.
WHAP!
UHN--!
HIYAHHH!
THEY'RE ESCAPING!
STOP THEM!
20.

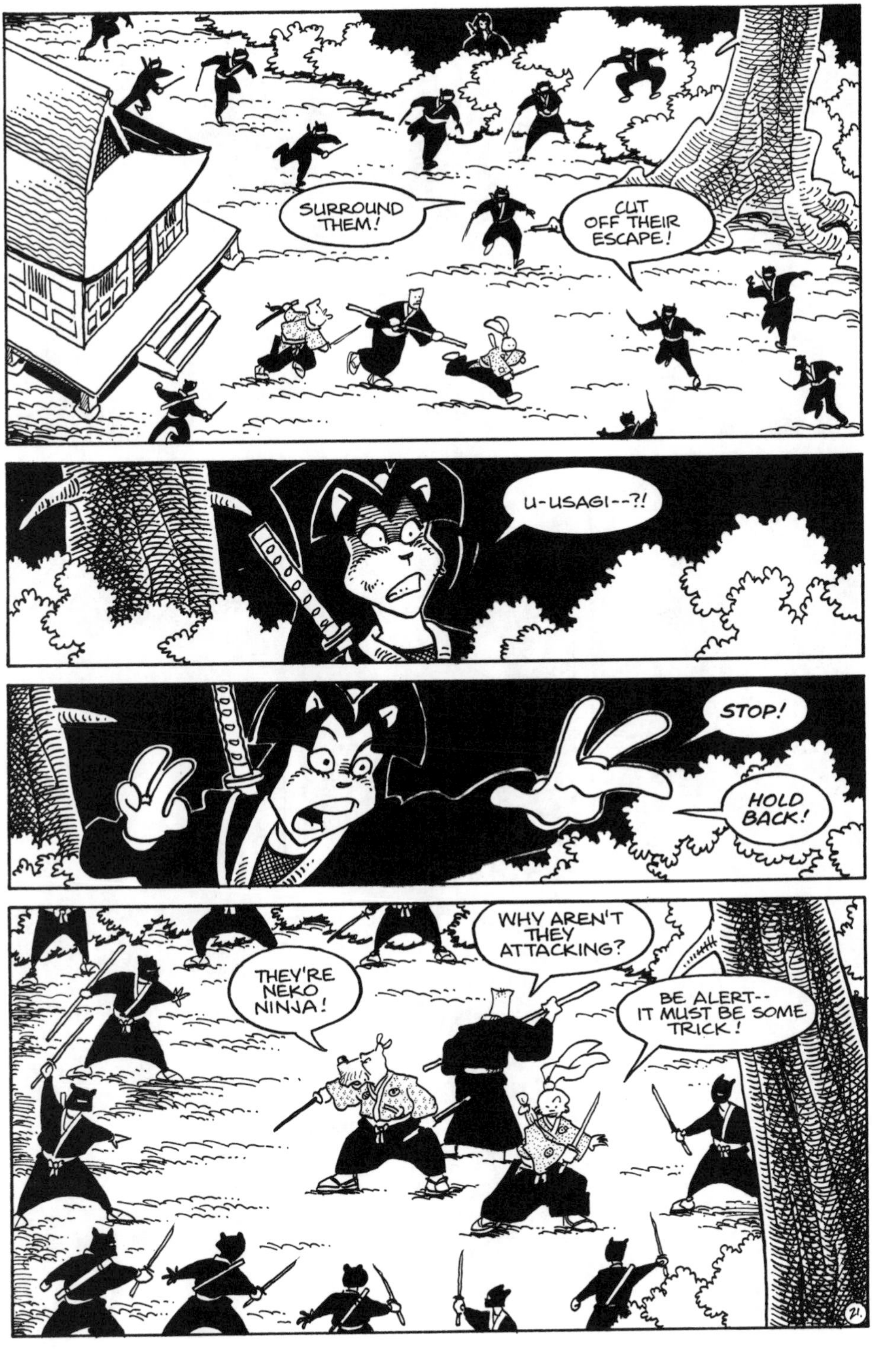
SURROUND THEM!
CUT OFF THEIR ESCAPE!
U-USAGI--?!
STOP!
HOLD BACK!
WHY AREN'T THEY ATTACKING?
THEY'RE NEKO NINJA!
BE ALERT-- IT MUST BE SOME TRICK!
21.

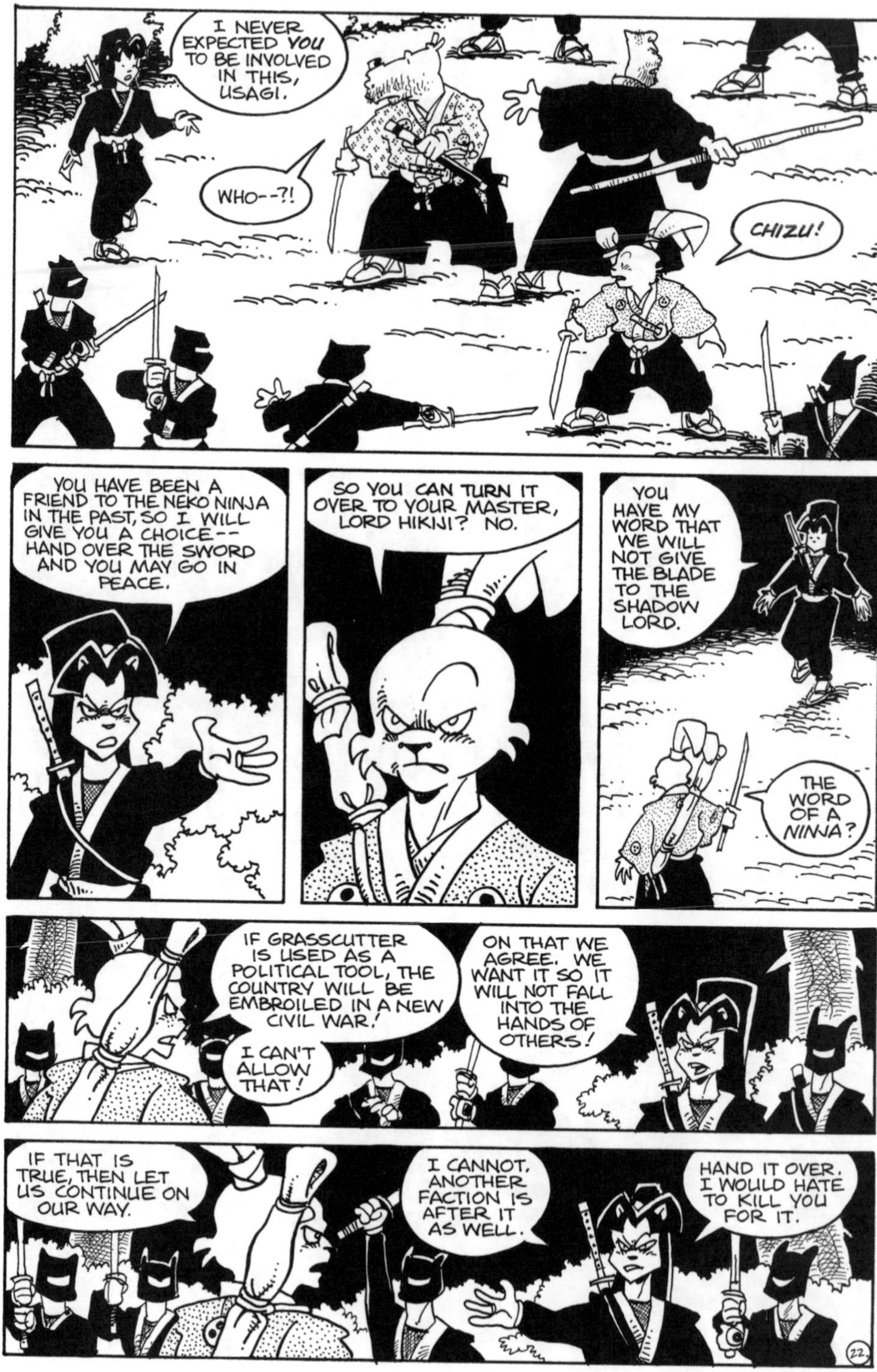
I NEVER EXPECTED YOU TO BE INVOLVED IN THIS, USAGI.
WHO--?!
CHIZU!
YOU HAVE BEEN A FRIEND TO THE NEKO NINJA IN THE PAST, SO I WILL GIVE YOU A CHOICE-- HAND OVER THE SWORD AND YOU MAY GO IN PEACE.
SO YOU CAN TURN IT OVER TO YOUR MASTER, LORD HIKIJI? NO.
YOU HAVE MY WORD THAT WE WILL NOT GIVE THE BLADE TO THE SHADOW LORD.
THE WORD OF A NINJA?
IF GRASSCUTTER IS USED AS A POLITICAL TOOL, THE COUNTRY WILL BE EMBROILED IN A NEW CIVIL WAR!
I CAN'T ALLOW THAT!
ON THAT WE AGREE. WE WANT IT SO IT WILL NOT FALL INTO THE HANDS OF OTHERS!
IF THAT IS TRUE, THEN LET US CONTINUE ON OUR WAY.
I CANNOT. ANOTHER FACTION IS AFTER IT AS WELL.
HAND IT OVER. I WOULD HATE TO KILL YOU FOR IT.
22

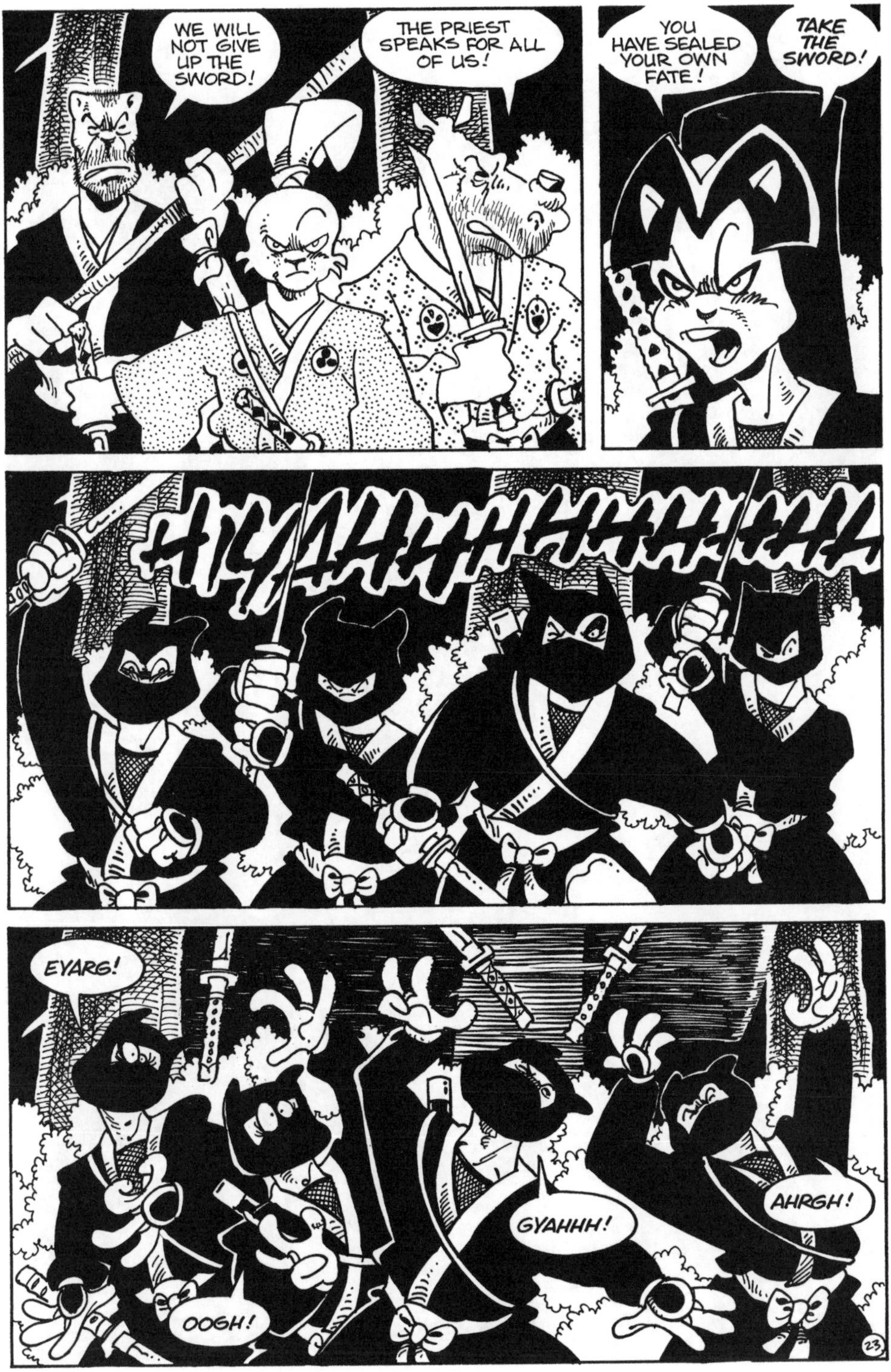
WE WILL NOT GIVE UP THE SWORD!
THE PRIEST SPEAKS FOR ALL OF US!
YOU HAVE SEALED YOUR OWN FATE!
TAKE THE SWORD!
HIYAAHHHHHHHHH
EYARG!
OOGH!
GYAHHH!
AHRGH!
23

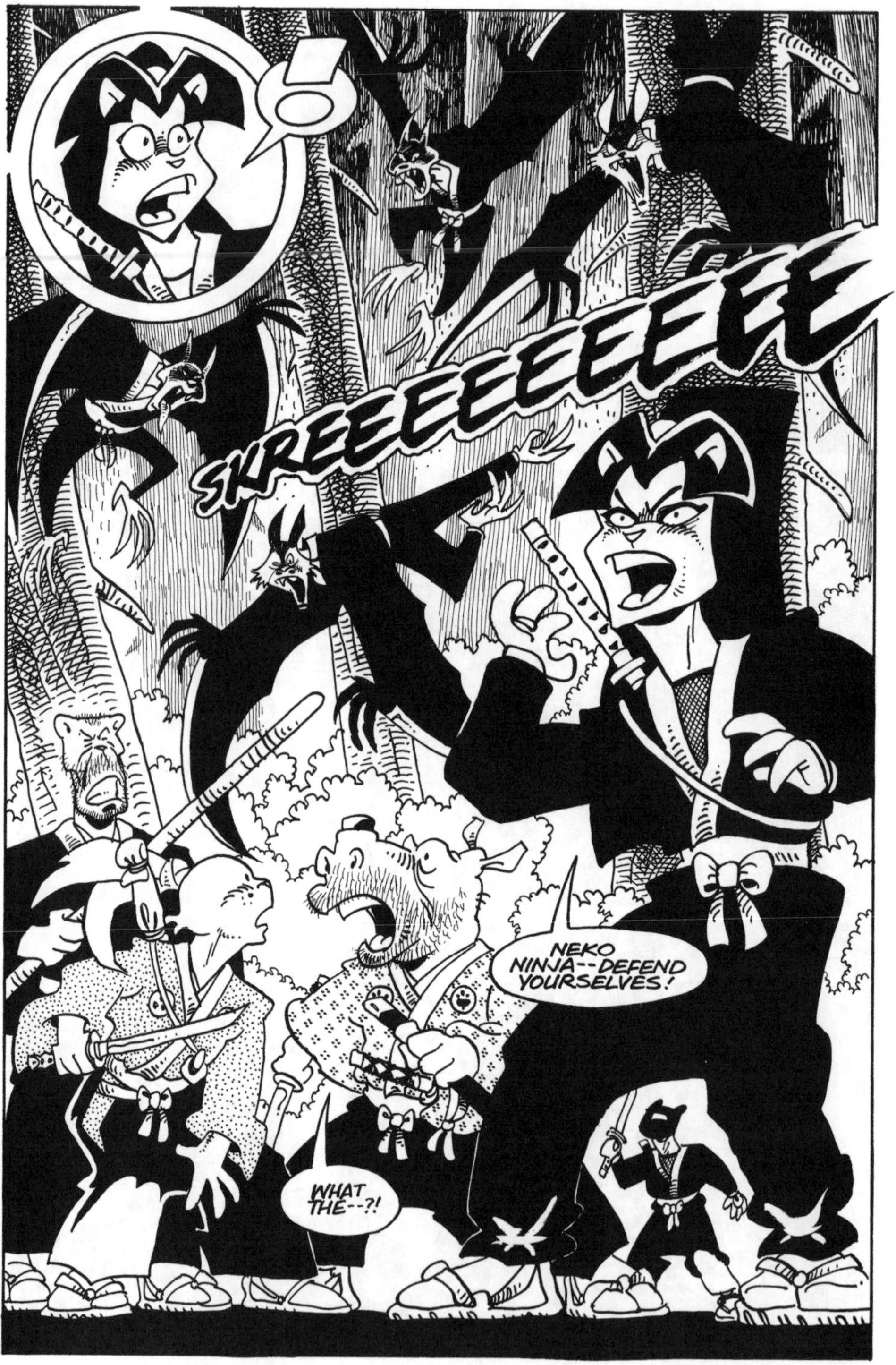
!
SKREEEEEEEEEEEE
NEKO NINJA--DEFEND YOURSELVES!
WHAT THE--?!

END OF CHAPTER 2

CHAPTER 3
THE HUNGER FOR DEATH

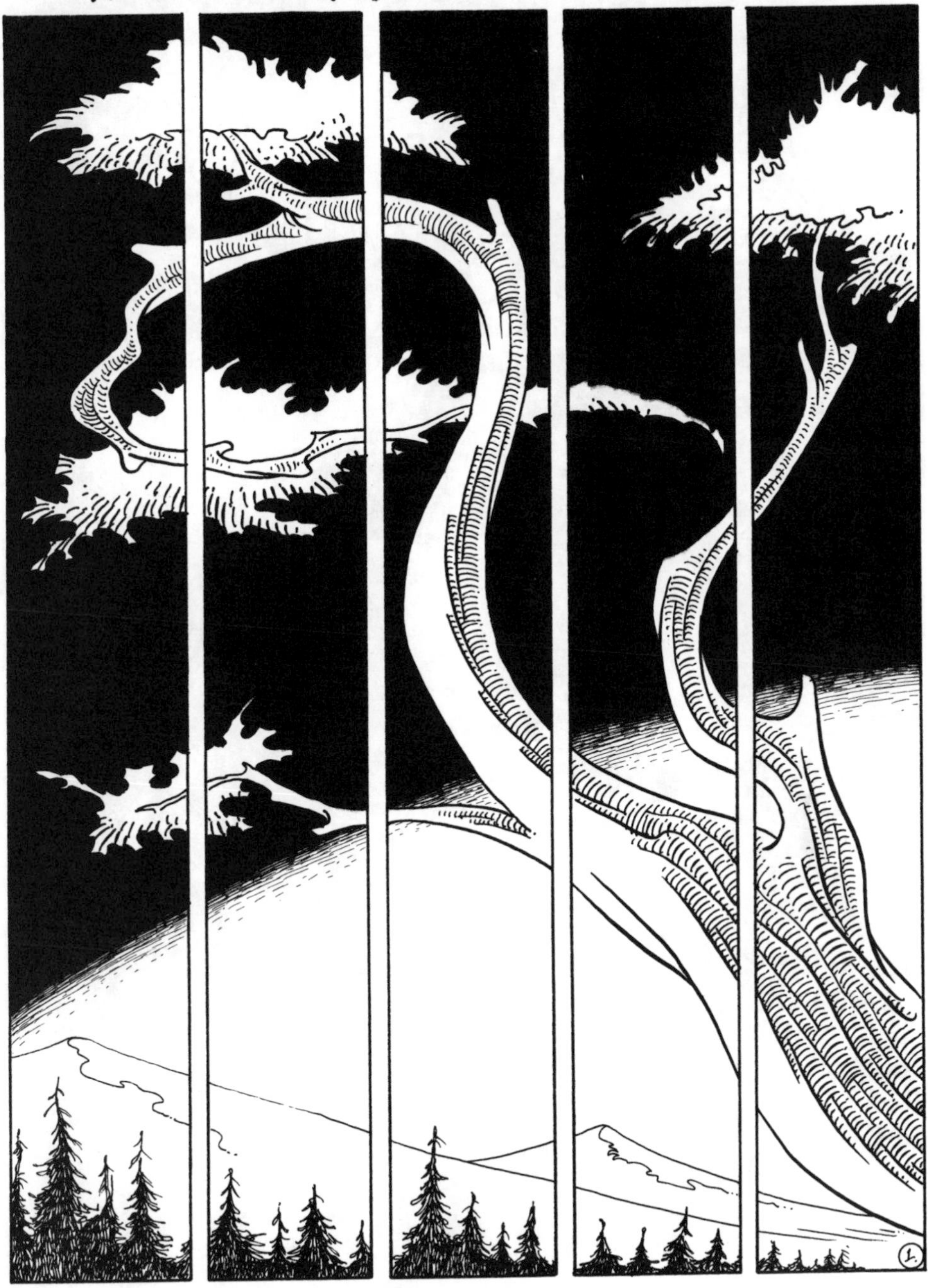

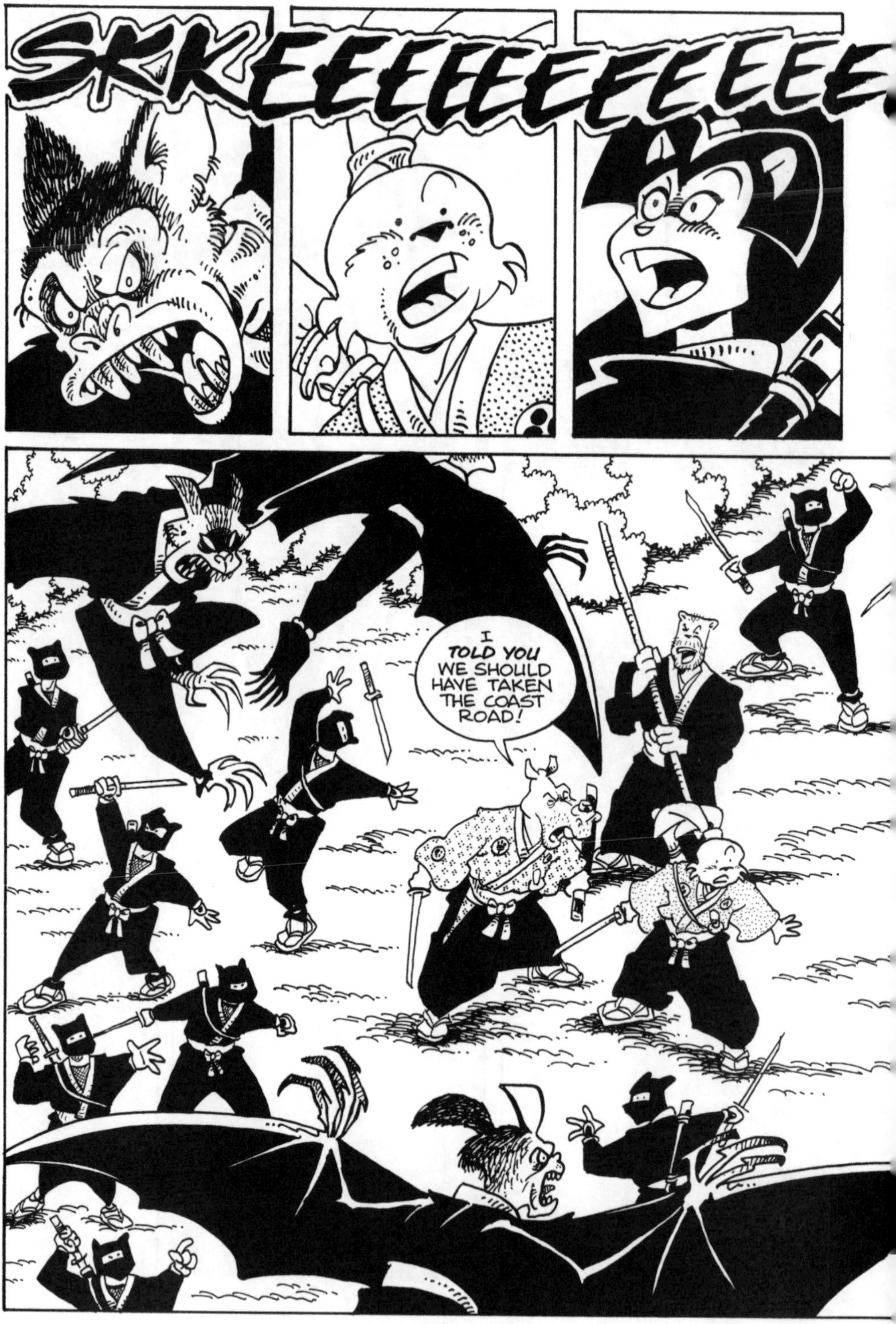
SKREEEEEEEEEEEEE
I TOLD YOU WE SHOULD HAVE TAKEN THE COAST ROAD!

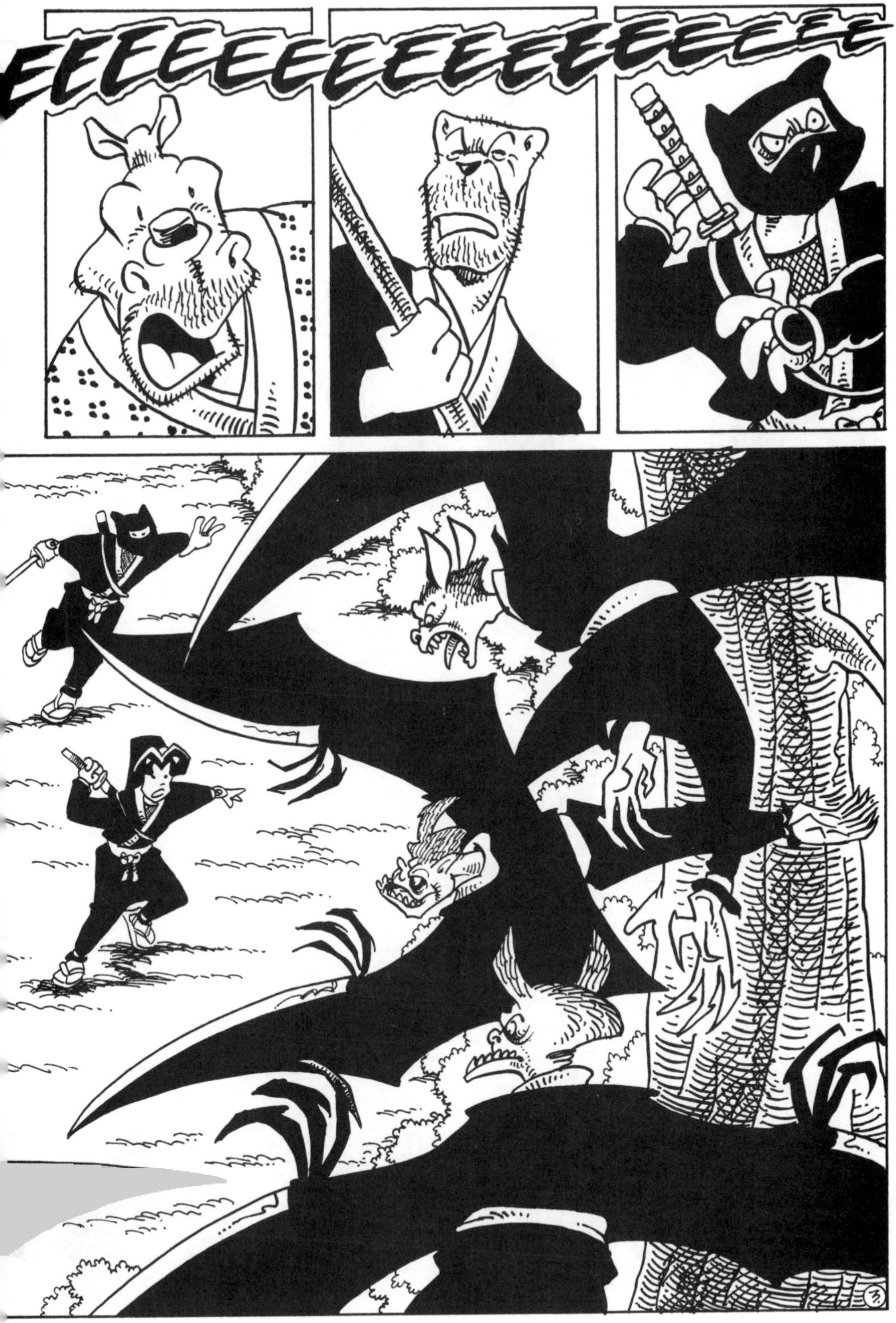
EEEEEEEEEEEEEEEEE

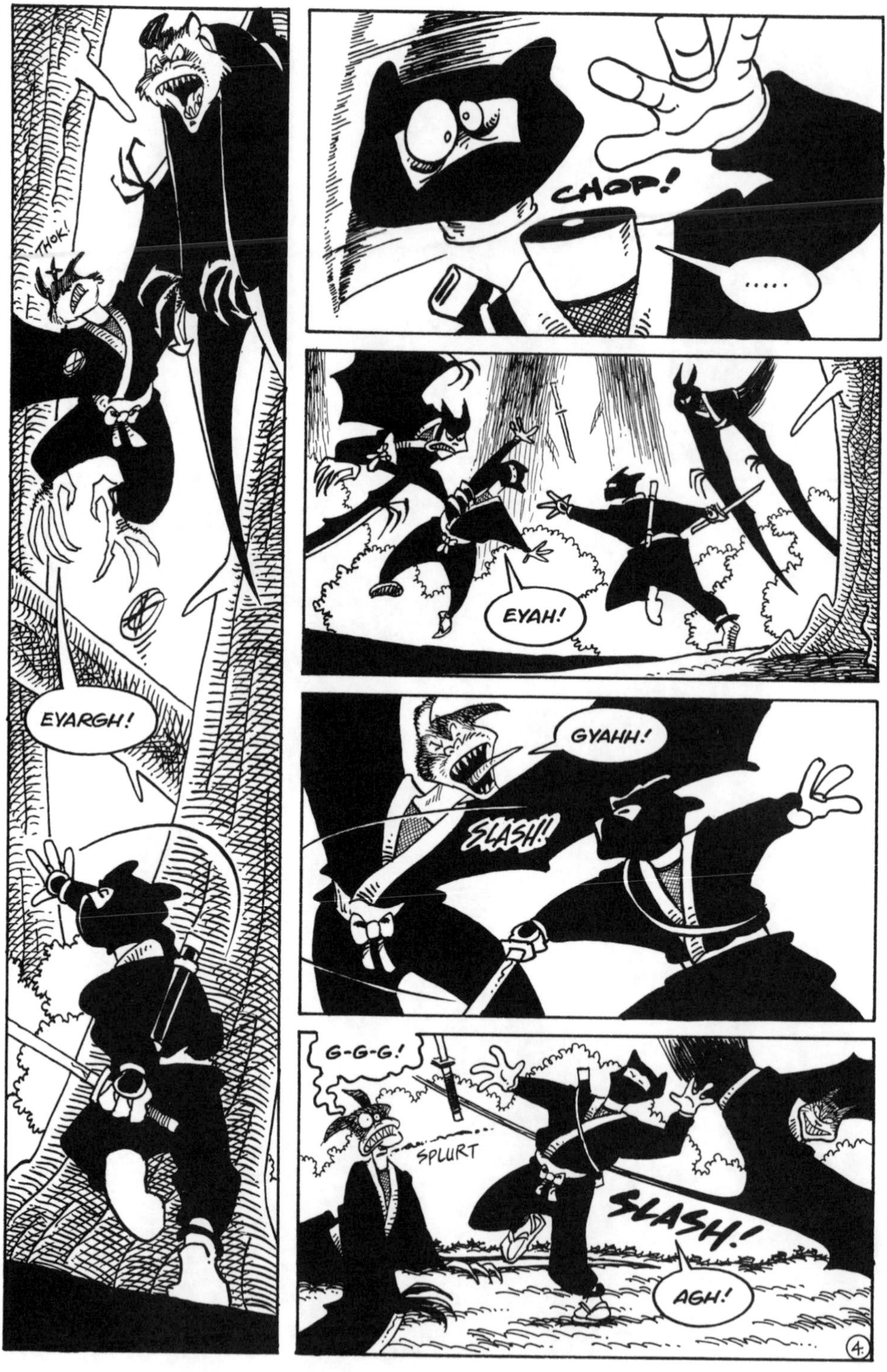
THOK!
EYARGH!
CHOP!
.....
EYAH!
GYAHH!
SLASH!
G-G-G!
SPLURT
SLASH!
AGH!
4

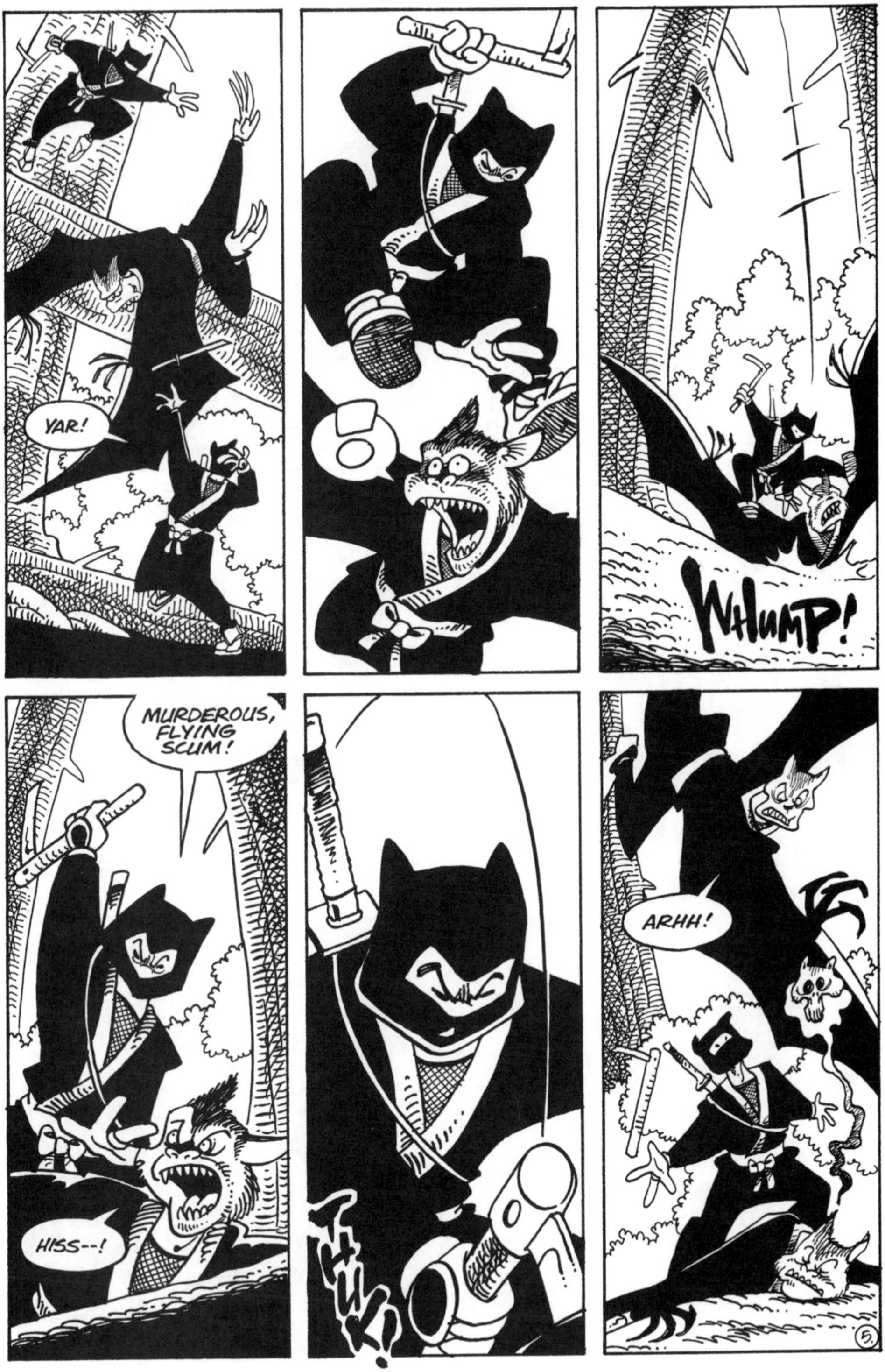
YAR!
WHUMP!
MURDEROUS, FLYING SCUM!
HISS--!
THUK!
ARHH!
5

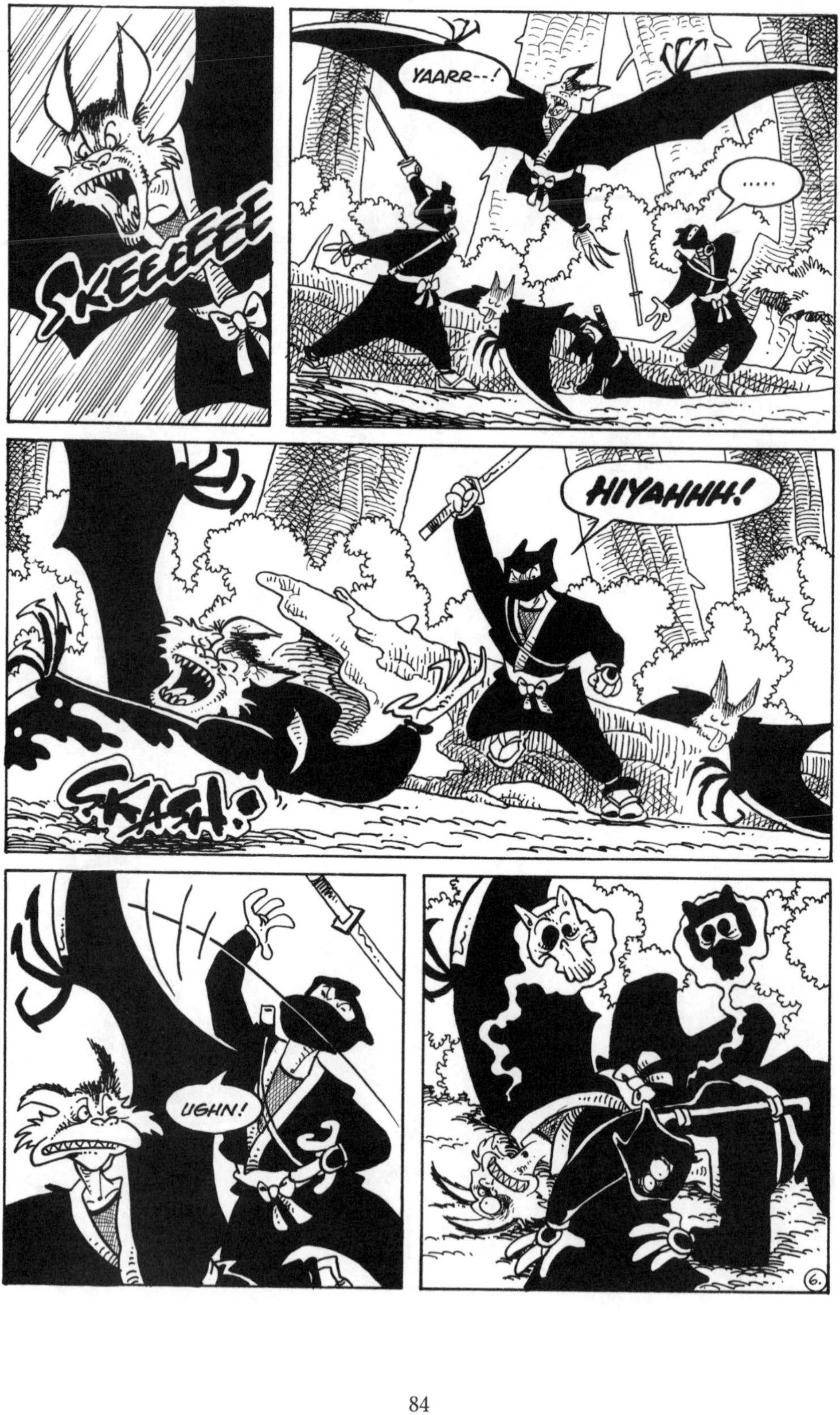
SKEEEEEE
YAARR--!
.....
HIYAHHH!
SKASH!
UGHN!
6.

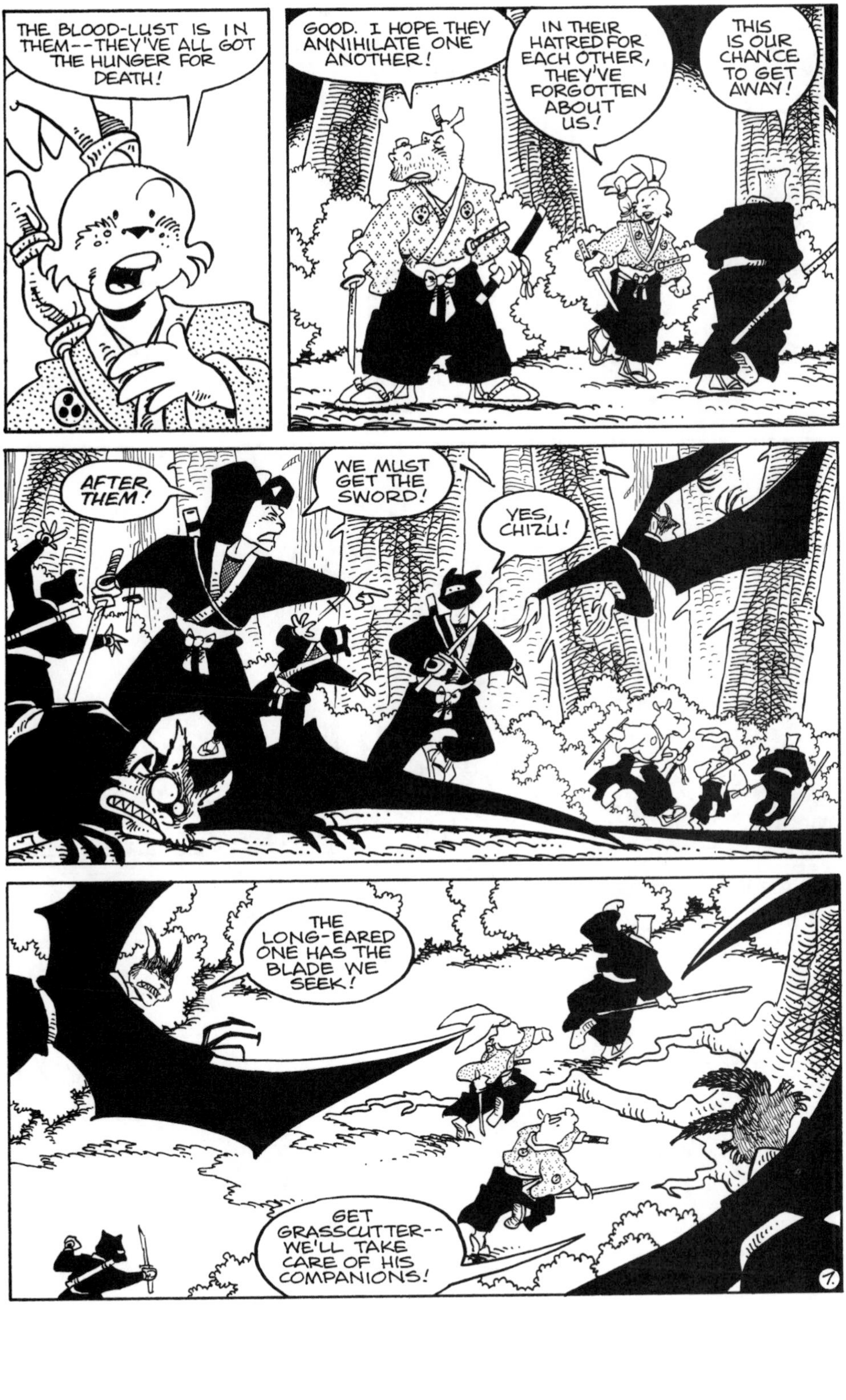
THE BLOOD-LUST IS IN THEM--THEY'VE ALL GOT THE HUNGER FOR DEATH!
GOOD. I HOPE THEY ANNIHILATE ONE ANOTHER!
IN THEIR HATRED FOR EACH OTHER, THEY'VE FORGOTTEN ABOUT US!
THIS IS OUR CHANCE TO GET AWAY!
AFTER THEM!
WE MUST GET THE SWORD!
YES, CHIZU!
THE LONG-EARED ONE HAS THE BLADE WE SEEK!
GET GRASSCUTTER--WE'LL TAKE CARE OF HIS COMPANIONS!
7.

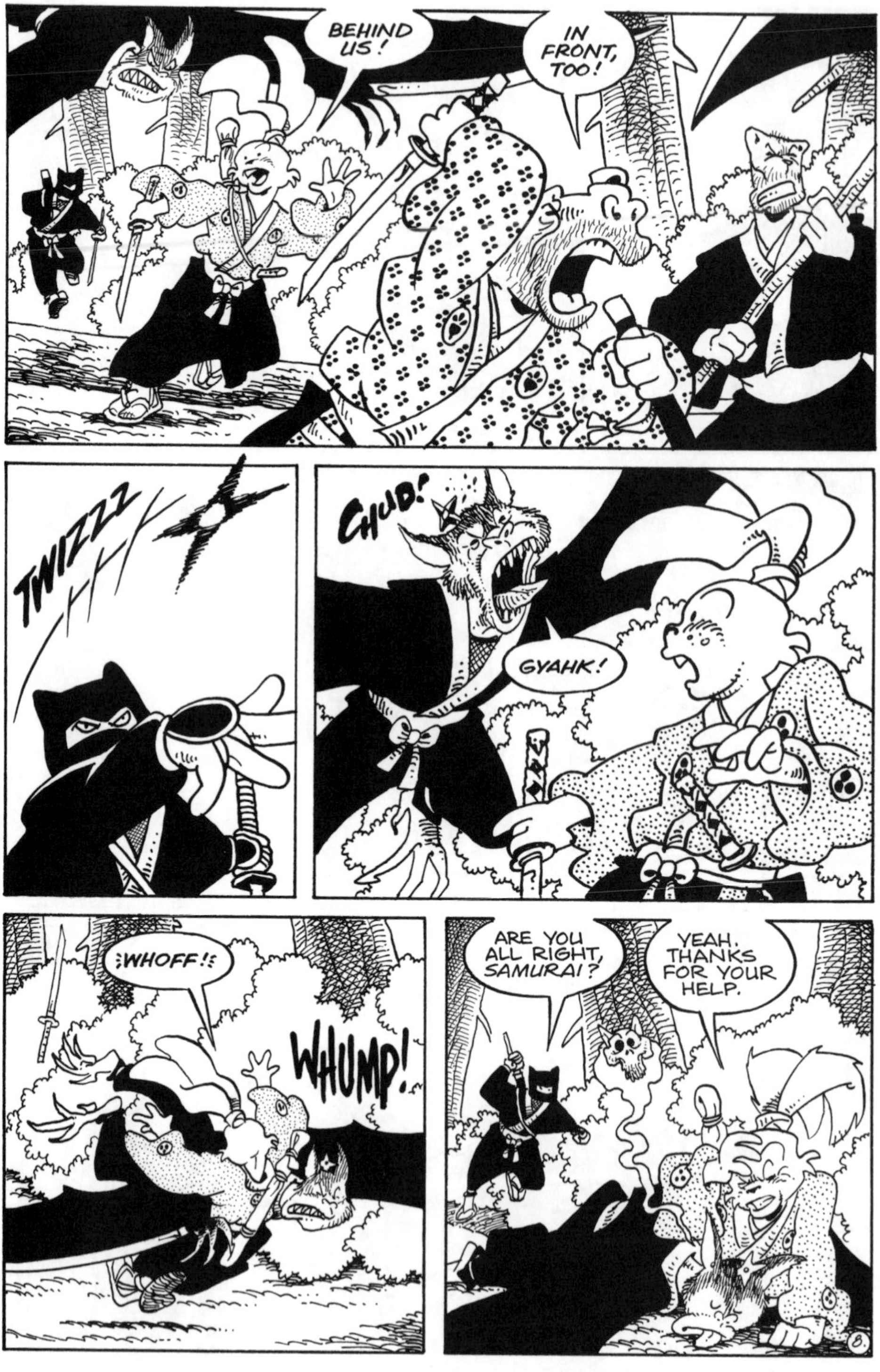
BEHIND US!
IN FRONT, TOO!
TWIZZZ
CHUD!
GYAHK!
WHOFF!
WHUMP!
ARE YOU ALL RIGHT, SAMURAI?
YEAH. THANKS FOR YOUR HELP.
8.

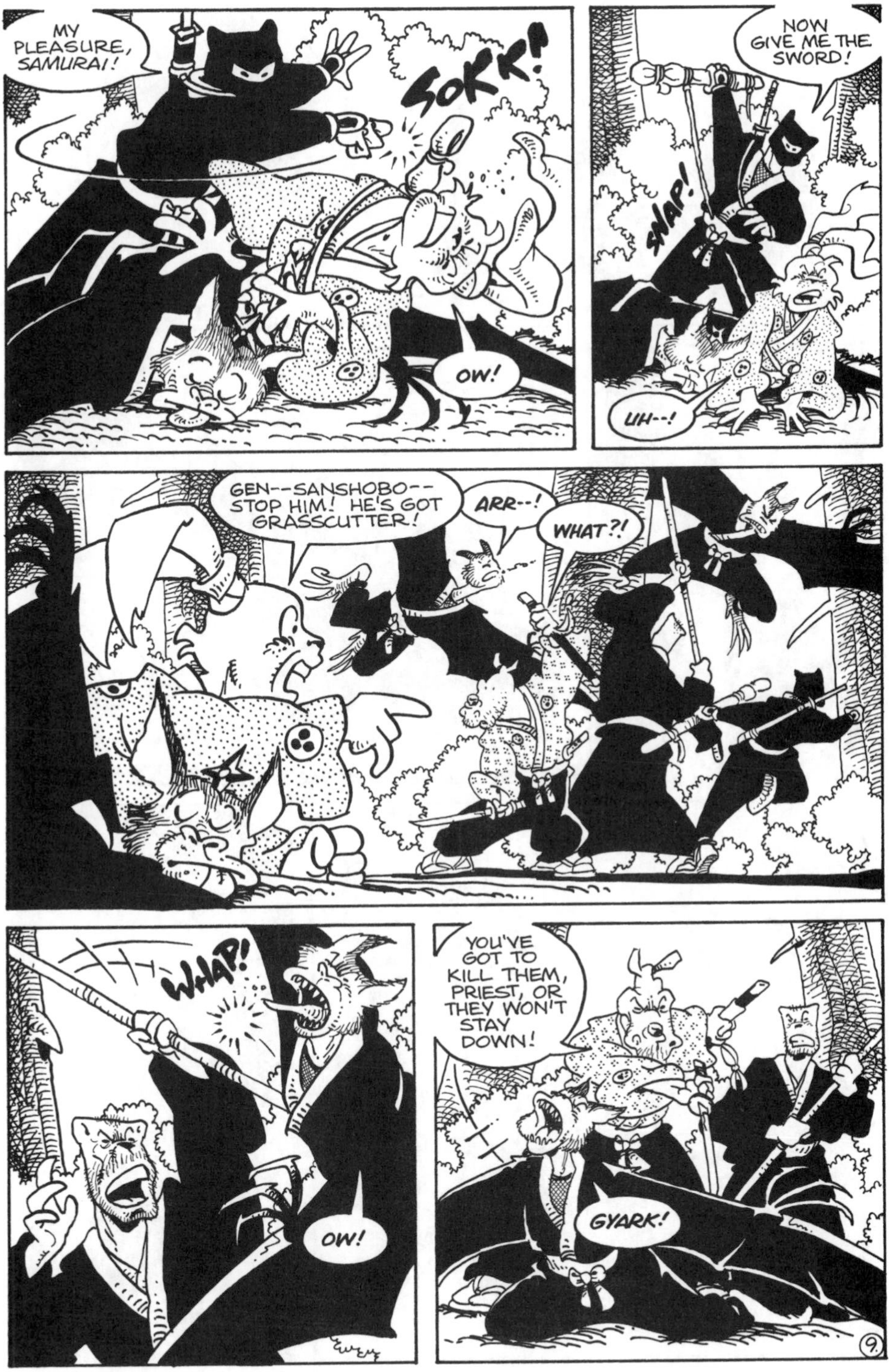
MY PLEASURE, SAMURAI!
SOKK!
OW!
NOW GIVE ME THE SWORD!
SNAP!
UH--!
GEN--SANSHOBO-- STOP HIM! HE'S GOT GRASSCUTTER!
ARR--!
WHAT?!
WHAP!
OW!
YOU'VE GOT TO KILL THEM, PRIEST, OR THEY WON'T STAY DOWN!
GYARK!
9.

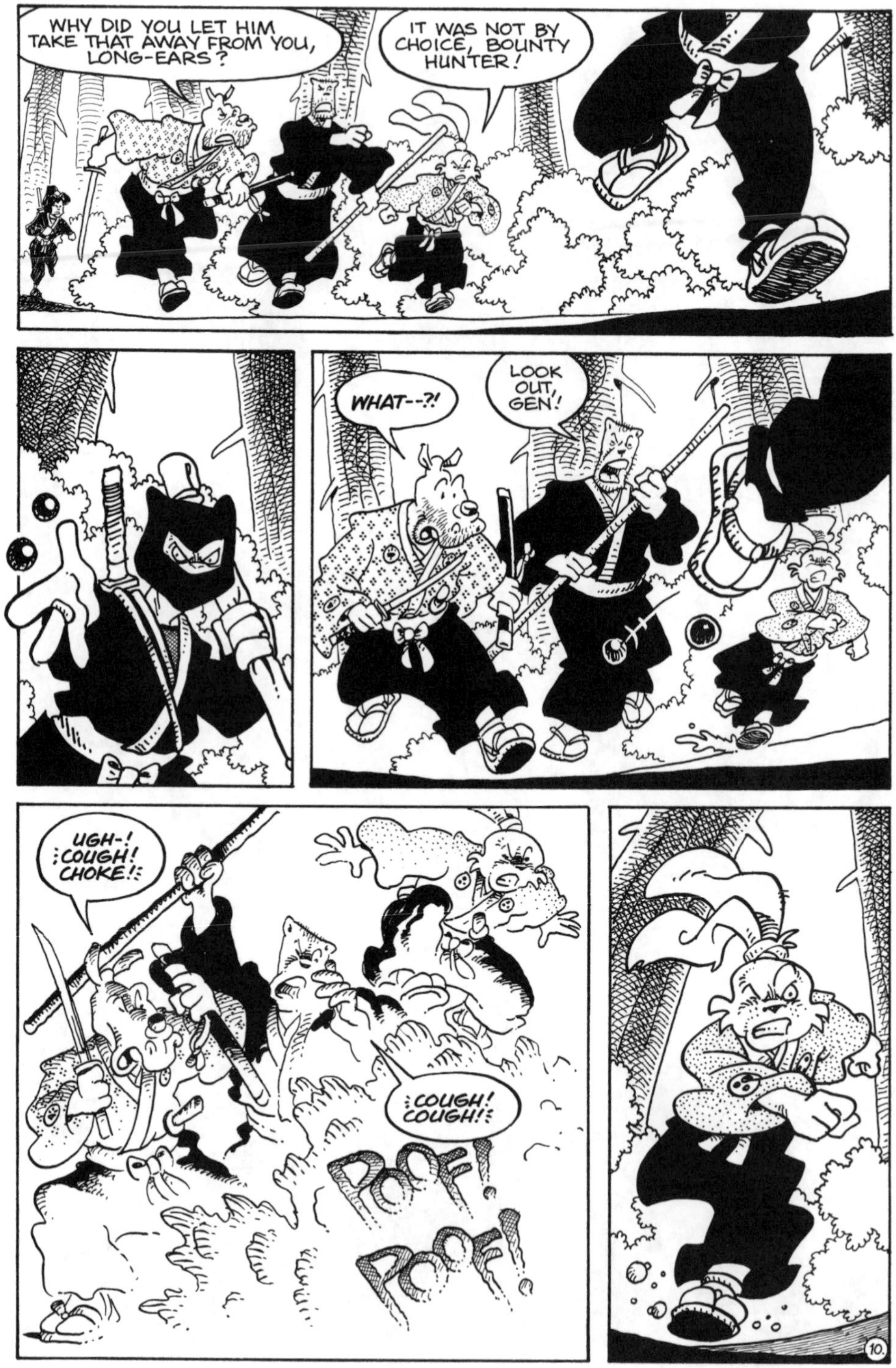
WHY DID YOU LET HIM TAKE THAT AWAY FROM YOU, LONG-EARS?
IT WAS NOT BY CHOICE, BOUNTY HUNTER!
WHAT--?!
LOOK OUT, GEN!
UGH-! COUGH! CHOKE!
COUGH! COUGH!
POOF! POOF!
10.

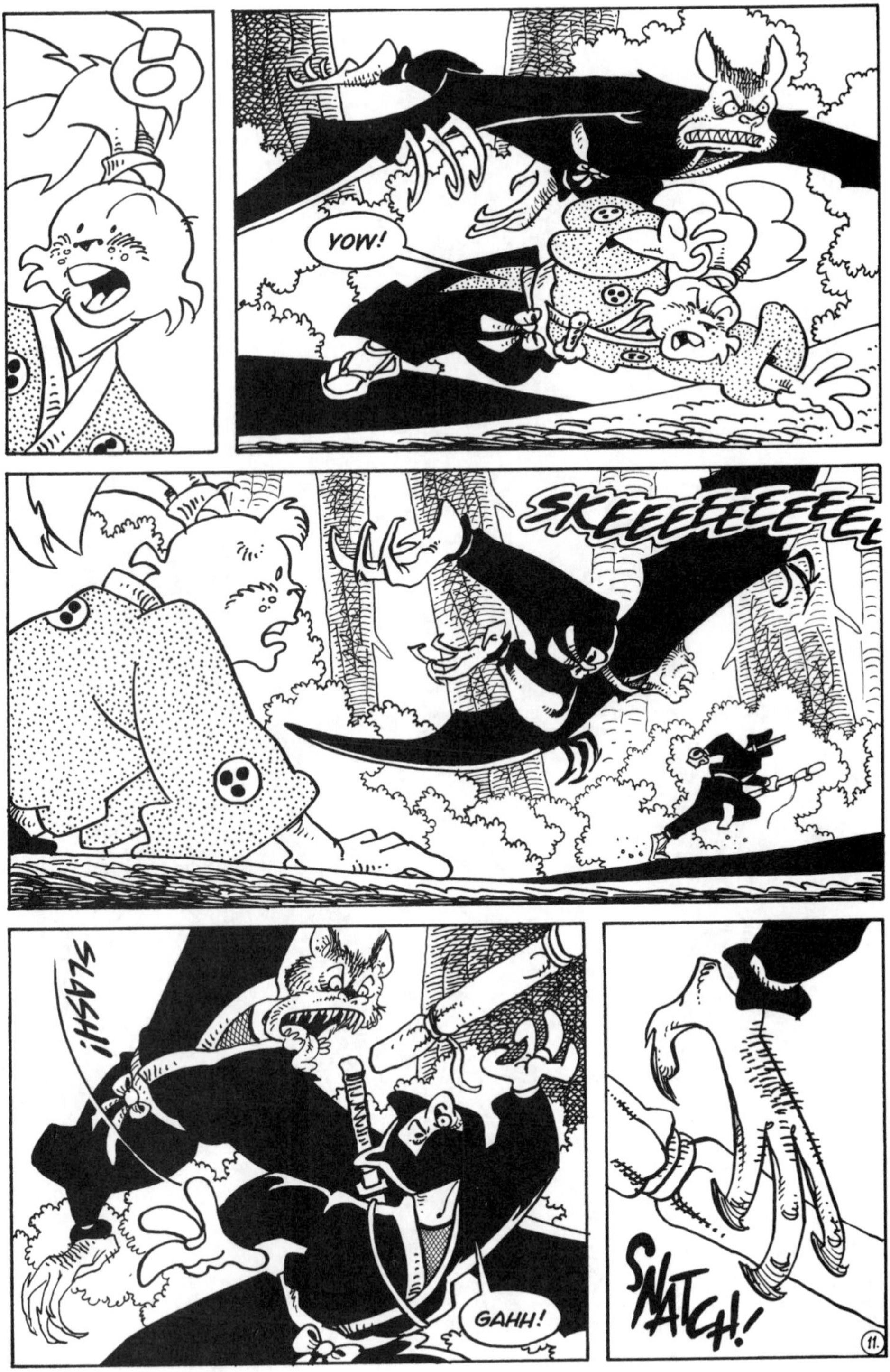
YOW!
SKEEEEEEEEEEE
SLASH!
GAHH!
SNATCH!
11.

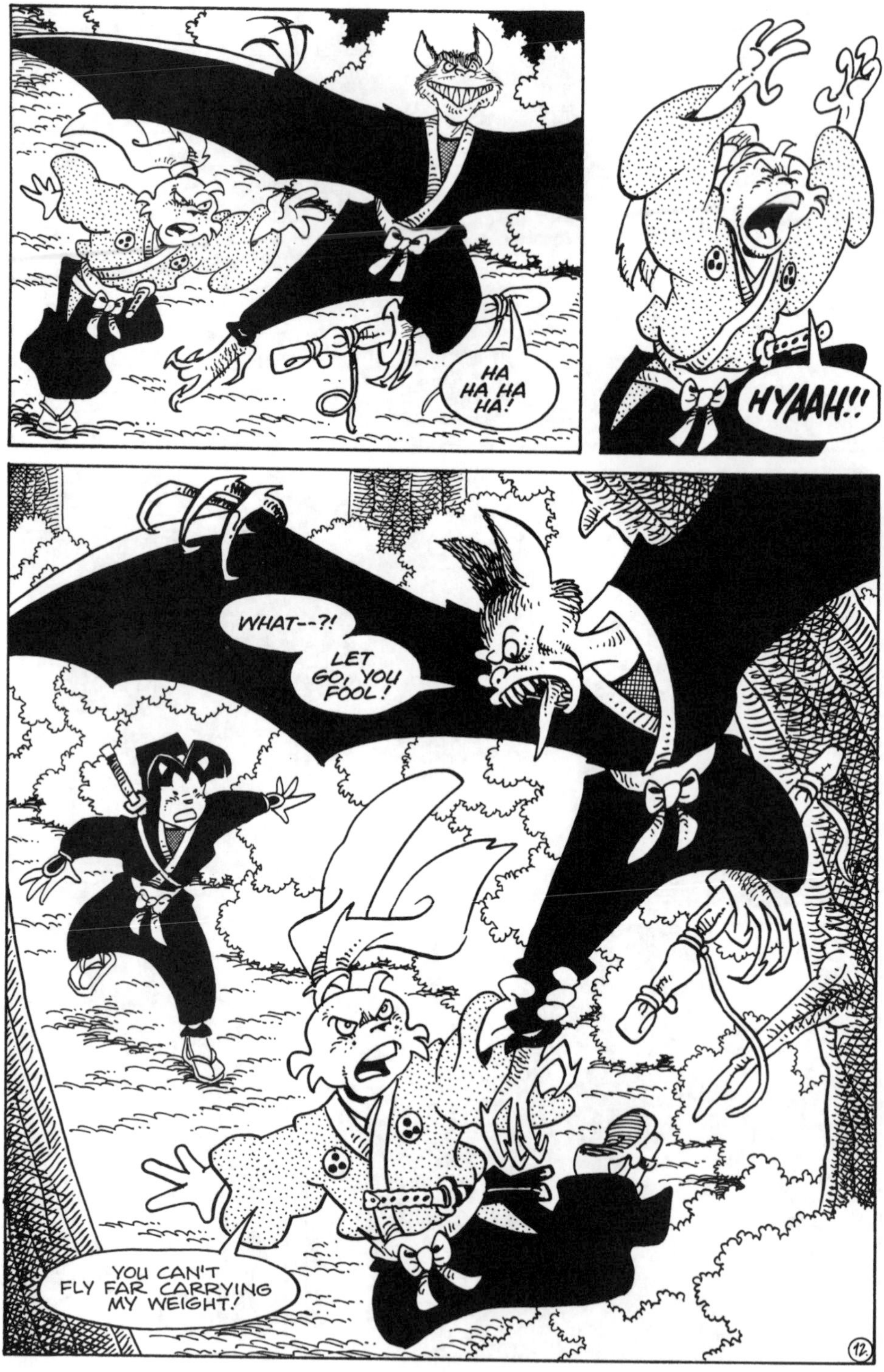

HA HA HA HA!
HYAAH!!
WHAT--?!
LET GO, YOU FOOL!
YOU CAN'T FLY FAR CARRYING MY WEIGHT!
12

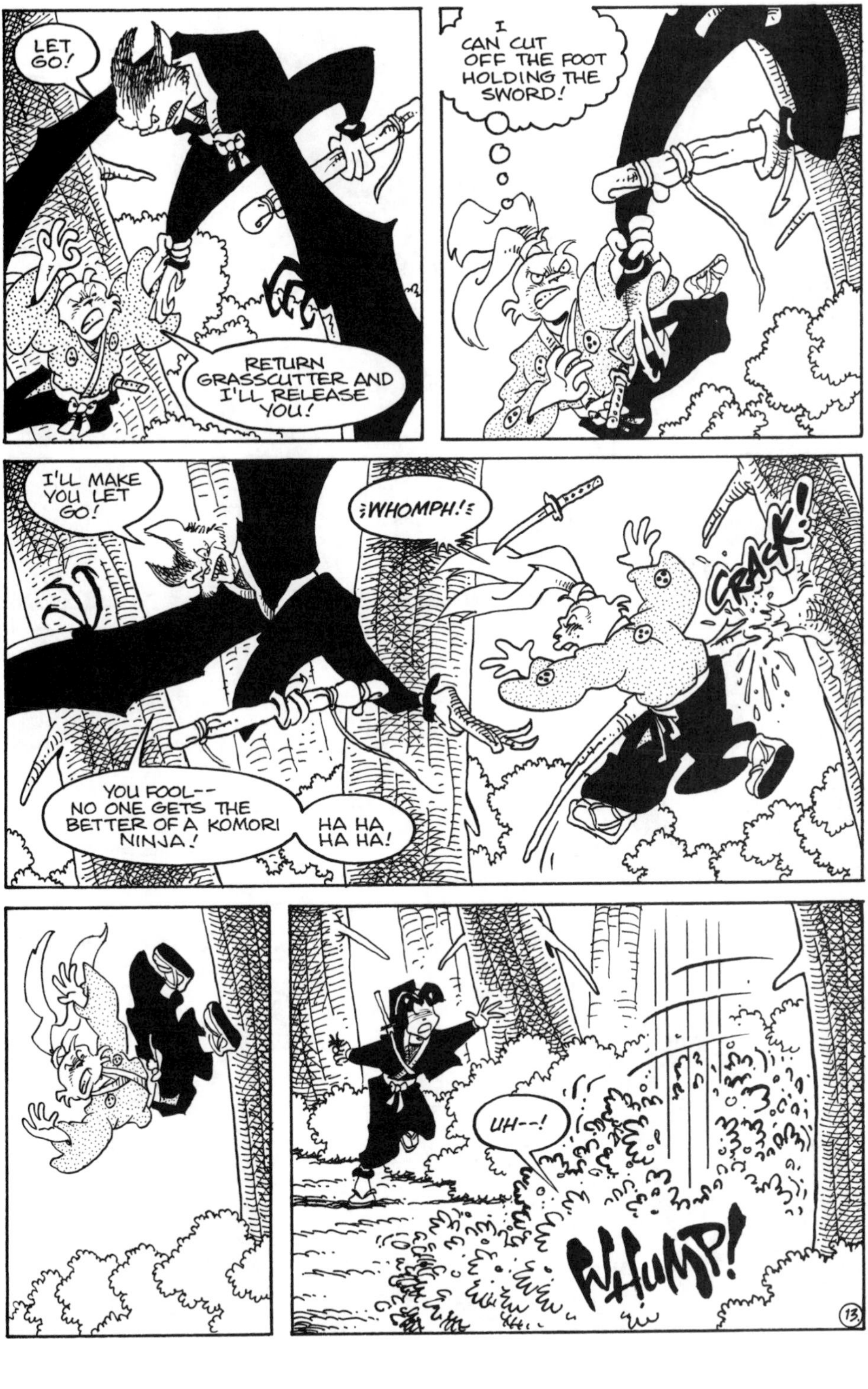
LET GO!
RETURN GRASSCUTTER AND I'LL RELEASE YOU!
I CAN CUT OFF THE FOOT HOLDING THE SWORD!
I'LL MAKE YOU LET GO!
WHOMPH!
CRACK!
YOU FOOL-- NO ONE GETS THE BETTER OF A KOMORI NINJA!
HA HA HA HA!
UH--!
WHUMP!
13

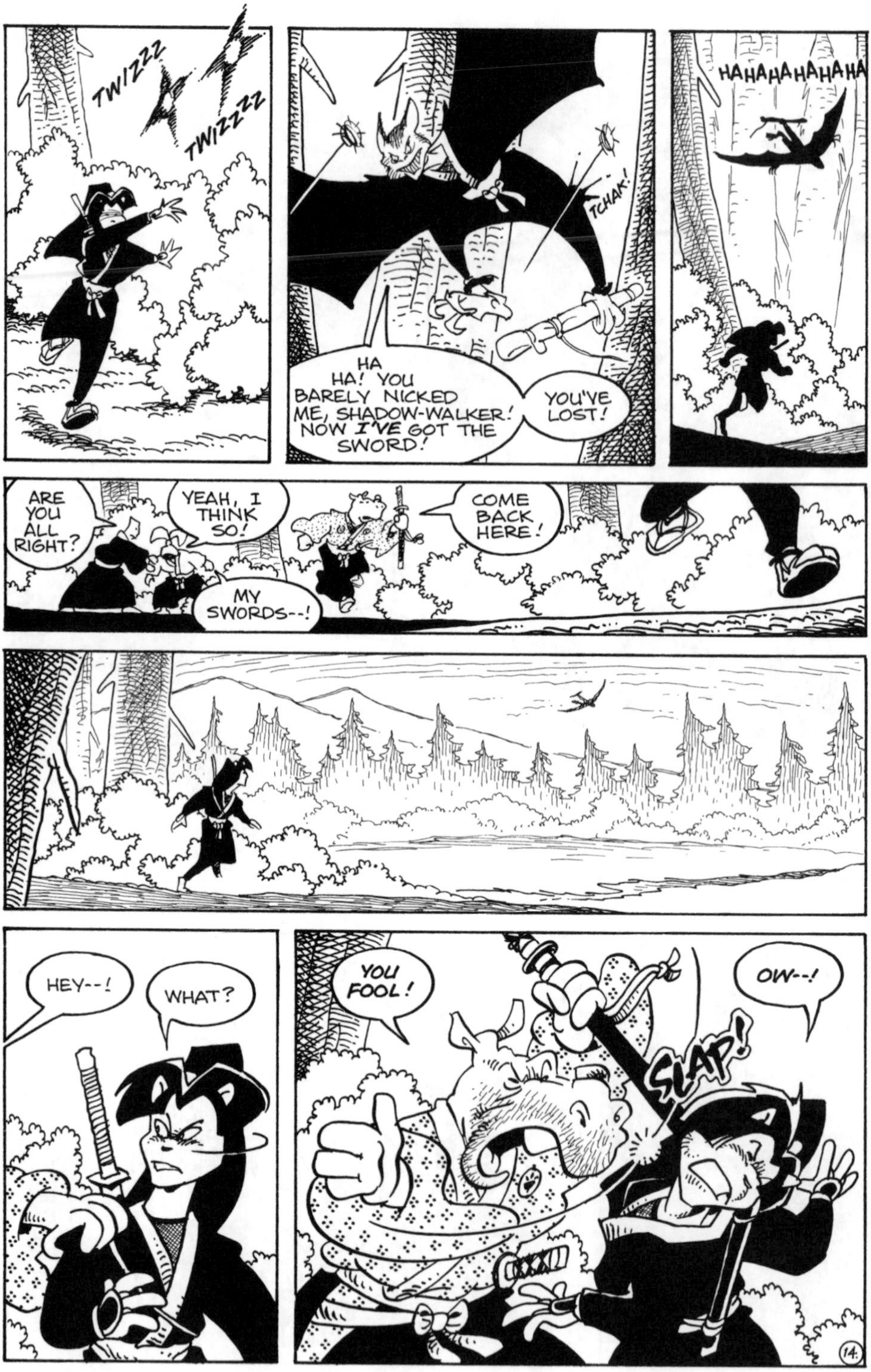
TWIZZZ
TWIZZZZ
HA HA! YOU BARELY NICKED ME, SHADOW-WALKER! NOW I'VE GOT THE SWORD!
YOU'VE LOST!
TCHAK!
HAHAHAHAHAHAHA
ARE YOU ALL RIGHT?
YEAH, I THINK SO!
MY SWORDS--!
COME BACK HERE!
HEY--!
WHAT?
YOU FOOL!
SLAP!
OW--!
14.

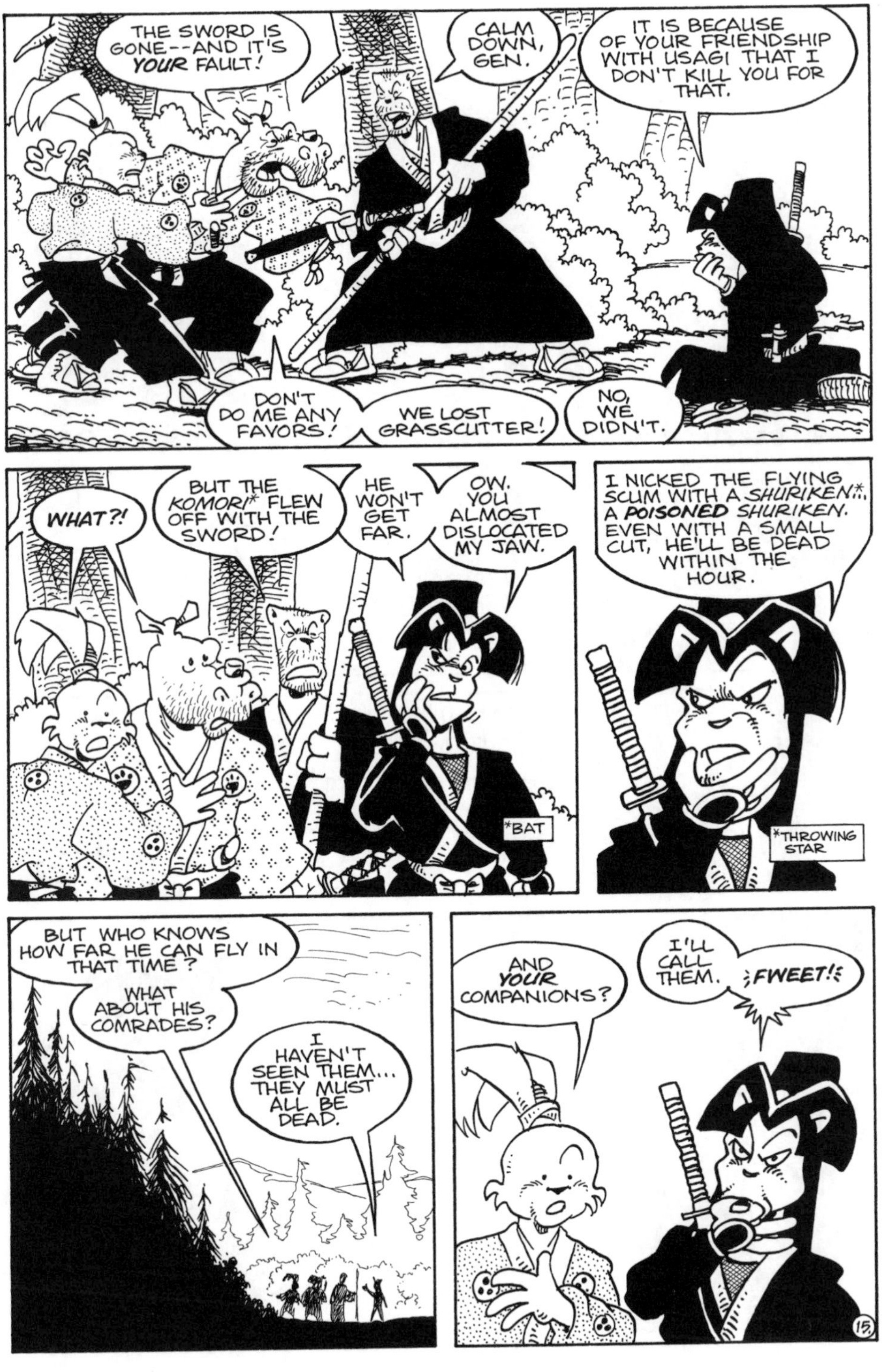

THE SWORD IS GONE--AND IT'S *YOUR* FAULT!
CALM DOWN, GEN.
IT IS BECAUSE OF YOUR FRIENDSHIP WITH USAGI THAT I DON'T KILL YOU FOR THAT.
DON'T DO ME ANY FAVORS!
WE LOST GRASSCUTTER!
NO, WE DIDN'T.
WHAT?!
BUT THE *KOMORI** FLEW OFF WITH THE SWORD!
HE WON'T GET FAR.
OW. YOU ALMOST DISLOCATED MY JAW.
*BAT
I NICKED THE FLYING SCUM WITH A *SHURIKEN*,* A **POISONED** *SHURIKEN*. EVEN WITH A SMALL CUT, HE'LL BE DEAD WITHIN THE HOUR.
*THROWING STAR
BUT WHO KNOWS HOW FAR HE CAN FLY IN THAT TIME?
WHAT ABOUT HIS COMRADES?
I HAVEN'T SEEN THEM... THEY MUST ALL BE DEAD.
AND *YOUR* COMPANIONS?
I'LL CALL THEM.
FWEET!
15

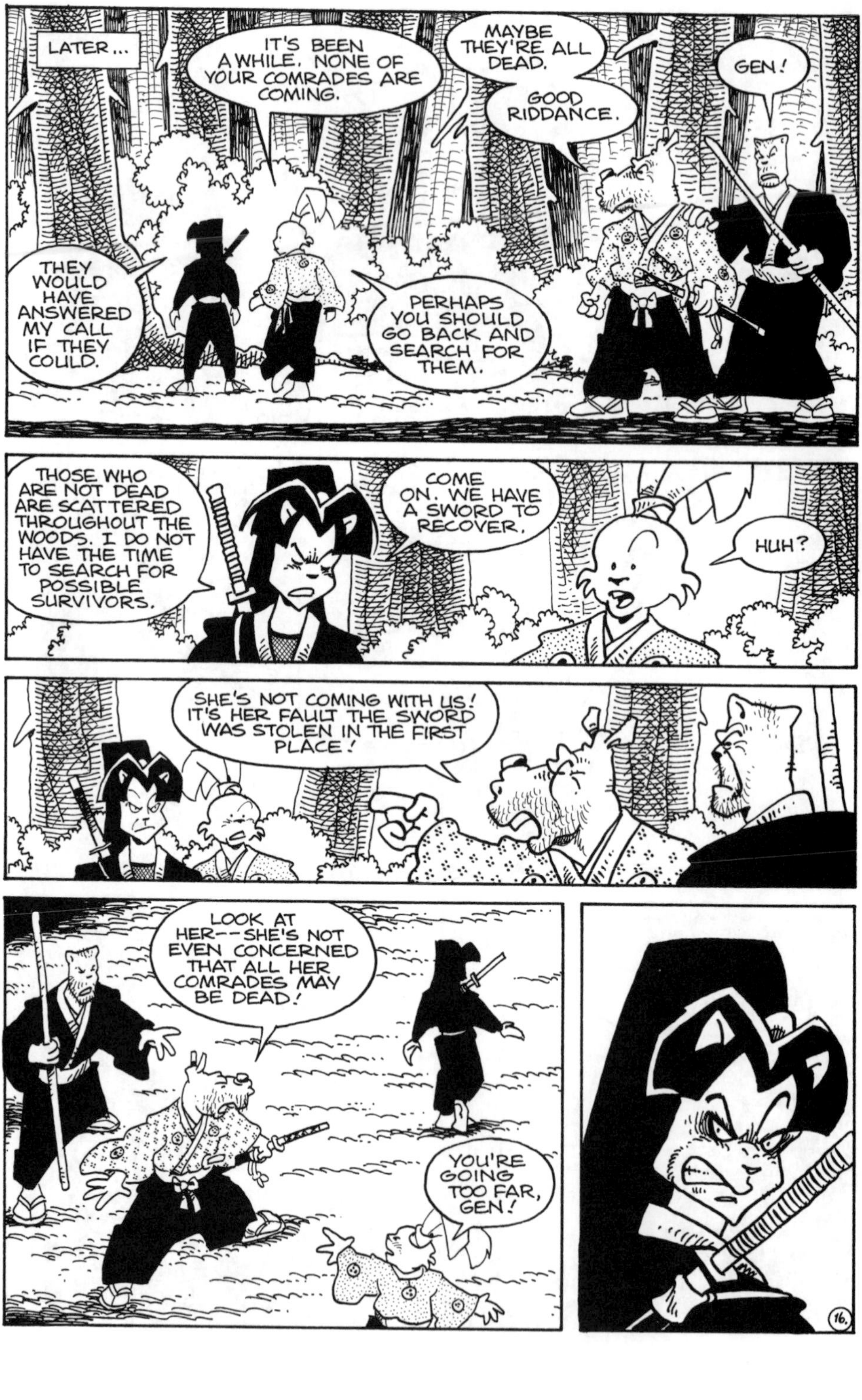
LATER...
IT'S BEEN A WHILE. NONE OF YOUR COMRADES ARE COMING.
MAYBE THEY'RE ALL DEAD.
GOOD RIDDANCE.
GEN!
THEY WOULD HAVE ANSWERED MY CALL IF THEY COULD.
PERHAPS YOU SHOULD GO BACK AND SEARCH FOR THEM.
THOSE WHO ARE NOT DEAD ARE SCATTERED THROUGHOUT THE WOODS. I DO NOT HAVE THE TIME TO SEARCH FOR POSSIBLE SURVIVORS.
COME ON. WE HAVE A SWORD TO RECOVER.
HUH?
SHE'S NOT COMING WITH US! IT'S HER FAULT THE SWORD WAS STOLEN IN THE FIRST PLACE!
LOOK AT HER--SHE'S NOT EVEN CONCERNED THAT ALL HER COMRADES MAY BE DEAD!
YOU'RE GOING TOO FAR, GEN!
16.

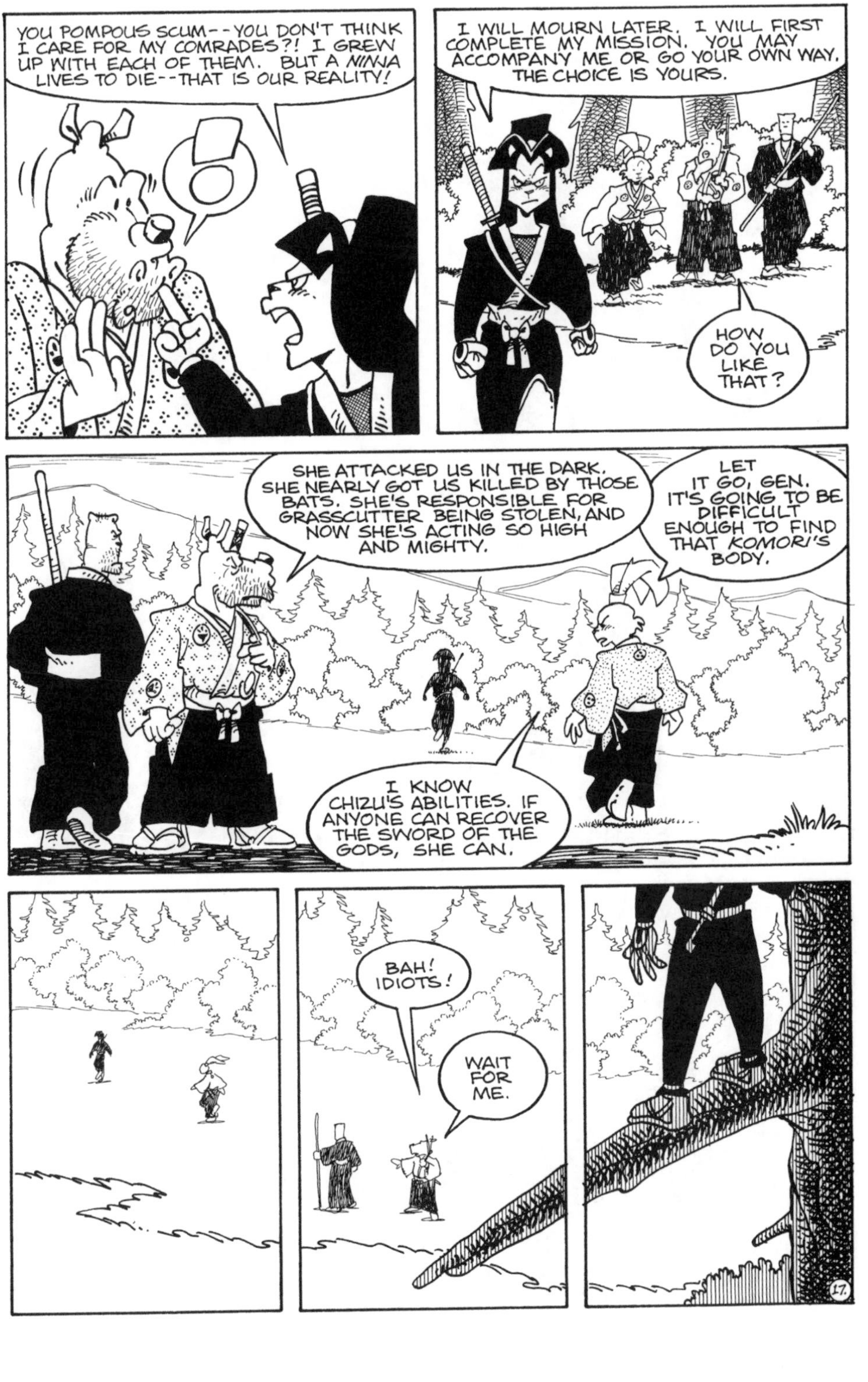
YOU POMPOUS SCUM--YOU DON'T THINK I CARE FOR MY COMRADES?! I GREW UP WITH EACH OF THEM. BUT A *NINJA* LIVES TO DIE--THAT IS OUR REALITY!
I WILL MOURN LATER. I WILL FIRST COMPLETE MY MISSION. YOU MAY ACCOMPANY ME OR GO YOUR OWN WAY. THE CHOICE IS YOURS.
HOW DO YOU LIKE THAT?
SHE ATTACKED US IN THE DARK. SHE NEARLY GOT US KILLED BY THOSE BATS. SHE'S RESPONSIBLE FOR GRASSCUTTER BEING STOLEN, AND NOW SHE'S ACTING SO HIGH AND MIGHTY.
LET IT GO, GEN. IT'S GOING TO BE DIFFICULT ENOUGH TO FIND THAT *KOMORI*'S BODY.
I KNOW CHIZU'S ABILITIES. IF ANYONE CAN RECOVER THE SWORD OF THE GODS, SHE CAN.
BAH! IDIOTS!
WAIT FOR ME.
17.

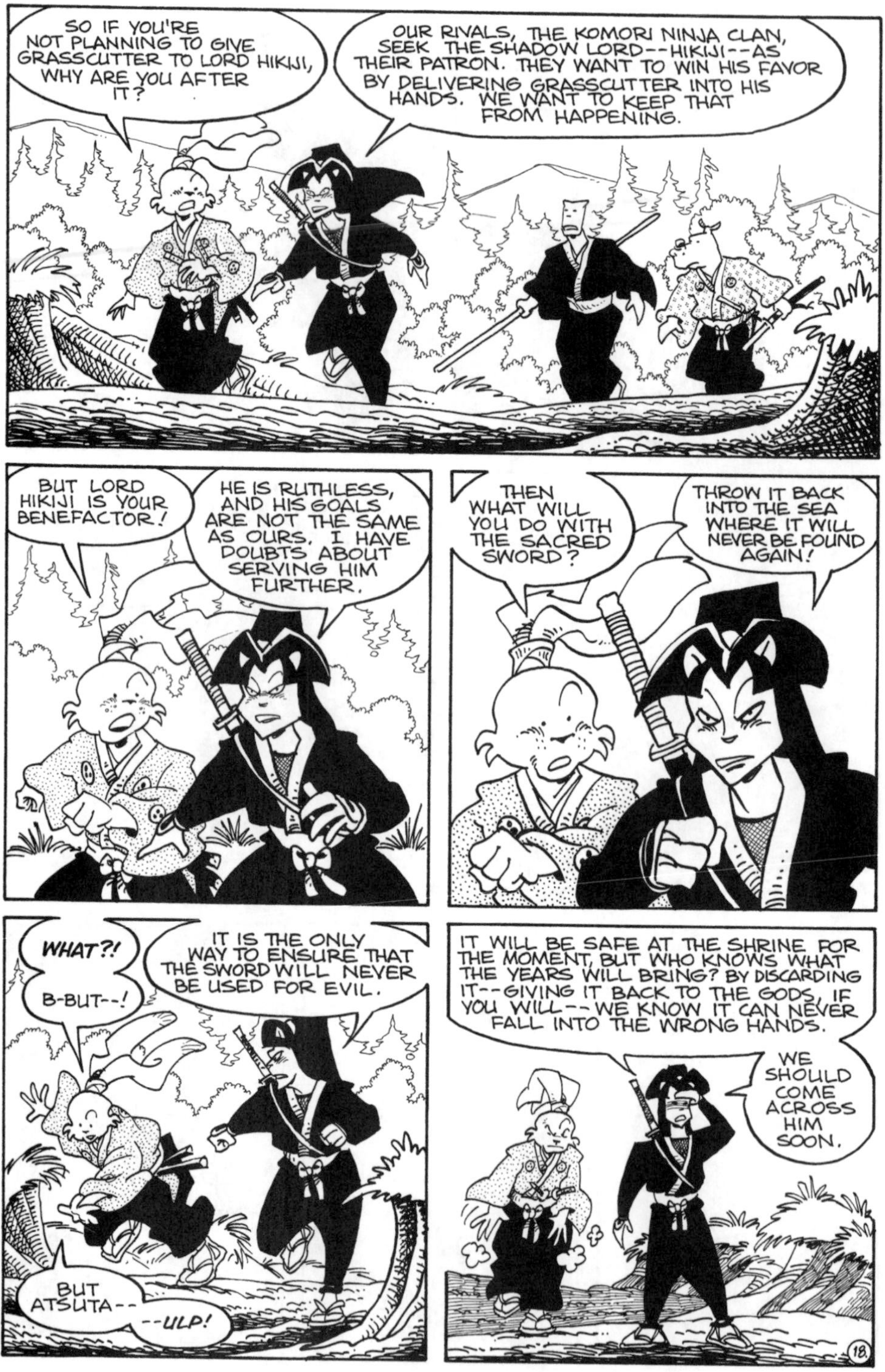
SO IF YOU'RE NOT PLANNING TO GIVE GRASSCUTTER TO LORD HIKIJI, WHY ARE YOU AFTER IT?
OUR RIVALS, THE KOMORI NINJA CLAN, SEEK THE SHADOW LORD--HIKIJI--AS THEIR PATRON. THEY WANT TO WIN HIS FAVOR BY DELIVERING GRASSCUTTER INTO HIS HANDS. WE WANT TO KEEP THAT FROM HAPPENING.
BUT LORD HIKIJI IS YOUR BENEFACTOR!
HE IS RUTHLESS, AND HIS GOALS ARE NOT THE SAME AS OURS. I HAVE DOUBTS ABOUT SERVING HIM FURTHER.
THEN WHAT WILL YOU DO WITH THE SACRED SWORD?
THROW IT BACK INTO THE SEA WHERE IT WILL NEVER BE FOUND AGAIN!
WHAT?!
B-BUT--!
IT IS THE ONLY WAY TO ENSURE THAT THE SWORD WILL NEVER BE USED FOR EVIL.
BUT ATSUTA--
--ULP!
IT WILL BE SAFE AT THE SHRINE FOR THE MOMENT, BUT WHO KNOWS WHAT THE YEARS WILL BRING? BY DISCARDING IT--GIVING IT BACK TO THE GODS, IF YOU WILL--WE KNOW IT CAN NEVER FALL INTO THE WRONG HANDS.
WE SHOULD COME ACROSS HIM SOON.
18

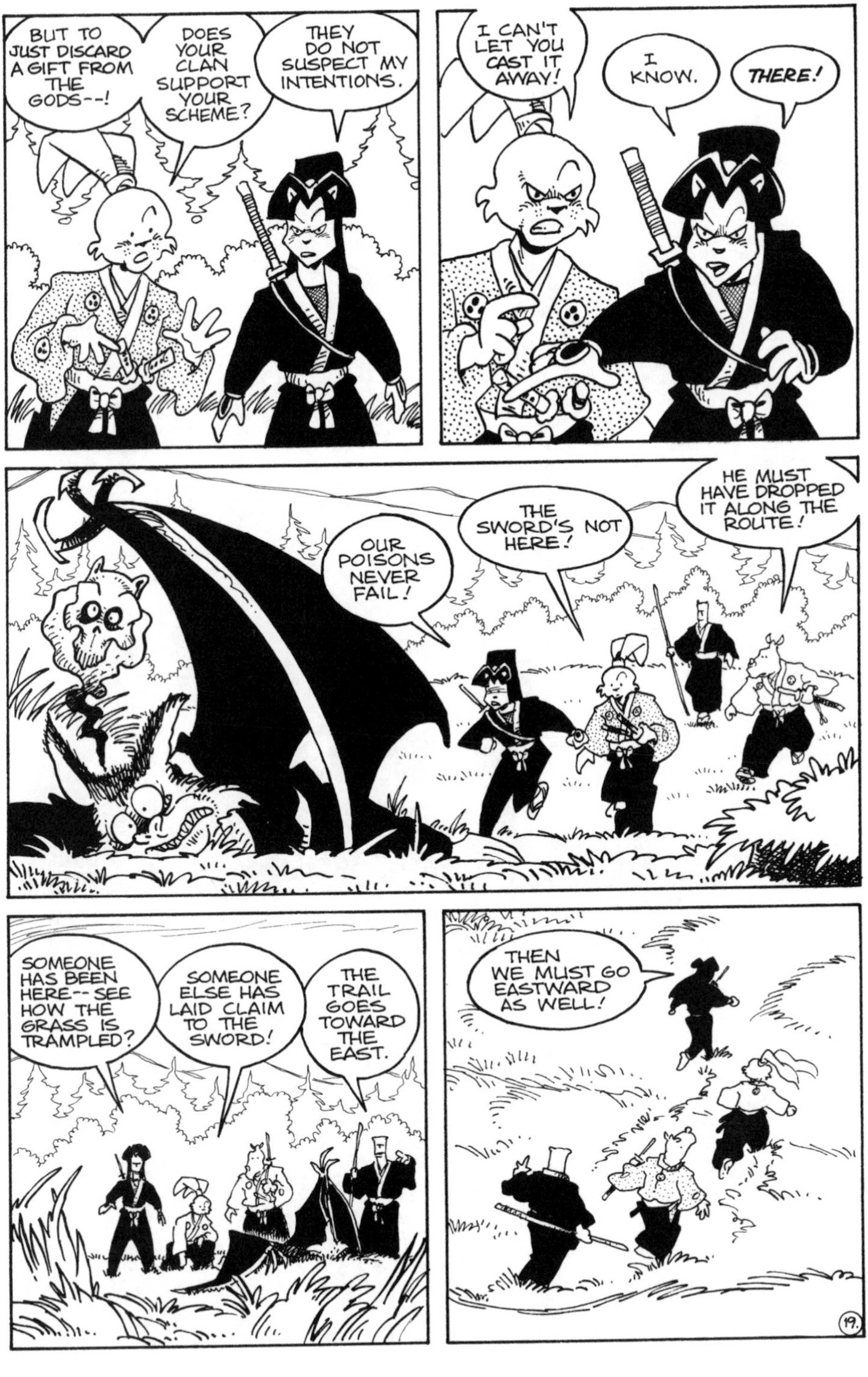
BUT TO JUST DISCARD A GIFT FROM THE GODS--!
DOES YOUR CLAN SUPPORT YOUR SCHEME?
THEY DO NOT SUSPECT MY INTENTIONS.
I CAN'T LET YOU CAST IT AWAY!
I KNOW.
THERE!
OUR POISONS NEVER FAIL!
THE SWORD'S NOT HERE!
HE MUST HAVE DROPPED IT ALONG THE ROUTE!
SOMEONE HAS BEEN HERE--SEE HOW THE GRASS IS TRAMPLED?
SOMEONE ELSE HAS LAID CLAIM TO THE SWORD!
THE TRAIL GOES TOWARD THE EAST.
THEN WE MUST GO EASTWARD AS WELL!
19.

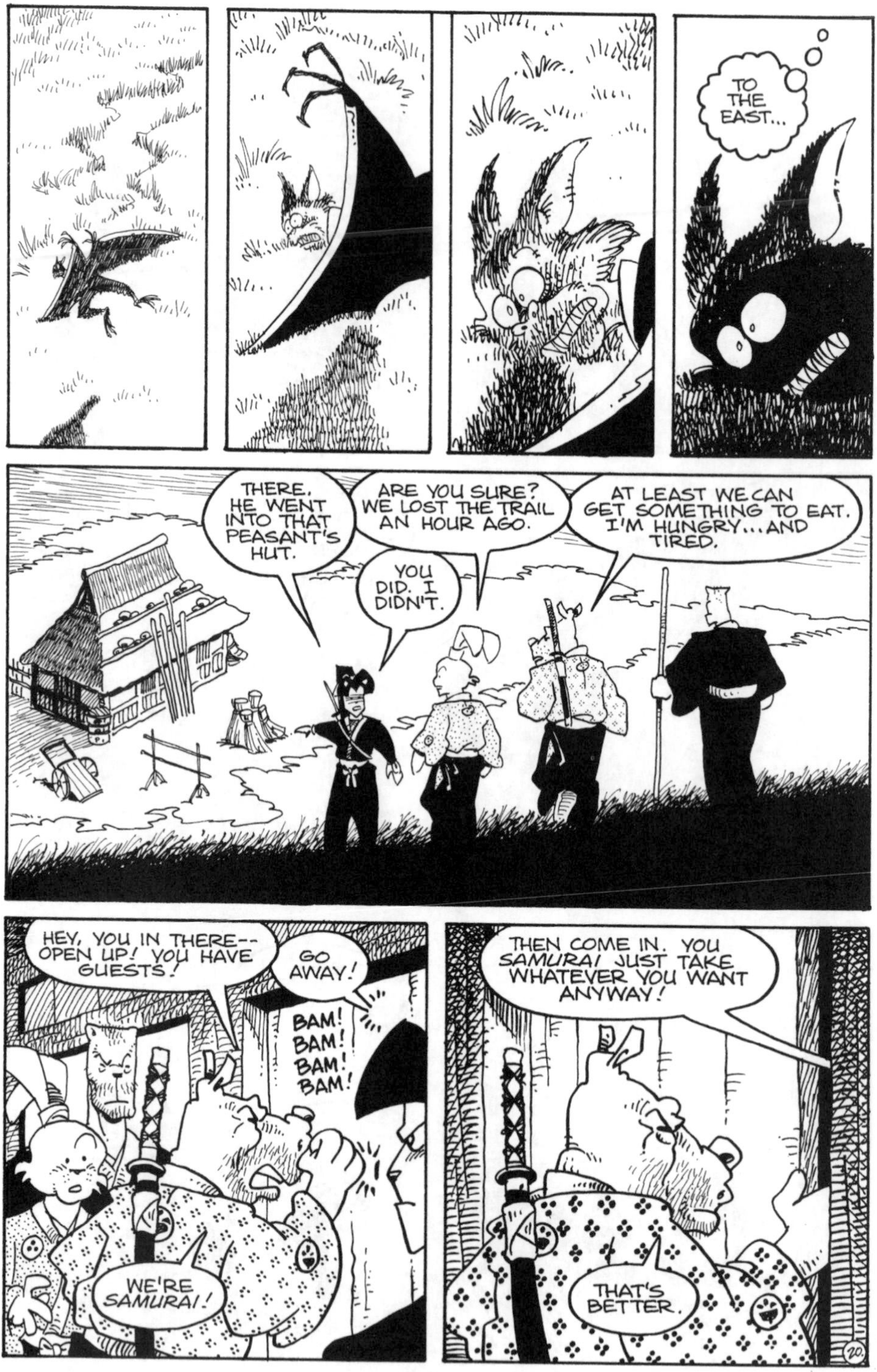
TO THE EAST...
THERE. HE WENT INTO THAT PEASANT'S HUT.
ARE YOU SURE? WE LOST THE TRAIL AN HOUR AGO.
YOU DID. I DIDN'T.
AT LEAST WE CAN GET SOMETHING TO EAT. I'M HUNGRY...AND TIRED.
HEY, YOU IN THERE-- OPEN UP! YOU HAVE GUESTS!
GO AWAY!
BAM! BAM! BAM! BAM!
WE'RE SAMURAI!
THEN COME IN. YOU SAMURAI JUST TAKE WHATEVER YOU WANT ANYWAY!
THAT'S BETTER.
20.

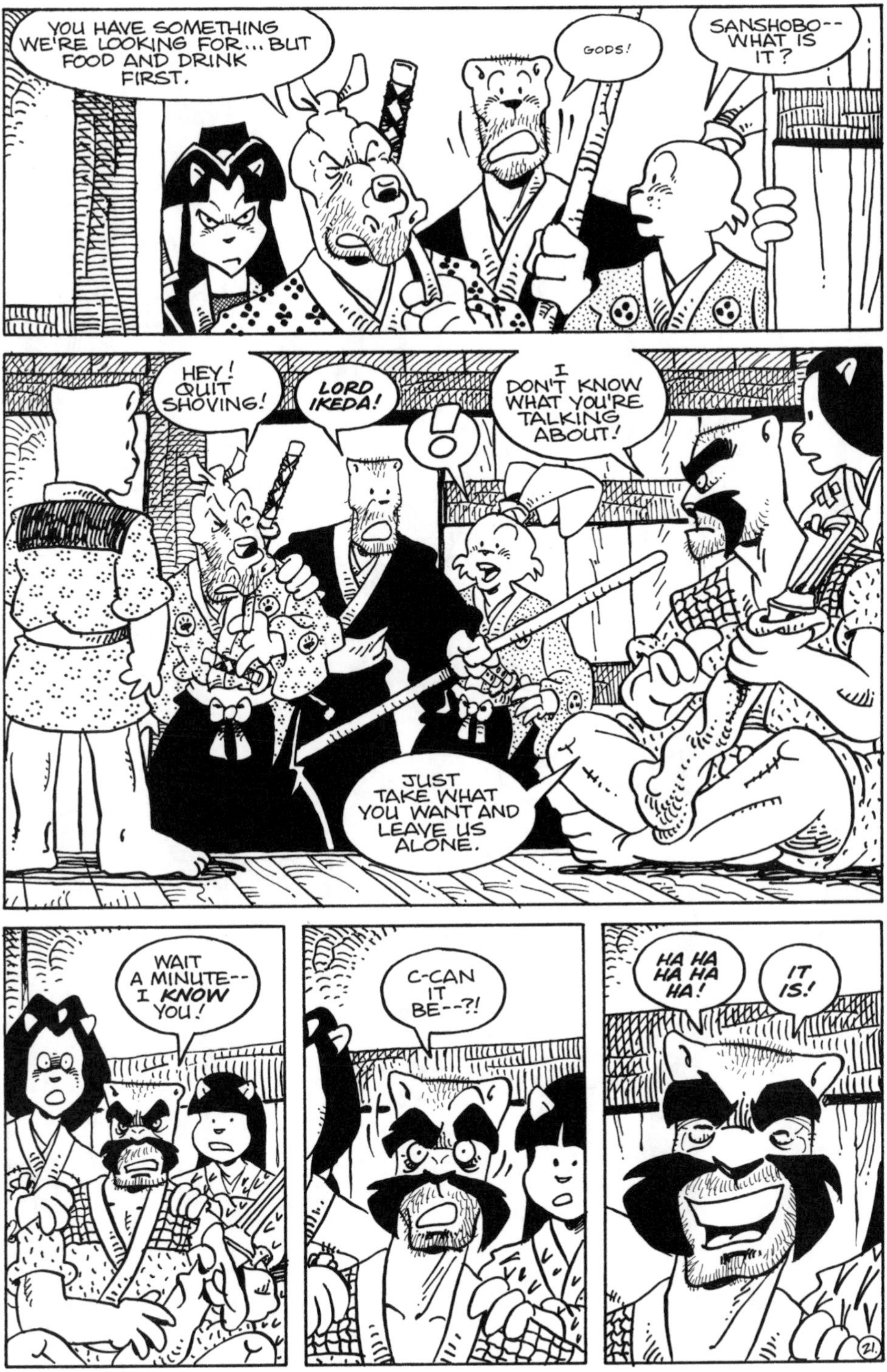
YOU HAVE SOMETHING WE'RE LOOKING FOR... BUT FOOD AND DRINK FIRST.
GODS!
SANSHOBO-- WHAT IS IT?
HEY! QUIT SHOVING!
LORD IKEDA!
!
I DON'T KNOW WHAT YOU'RE TALKING ABOUT!
JUST TAKE WHAT YOU WANT AND LEAVE US ALONE.
WAIT A MINUTE-- I KNOW YOU!
C-CAN IT BE--?!
HA HA HA HA HA!
IT IS!
21.

IT-- IT IS YOU!
OF COURSE, INUSHIRO, MY GOOD AND FAITHFUL FRIEND!
I-I BELIEVED YOU WERE KILLED IN THE REVOLT.
I BARELY ESCAPED AND HAVE BEEN LIVING IN HIDING THESE MANY YEARS!*
MY LORD!
GET UP, INUSHIRO. I AM A PEASANT NOW--A LORD NO LONGER.
IT IS GOOD TO SEE YOU AGAIN, MY FRIEND.
BUT YOU TRAVEL WITH INTERESTING COMPANIONS...TWO SAMURAI--
*UY: BOOK 11 SEASONS
--AND A NEKO NINJA.
WHAT ARE YOU INVOLVED IN, INUSHIRO?
22

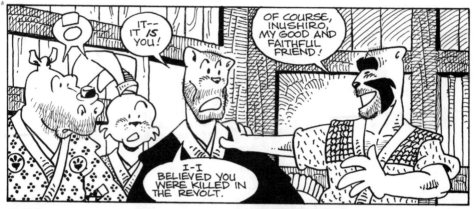

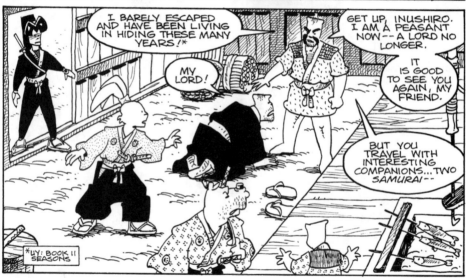

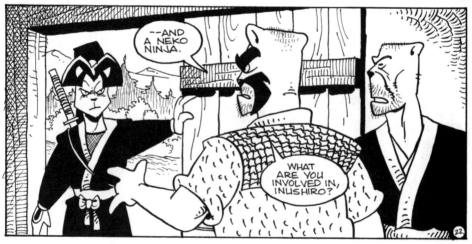

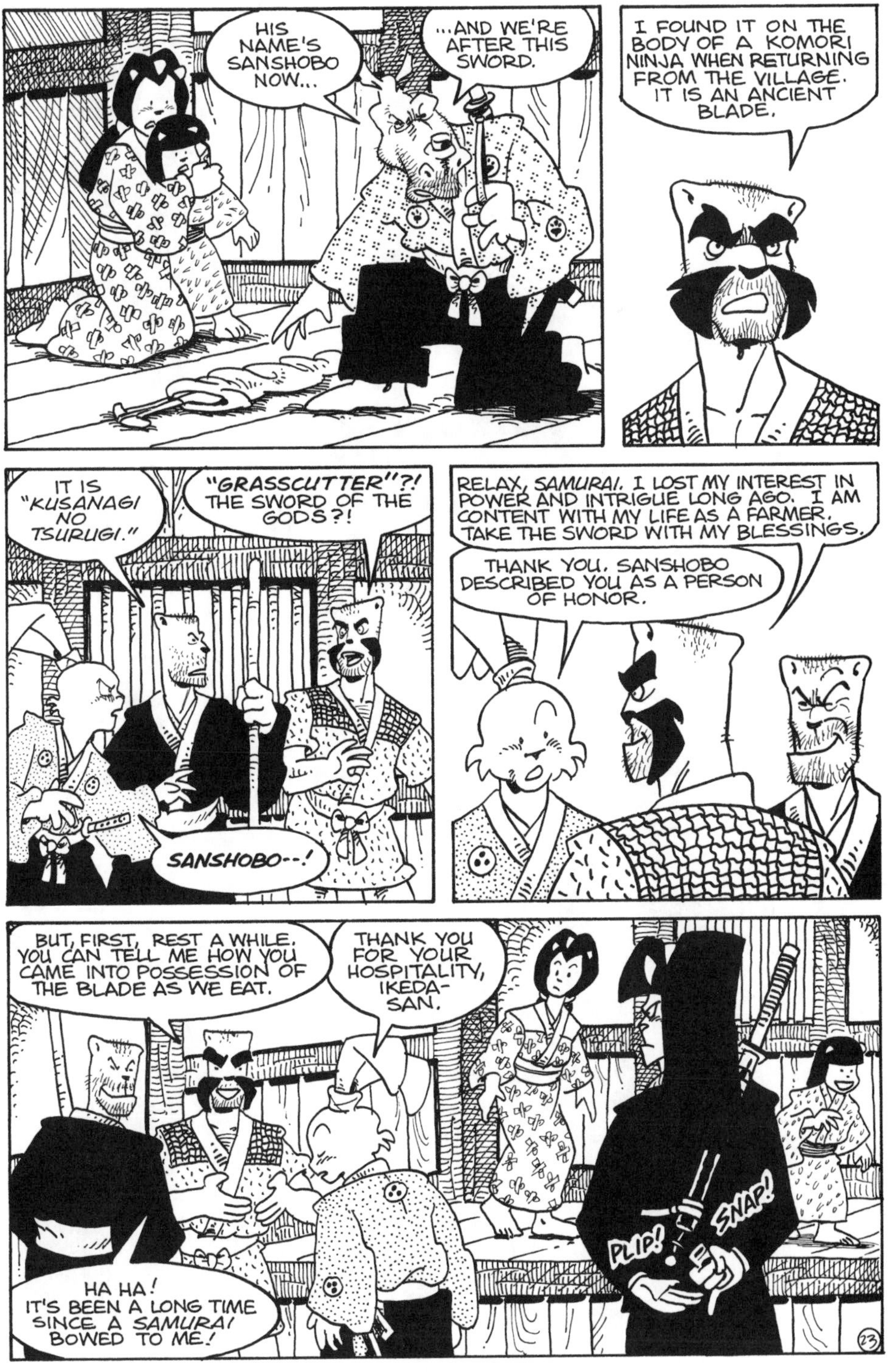
HIS NAME'S SANSHOBO NOW...
...AND WE'RE AFTER THIS SWORD.
I FOUND IT ON THE BODY OF A KOMORI NINJA WHEN RETURNING FROM THE VILLAGE. IT IS AN ANCIENT BLADE.
IT IS "KUSANAGI NO TSURUGI."
"GRASSCUTTER"?! THE SWORD OF THE GODS?!
SANSHOBO--!
RELAX, SAMURAI. I LOST MY INTEREST IN POWER AND INTRIGUE LONG AGO. I AM CONTENT WITH MY LIFE AS A FARMER. TAKE THE SWORD WITH MY BLESSINGS.
THANK YOU. SANSHOBO DESCRIBED YOU AS A PERSON OF HONOR.
BUT, FIRST, REST A WHILE. YOU CAN TELL ME HOW YOU CAME INTO POSSESSION OF THE BLADE AS WE EAT.
THANK YOU FOR YOUR HOSPITALITY, IKEDA-SAN.
HA HA! IT'S BEEN A LONG TIME SINCE A SAMURAI BOWED TO ME!
PLIP!
SNAP!
23

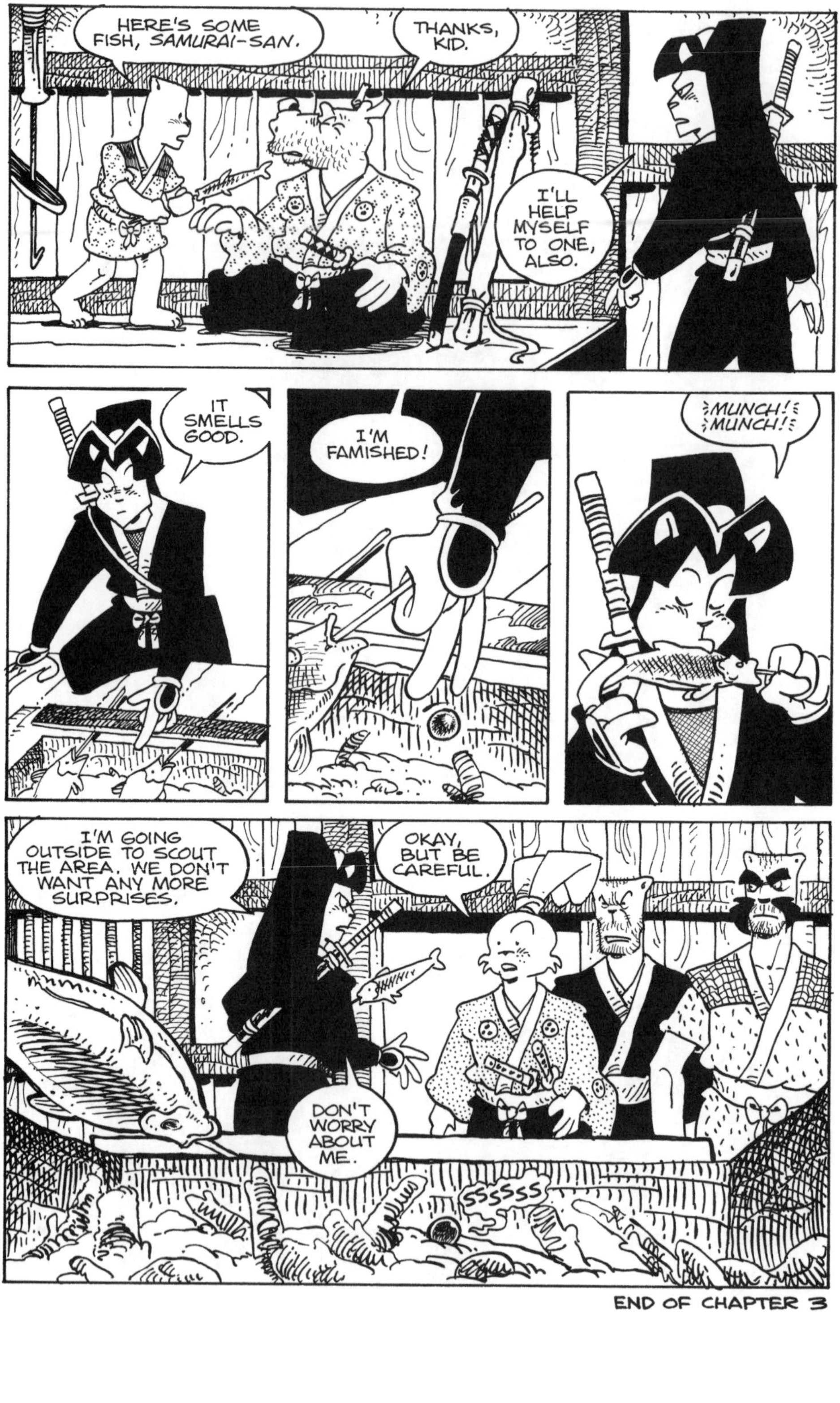
HERE'S SOME FISH, SAMURAI-SAN.
THANKS, KID.
I'LL HELP MYSELF TO ONE, ALSO.
IT SMELLS GOOD.
I'M FAMISHED!
MUNCH! MUNCH!
I'M GOING OUTSIDE TO SCOUT THE AREA. WE DON'T WANT ANY MORE SURPRISES.
OKAY, BUT BE CAREFUL.
DON'T WORRY ABOUT ME.
SSSSSS

END OF CHAPTER 3

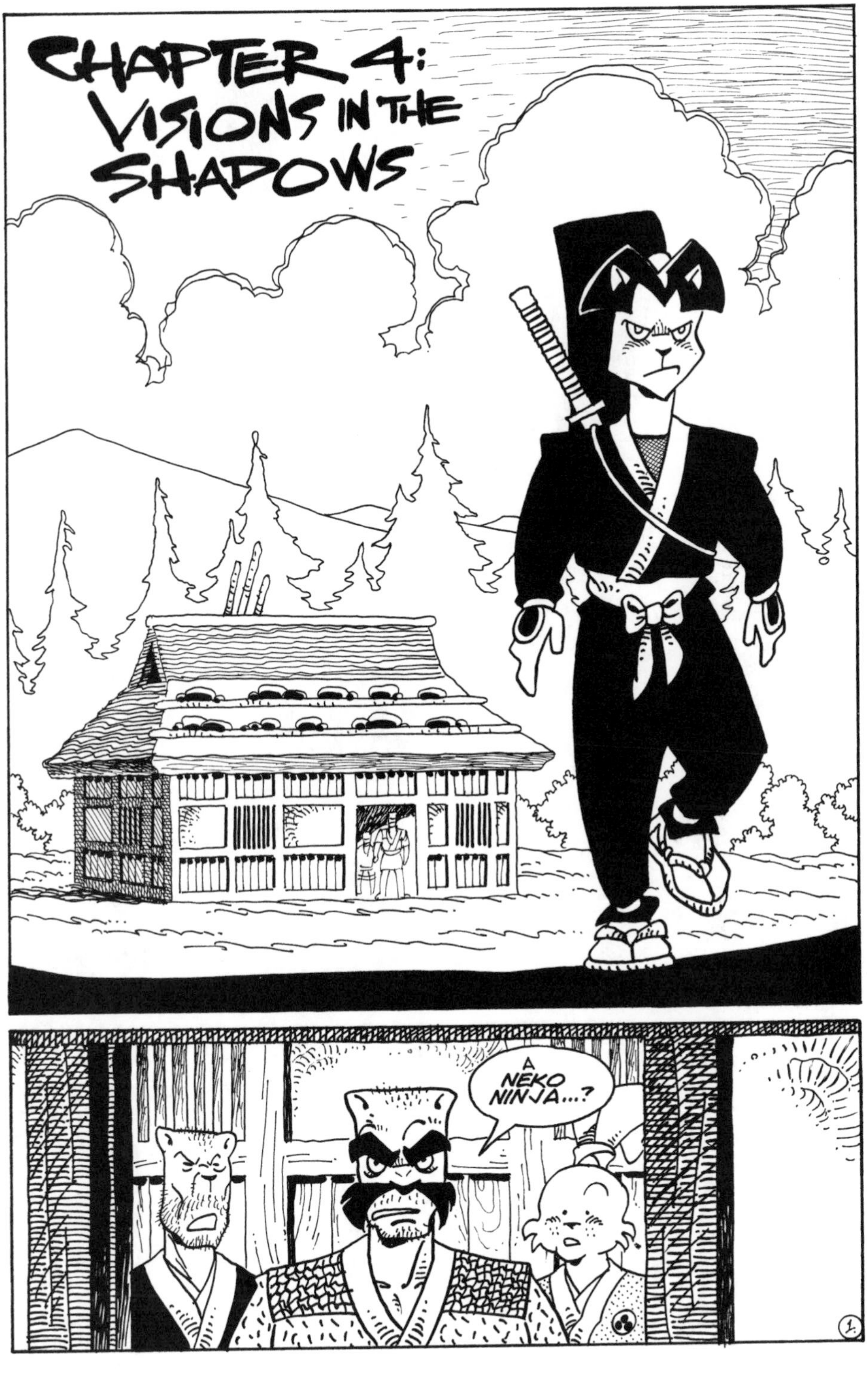
CHAPTER 4:
VISIONS IN THE
SHADOWS
A NEKO NINJA...?
1

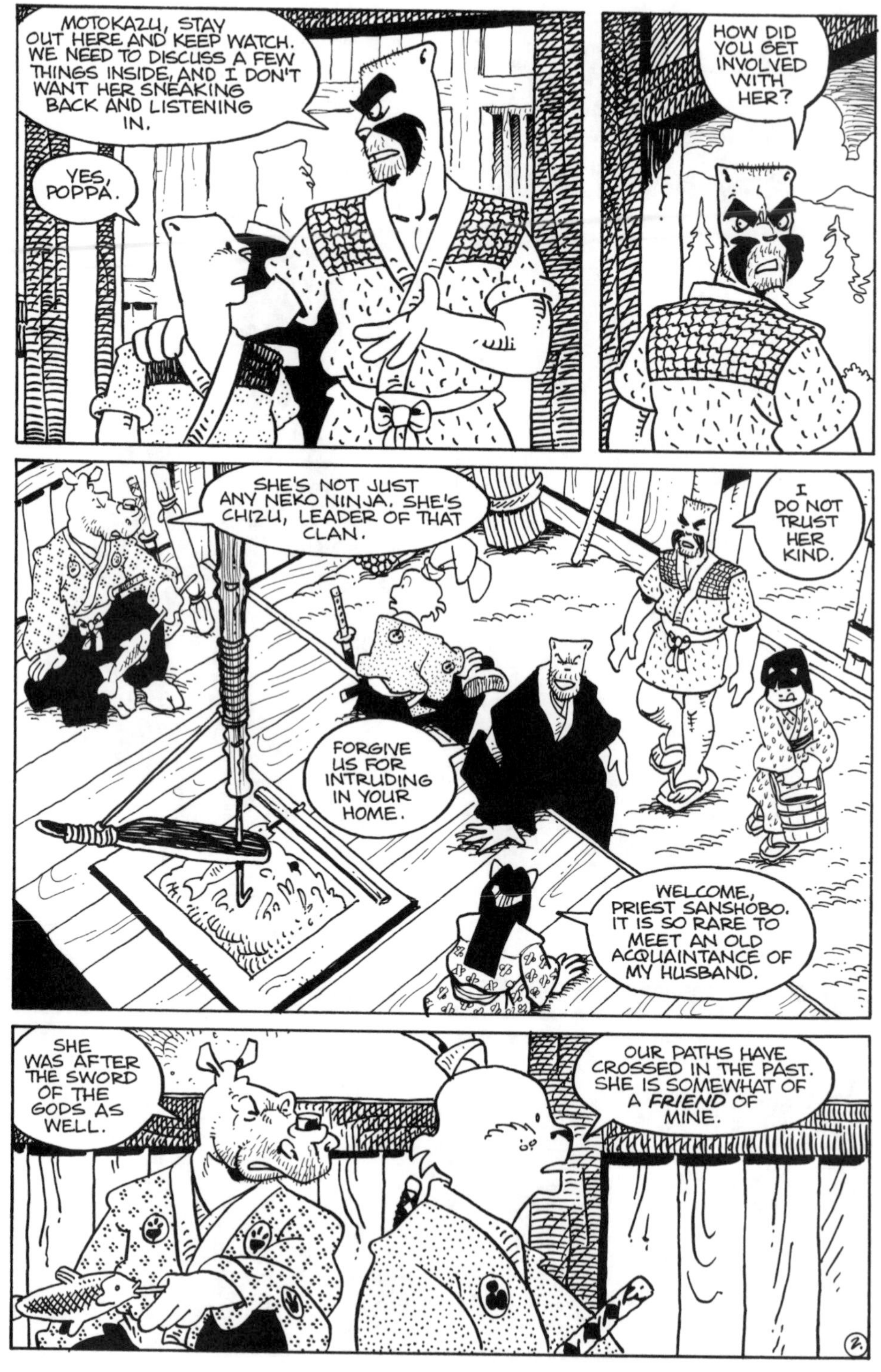
MOTOKAZU, STAY OUT HERE AND KEEP WATCH. WE NEED TO DISCUSS A FEW THINGS INSIDE, AND I DON'T WANT HER SNEAKING BACK AND LISTENING IN.
YES, POPPA.
HOW DID YOU GET INVOLVED WITH HER?
SHE'S NOT JUST ANY NEKO NINJA. SHE'S CHIZU, LEADER OF THAT CLAN.
I DO NOT TRUST HER KIND.
FORGIVE US FOR INTRUDING IN YOUR HOME.
WELCOME, PRIEST SANSHOBO. IT IS SO RARE TO MEET AN OLD ACQUAINTANCE OF MY HUSBAND.
SHE WAS AFTER THE SWORD OF THE GODS AS WELL.
OUR PATHS HAVE CROSSED IN THE PAST. SHE IS SOMEWHAT OF A FRIEND OF MINE.
2.

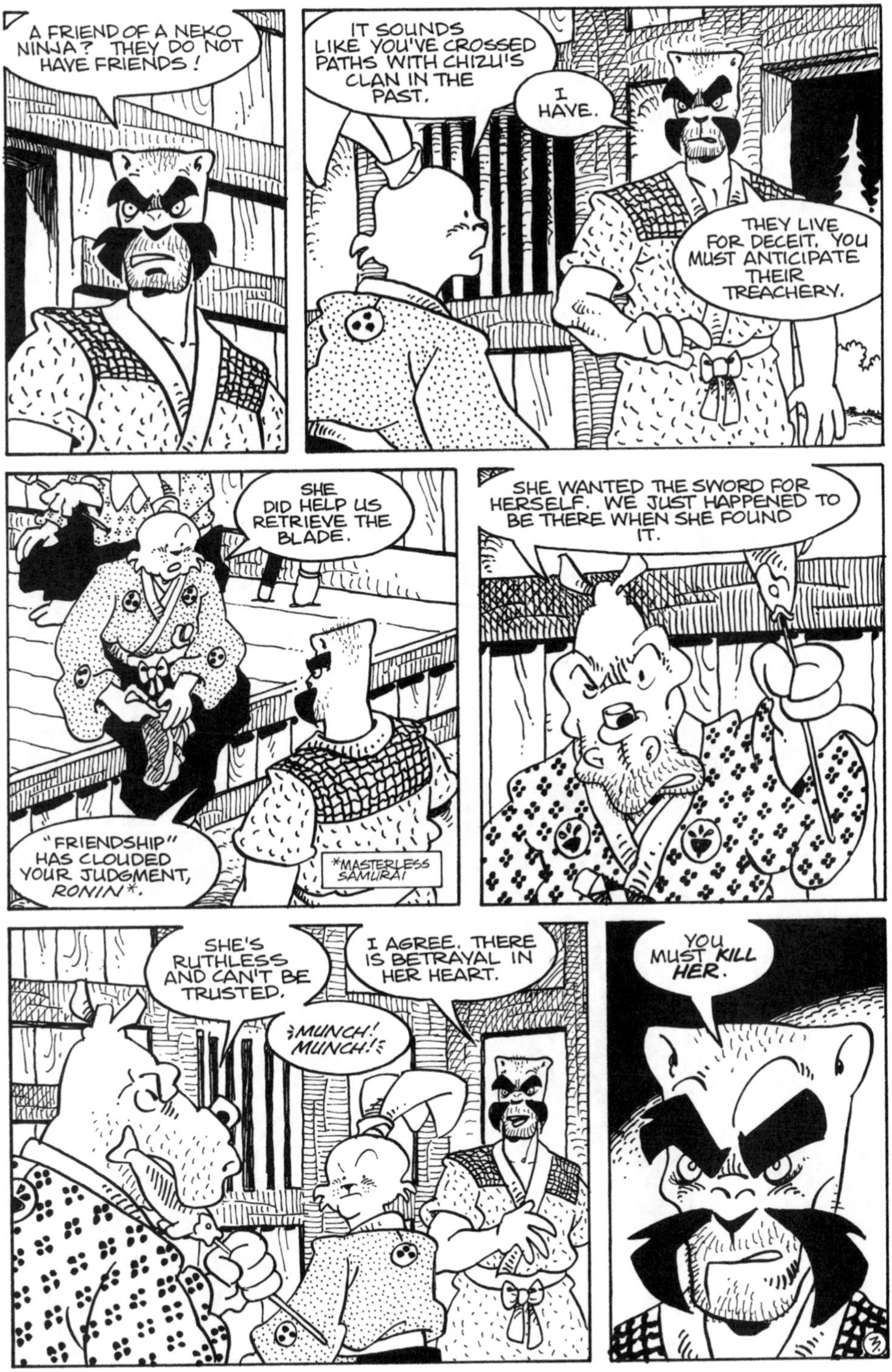
A FRIEND OF A NEKO NINJA? THEY DO NOT HAVE FRIENDS!
IT SOUNDS LIKE YOU'VE CROSSED PATHS WITH CHIZU'S CLAN IN THE PAST.
I HAVE.
THEY LIVE FOR DECEIT. YOU MUST ANTICIPATE THEIR TREACHERY.
SHE DID HELP US RETRIEVE THE BLADE.
"FRIENDSHIP" HAS CLOUDED YOUR JUDGMENT, RONIN*.
*MASTERLESS SAMURAI
SHE WANTED THE SWORD FOR HERSELF. WE JUST HAPPENED TO BE THERE WHEN SHE FOUND IT.
SHE'S RUTHLESS AND CAN'T BE TRUSTED.
MUNCH! MUNCH!
I AGREE. THERE IS BETRAYAL IN HER HEART.
YOU MUST KILL HER.
3.

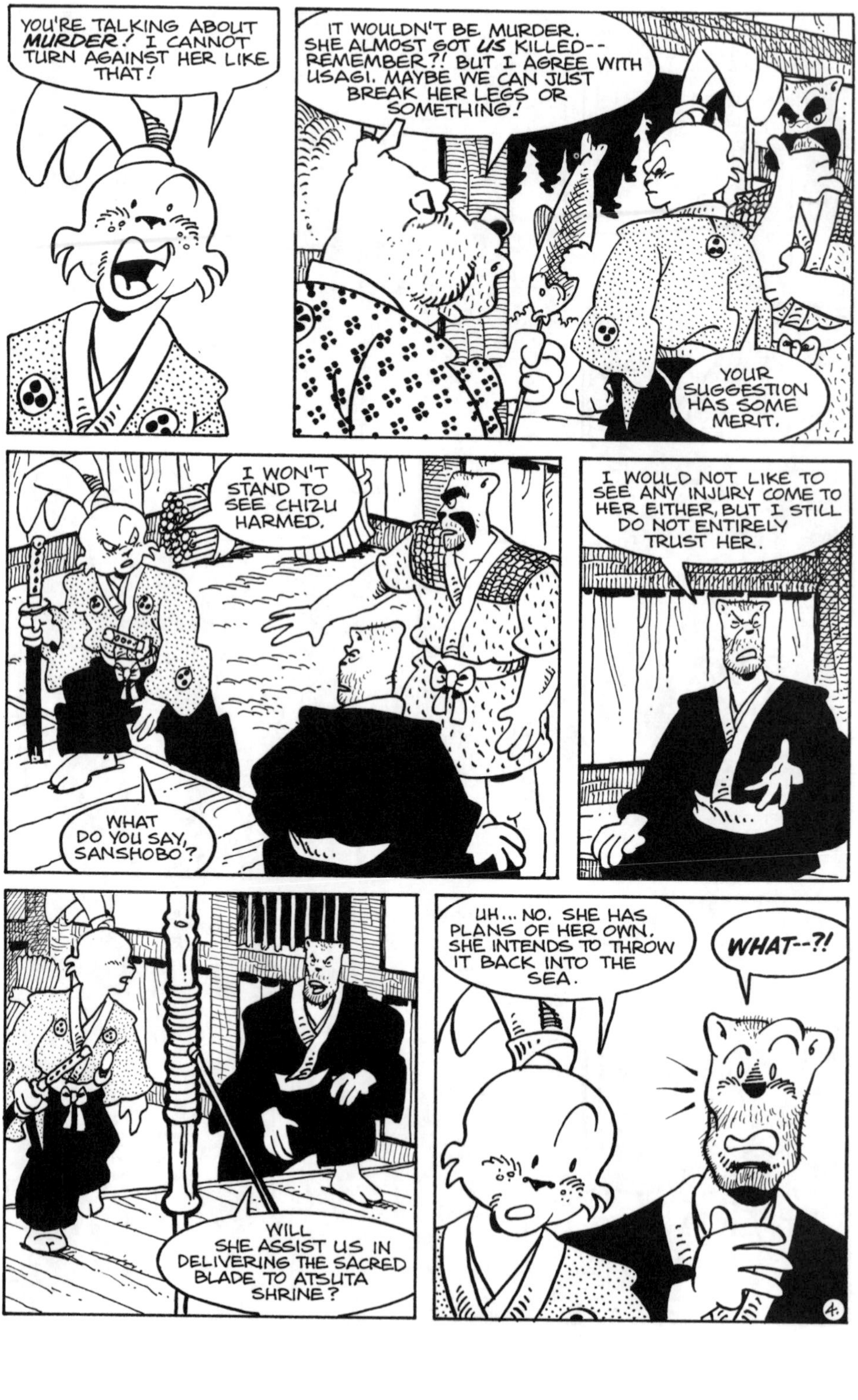
YOU'RE TALKING ABOUT MURDER! I CANNOT TURN AGAINST HER LIKE THAT!
IT WOULDN'T BE MURDER. SHE ALMOST GOT US KILLED-- REMEMBER?! BUT I AGREE WITH USAGI. MAYBE WE CAN JUST BREAK HER LEGS OR SOMETHING!
YOUR SUGGESTION HAS SOME MERIT.
I WON'T STAND TO SEE CHIZU HARMED.
WHAT DO YOU SAY, SANSHOBO?
I WOULD NOT LIKE TO SEE ANY INJURY COME TO HER EITHER, BUT I STILL DO NOT ENTIRELY TRUST HER.
WILL SHE ASSIST US IN DELIVERING THE SACRED BLADE TO ATSUTA SHRINE?
UH... NO. SHE HAS PLANS OF HER OWN. SHE INTENDS TO THROW IT BACK INTO THE SEA.
WHAT--?!
4.

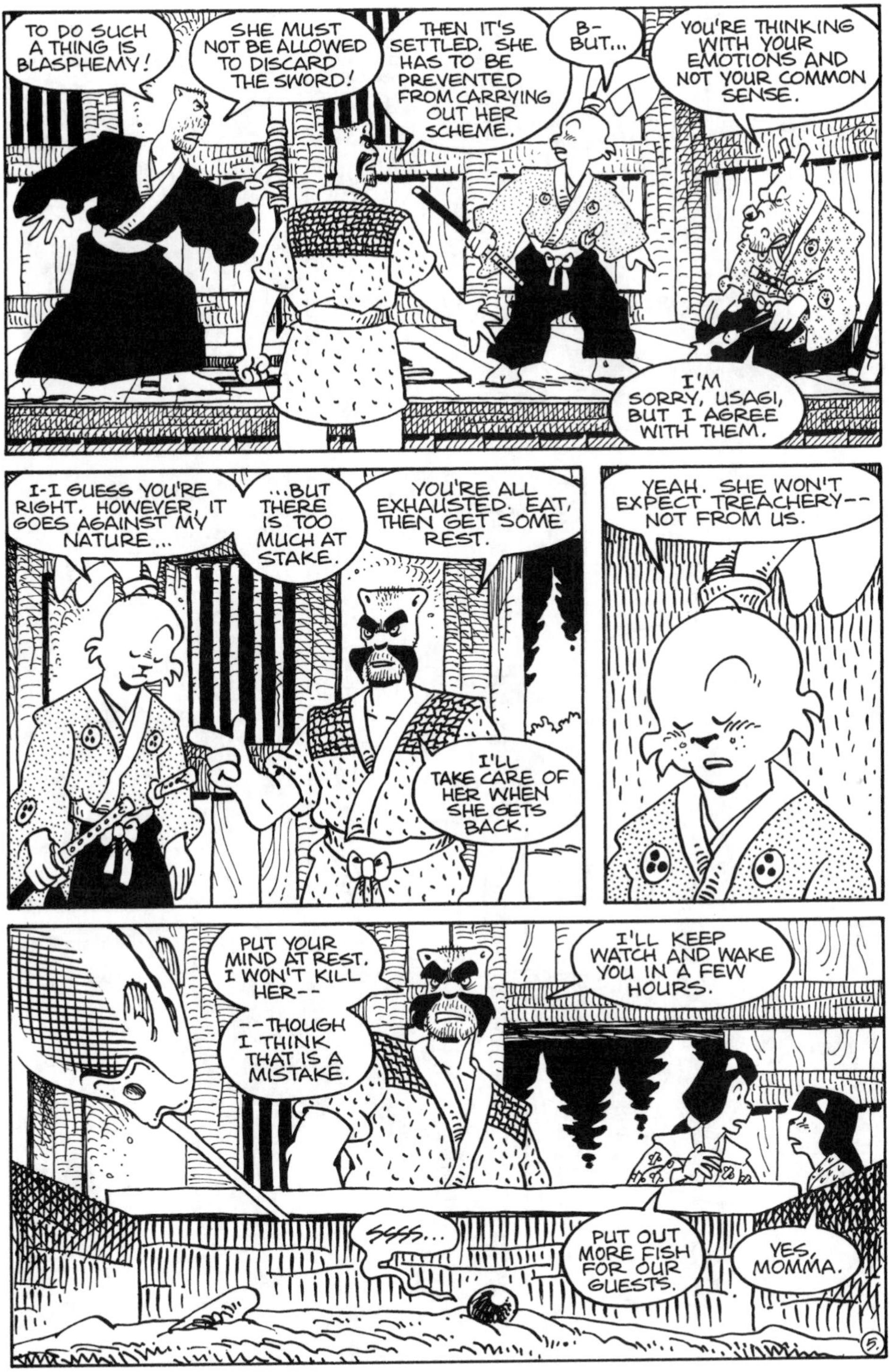
TO DO SUCH A THING IS BLASPHEMY!
SHE MUST NOT BE ALLOWED TO DISCARD THE SWORD!
THEN IT'S SETTLED. SHE HAS TO BE PREVENTED FROM CARRYING OUT HER SCHEME.
B-BUT...
YOU'RE THINKING WITH YOUR EMOTIONS AND NOT YOUR COMMON SENSE.
I'M SORRY, USAGI, BUT I AGREE WITH THEM.
I-I GUESS YOU'RE RIGHT. HOWEVER, IT GOES AGAINST MY NATURE...
...BUT THERE IS TOO MUCH AT STAKE.
YOU'RE ALL EXHAUSTED. EAT, THEN GET SOME REST.
I'LL TAKE CARE OF HER WHEN SHE GETS BACK.
YEAH. SHE WON'T EXPECT TREACHERY--NOT FROM US.
PUT YOUR MIND AT REST. I WON'T KILL HER--
--THOUGH I THINK THAT IS A MISTAKE.
I'LL KEEP WATCH AND WAKE YOU IN A FEW HOURS.
SSSS...
PUT OUT MORE FISH FOR OUR GUESTS.
YES, MOMMA.
5.

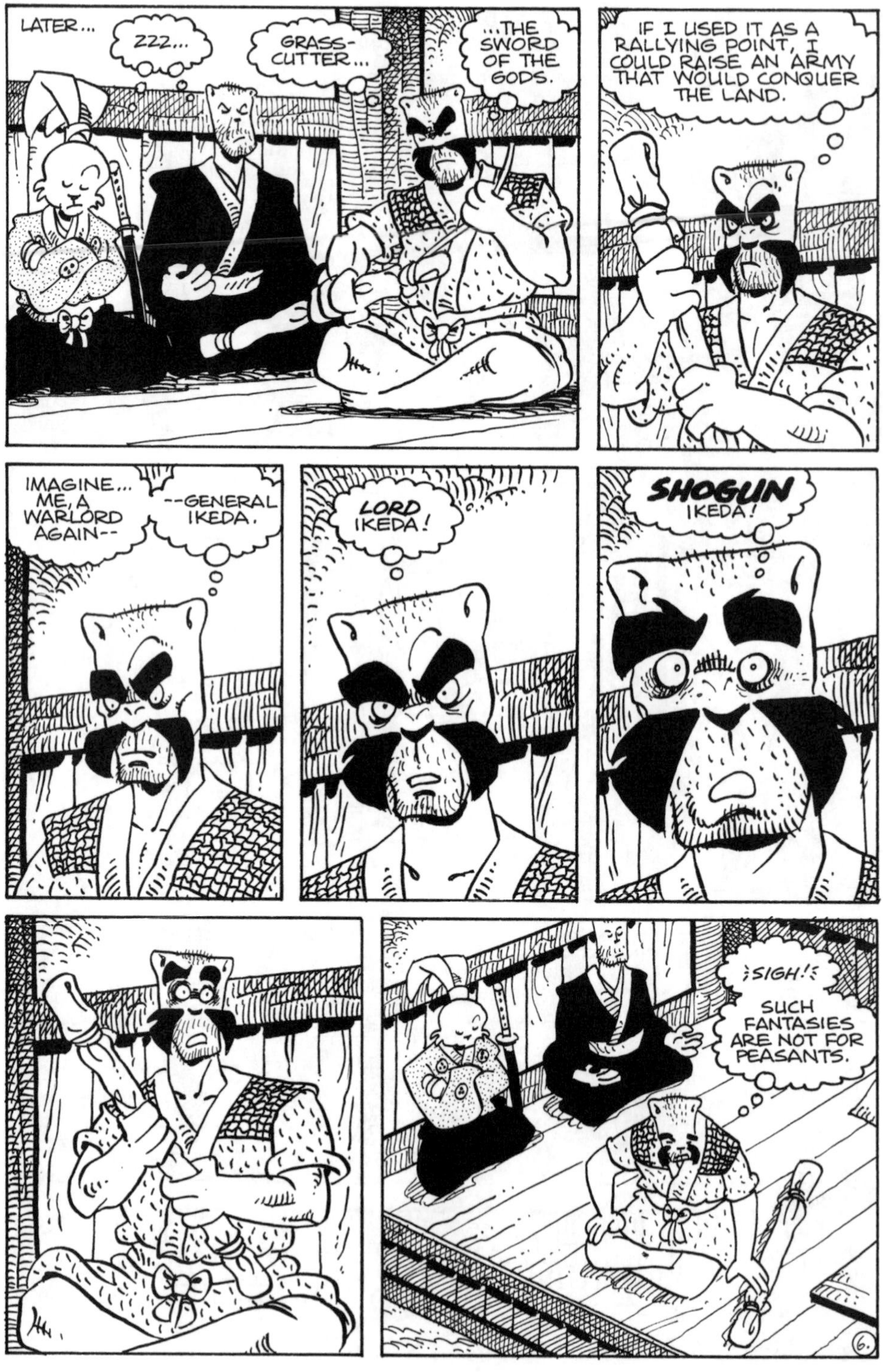
LATER...
ZZZ...
GRASS-CUTTER...
...THE SWORD OF THE GODS.
IF I USED IT AS A RALLYING POINT, I COULD RAISE AN ARMY THAT WOULD CONQUER THE LAND.
IMAGINE... ME, A WARLORD AGAIN--
--GENERAL IKEDA.
LORD IKEDA!
SHOGUN IKEDA!
SIGH!
SUCH FANTASIES ARE NOT FOR PEASANTS.
6.

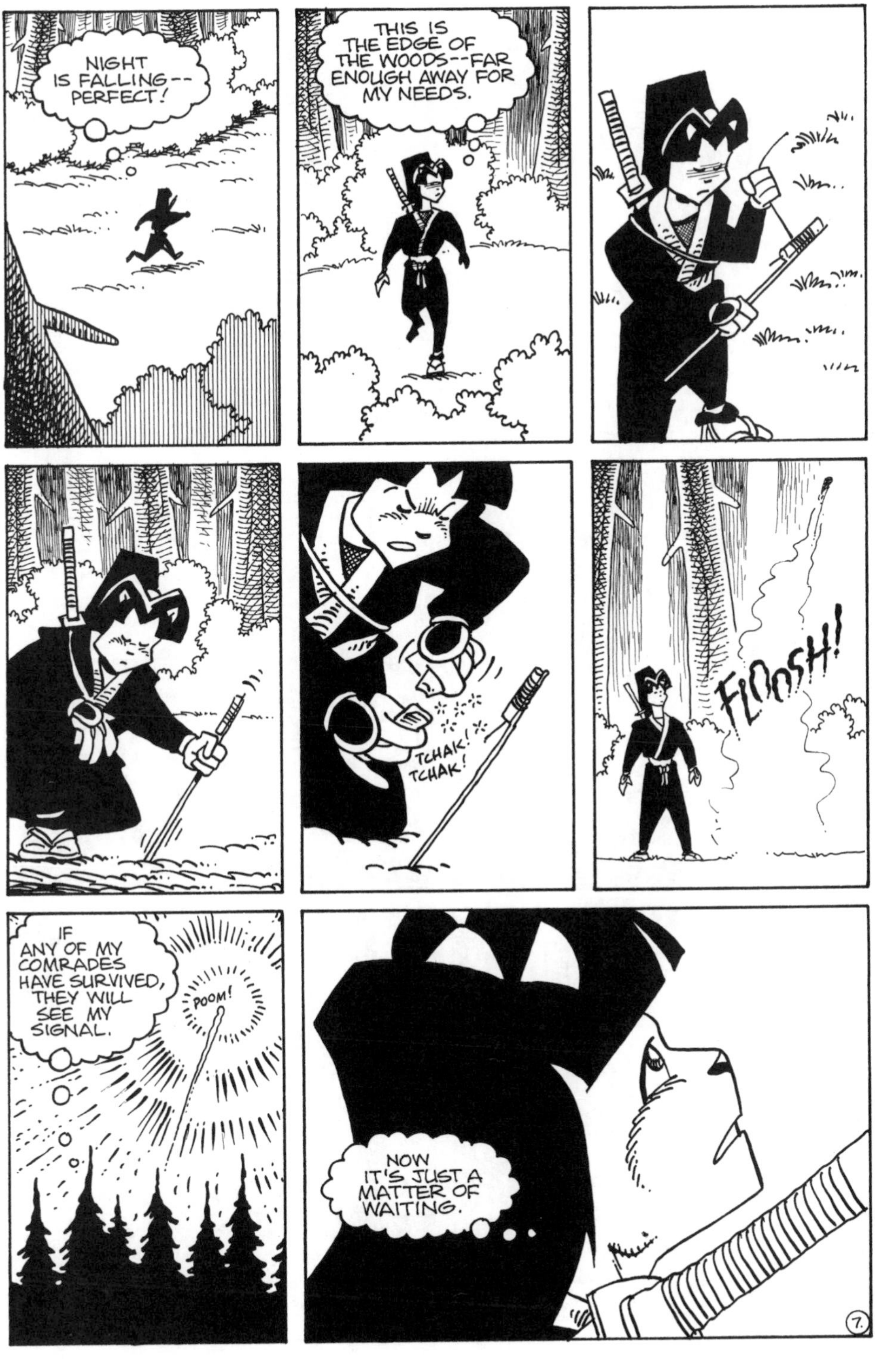
NIGHT IS FALLING-- PERFECT!
THIS IS THE EDGE OF THE WOODS--FAR ENOUGH AWAY FOR MY NEEDS.
TCHAK! TCHAK!
FLOOSH!
IF ANY OF MY COMRADES HAVE SURVIVED, THEY WILL SEE MY SIGNAL.
POOM!
NOW IT'S JUST A MATTER OF WAITING.
7.

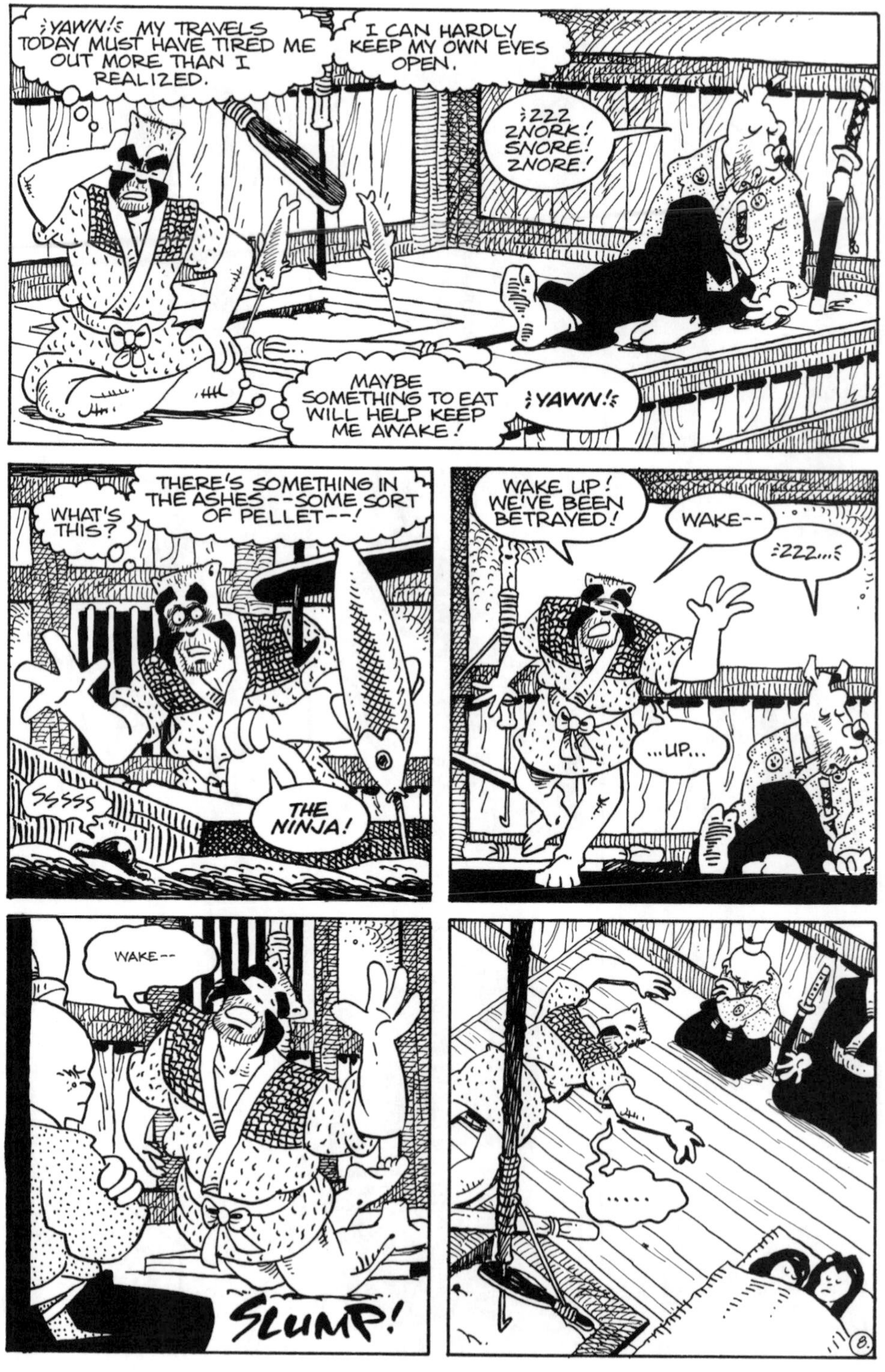

YAWN! MY TRAVELS TODAY MUST HAVE TIRED ME OUT MORE THAN I REALIZED.
I CAN HARDLY KEEP MY OWN EYES OPEN.
ZZZ ZNORK! SNORE! ZNORE!
MAYBE SOMETHING TO EAT WILL HELP KEEP ME AWAKE!
YAWN!
WHAT'S THIS?
THERE'S SOMETHING IN THE ASHES--SOME SORT OF PELLET--!
SSSSS
THE NINJA!
WAKE UP! WE'VE BEEN BETRAYED!
WAKE--
ZZZ...
...UP...
WAKE--
SLUMP!
.....
8.

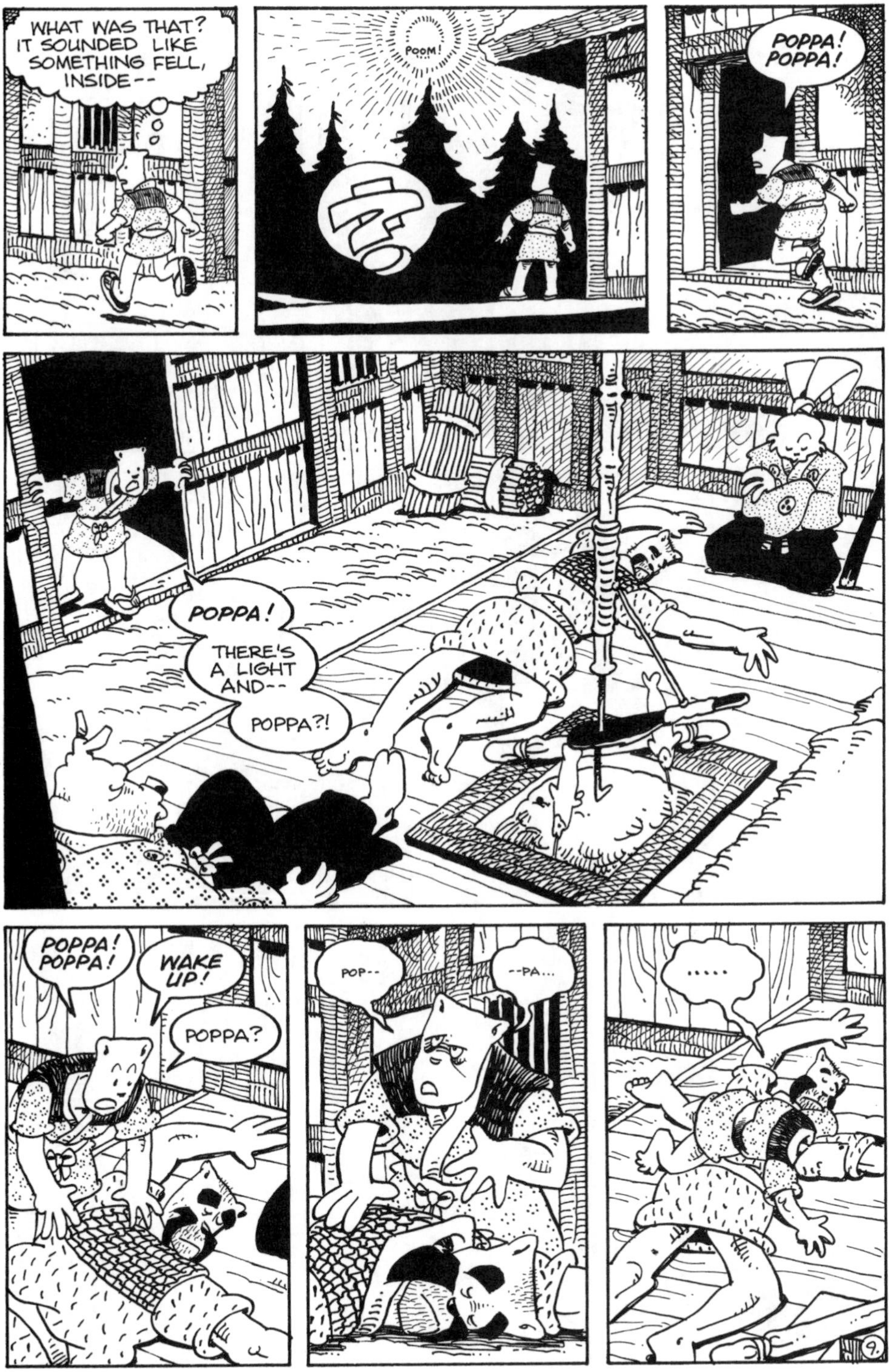
WHAT WAS THAT? IT SOUNDED LIKE SOMETHING FELL, INSIDE--
POOM!
POPPA! POPPA!
POPPA!
THERE'S A LIGHT AND--
POPPA?!
POPPA! POPPA!
WAKE UP!
POPPA?
POP--
--PA...
.....
9.

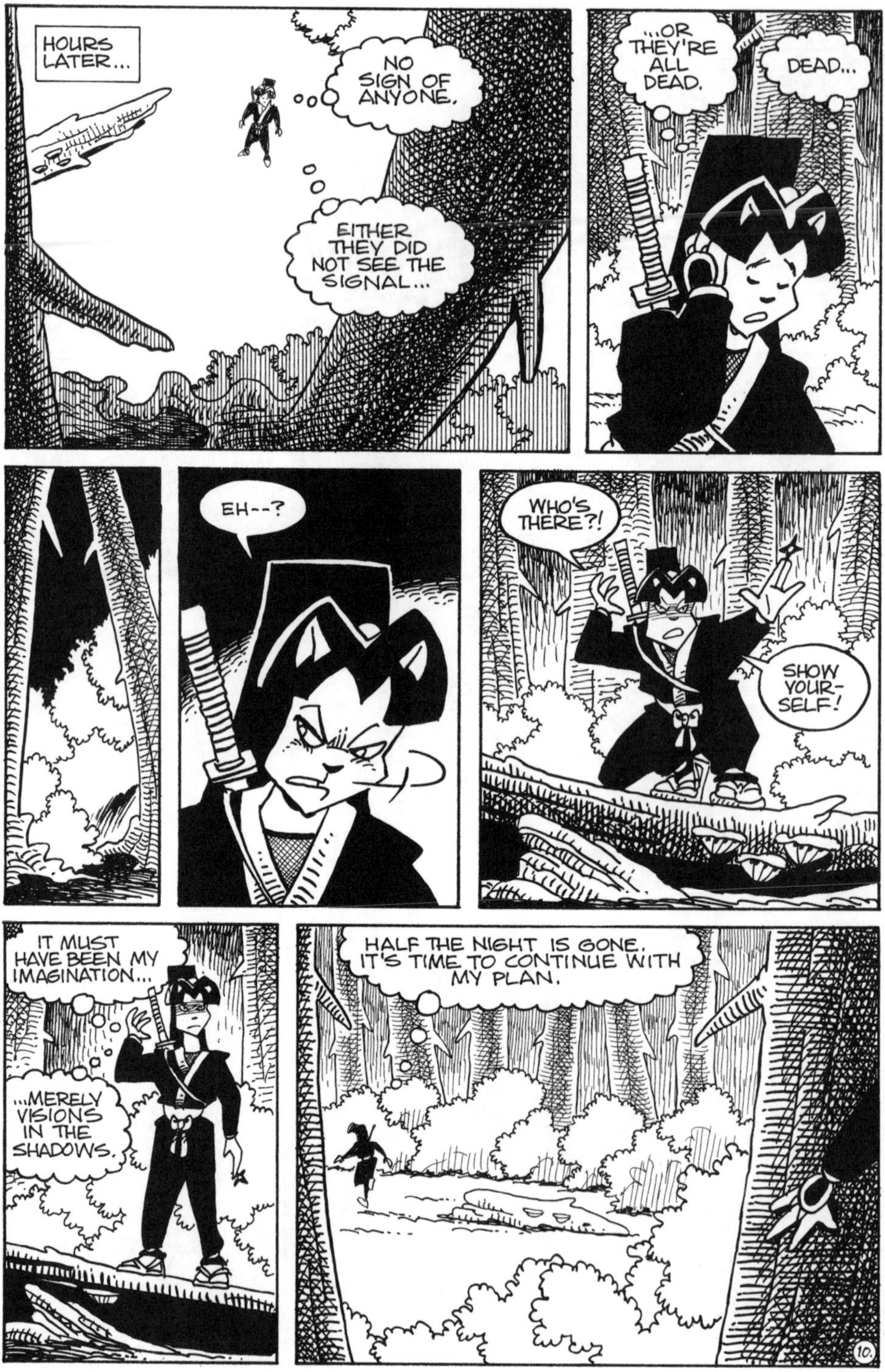
HOURS LATER...
NO SIGN OF ANYONE.
EITHER THEY DID NOT SEE THE SIGNAL...
...OR THEY'RE ALL DEAD.
DEAD...
EH--?
WHO'S THERE?!
SHOW YOURSELF!
IT MUST HAVE BEEN MY IMAGINATION...
...MERELY VISIONS IN THE SHADOWS.
HALF THE NIGHT IS GONE. IT'S TIME TO CONTINUE WITH MY PLAN.
10.

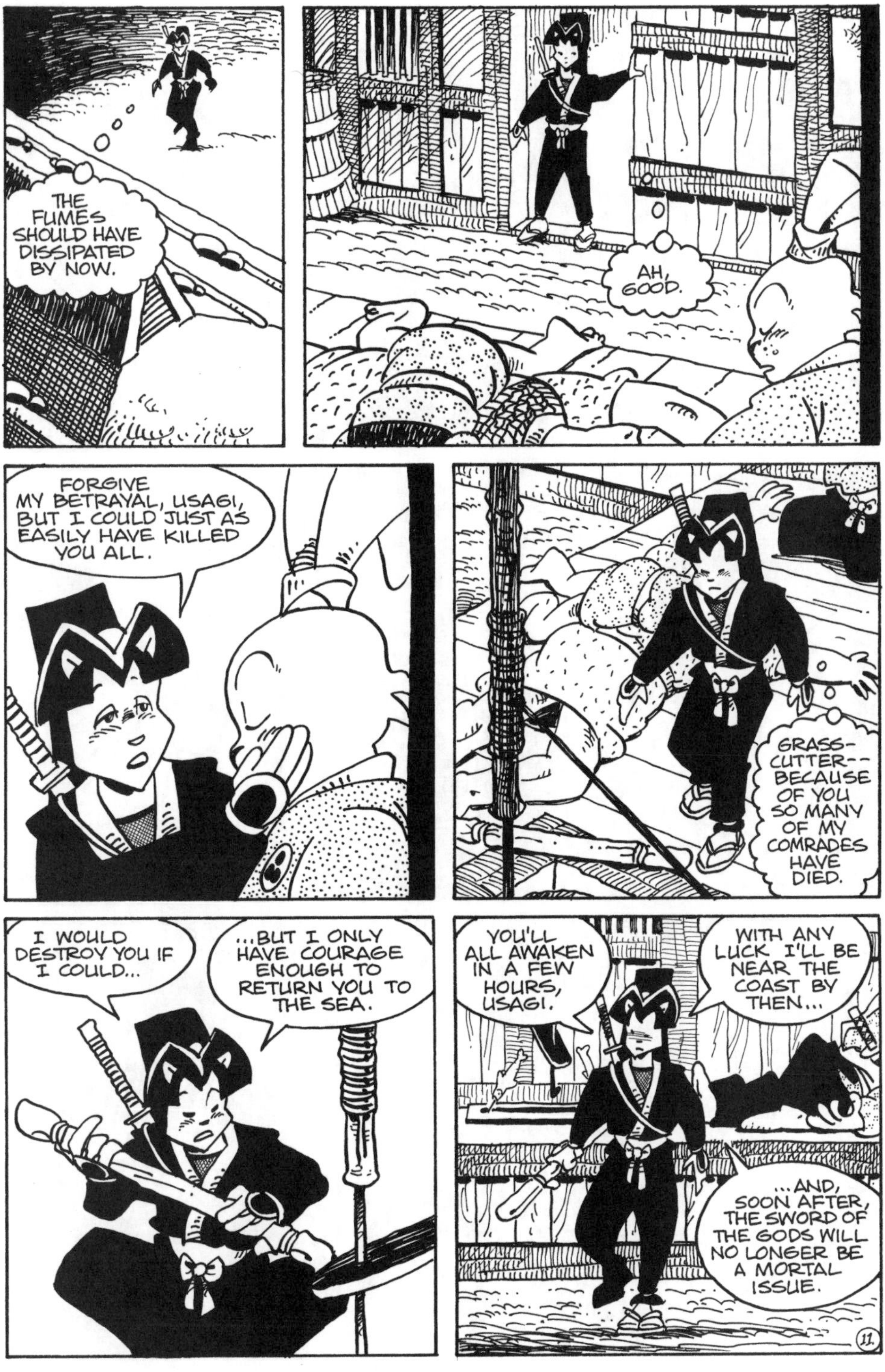

THE FUMES SHOULD HAVE DISSIPATED BY NOW.
AH, GOOD.
FORGIVE MY BETRAYAL, USAGI, BUT I COULD JUST AS EASILY HAVE KILLED YOU ALL.
GRASS-CUTTER-- BECAUSE OF YOU SO MANY OF MY COMRADES HAVE DIED.
I WOULD DESTROY YOU IF I COULD...
...BUT I ONLY HAVE COURAGE ENOUGH TO RETURN YOU TO THE SEA.
YOU'LL ALL AWAKEN IN A FEW HOURS, USAGI.
WITH ANY LUCK I'LL BE NEAR THE COAST BY THEN...
...AND, SOON AFTER, THE SWORD OF THE GODS WILL NO LONGER BE A MORTAL ISSUE.
11

ZZZ...

THERE IS A SCORE I HAVE TO SETTLE WITH YOU, BOUNTY HUNTER.

;ZNORE!;

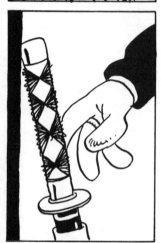

ZWIT!

THUNK!

12.

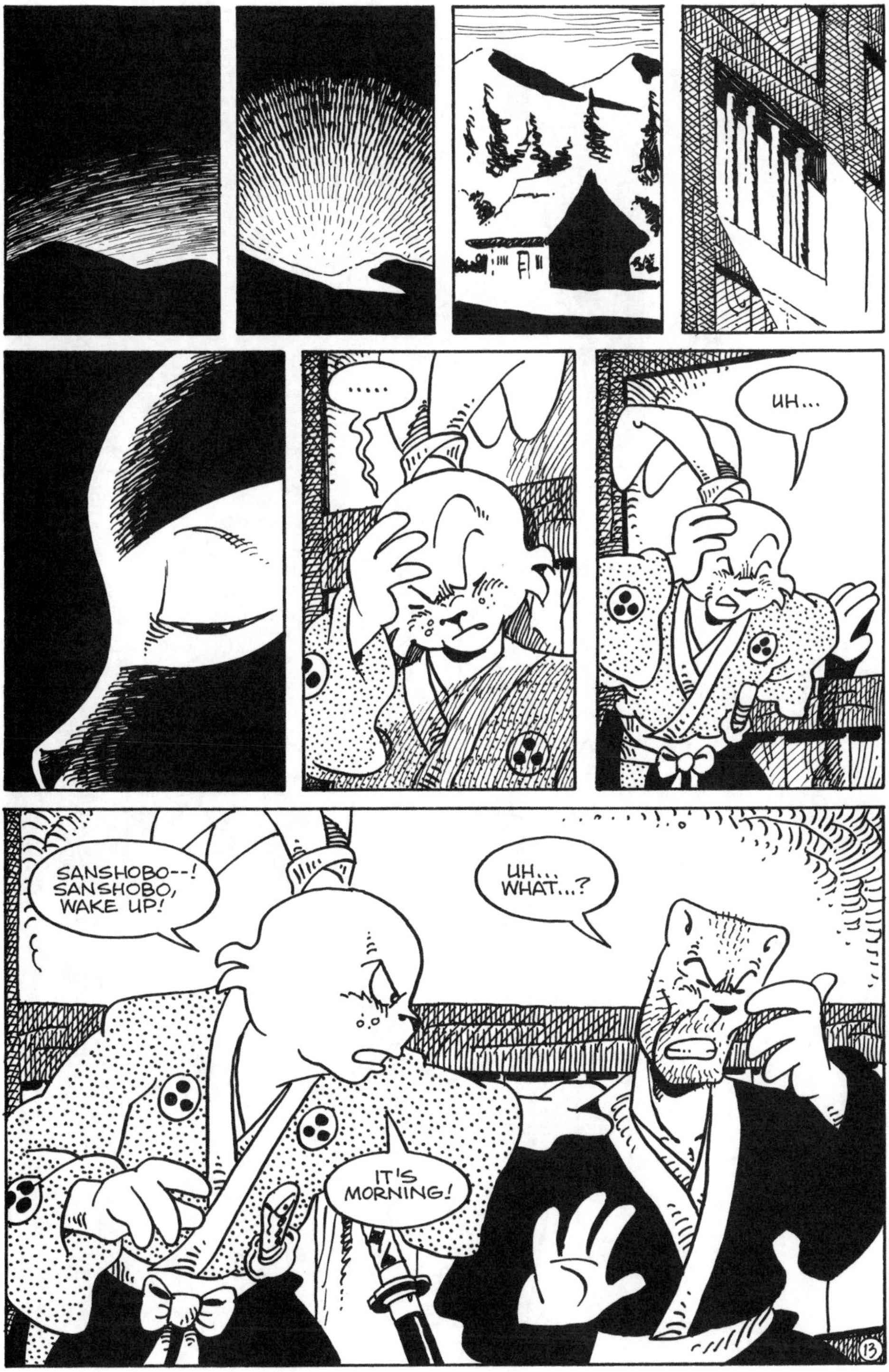
......
UH...
SANSHOBO--! SANSHOBO, WAKE UP!
UH... WHAT...?
IT'S MORNING!
13

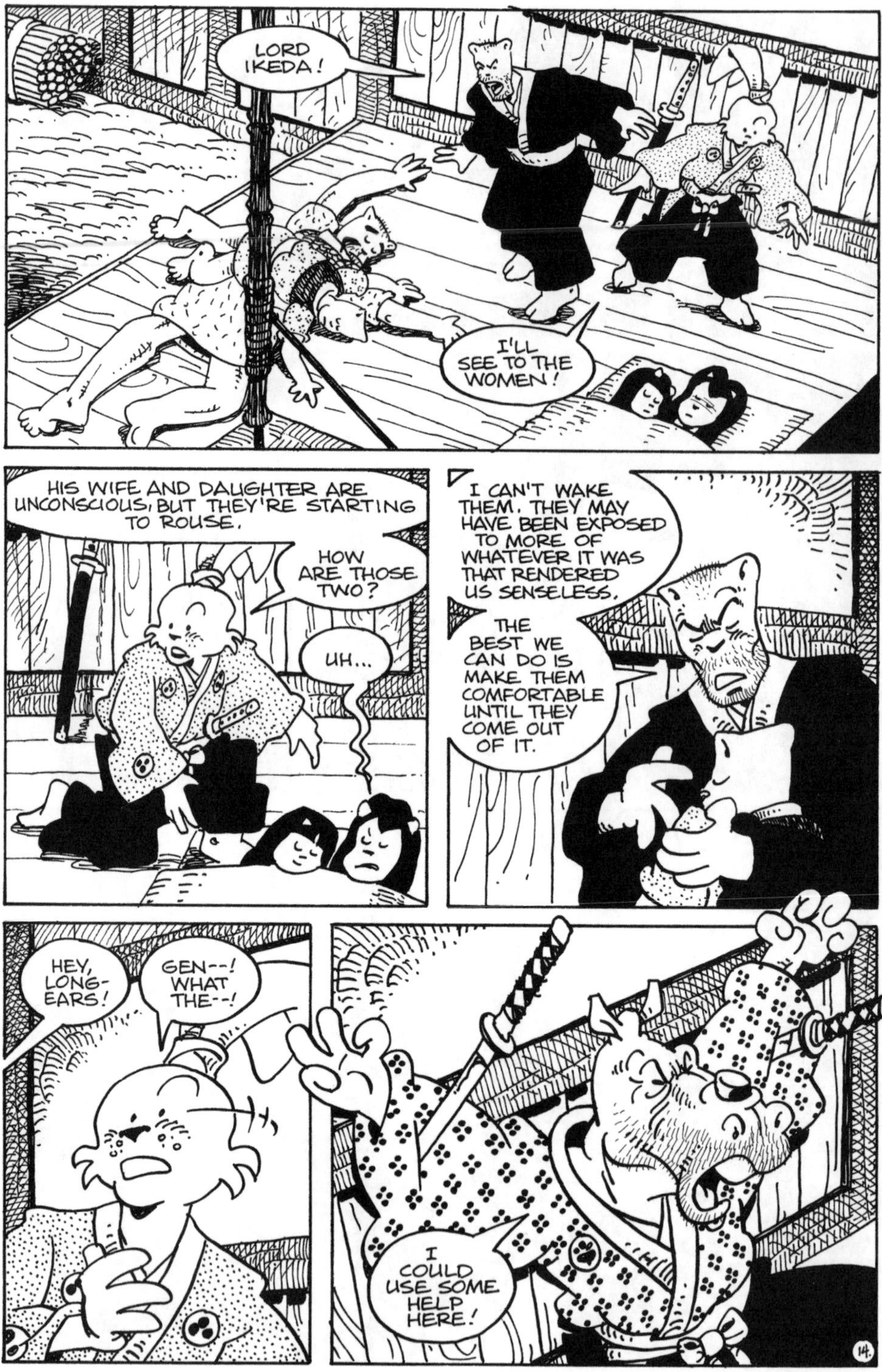
LORD IKEDA!
I'LL SEE TO THE WOMEN!
HIS WIFE AND DAUGHTER ARE UNCONSCIOUS, BUT THEY'RE STARTING TO ROUSE.
HOW ARE THOSE TWO?
UH...
I CAN'T WAKE THEM. THEY MAY HAVE BEEN EXPOSED TO MORE OF WHATEVER IT WAS THAT RENDERED US SENSELESS.
THE BEST WE CAN DO IS MAKE THEM COMFORTABLE UNTIL THEY COME OUT OF IT.
HEY, LONG-EARS!
GEN--! WHAT THE--!
I COULD USE SOME HELP HERE!
14.

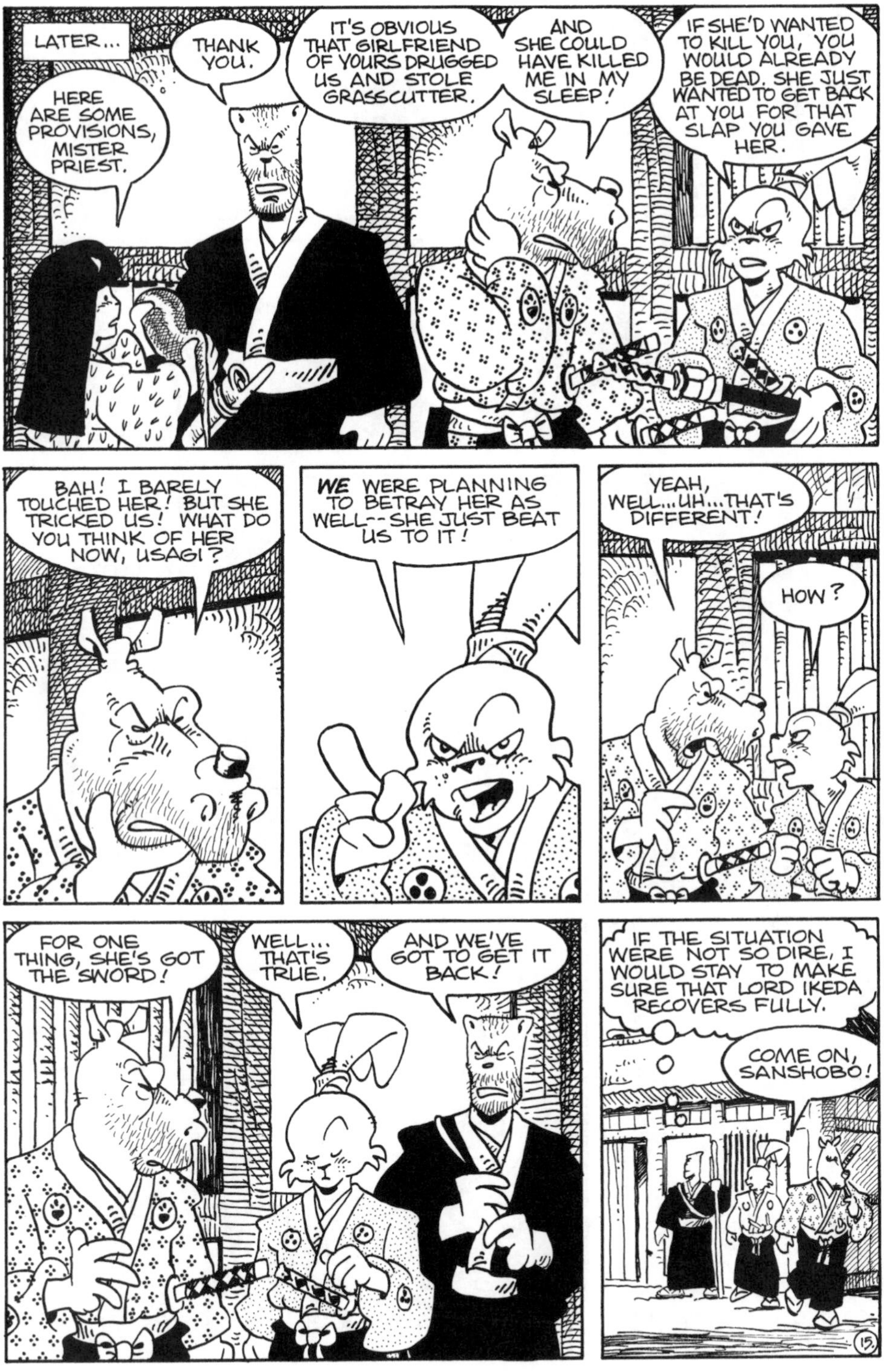
LATER...
HERE ARE SOME PROVISIONS, MISTER PRIEST.
THANK YOU.
IT'S OBVIOUS THAT GIRLFRIEND OF YOURS DRUGGED US AND STOLE GRASSCUTTER.
AND SHE COULD HAVE KILLED ME IN MY SLEEP!
IF SHE'D WANTED TO KILL YOU, YOU WOULD ALREADY BE DEAD. SHE JUST WANTED TO GET BACK AT YOU FOR THAT SLAP YOU GAVE HER.
BAH! I BARELY TOUCHED HER! BUT SHE TRICKED US! WHAT DO YOU THINK OF HER NOW, USAGI?
WE WERE PLANNING TO BETRAY HER AS WELL--SHE JUST BEAT US TO IT!
YEAH, WELL...UH...THAT'S DIFFERENT!
HOW?
FOR ONE THING, SHE'S GOT THE SWORD!
WELL... THAT'S TRUE.
AND WE'VE GOT TO GET IT BACK!
IF THE SITUATION WERE NOT SO DIRE, I WOULD STAY TO MAKE SURE THAT LORD IKEDA RECOVERS FULLY.
COME ON, SANSHOBO!
15

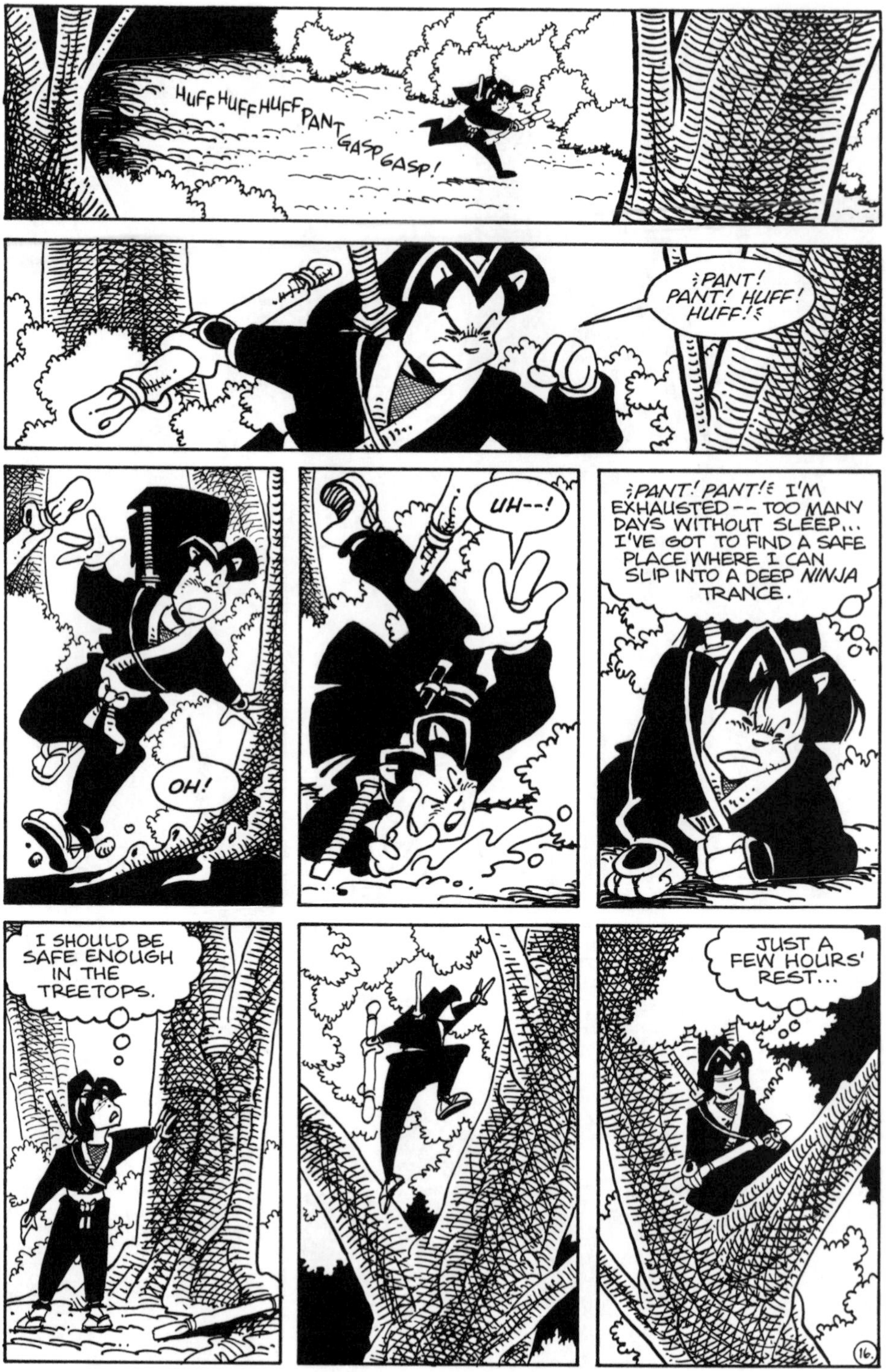
HUFF HUFF HUFF PANT GASP GASP!
PANT! PANT! HUFF! HUFF!
OH!
UH--!
PANT! PANT! I'M EXHAUSTED -- TOO MANY DAYS WITHOUT SLEEP... I'VE GOT TO FIND A SAFE PLACE WHERE I CAN SLIP INTO A DEEP NINJA TRANCE.
I SHOULD BE SAFE ENOUGH IN THE TREETOPS.
JUST A FEW HOURS' REST...
16.

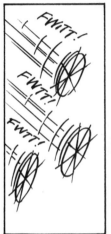

FWITT!

FWITT!

FWITT!

TOK!

TOK!

TOK!

THE MYSTERIOUS *NINJA* ASSASSIN IS BACK.

I *MUST* BE WEARY. HE ALMOST CAUGHT ME UNAWARES.

WHERE IS HE?

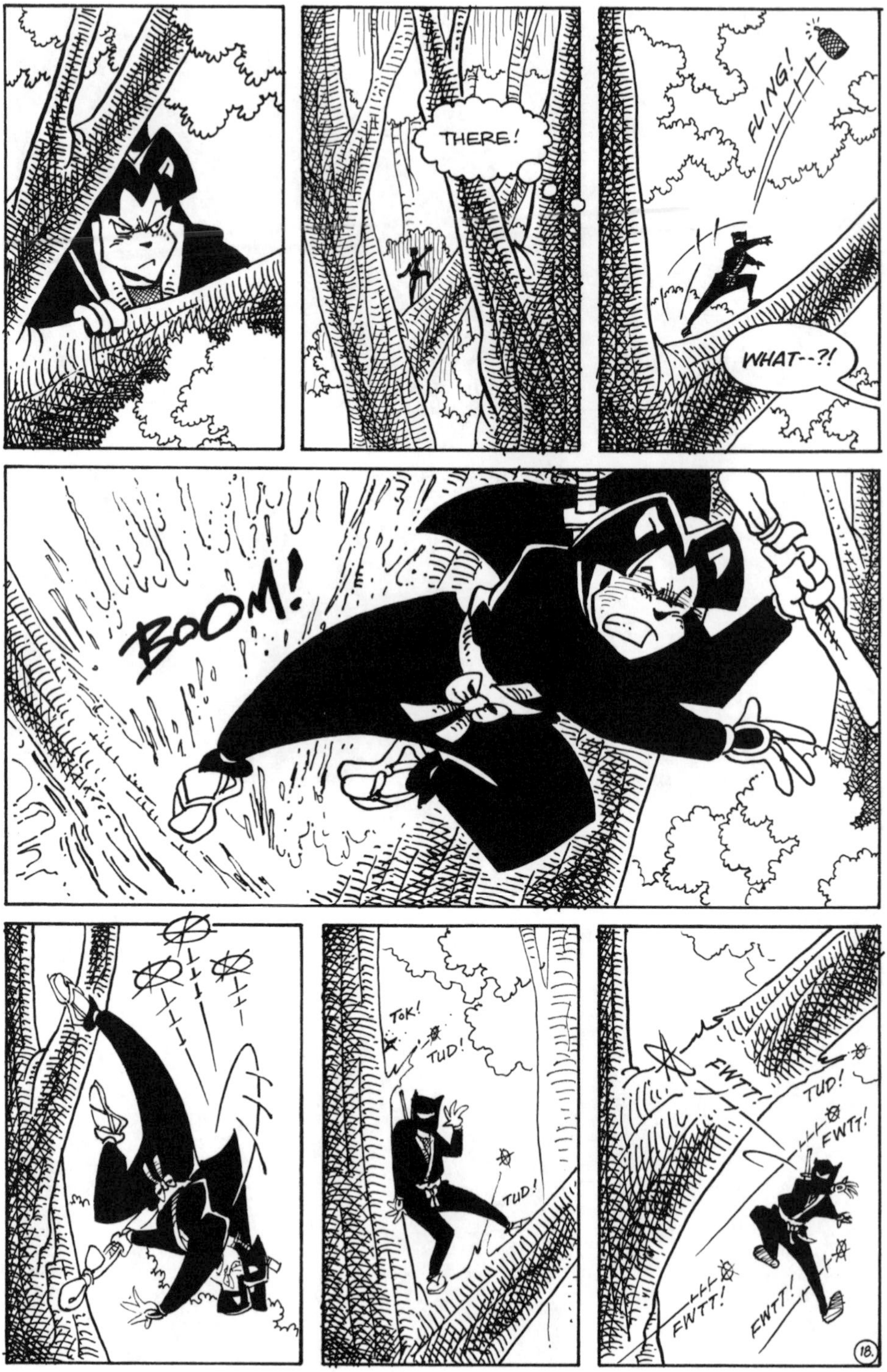
THERE!
FLING!
WHAT--?!
BOOM!
TOK!
TUD!
TUD!
FWTT!
TUD!
FWTT!
FWTT!
FWTT!
18.

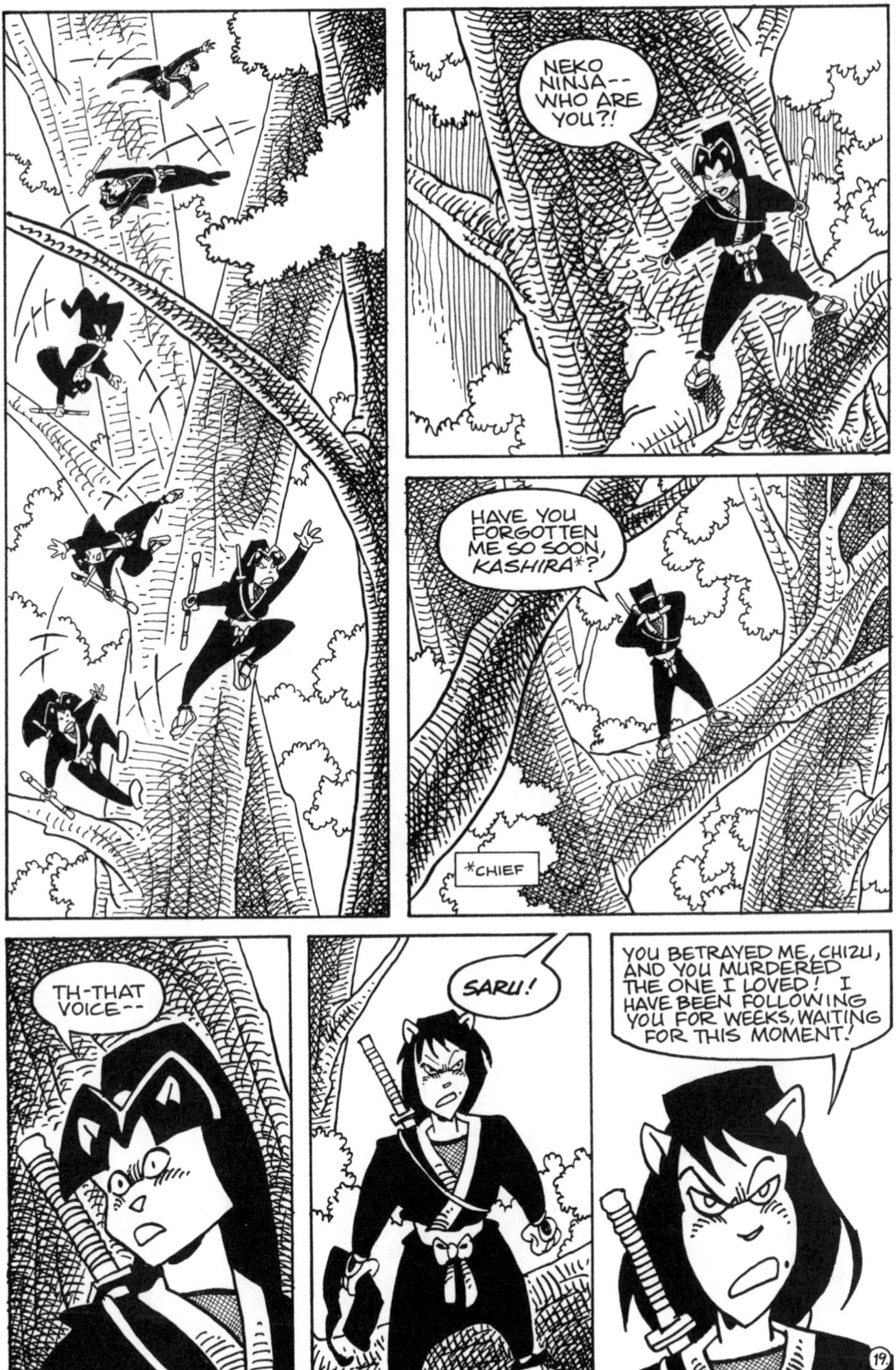
NEKO NINJA-- WHO ARE YOU?!
HAVE YOU FORGOTTEN ME SO SOON, KASHIRA*?
*CHIEF
TH-THAT VOICE--
SARU!
YOU BETRAYED ME, CHIZU, AND YOU MURDERED THE ONE I LOVED! I HAVE BEEN FOLLOWING YOU FOR WEEKS, WAITING FOR THIS MOMENT!
19.

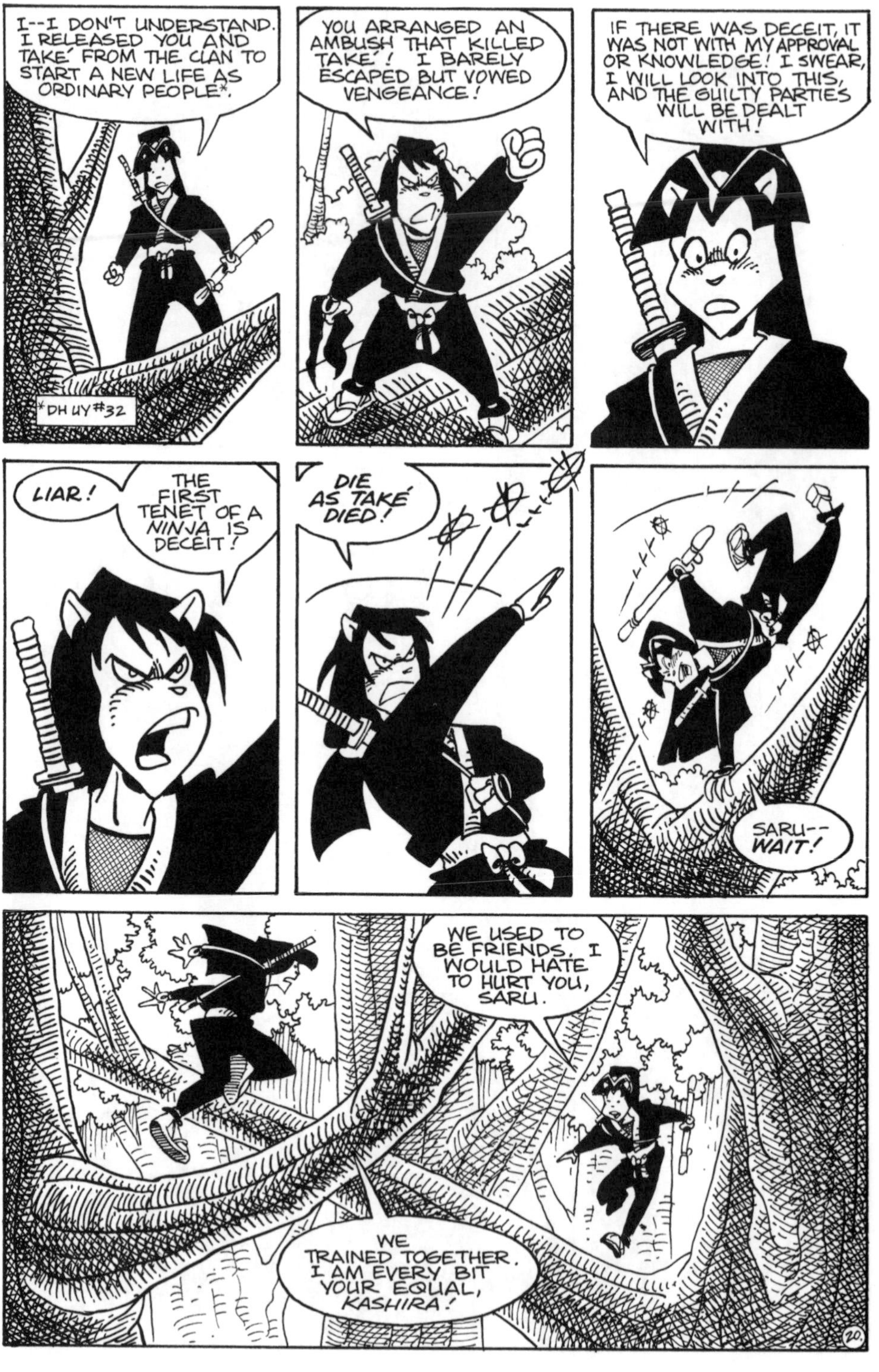
I--I DON'T UNDERSTAND. I RELEASED YOU AND TAKE' FROM THE CLAN TO START A NEW LIFE AS ORDINARY PEOPLE*.
*DH UY #32
YOU ARRANGED AN AMBUSH THAT KILLED TAKE'! I BARELY ESCAPED BUT VOWED VENGEANCE!
IF THERE WAS DECEIT, IT WAS NOT WITH MY APPROVAL OR KNOWLEDGE! I SWEAR, I WILL LOOK INTO THIS, AND THE GUILTY PARTIES WILL BE DEALT WITH!
LIAR!
THE FIRST TENET OF A *NINJA* IS DECEIT!
DIE AS TAKÉ DIED!
SARU-- *WAIT!*
WE USED TO BE FRIENDS. I WOULD HATE TO HURT YOU, SARU.
WE TRAINED TOGETHER. I AM EVERY BIT YOUR EQUAL, *KASHIRA!*
20

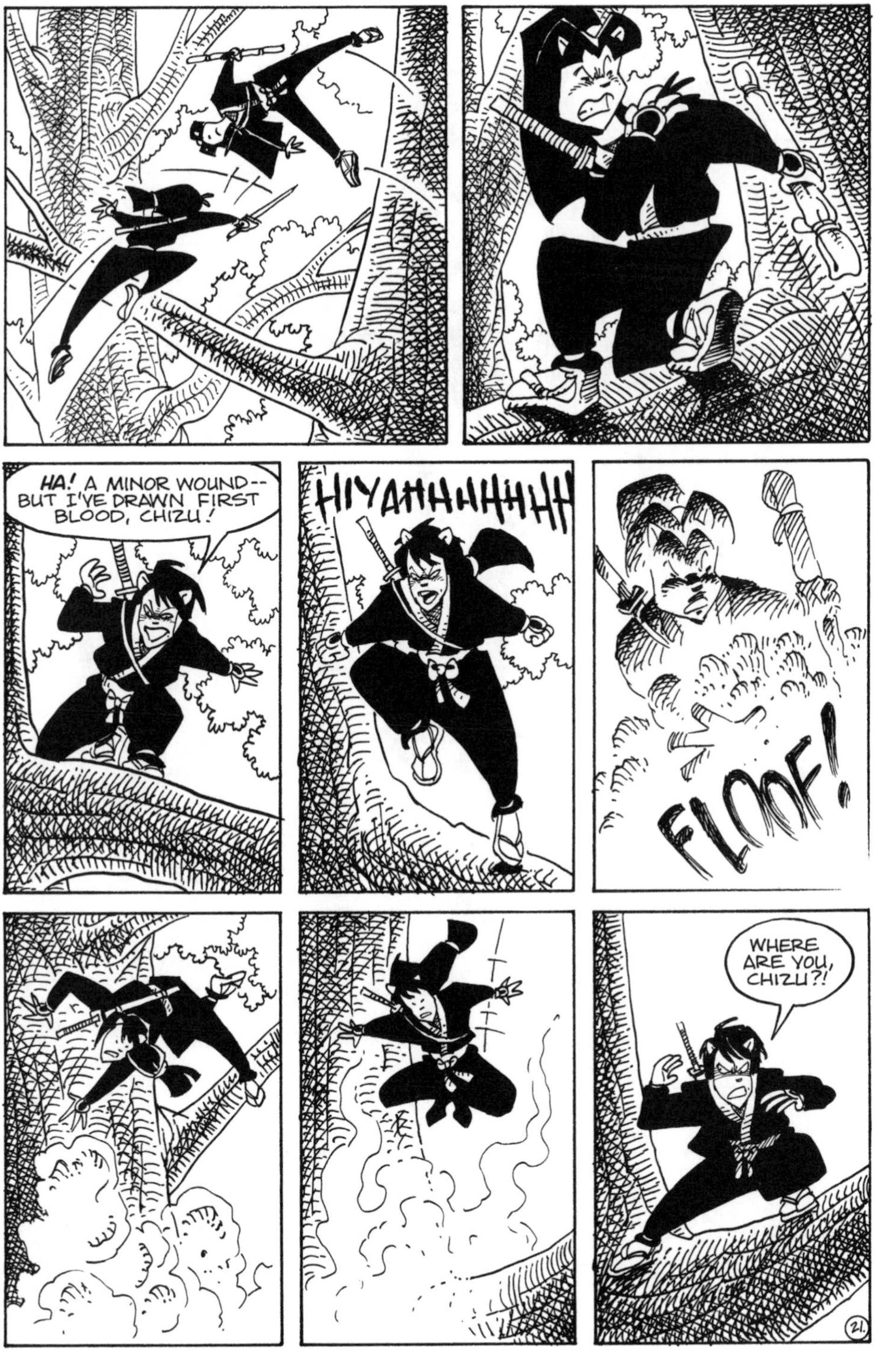
HA! A MINOR WOUND--
BUT I'VE DRAWN FIRST
BLOOD, CHIZU!
HIYAHHHHHHH
FLOOF!
WHERE
ARE YOU,
CHIZU?!
21.

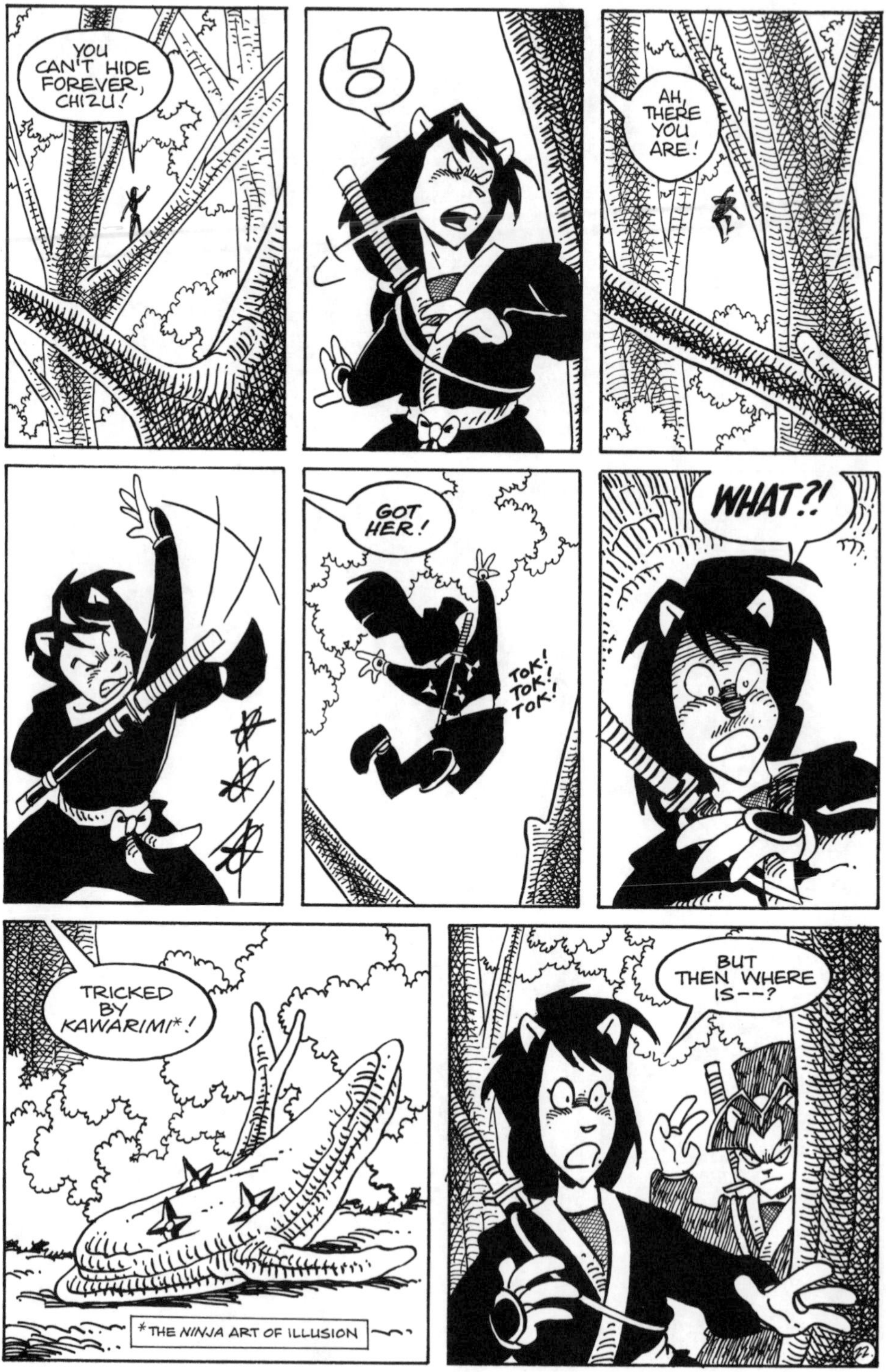
YOU CAN'T HIDE FOREVER, CHIZU!
!
AH, THERE YOU ARE!
GOT HER!
TOK! TOK! TOK!
WHAT?!
TRICKED BY KAWARIMI*!
*THE NINJA ART OF ILLUSION
BUT THEN WHERE IS--?
22

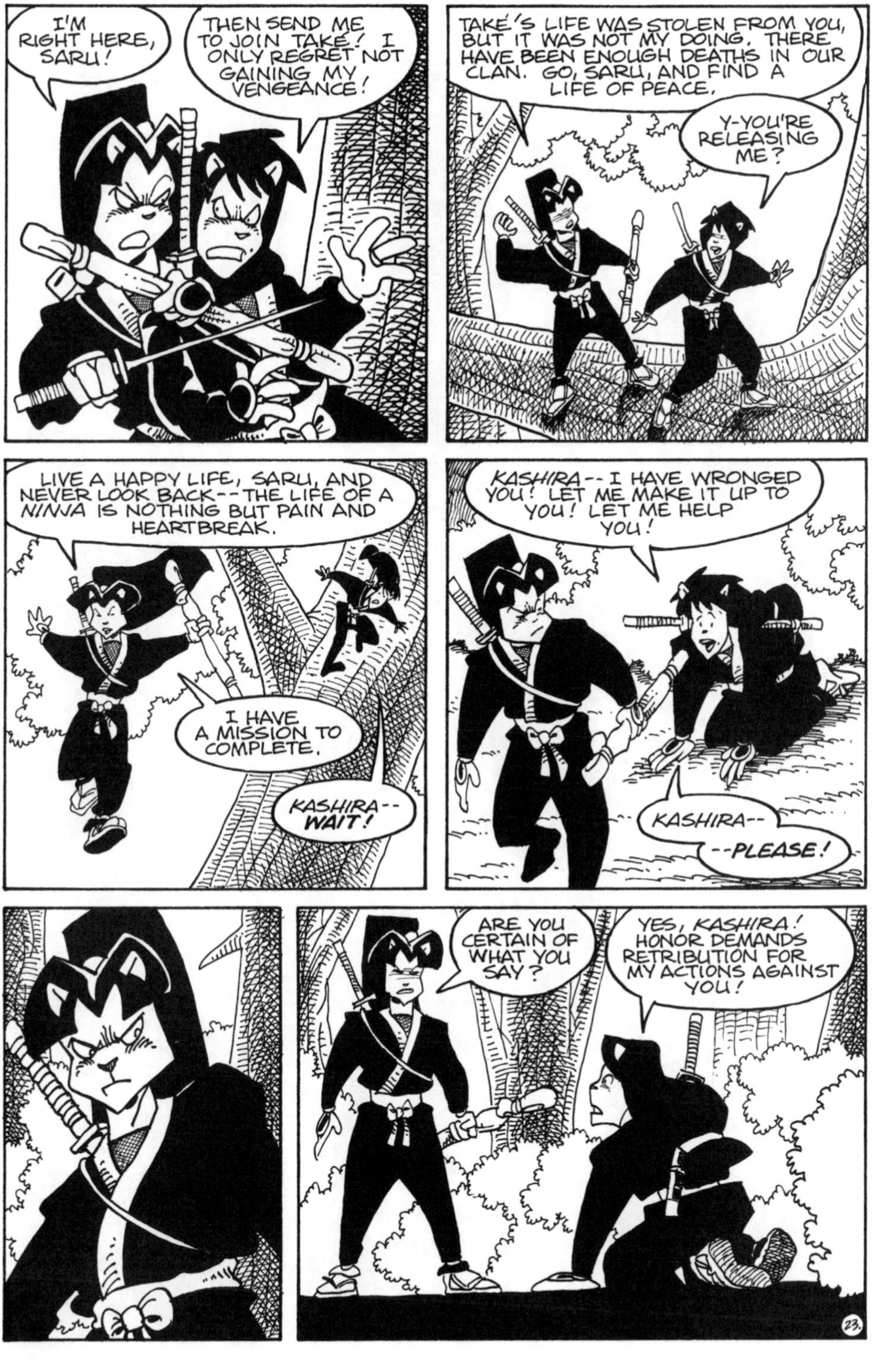
I'M RIGHT HERE, SARU!
THEN SEND ME TO JOIN TAKE! I ONLY REGRET NOT GAINING MY VENGEANCE!
TAKE'S LIFE WAS STOLEN FROM YOU, BUT IT WAS NOT MY DOING. THERE HAVE BEEN ENOUGH DEATHS IN OUR CLAN. GO, SARU, AND FIND A LIFE OF PEACE.
Y-YOU'RE RELEASING ME?
LIVE A HAPPY LIFE, SARU, AND NEVER LOOK BACK--THE LIFE OF A *NINJA* IS NOTHING BUT PAIN AND HEARTBREAK.
I HAVE A MISSION TO COMPLETE.
KASHIRA-- ***WAIT!***
KASHIRA--I HAVE WRONGED YOU! LET ME MAKE IT UP TO YOU! LET ME HELP YOU!
KASHIRA--
--***PLEASE!***
ARE YOU CERTAIN OF WHAT YOU SAY?
YES, *KASHIRA*! HONOR DEMANDS RETRIBUTION FOR MY ACTIONS AGAINST YOU!
23.

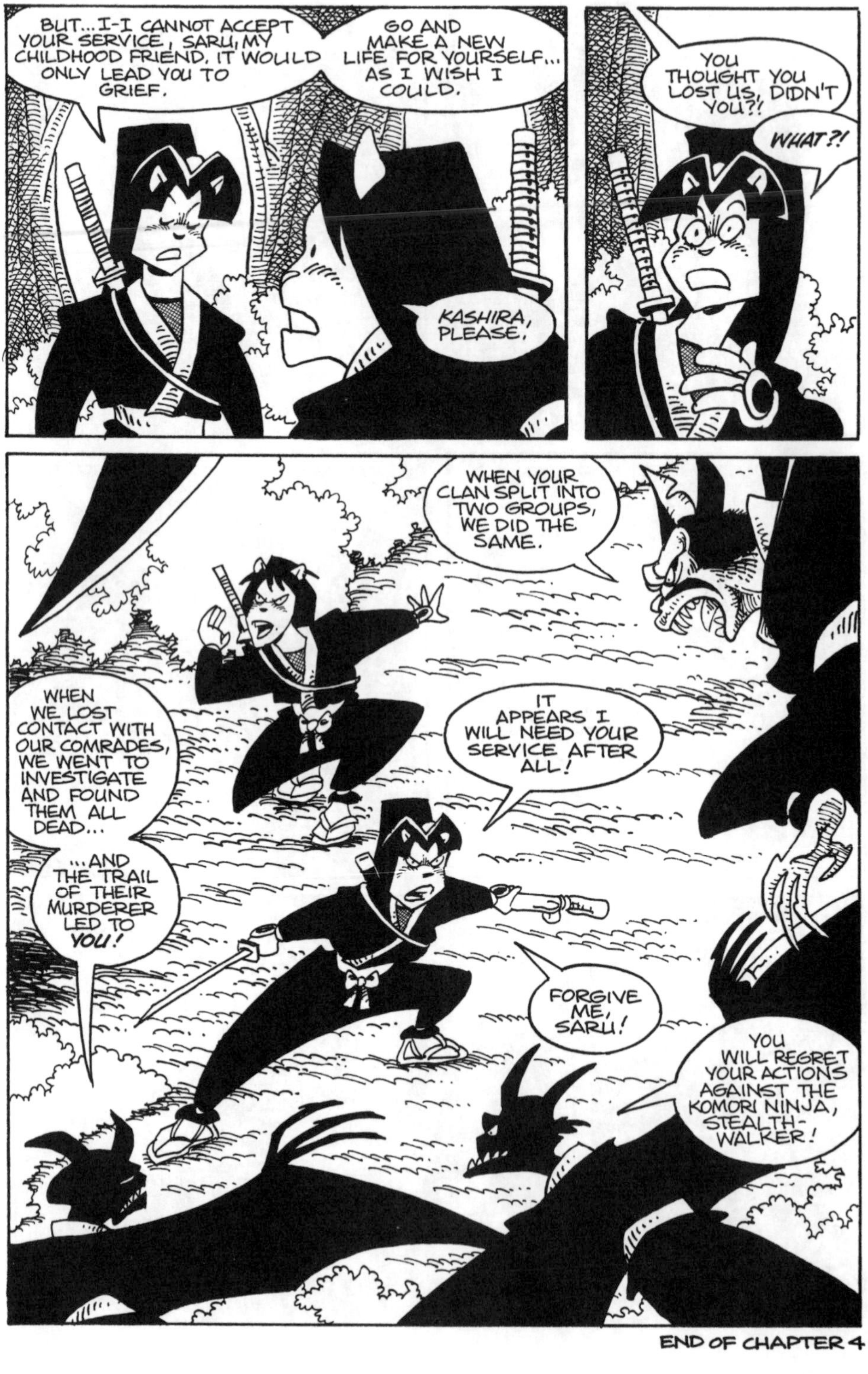
BUT... I-I CANNOT ACCEPT YOUR SERVICE, SARU, MY CHILDHOOD FRIEND. IT WOULD ONLY LEAD YOU TO GRIEF.
GO AND MAKE A NEW LIFE FOR YOURSELF... AS I WISH I COULD.
KASHIRA, PLEASE.
YOU THOUGHT YOU LOST US, DIDN'T YOU?!
WHAT?!
WHEN YOUR CLAN SPLIT INTO TWO GROUPS, WE DID THE SAME.
WHEN WE LOST CONTACT WITH OUR COMRADES, WE WENT TO INVESTIGATE AND FOUND THEM ALL DEAD...
...AND THE TRAIL OF THEIR MURDERER LED TO YOU!
IT APPEARS I WILL NEED YOUR SERVICE AFTER ALL!
FORGIVE ME, SARU!
YOU WILL REGRET YOUR ACTIONS AGAINST THE KOMORI NINJA, STEALTH-WALKER!
END OF CHAPTER 4

CHAPTER 5
THE FEEL OF SALT

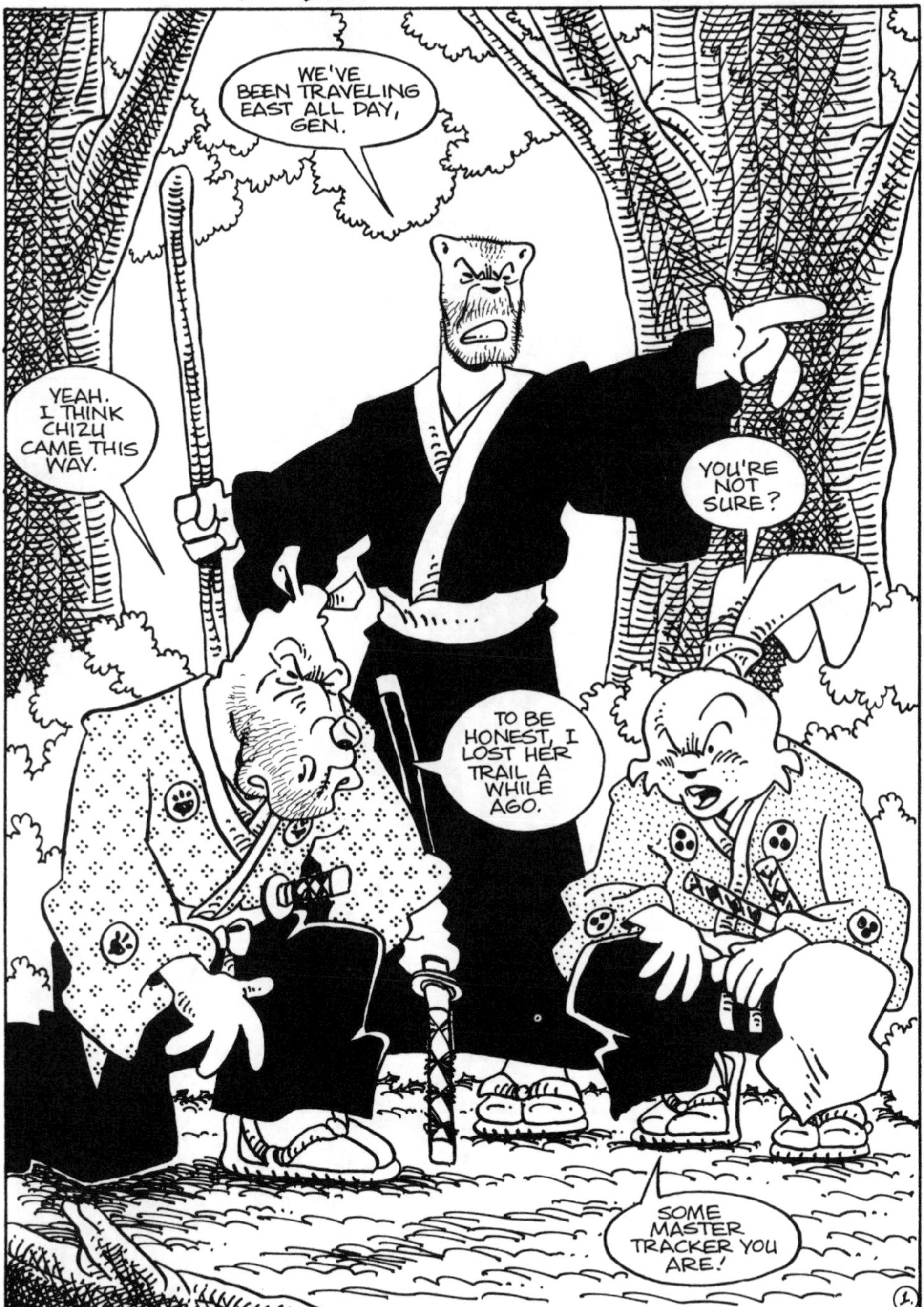

WE'VE BEEN TRAVELING EAST ALL DAY, GEN.
YEAH. I THINK CHIZU CAME THIS WAY.
YOU'RE NOT SURE?
TO BE HONEST, I LOST HER TRAIL A WHILE AGO.
SOME MASTER TRACKER YOU ARE!
1.

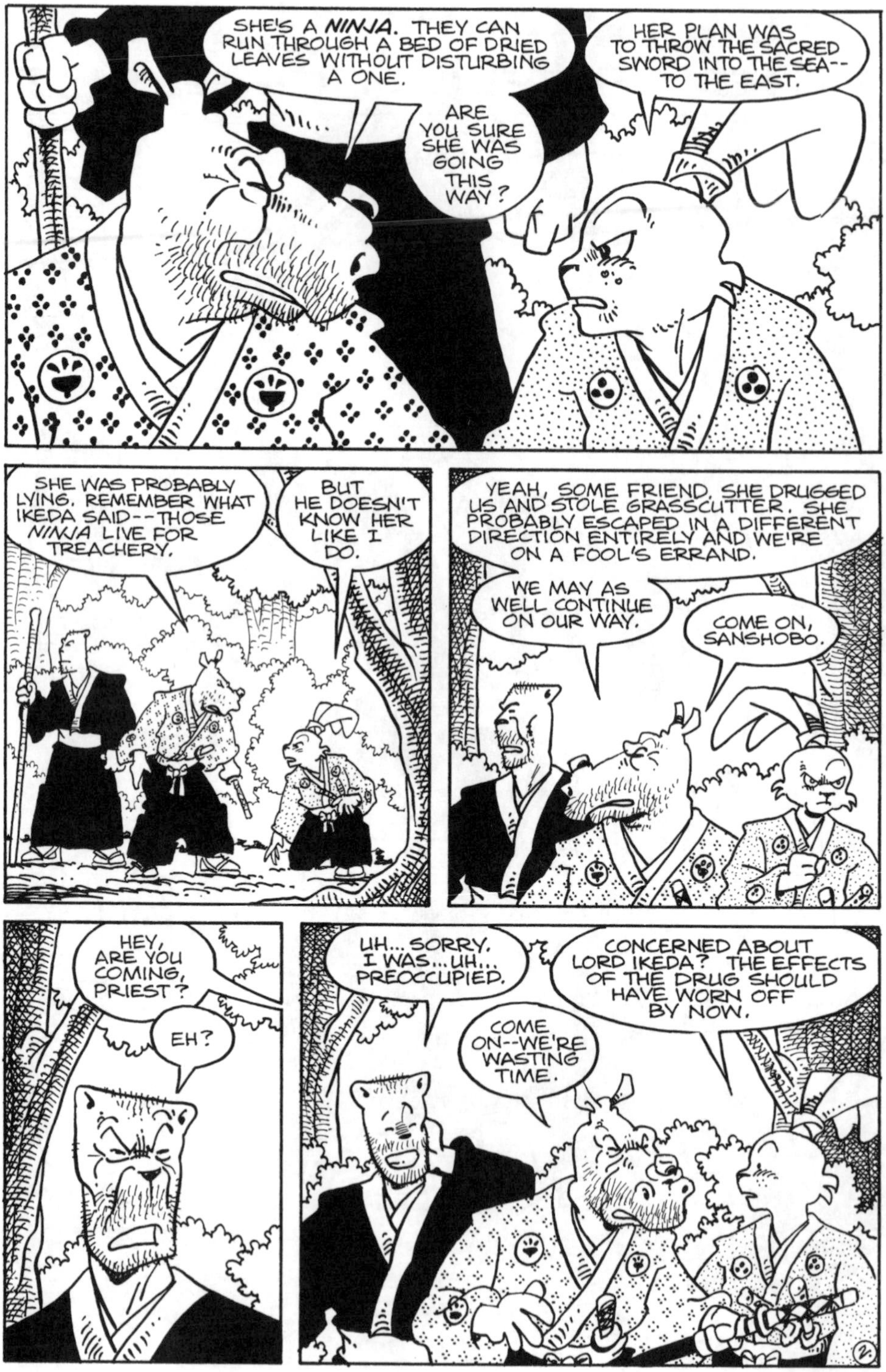
SHE'S A NINJA. THEY CAN RUN THROUGH A BED OF DRIED LEAVES WITHOUT DISTURBING A ONE.
ARE YOU SURE SHE WAS GOING THIS WAY?
HER PLAN WAS TO THROW THE SACRED SWORD INTO THE SEA-- TO THE EAST.
SHE WAS PROBABLY LYING. REMEMBER WHAT IKEDA SAID--THOSE NINJA LIVE FOR TREACHERY.
BUT HE DOESN'T KNOW HER LIKE I DO.
YEAH, SOME FRIEND. SHE DRUGGED US AND STOLE GRASSCUTTER. SHE PROBABLY ESCAPED IN A DIFFERENT DIRECTION ENTIRELY AND WE'RE ON A FOOL'S ERRAND.
WE MAY AS WELL CONTINUE ON OUR WAY.
COME ON, SANSHOBO.
HEY, ARE YOU COMING, PRIEST?
EH?
UH... SORRY. I WAS... UH... PREOCCUPIED.
CONCERNED ABOUT LORD IKEDA? THE EFFECTS OF THE DRUG SHOULD HAVE WORN OFF BY NOW.
COME ON--WE'RE WASTING TIME.
2.

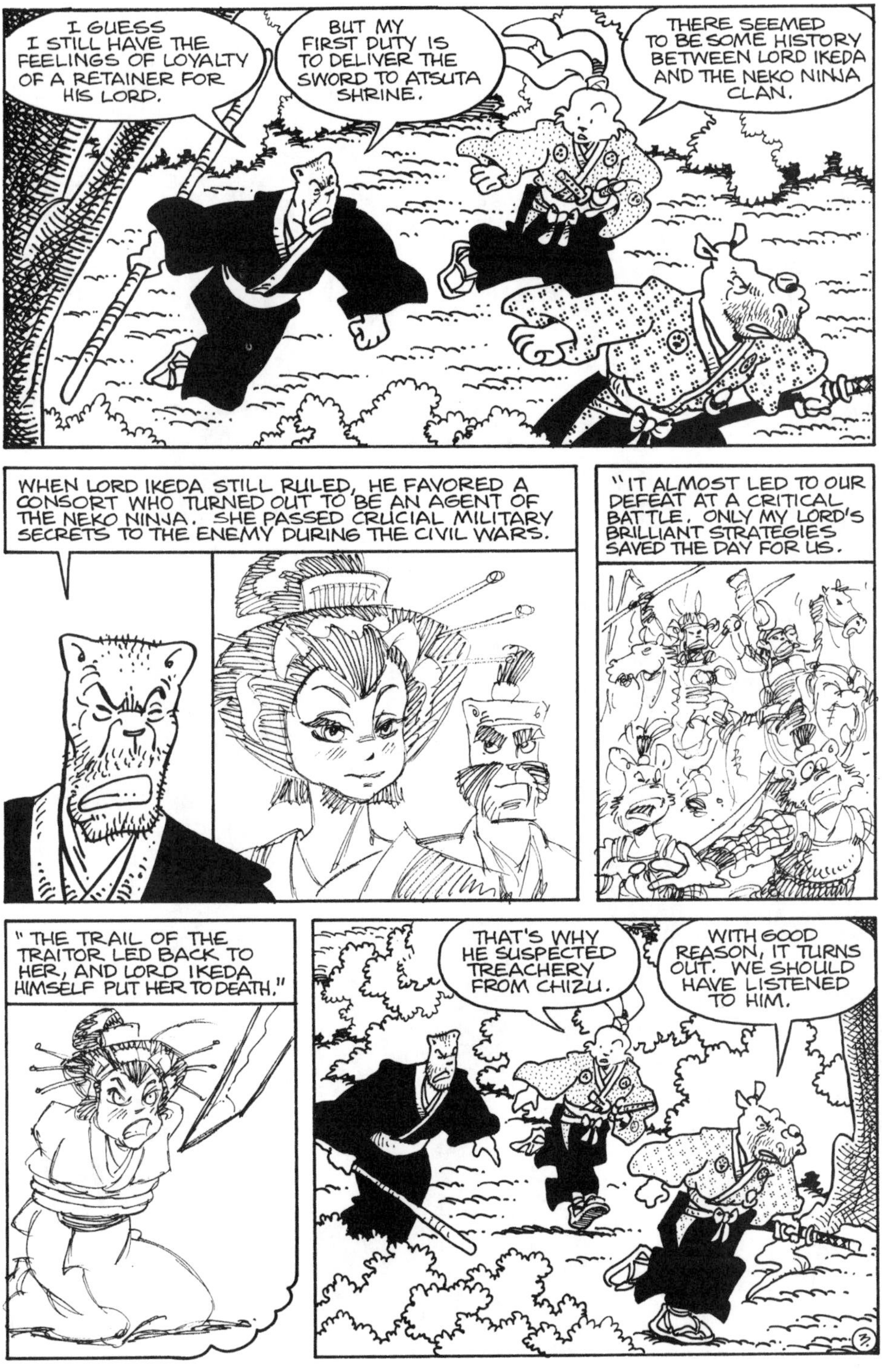
I GUESS I STILL HAVE THE FEELINGS OF LOYALTY OF A RETAINER FOR HIS LORD.
BUT MY FIRST DUTY IS TO DELIVER THE SWORD TO ATSUTA SHRINE.
THERE SEEMED TO BE SOME HISTORY BETWEEN LORD IKEDA AND THE NEKO NINJA CLAN.
WHEN LORD IKEDA STILL RULED, HE FAVORED A CONSORT WHO TURNED OUT TO BE AN AGENT OF THE NEKO NINJA. SHE PASSED CRUCIAL MILITARY SECRETS TO THE ENEMY DURING THE CIVIL WARS.
"IT ALMOST LED TO OUR DEFEAT AT A CRITICAL BATTLE. ONLY MY LORD'S BRILLIANT STRATEGIES SAVED THE DAY FOR US.
" THE TRAIL OF THE TRAITOR LED BACK TO HER, AND LORD IKEDA HIMSELF PUT HER TO DEATH."
THAT'S WHY HE SUSPECTED TREACHERY FROM CHIZU.
WITH GOOD REASON, IT TURNS OUT. WE SHOULD HAVE LISTENED TO HIM.
3.

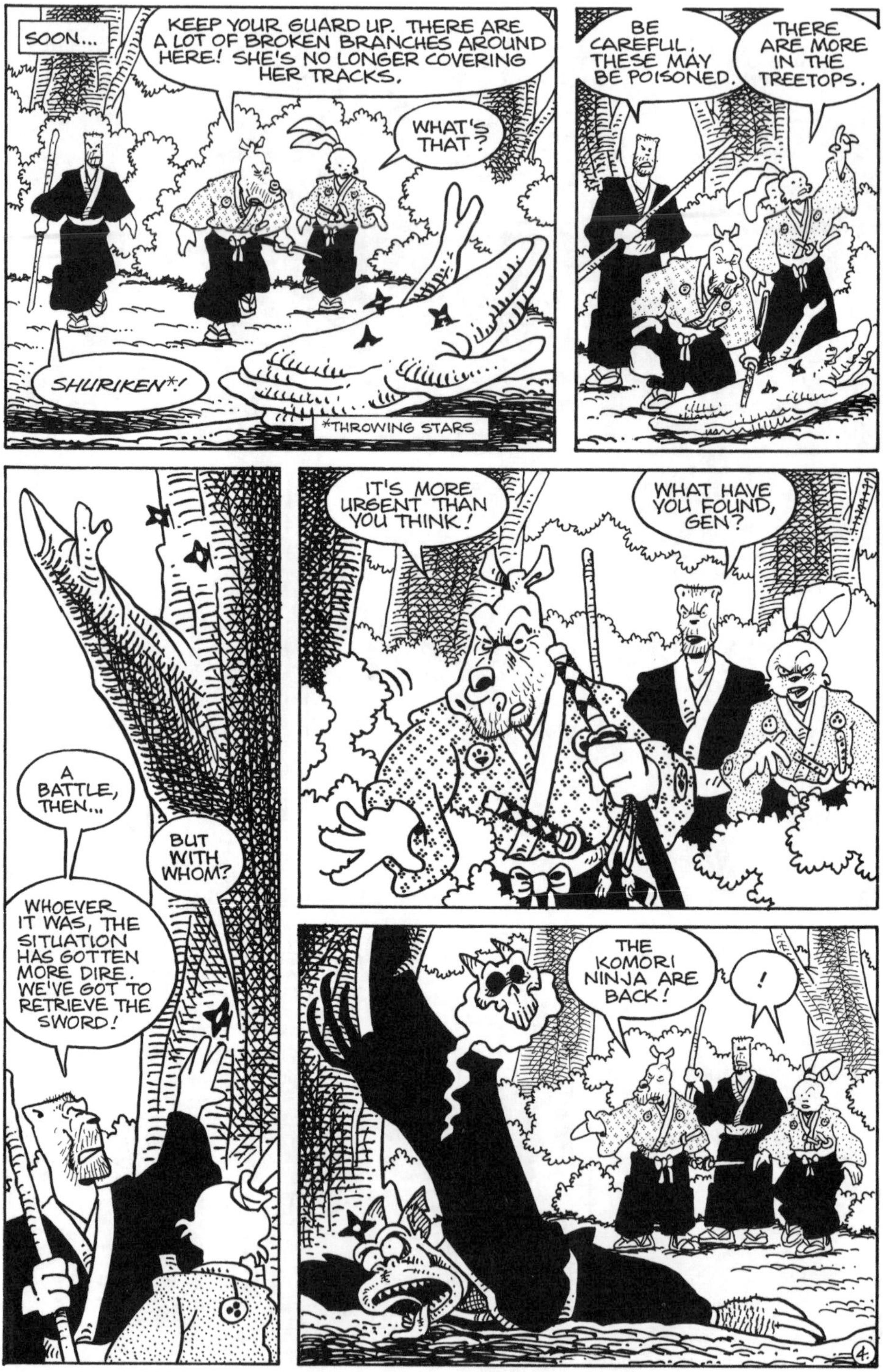
SOON...
KEEP YOUR GUARD UP. THERE ARE A LOT OF BROKEN BRANCHES AROUND HERE! SHE'S NO LONGER COVERING HER TRACKS.
WHAT'S THAT?
SHURIKEN*!
*THROWING STARS
BE CAREFUL, THESE MAY BE POISONED.
THERE ARE MORE IN THE TREETOPS.
A BATTLE, THEN...
BUT WITH WHOM?
WHOEVER IT WAS, THE SITUATION HAS GOTTEN MORE DIRE. WE'VE GOT TO RETRIEVE THE SWORD!
IT'S MORE URGENT THAN YOU THINK!
WHAT HAVE YOU FOUND, GEN?
THE KOMORI NINJA ARE BACK!
!
4.

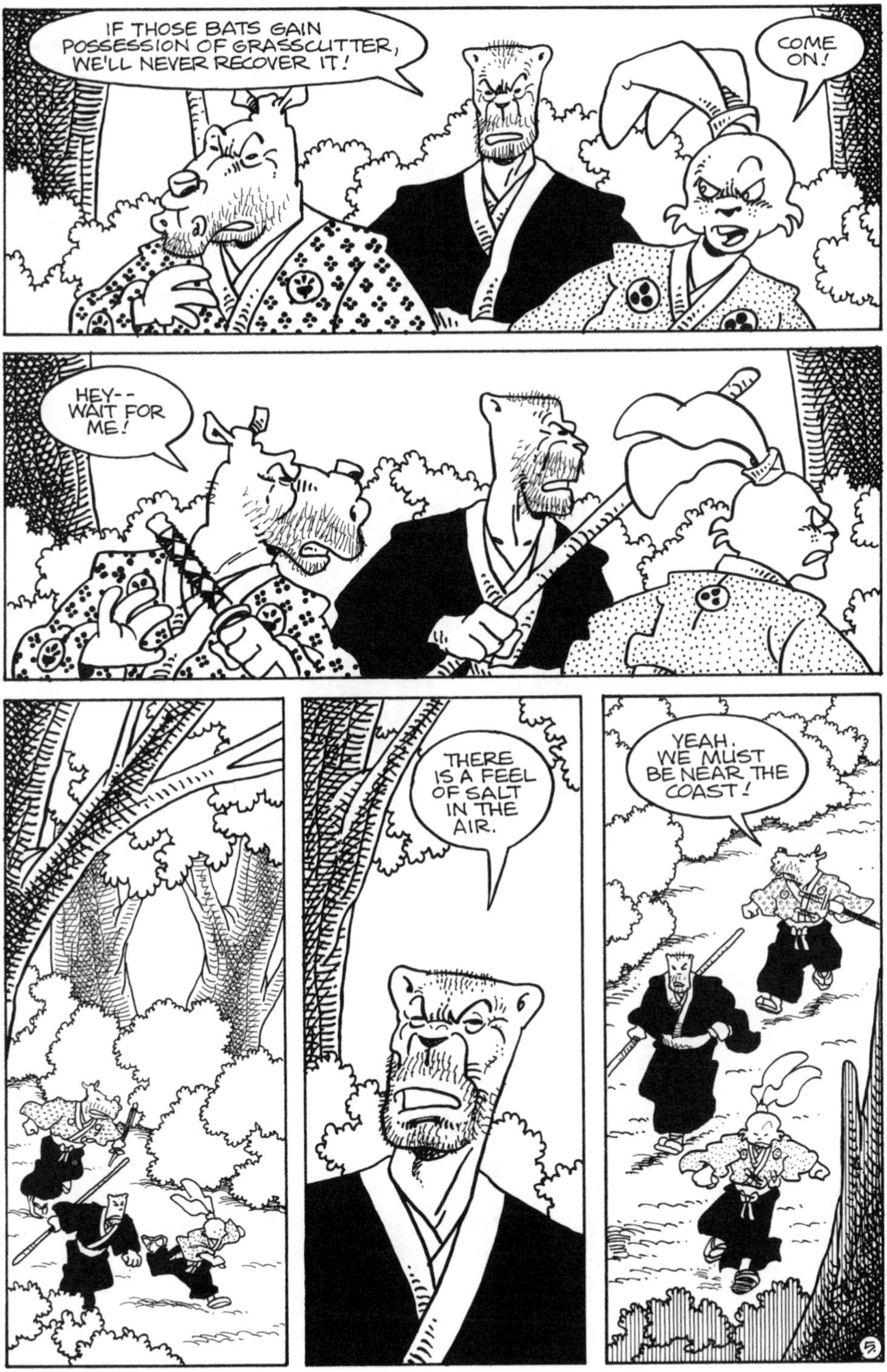
IF THOSE BATS GAIN POSSESSION OF GRASSCUTTER, WE'LL NEVER RECOVER IT!
COME ON!
HEY-- WAIT FOR ME!
THERE IS A FEEL OF SALT IN THE AIR.
YEAH. WE MUST BE NEAR THE COAST!

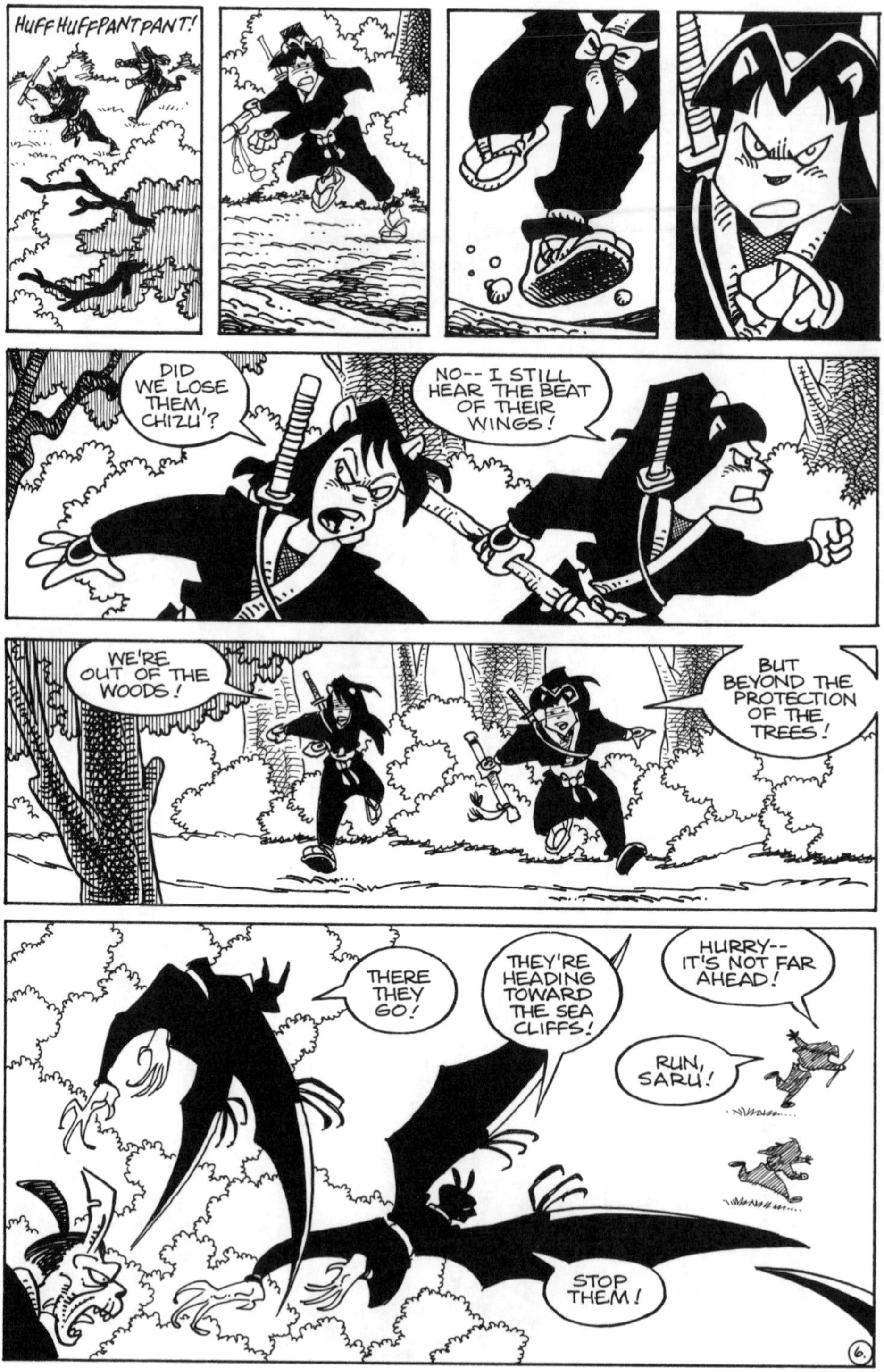
HUFF HUFF PANT PANT!
DID WE LOSE THEM, CHIZU?
NO-- I STILL HEAR THE BEAT OF THEIR WINGS!
WE'RE OUT OF THE WOODS!
BUT BEYOND THE PROTECTION OF THE TREES!
THERE THEY GO!
THEY'RE HEADING TOWARD THE SEA CLIFFS!
HURRY-- IT'S NOT FAR AHEAD!
RUN, SARU!
STOP THEM!
6.

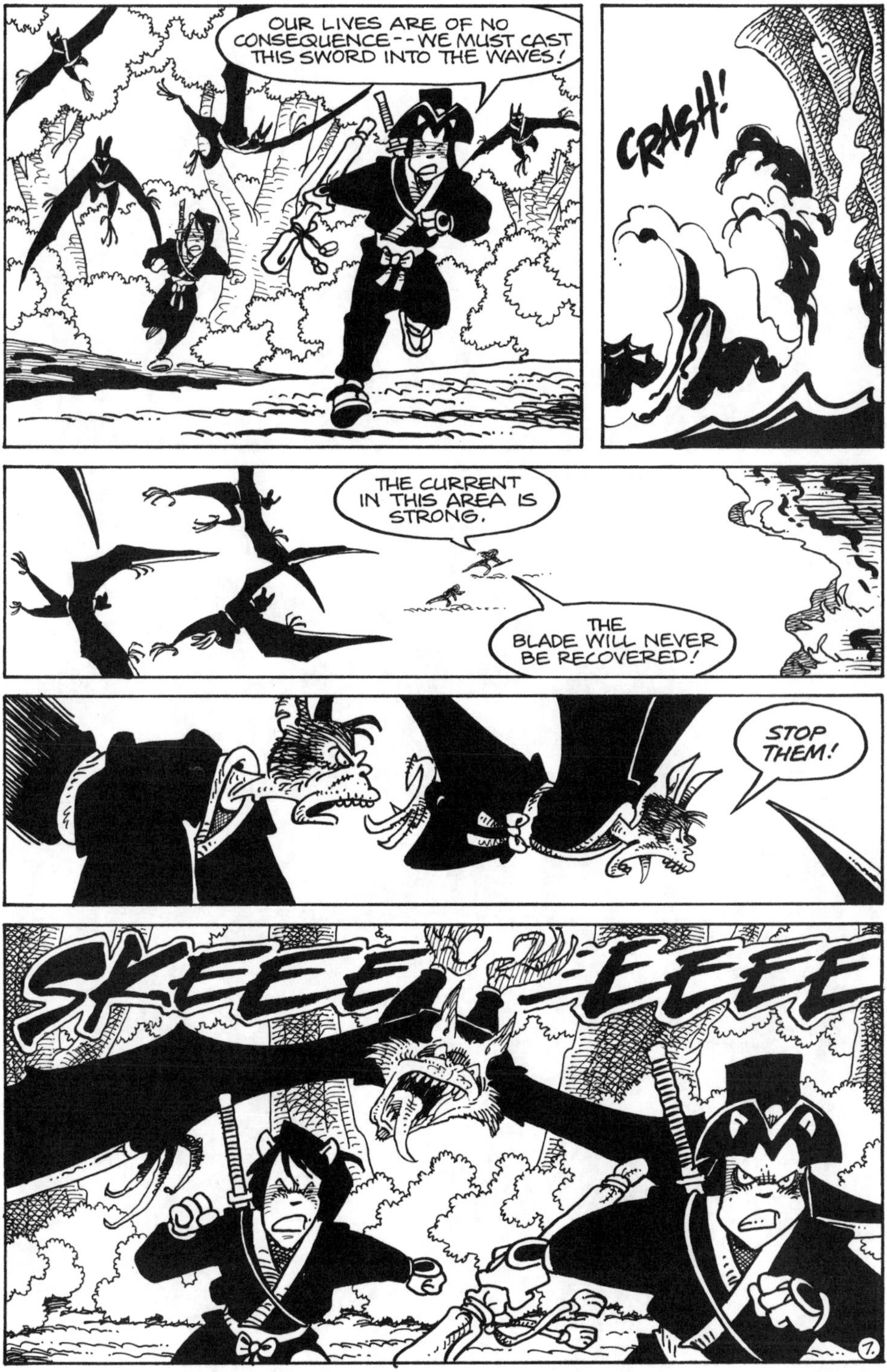
OUR LIVES ARE OF NO CONSEQUENCE--WE MUST CAST THIS SWORD INTO THE WAVES!
CRASH!
THE CURRENT IN THIS AREA IS STRONG.
THE BLADE WILL NEVER BE RECOVERED!
STOP THEM!
SKEEEE-EEEE
7.

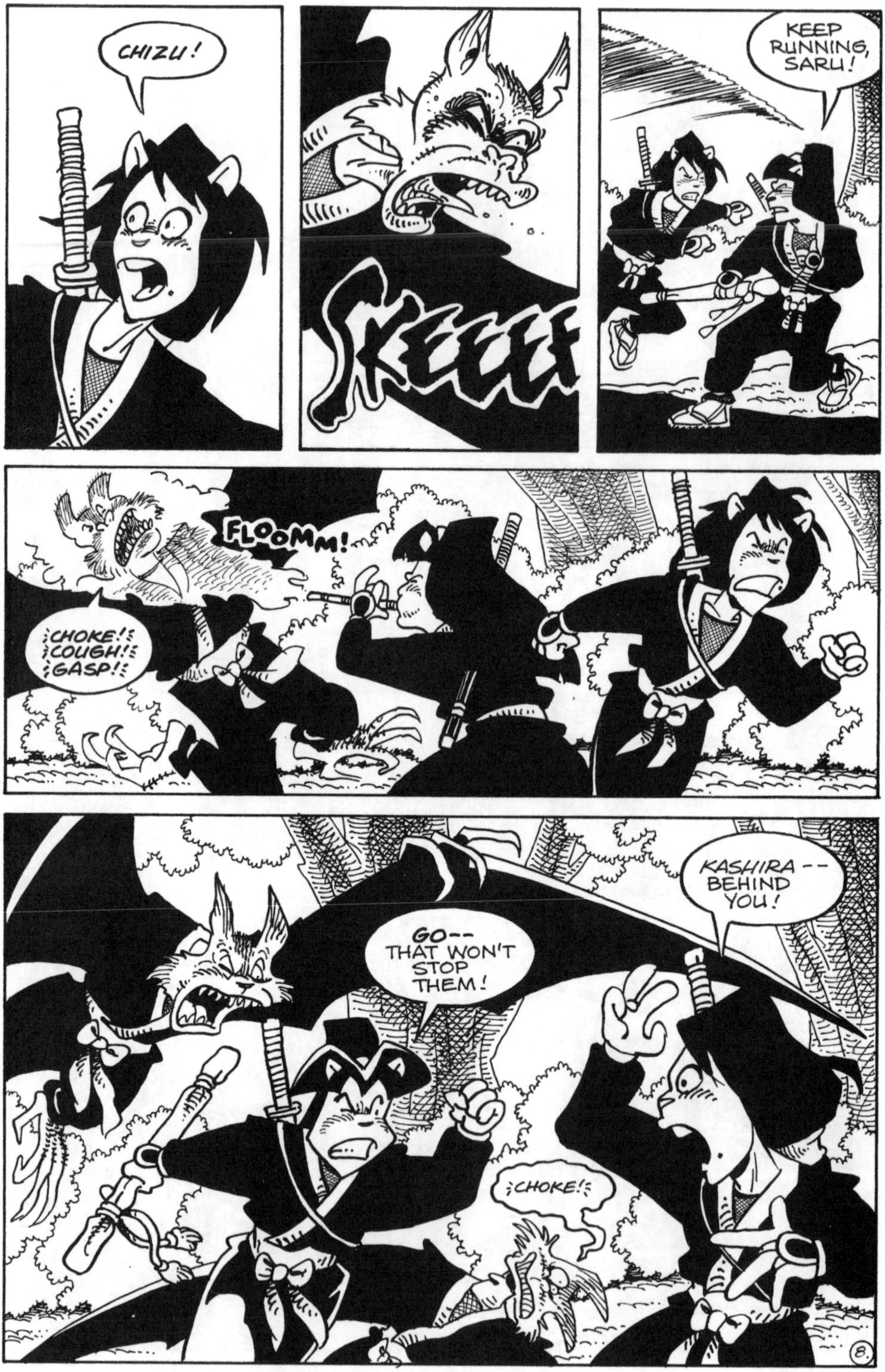
CHIZU!
SKEEEE
KEEP RUNNING, SARU!
FLOOMM!
CHOKE! COUGH! GASP!
KASHIRA -- BEHIND YOU!
GO-- THAT WON'T STOP THEM!
CHOKE!
8.

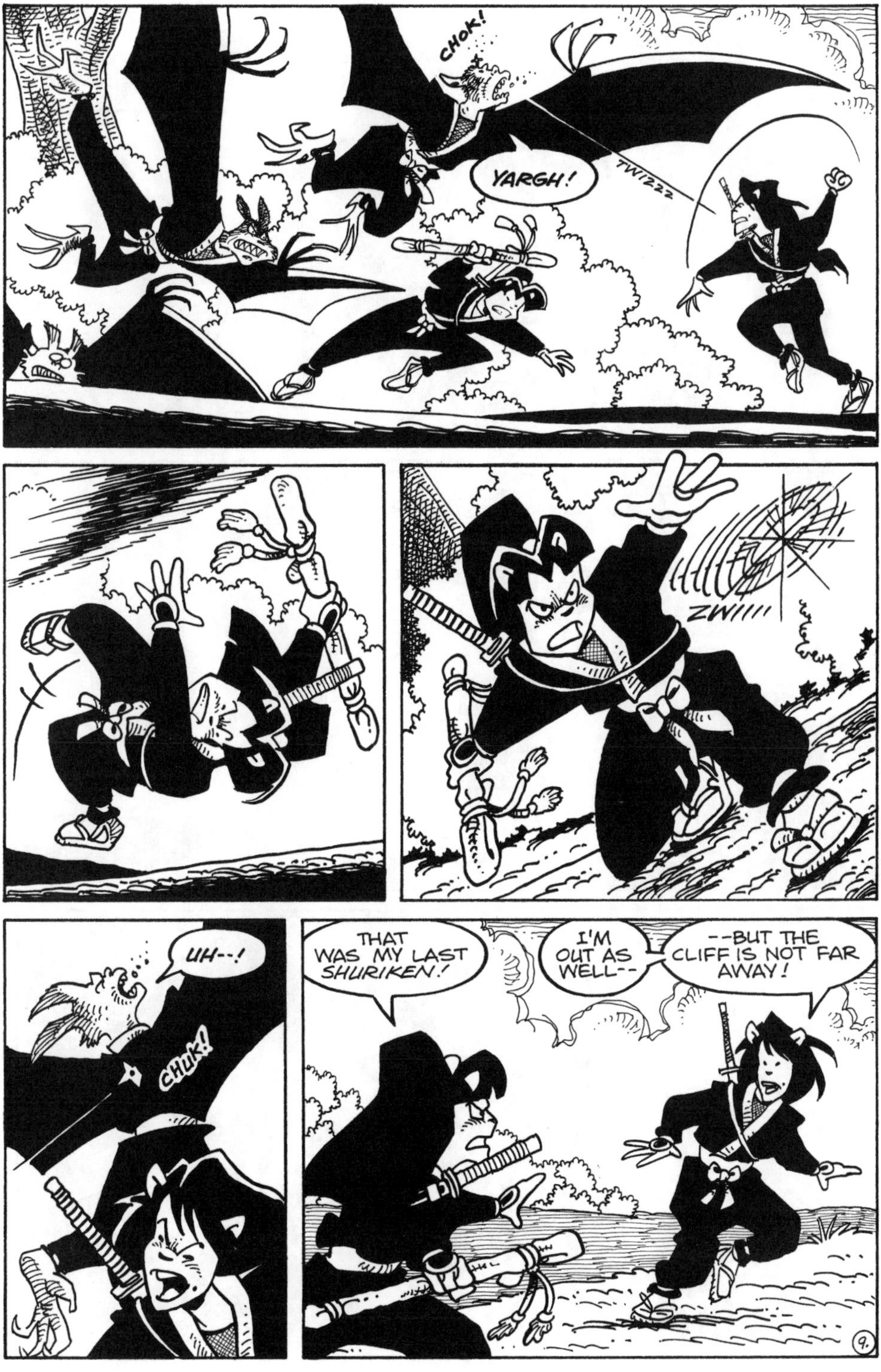
CHOK!
YARGH!
TWIZZZ
ZWIIII
UH--!
CHOK!
THAT WAS MY LAST SHURIKEN!
I'M OUT AS WELL--
--BUT THE CLIFF IS NOT FAR AWAY!
9.

SARU--TAKE THE SWORD AND HURL IT OVER THE CLIFF!
I'LL HOLD THEM OFF!
IT'S TOO LATE, CHIZU!
THEY'VE CUT US OFF FROM THE EDGE!
WE'VE GOT TO CAST IT INTO THE WAVES--REGARDLESS OF WHAT HAPPENS TO US!
UH--!
SLASH!
CHIZU!
10.

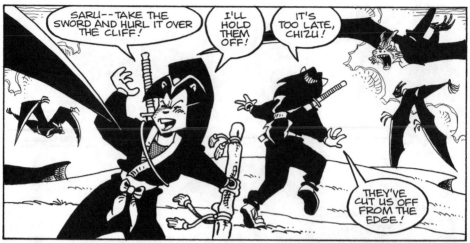

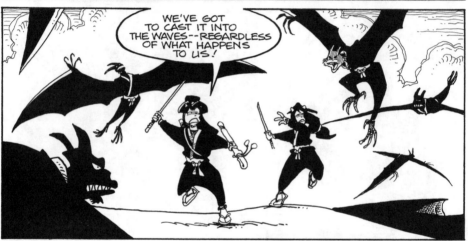

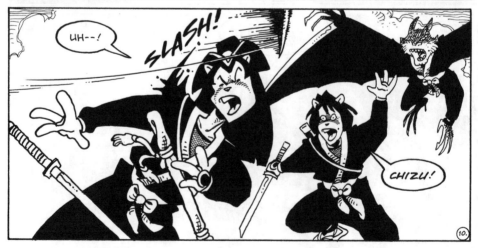

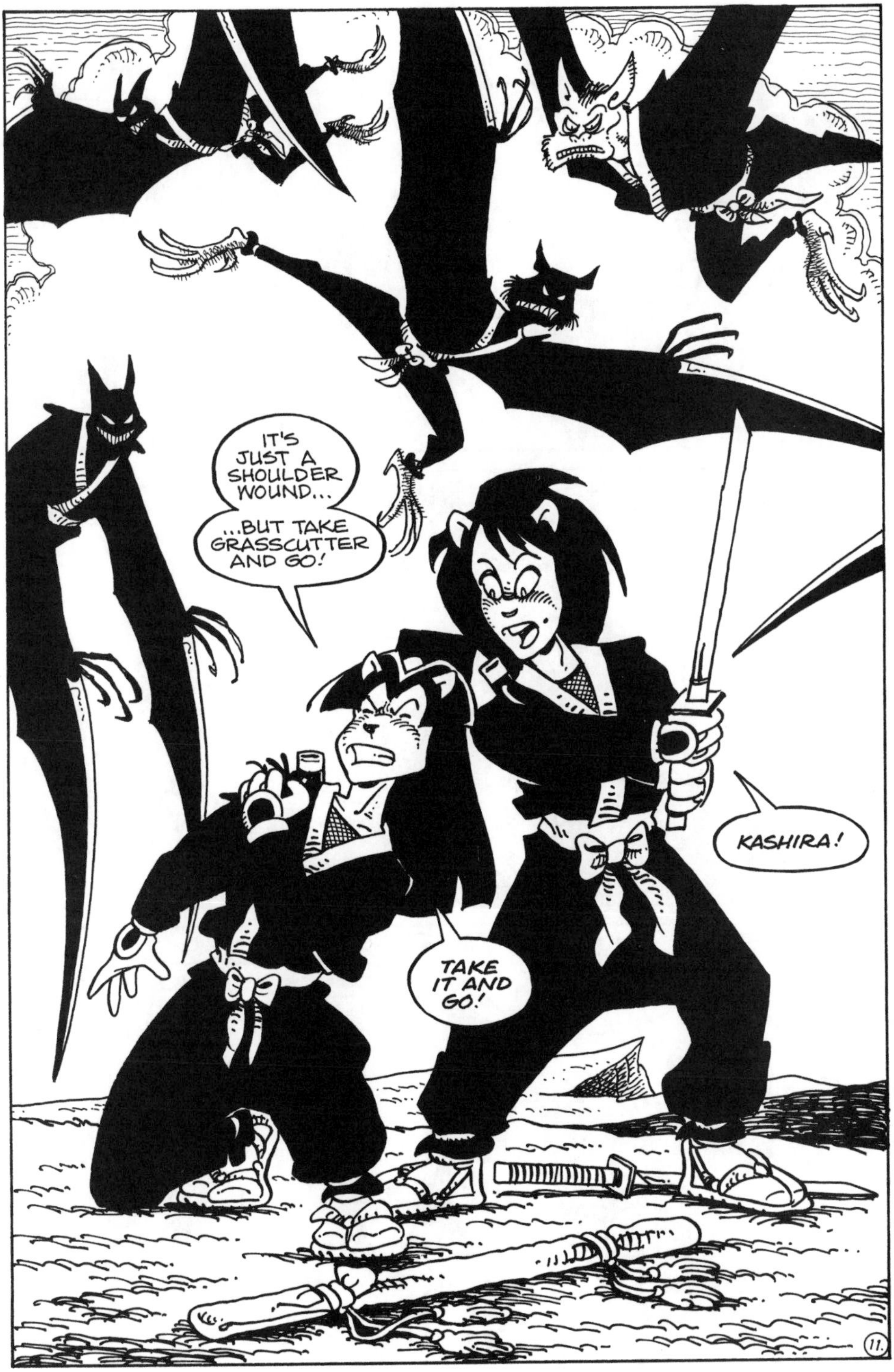
IT'S JUST A SHOULDER WOUND...
...BUT TAKE GRASSCUTTER AND GO!
KASHIRA!
TAKE IT AND GO!
11.

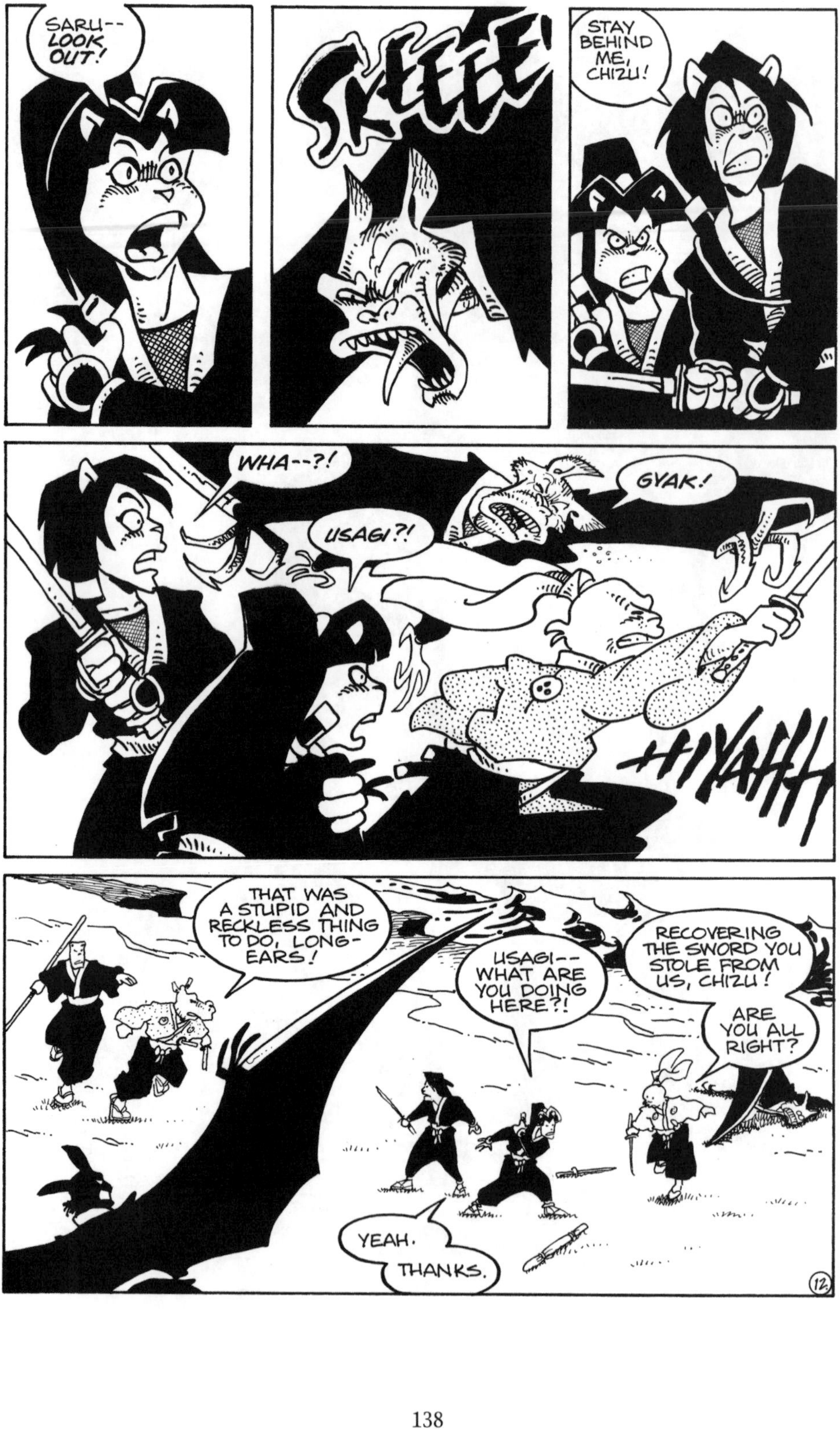
SARU-- LOOK OUT!
SKEEEE!
STAY BEHIND ME, CHIZU!
WHA--?!
USAGI?!
GYAK!
HIYAHH
THAT WAS A STUPID AND RECKLESS THING TO DO, LONG-EARS!
USAGI-- WHAT ARE YOU DOING HERE?!
RECOVERING THE SWORD YOU STOLE FROM US, CHIZU!
ARE YOU ALL RIGHT?
YEAH.
THANKS.
12

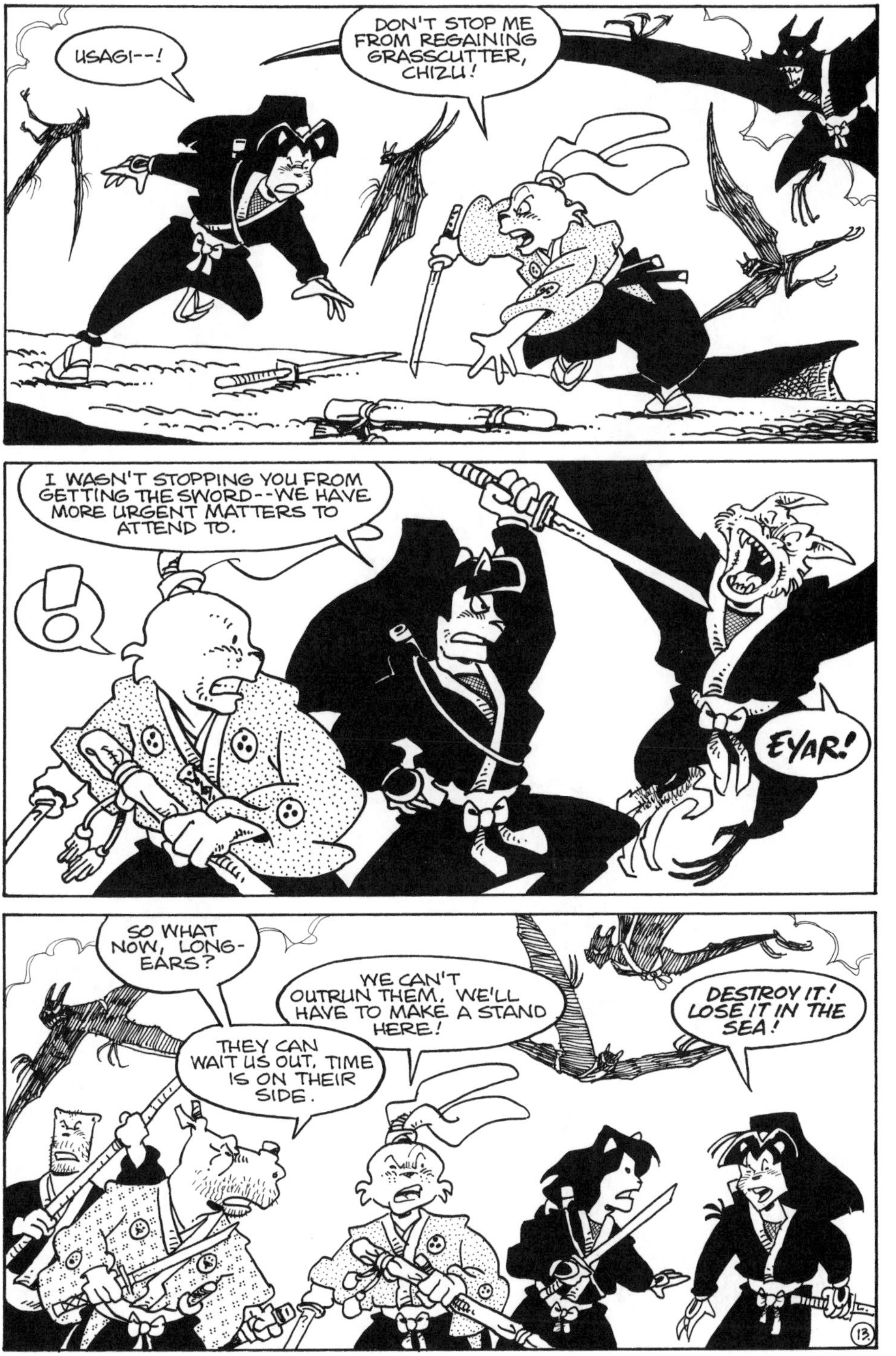
USAGI--!
DON'T STOP ME FROM REGAINING GRASSCUTTER, CHIZU!
I WASN'T STOPPING YOU FROM GETTING THE SWORD--WE HAVE MORE URGENT MATTERS TO ATTEND TO.
!
EYAR!
SO WHAT NOW, LONG-EARS?
THEY CAN WAIT US OUT. TIME IS ON THEIR SIDE.
WE CAN'T OUTRUN THEM. WE'LL HAVE TO MAKE A STAND HERE!
DESTROY IT! LOSE IT IN THE SEA!
13

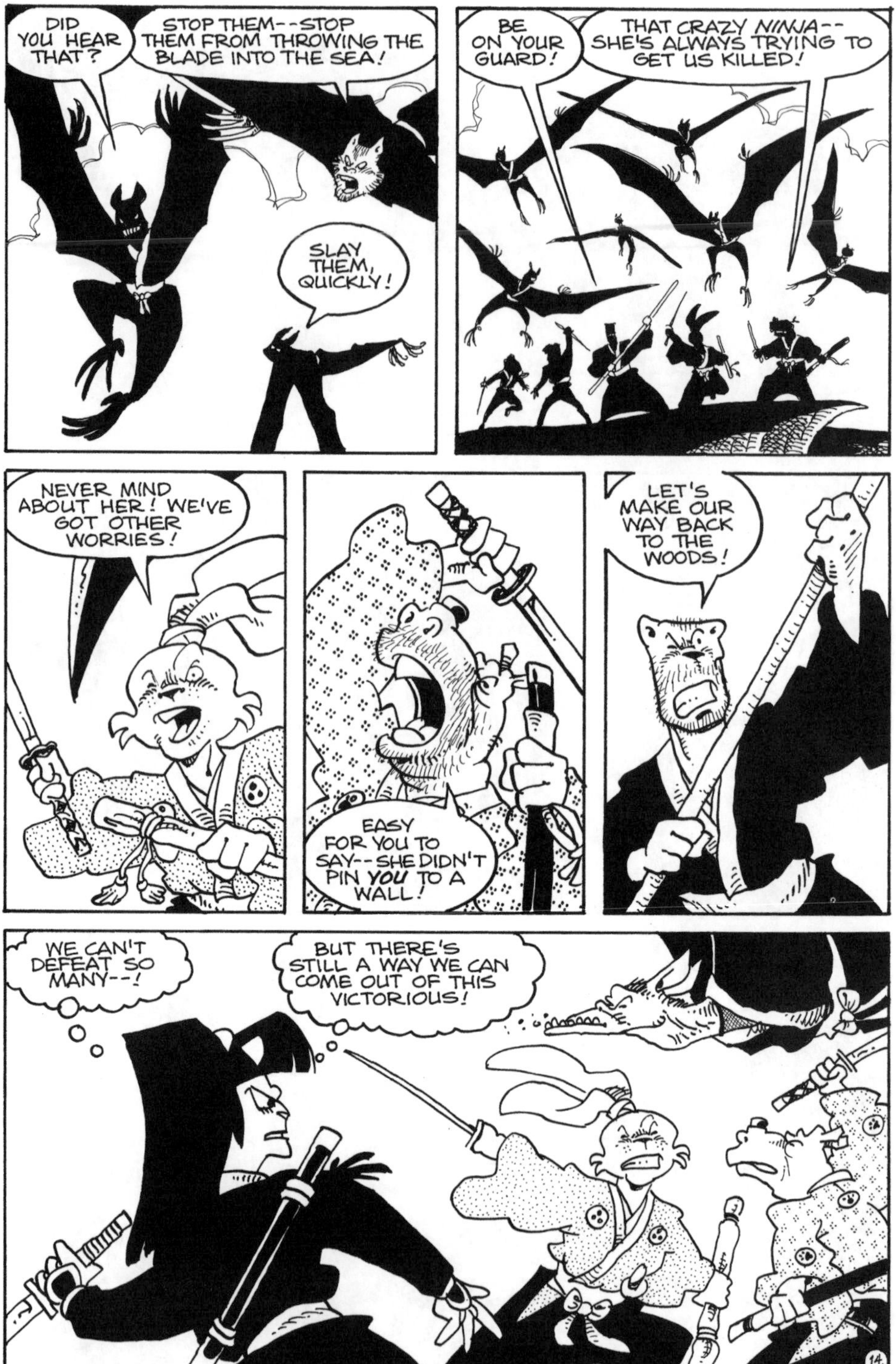
DID YOU HEAR THAT?
STOP THEM--STOP THEM FROM THROWING THE BLADE INTO THE SEA!
SLAY THEM, QUICKLY!
BE ON YOUR GUARD!
THAT CRAZY NINJA-- SHE'S ALWAYS TRYING TO GET US KILLED!
NEVER MIND ABOUT HER! WE'VE GOT OTHER WORRIES!
EASY FOR YOU TO SAY--SHE DIDN'T PIN YOU TO A WALL!
LET'S MAKE OUR WAY BACK TO THE WOODS!
WE CAN'T DEFEAT SO MANY--!
BUT THERE'S STILL A WAY WE CAN COME OUT OF THIS VICTORIOUS!
14.

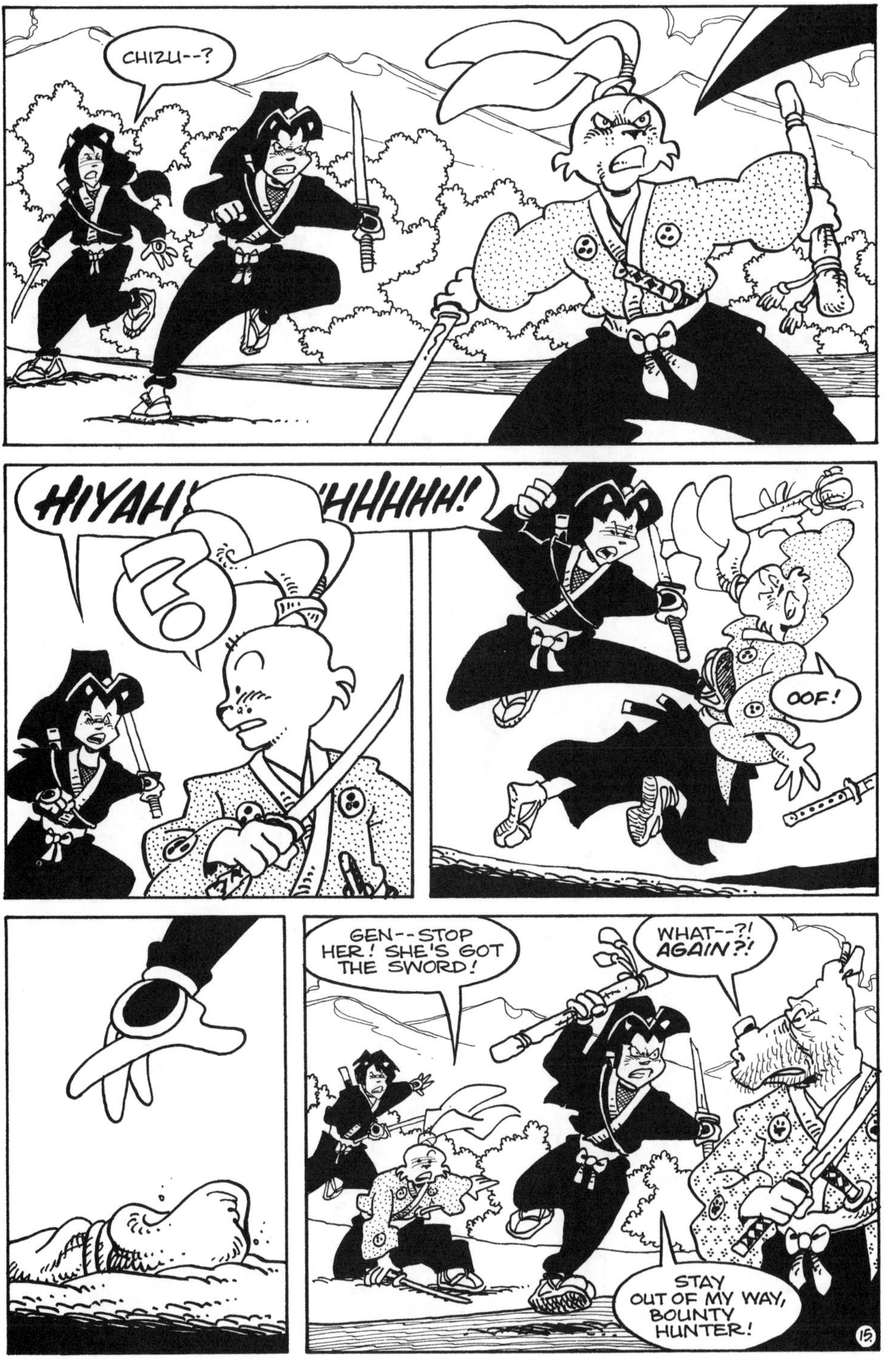
CHIZU--?
HIYAH HHHHHH!
?
OOF!
GEN--STOP HER! SHE'S GOT THE SWORD!
WHAT--?! AGAIN?!
STAY OUT OF MY WAY, BOUNTY HUNTER!
15

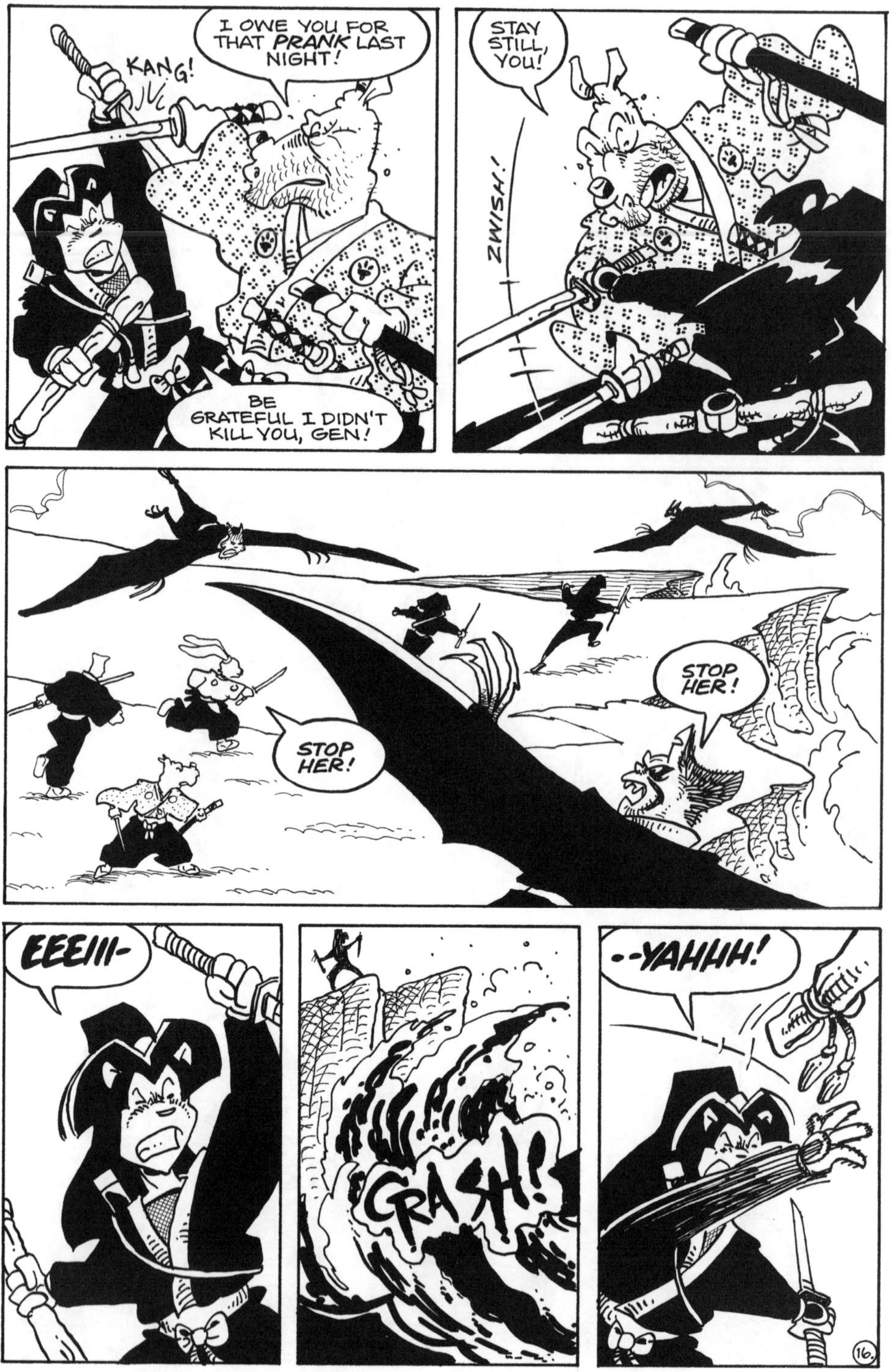
KANG!
I OWE YOU FOR THAT PRANK LAST NIGHT!
BE GRATEFUL I DIDN'T KILL YOU, GEN!
STAY STILL, YOU!
ZWISH!
STOP HER!
STOP HER!
EEEIII-
CRASH!
--YAHHH!
16.

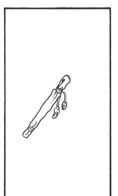
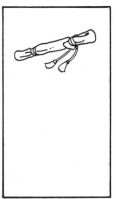
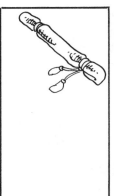

SKEEEE

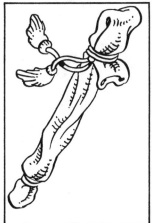

SNATCH!

NO!

HA HA HA HA HA! YOU'RE BEATEN, SHADOW-WALKER!

WE, OF THE KOMORI NINJA, WILL ALWAYS WIN OUT IN THE END!

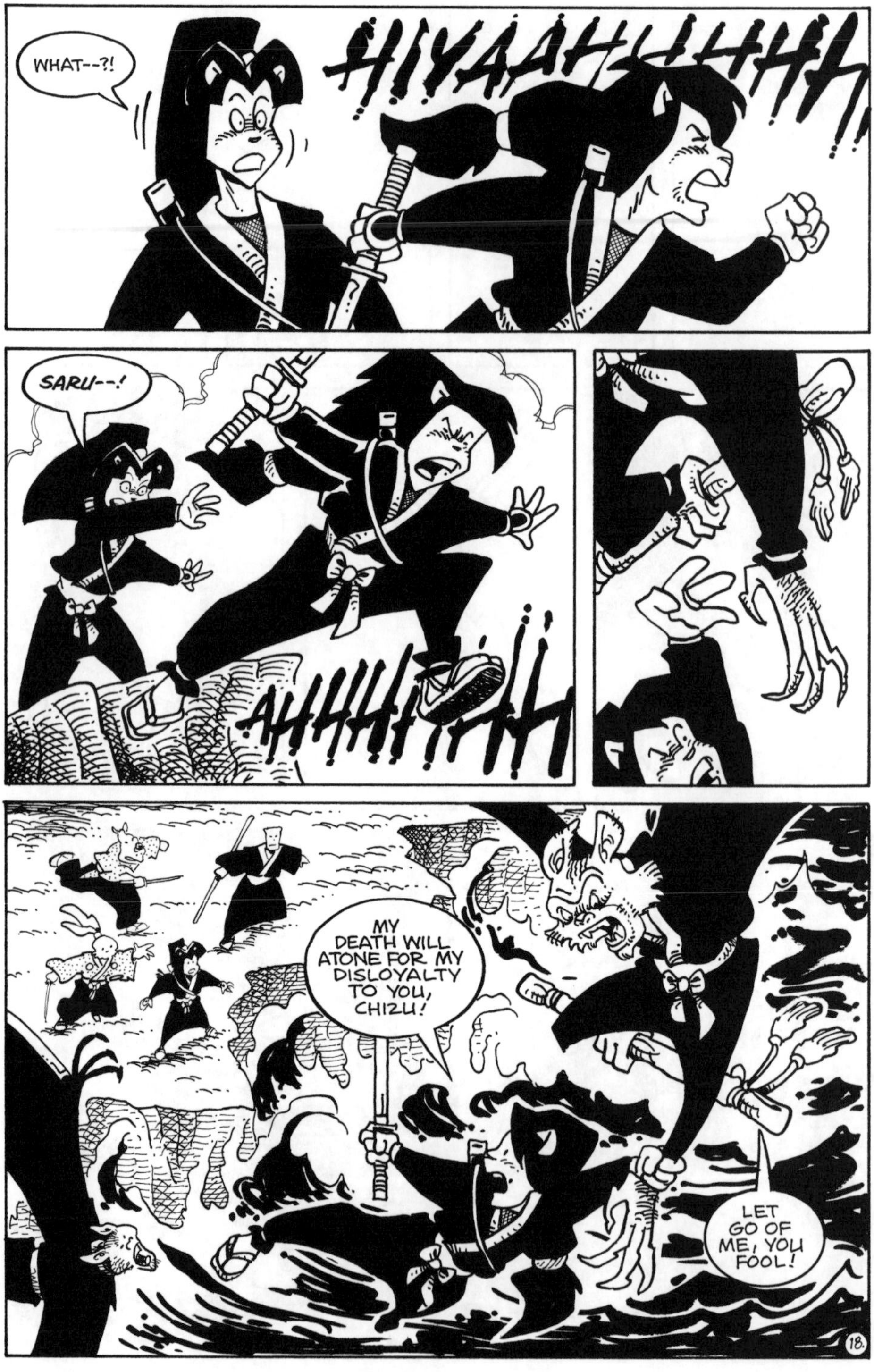
WHAT--?!
HIYAAAHHHHHH!!
SARU--!
AHHHHHHH!!
MY DEATH WILL ATONE FOR MY DISLOYALTY TO YOU, CHIZU!
LET GO OF ME, YOU FOOL!
18.

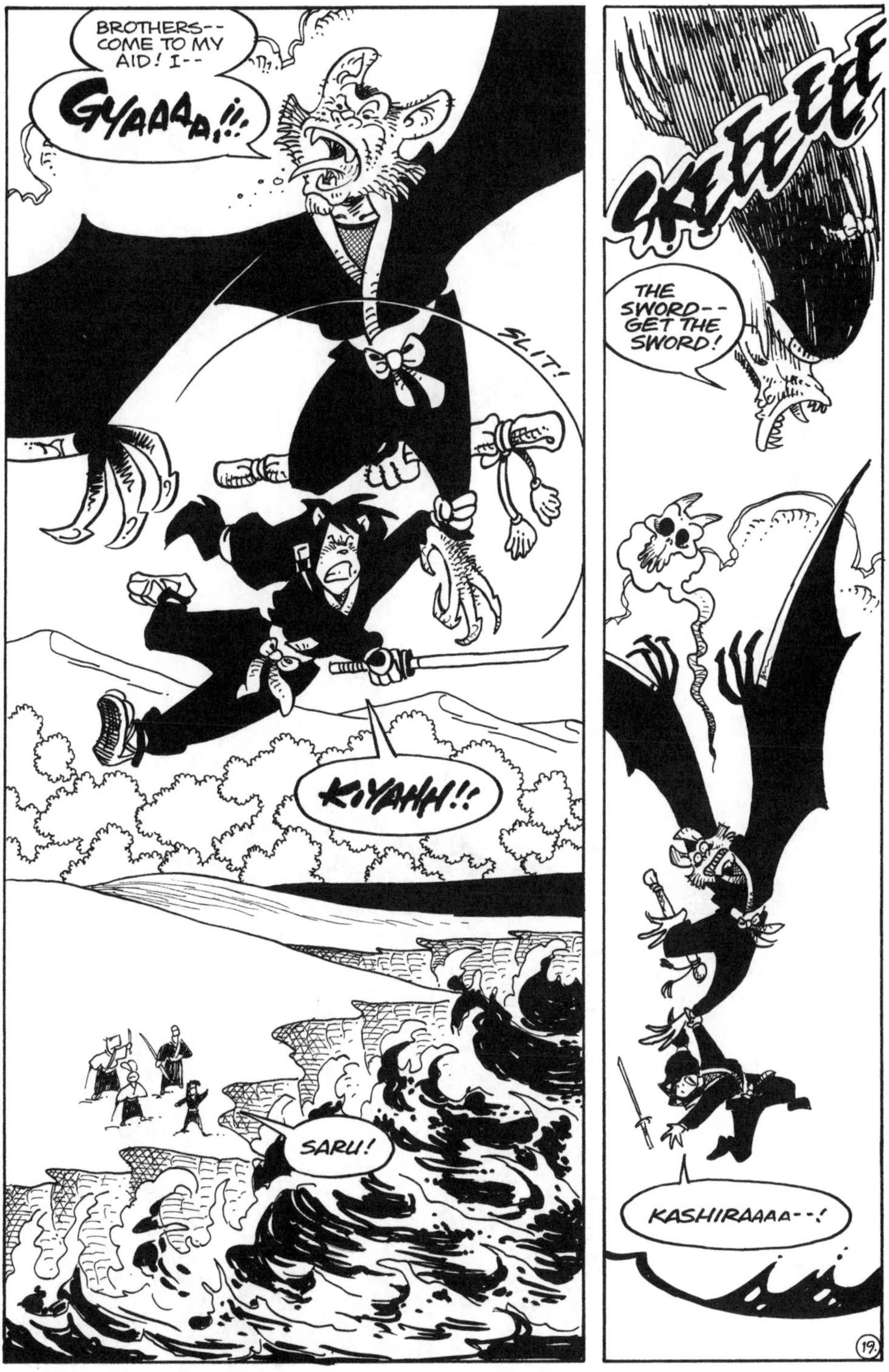
BROTHERS-- COME TO MY AID! I--
GYAAAA!!!
SLIT!
KIYAHH!!
SARU!
SKEEEEEE
THE SWORD-- GET THE SWORD!
KASHIRAAAA--!
19

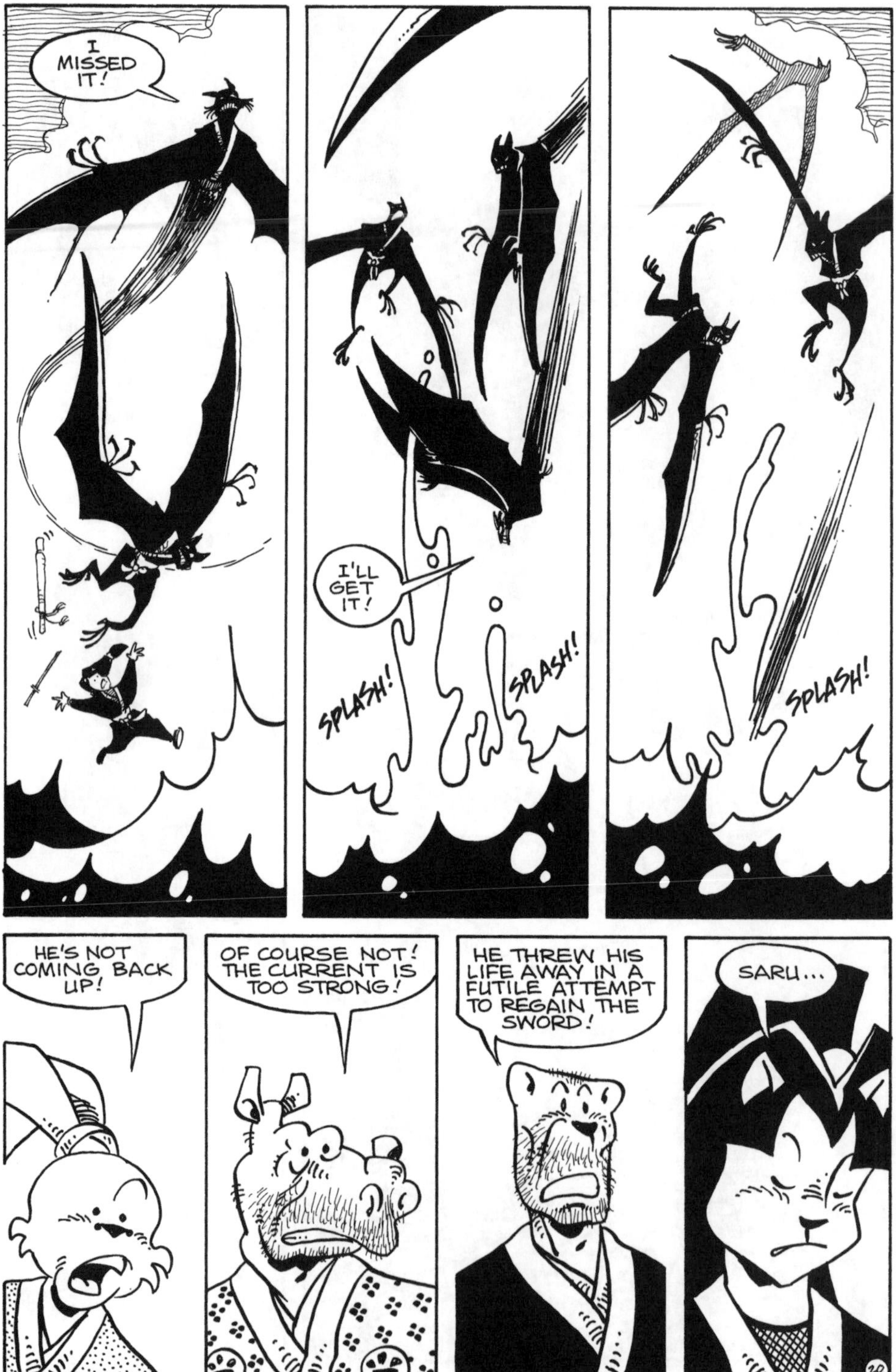
I MISSED IT!
I'LL GET IT!
SPLASH!
SPLASH!
SPLASH!
HE'S NOT COMING BACK UP!
OF COURSE NOT! THE CURRENT IS TOO STRONG!
HE THREW HIS LIFE AWAY IN A FUTILE ATTEMPT TO REGAIN THE SWORD!
SARU...
20.

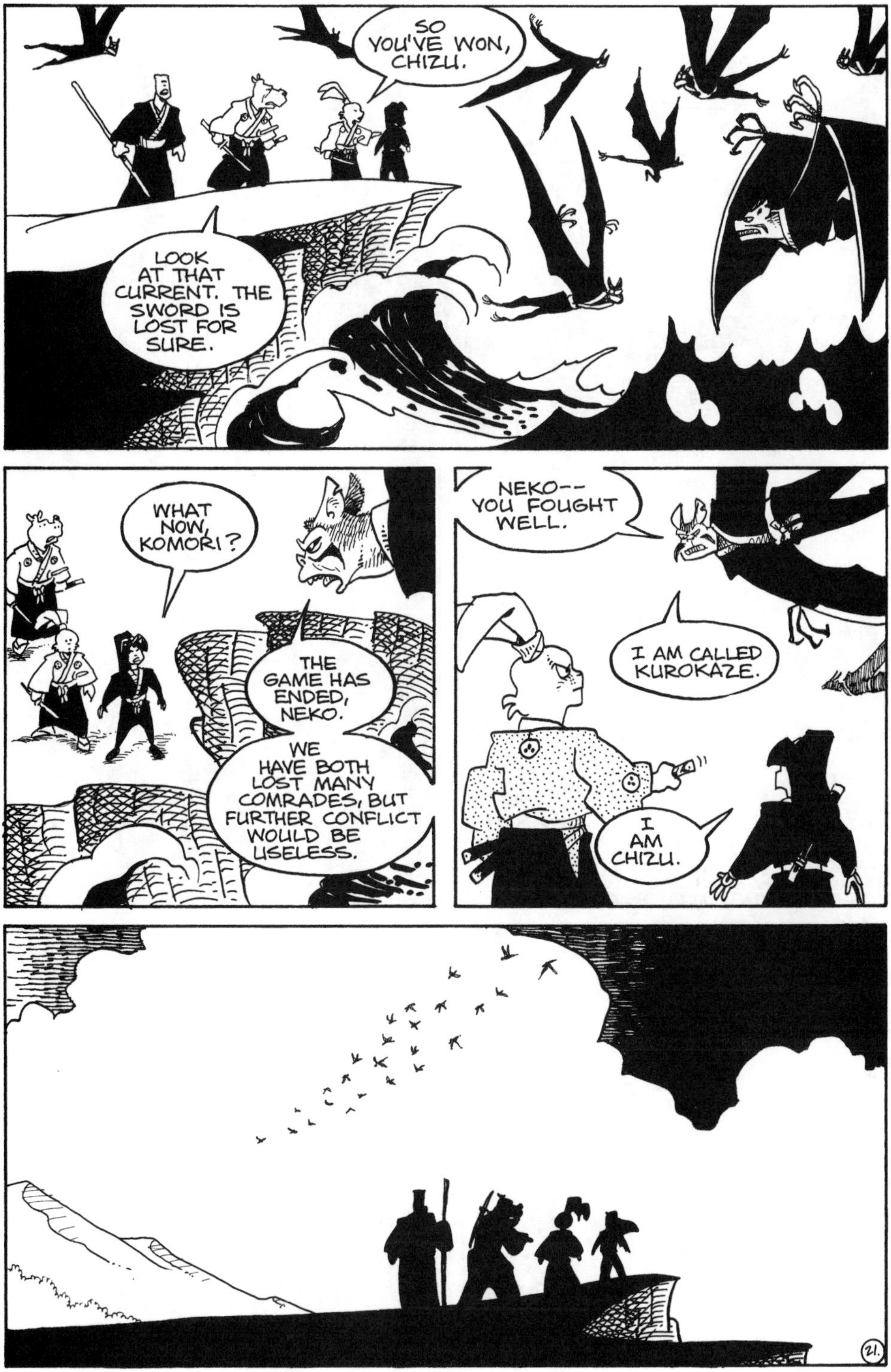
SO YOU'VE WON, CHIZU.
LOOK AT THAT CURRENT. THE SWORD IS LOST FOR SURE.
WHAT NOW, KOMORI?
THE GAME HAS ENDED, NEKO.
WE HAVE BOTH LOST MANY COMRADES, BUT FURTHER CONFLICT WOULD BE USELESS.
NEKO-- YOU FOUGHT WELL.
I AM CALLED KUROKAZE.
I AM CHIZU.
21.

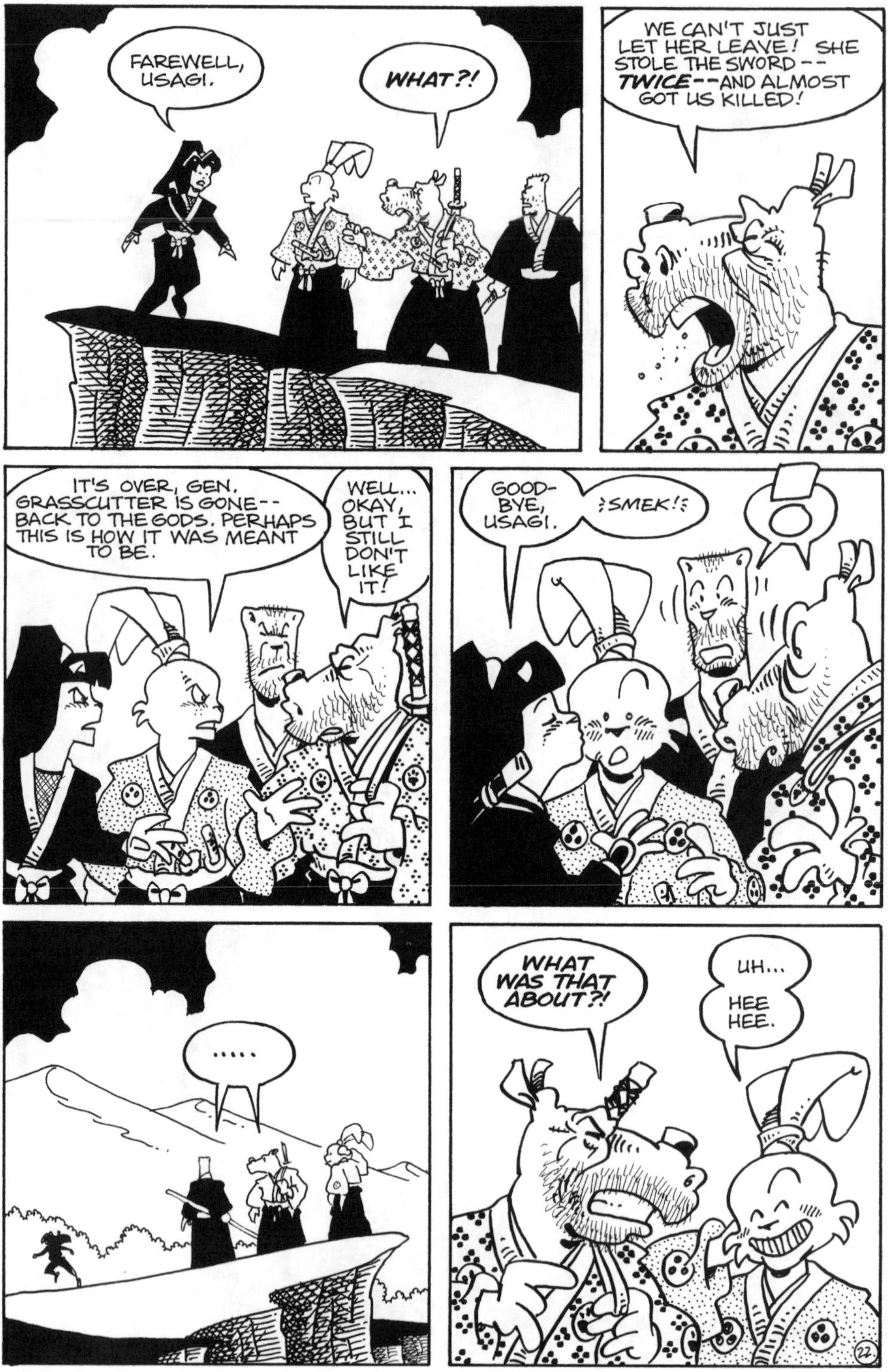
FAREWELL, USAGI.
WHAT?!
WE CAN'T JUST LET HER LEAVE! SHE STOLE THE SWORD -- TWICE -- AND ALMOST GOT US KILLED!
IT'S OVER, GEN. GRASSCUTTER IS GONE-- BACK TO THE GODS. PERHAPS THIS IS HOW IT WAS MEANT TO BE.
WELL... OKAY, BUT I STILL DON'T LIKE IT!
GOOD-BYE, USAGI.
SMEK!
!
.....
WHAT WAS THAT ABOUT?!
UH...
HEE HEE.
22

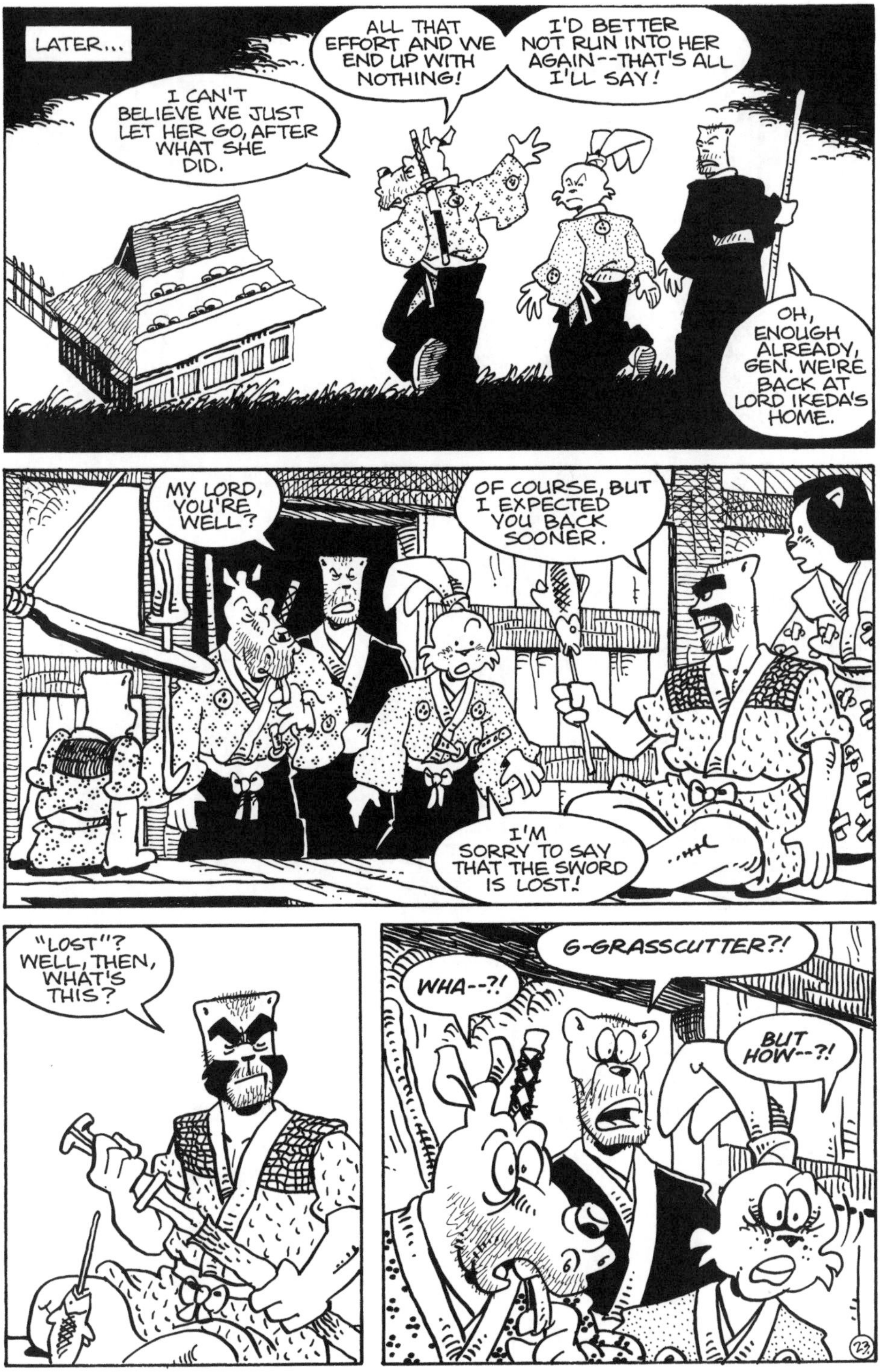
LATER...
I CAN'T BELIEVE WE JUST LET HER GO, AFTER WHAT SHE DID.
ALL THAT EFFORT AND WE END UP WITH NOTHING!
I'D BETTER NOT RUN INTO HER AGAIN--THAT'S ALL I'LL SAY!
OH, ENOUGH ALREADY, GEN. WE'RE BACK AT LORD IKEDA'S HOME.
MY LORD, YOU'RE WELL?
OF COURSE, BUT I EXPECTED YOU BACK SOONER.
I'M SORRY TO SAY THAT THE SWORD IS LOST!
"LOST"? WELL, THEN, WHAT'S THIS?
WHA--?!
G-GRASSCUTTER?!
BUT HOW--?!
23

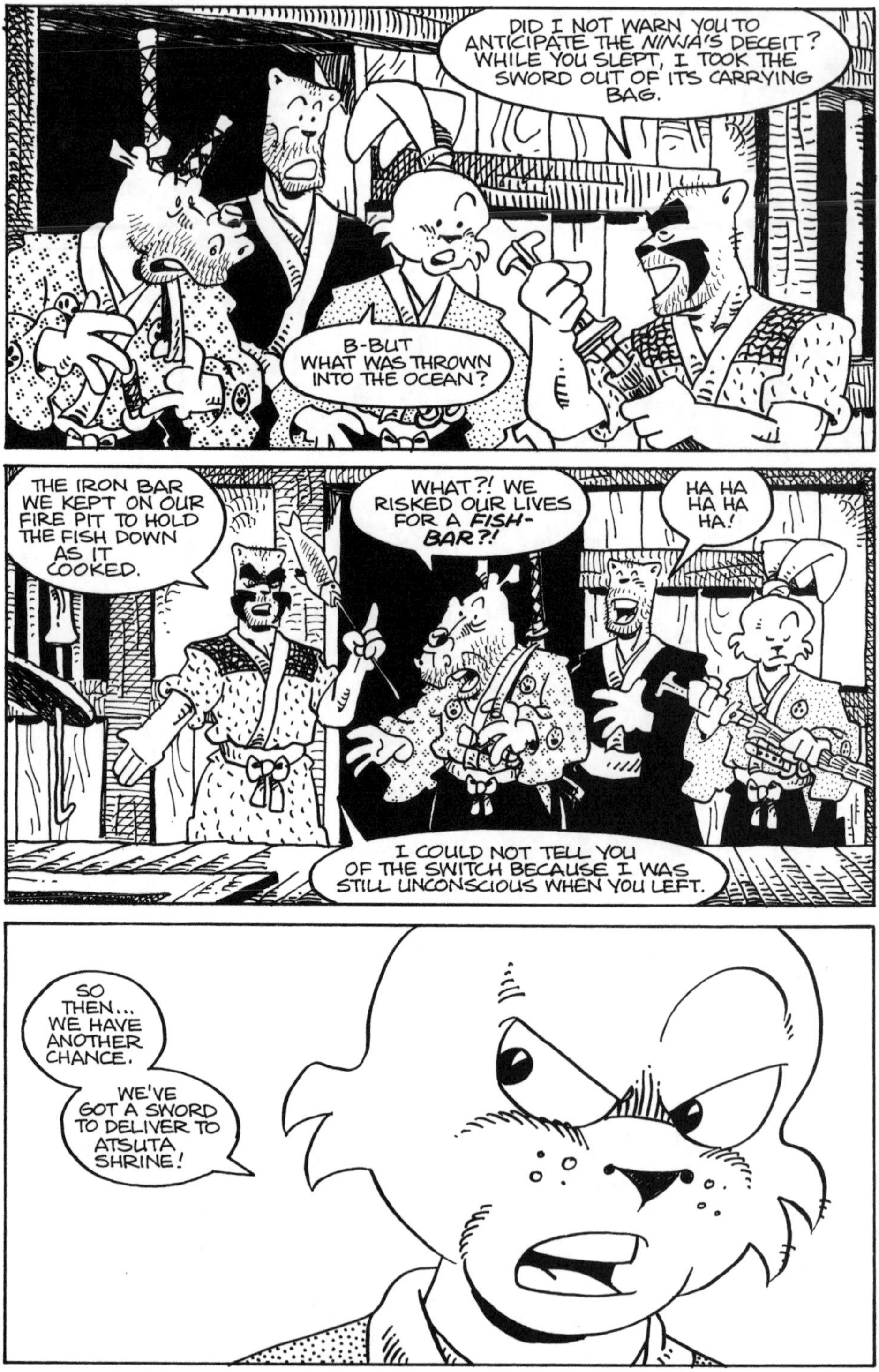
DID I NOT WARN YOU TO ANTICIPATE THE NINJA'S DECEIT? WHILE YOU SLEPT, I TOOK THE SWORD OUT OF ITS CARRYING BAG.
B-BUT WHAT WAS THROWN INTO THE OCEAN?
THE IRON BAR WE KEPT ON OUR FIRE PIT TO HOLD THE FISH DOWN AS IT COOKED.
WHAT?! WE RISKED OUR LIVES FOR A FISH-BAR?!
HA HA HA HA HA!
I COULD NOT TELL YOU OF THE SWITCH BECAUSE I WAS STILL UNCONSCIOUS WHEN YOU LEFT.
SO THEN... WE HAVE ANOTHER CHANCE.
WE'VE GOT A SWORD TO DELIVER TO ATSUTA SHRINE!

END OF CHAPTER 5

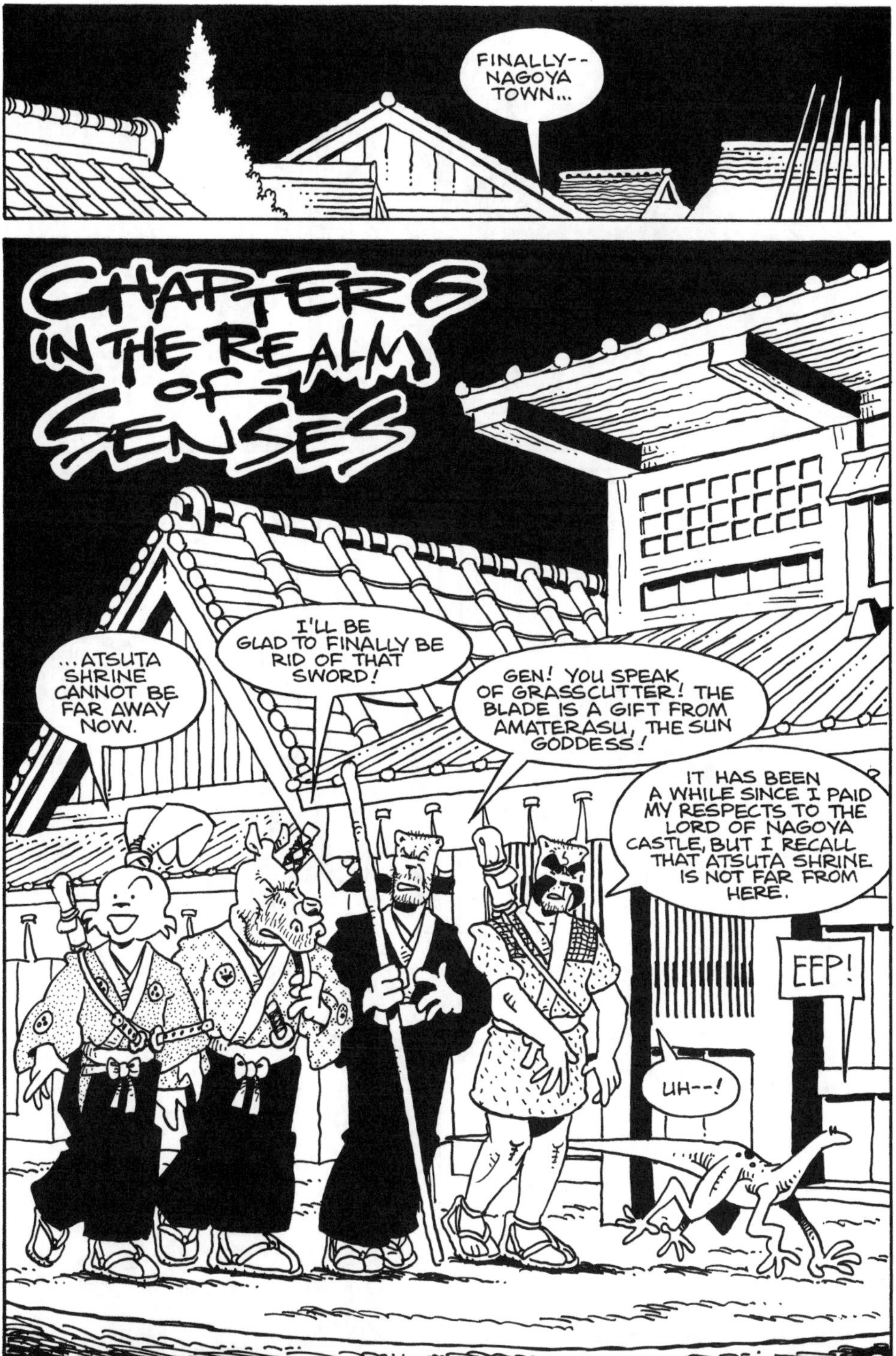
FINALLY--
NAGOYA
TOWN...
CHAPTER 6
IN THE REALM
OF
SENSES
...ATSUTA
SHRINE
CANNOT BE
FAR AWAY
NOW.
I'LL BE
GLAD TO FINALLY BE
RID OF THAT
SWORD!
GEN! YOU SPEAK
OF GRASSCUTTER! THE
BLADE IS A GIFT FROM
AMATERASU, THE SUN
GODDESS!
IT HAS BEEN
A WHILE SINCE I PAID
MY RESPECTS TO THE
LORD OF NAGOYA
CASTLE, BUT I RECALL
THAT ATSUTA SHRINE
IS NOT FAR FROM
HERE.
EEP!
UH--!
1.

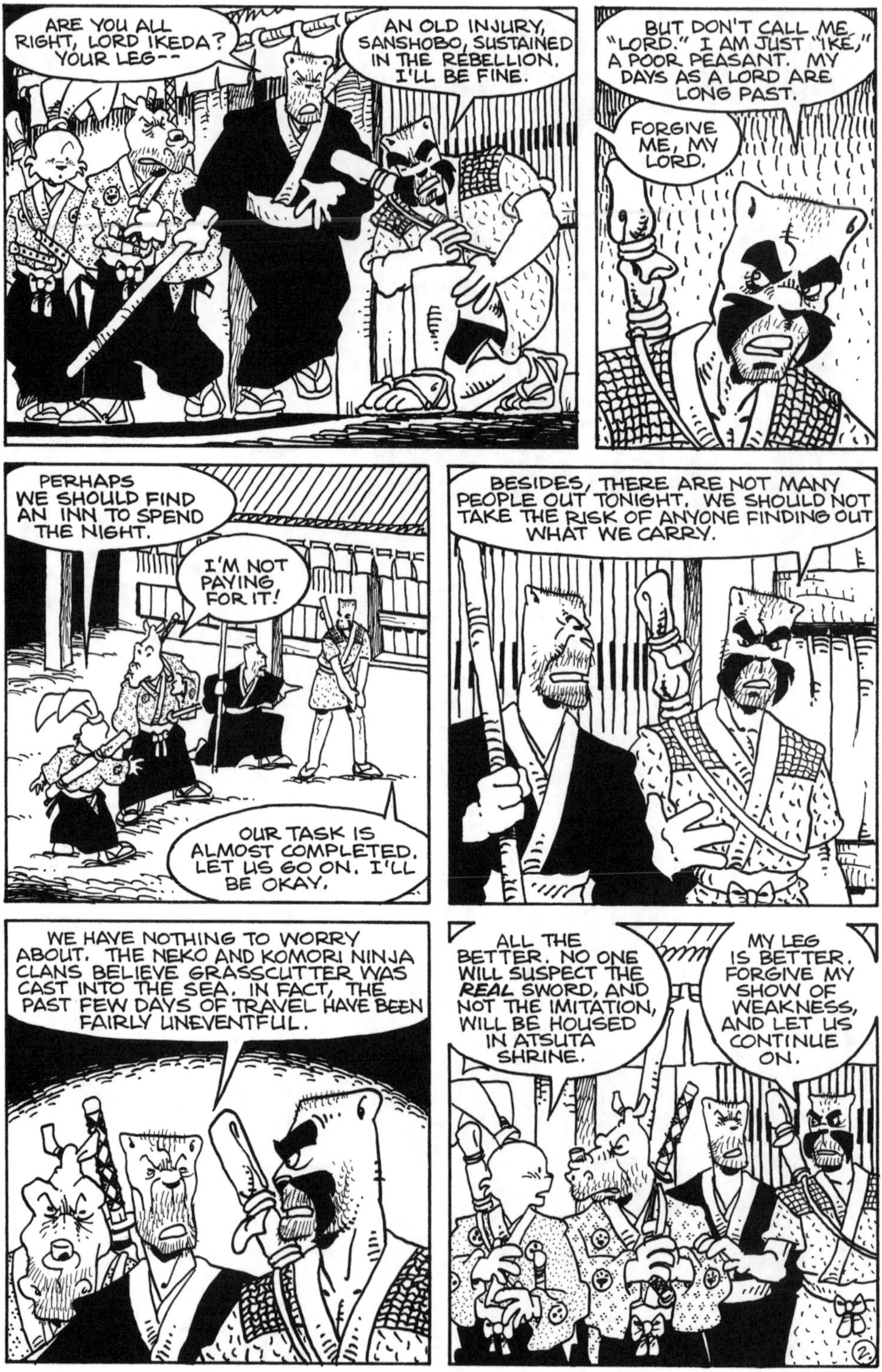
ARE YOU ALL RIGHT, LORD IKEDA? YOUR LEG--
AN OLD INJURY, SANSHOBO, SUSTAINED IN THE REBELLION. I'LL BE FINE.
BUT DON'T CALL ME "LORD." I AM JUST "IKE," A POOR PEASANT. MY DAYS AS A LORD ARE LONG PAST.
FORGIVE ME, MY LORD.
PERHAPS WE SHOULD FIND AN INN TO SPEND THE NIGHT.
I'M NOT PAYING FOR IT!
OUR TASK IS ALMOST COMPLETED. LET US GO ON. I'LL BE OKAY.
BESIDES, THERE ARE NOT MANY PEOPLE OUT TONIGHT. WE SHOULD NOT TAKE THE RISK OF ANYONE FINDING OUT WHAT WE CARRY.
WE HAVE NOTHING TO WORRY ABOUT. THE NEKO AND KOMORI NINJA CLANS BELIEVE GRASSCUTTER WAS CAST INTO THE SEA. IN FACT, THE PAST FEW DAYS OF TRAVEL HAVE BEEN FAIRLY UNEVENTFUL.
ALL THE BETTER. NO ONE WILL SUSPECT THE REAL SWORD, AND NOT THE IMITATION, WILL BE HOUSED IN ATSUTA SHRINE.
MY LEG IS BETTER. FORGIVE MY SHOW OF WEAKNESS, AND LET US CONTINUE ON.
2

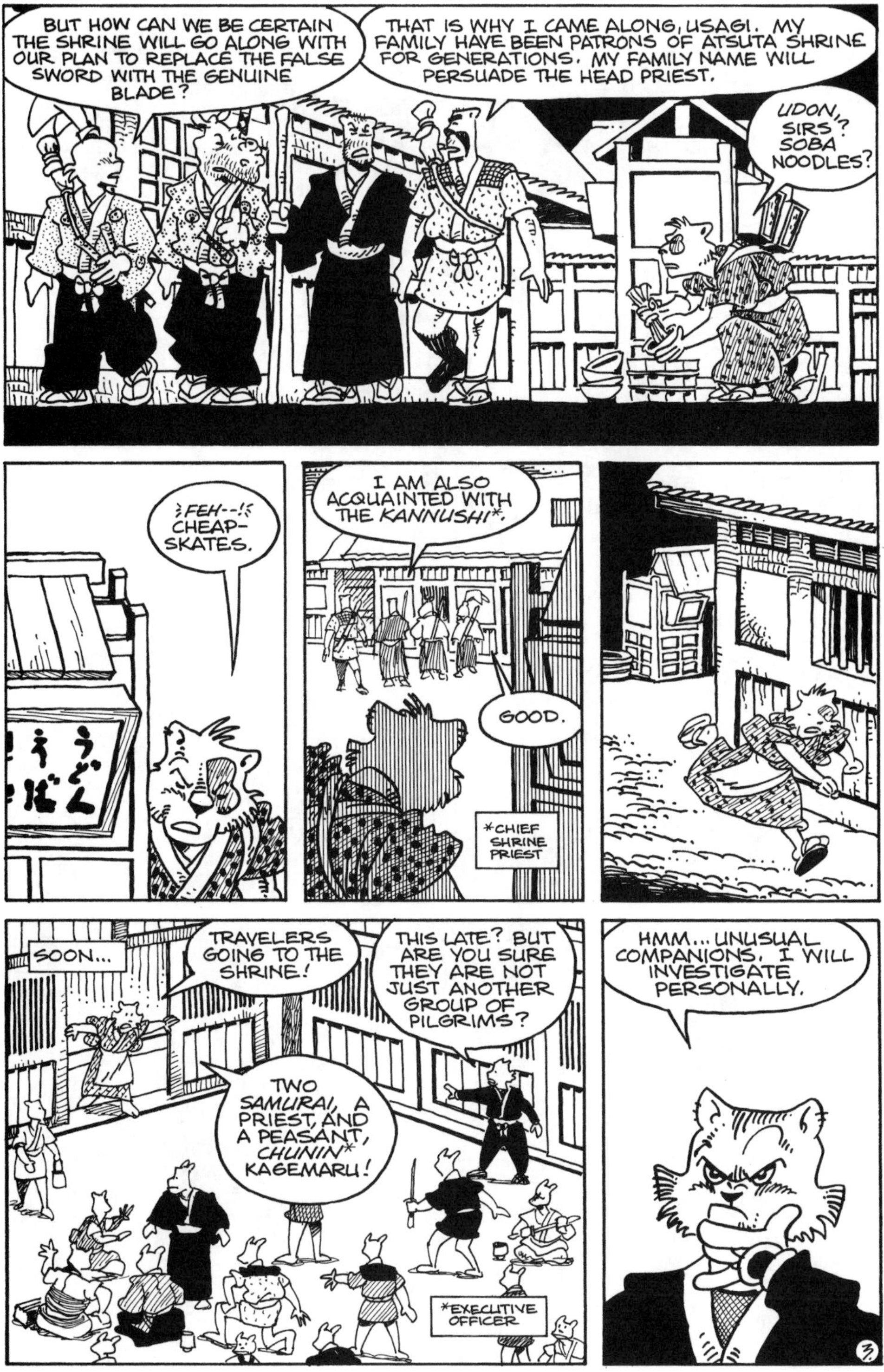
BUT HOW CAN WE BE CERTAIN THE SHRINE WILL GO ALONG WITH OUR PLAN TO REPLACE THE FALSE SWORD WITH THE GENUINE BLADE?
THAT IS WHY I CAME ALONG, USAGI. MY FAMILY HAVE BEEN PATRONS OF ATSUTA SHRINE FOR GENERATIONS. MY FAMILY NAME WILL PERSUADE THE HEAD PRIEST.
UDON, SIRS? SOBA NOODLES?
FEH--! CHEAPSKATES.
I AM ALSO ACQUAINTED WITH THE KANNUSHI*.
GOOD.
*CHIEF SHRINE PRIEST
SOON...
TRAVELERS GOING TO THE SHRINE!
THIS LATE? BUT ARE YOU SURE THEY ARE NOT JUST ANOTHER GROUP OF PILGRIMS?
TWO SAMURAI, A PRIEST, AND A PEASANT, CHUNIN* KAGEMARU!
*EXECUTIVE OFFICER
HMM... UNUSUAL COMPANIONS. I WILL INVESTIGATE PERSONALLY.
3.

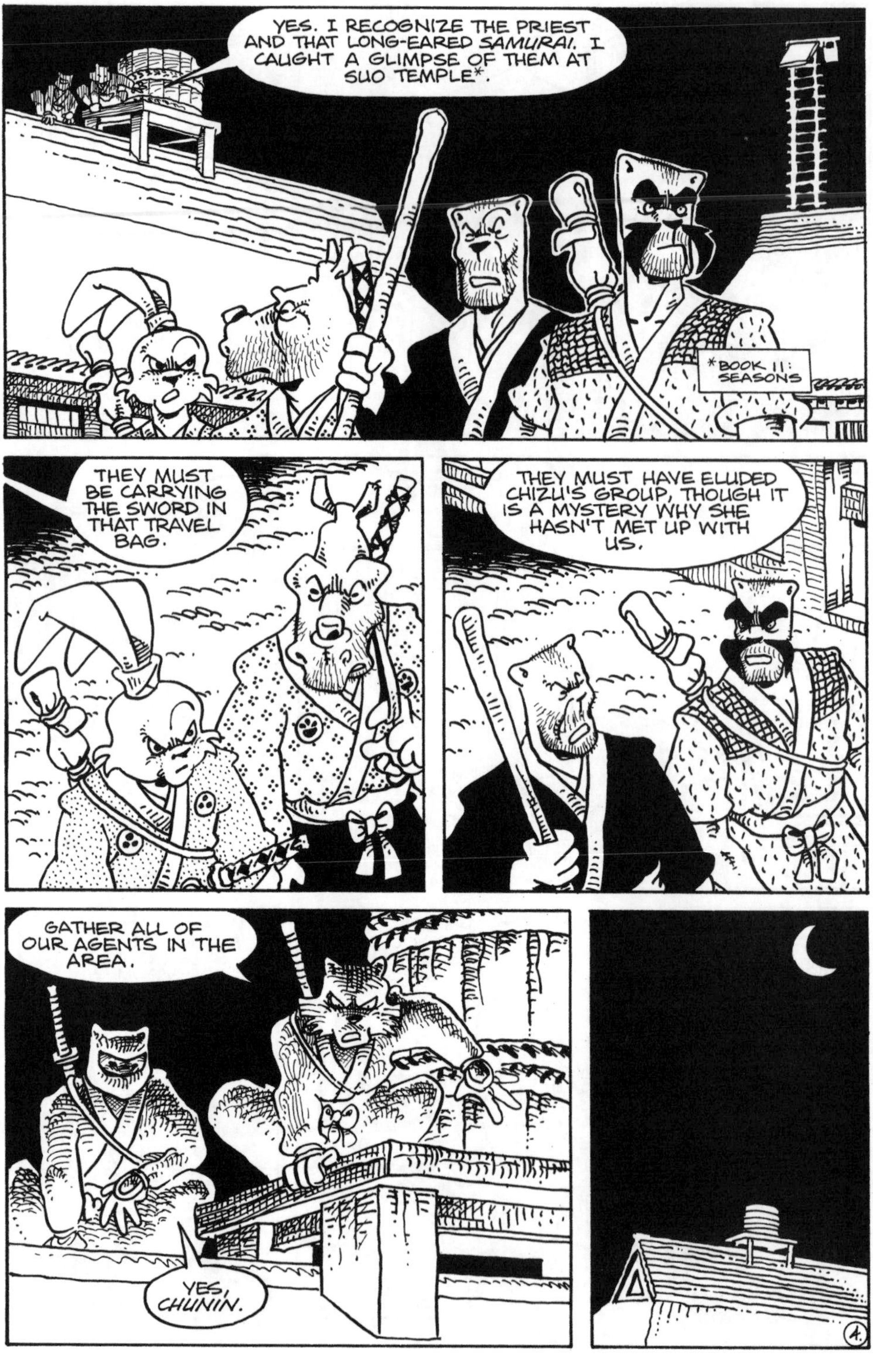
YES. I RECOGNIZE THE PRIEST AND THAT LONG-EARED SAMURAI. I CAUGHT A GLIMPSE OF THEM AT SUO TEMPLE*.
*BOOK 11: SEASONS
THEY MUST BE CARRYING THE SWORD IN THAT TRAVEL BAG.
THEY MUST HAVE ELUDED CHIZU'S GROUP, THOUGH IT IS A MYSTERY WHY SHE HASN'T MET UP WITH US.
GATHER ALL OF OUR AGENTS IN THE AREA.
YES, CHUNIN.

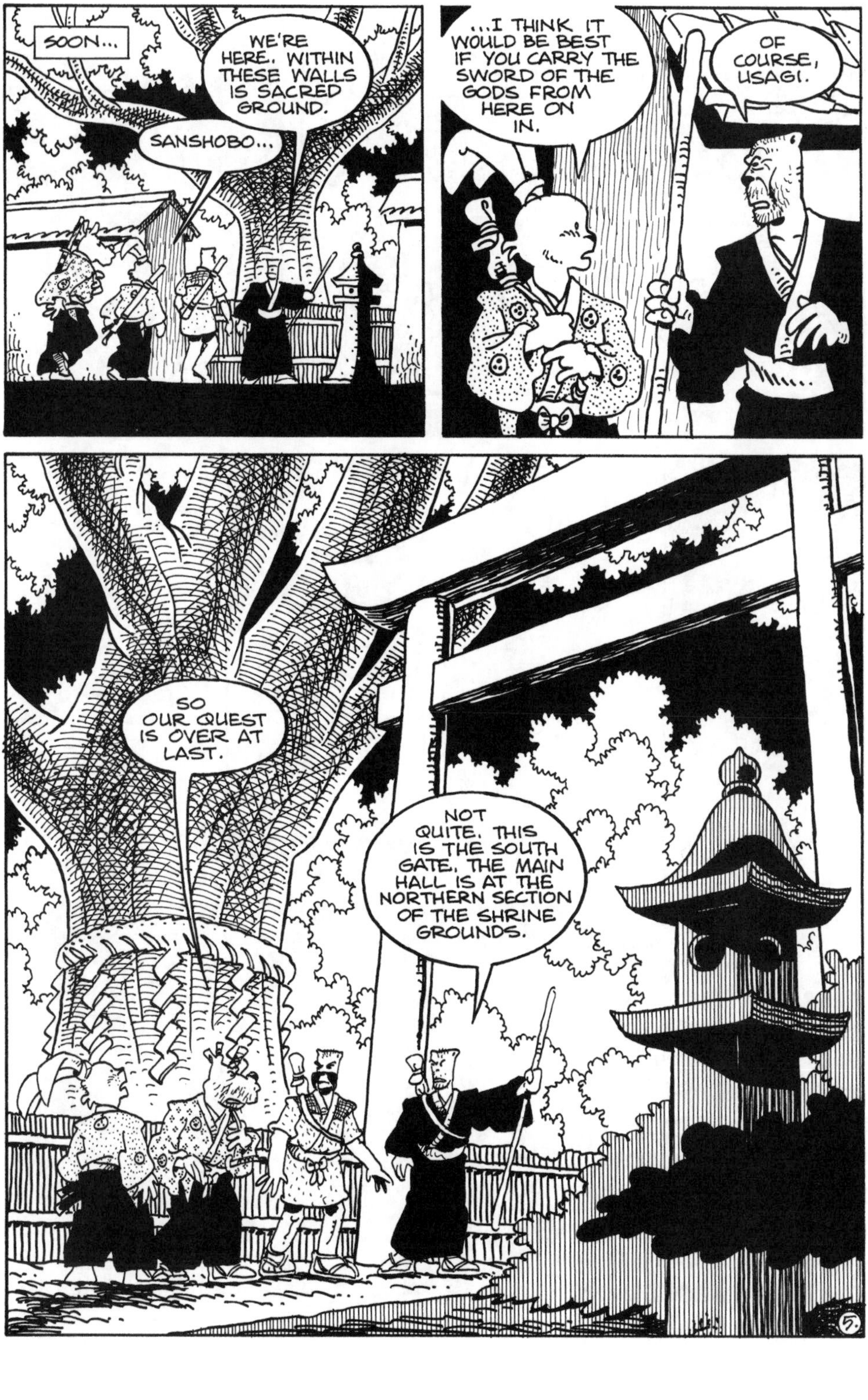
SOON...
SANSHOBO...
WE'RE HERE. WITHIN THESE WALLS IS SACRED GROUND.
...I THINK IT WOULD BE BEST IF YOU CARRY THE SWORD OF THE GODS FROM HERE ON IN.
OF COURSE, USAGI.
SO OUR QUEST IS OVER AT LAST.
NOT QUITE. THIS IS THE SOUTH GATE. THE MAIN HALL IS AT THE NORTHERN SECTION OF THE SHRINE GROUNDS.
5.

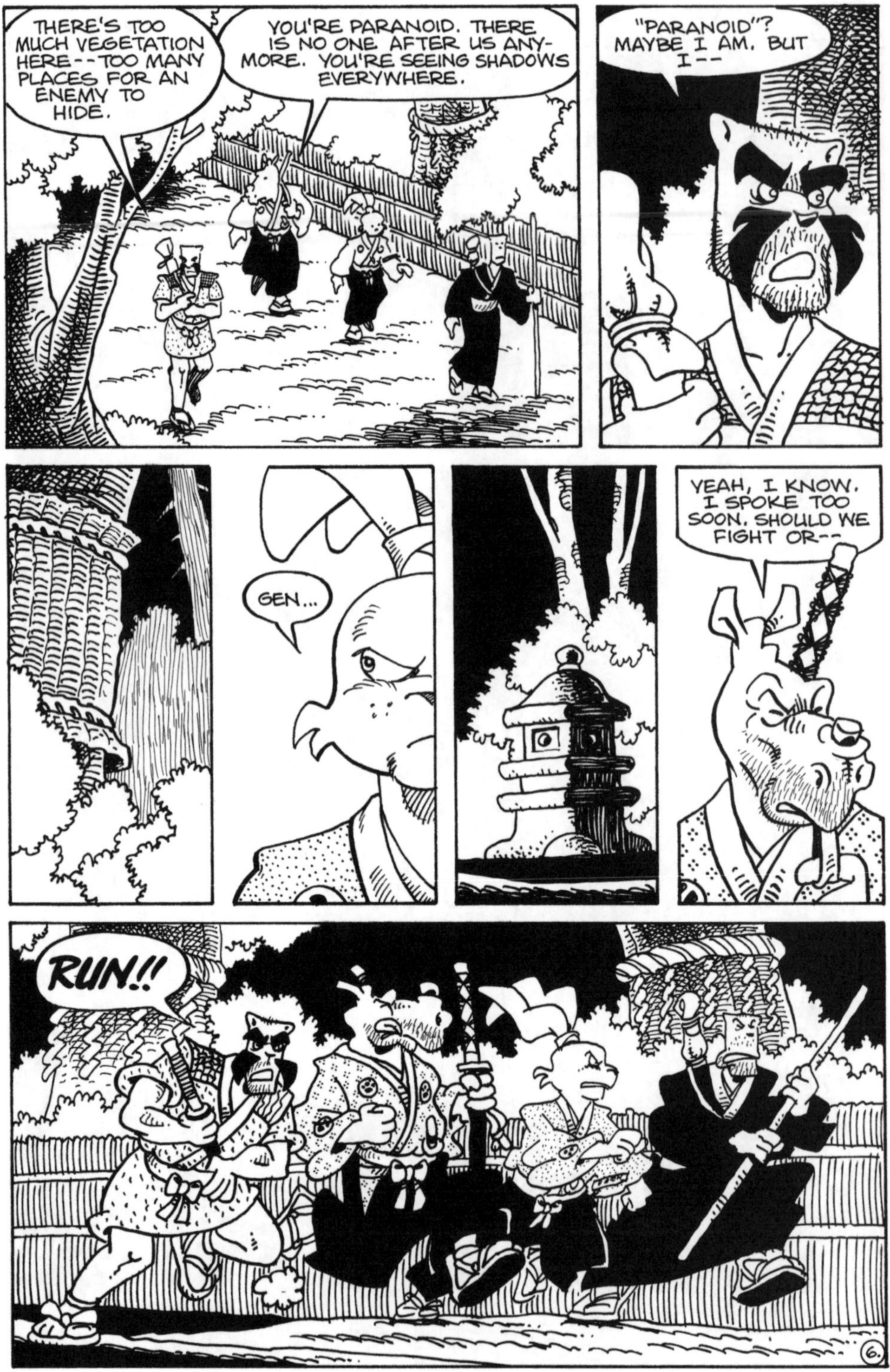
THERE'S TOO MUCH VEGETATION HERE--TOO MANY PLACES FOR AN ENEMY TO HIDE.
YOU'RE PARANOID. THERE IS NO ONE AFTER US ANY-MORE. YOU'RE SEEING SHADOWS EVERYWHERE.
"PARANOID"? MAYBE I AM. BUT I--
GEN...
YEAH, I KNOW. I SPOKE TOO SOON. SHOULD WE FIGHT OR--
RUN!!
6.

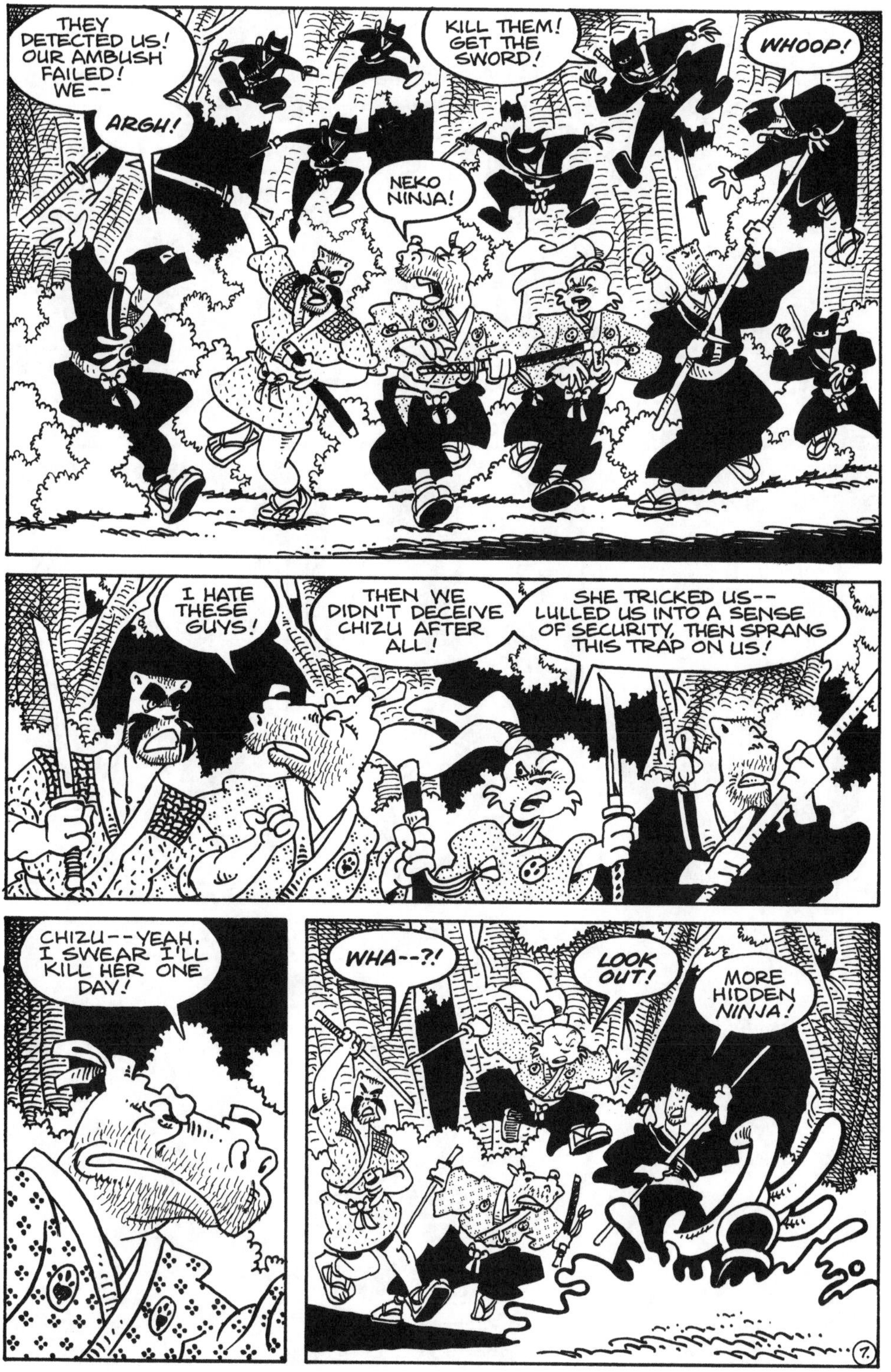
THEY DETECTED US! OUR AMBUSH FAILED! WE--
ARGH!
KILL THEM! GET THE SWORD!
WHOOP!
NEKO NINJA!
I HATE THESE GUYS!
THEN WE DIDN'T DECEIVE CHIZU AFTER ALL!
SHE TRICKED US-- LULLED US INTO A SENSE OF SECURITY, THEN SPRANG THIS TRAP ON US!
CHIZU--YEAH. I SWEAR I'LL KILL HER ONE DAY!
WHA--?!
LOOK OUT!
MORE HIDDEN NINJA!
7.

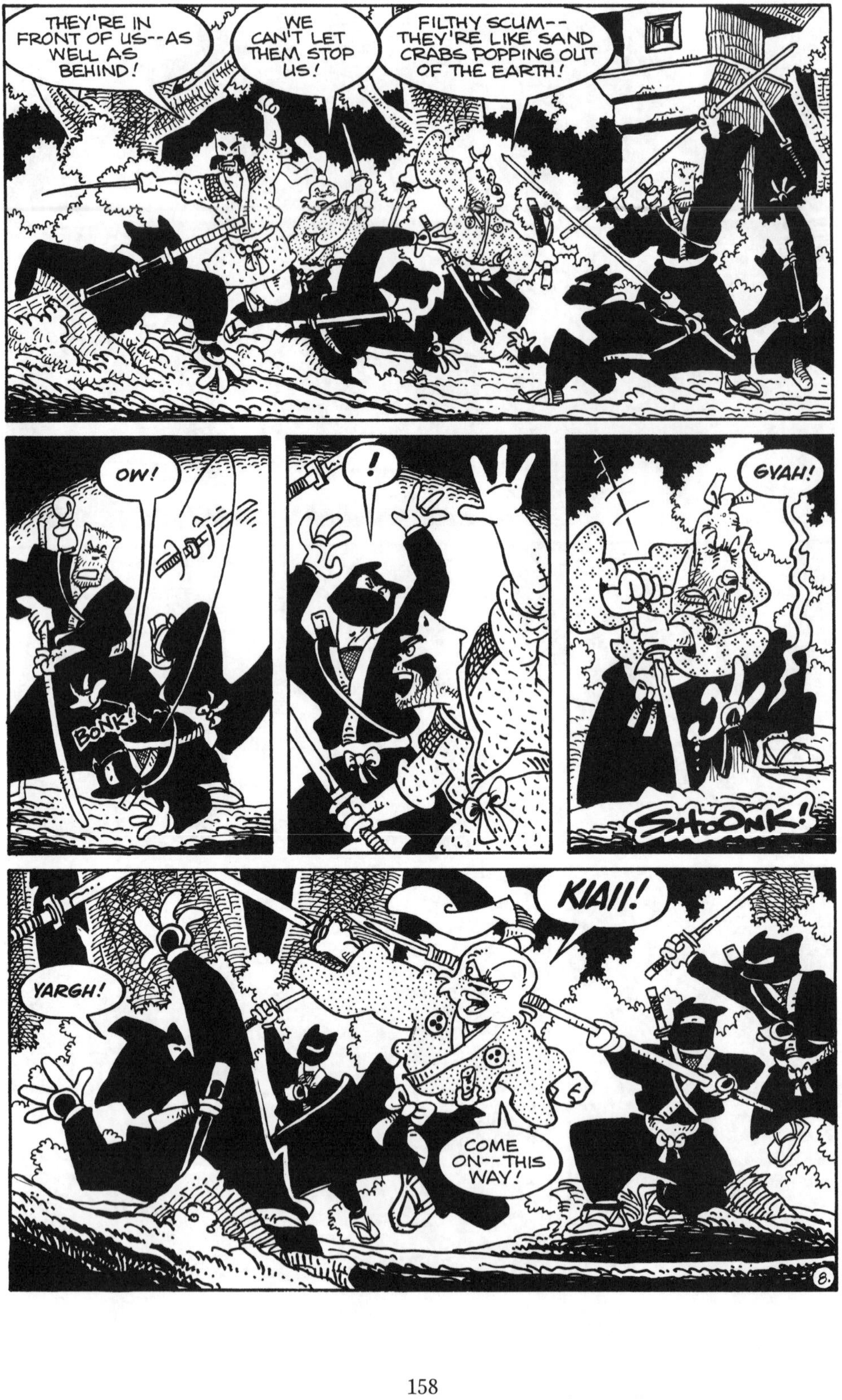

THEY'RE IN FRONT OF US--AS WELL AS BEHIND!
WE CAN'T LET THEM STOP US!
FILTHY SCUM-- THEY'RE LIKE SAND CRABS POPPING OUT OF THE EARTH!
OW!
BONK!
!
GYAH!
SHOONK!
KIAII!
YARGH!
COME ON--THIS WAY!
8.

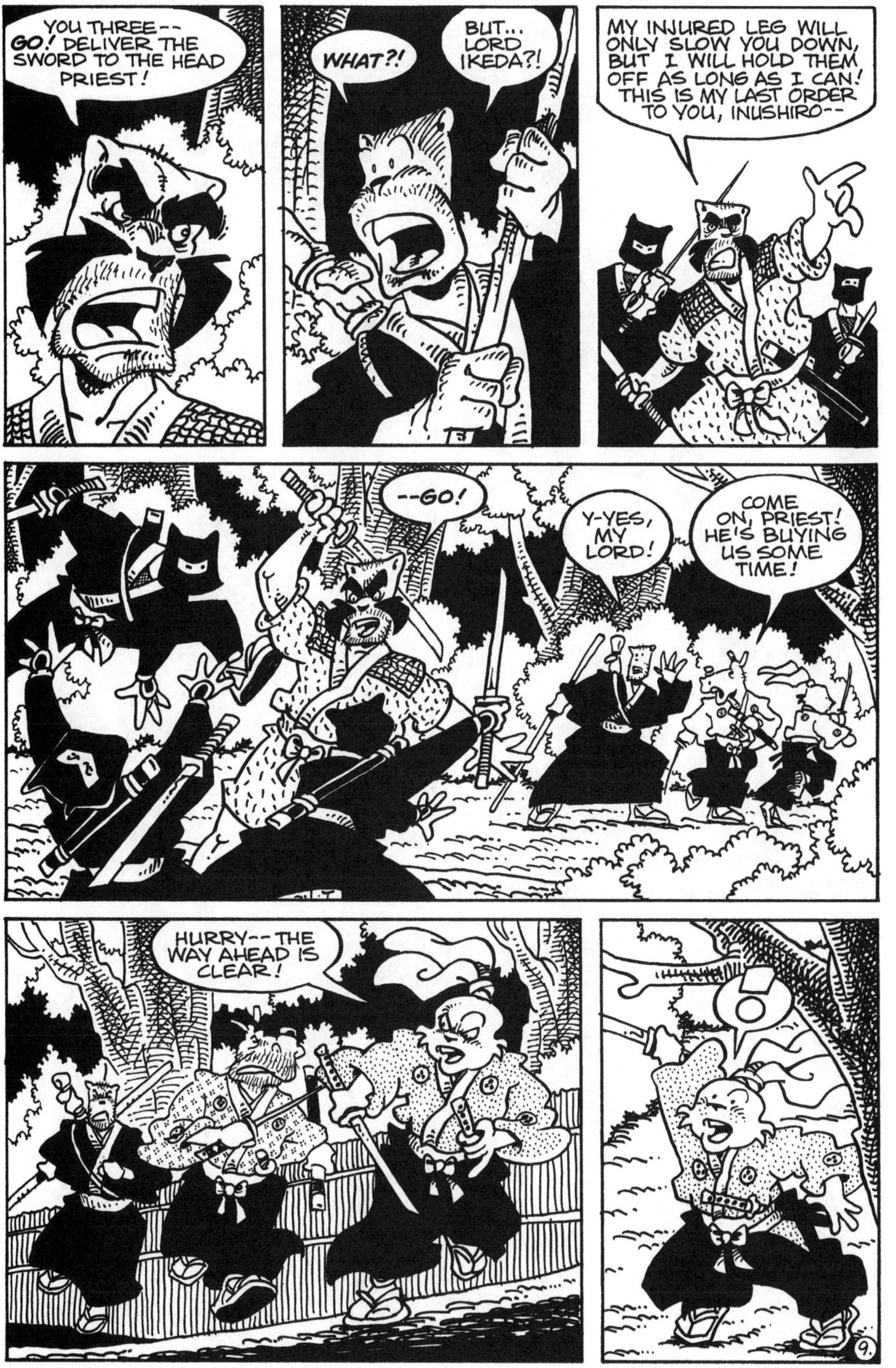

YOU THREE-- GO! DELIVER THE SWORD TO THE HEAD PRIEST!
WHAT?!
BUT... LORD IKEDA?!
MY INJURED LEG WILL ONLY SLOW YOU DOWN, BUT I WILL HOLD THEM OFF AS LONG AS I CAN! THIS IS MY LAST ORDER TO YOU, INUSHIRO--
--GO!
Y-YES, MY LORD!
COME ON, PRIEST! HE'S BUYING US SOME TIME!
HURRY-- THE WAY AHEAD IS CLEAR!
!
9.

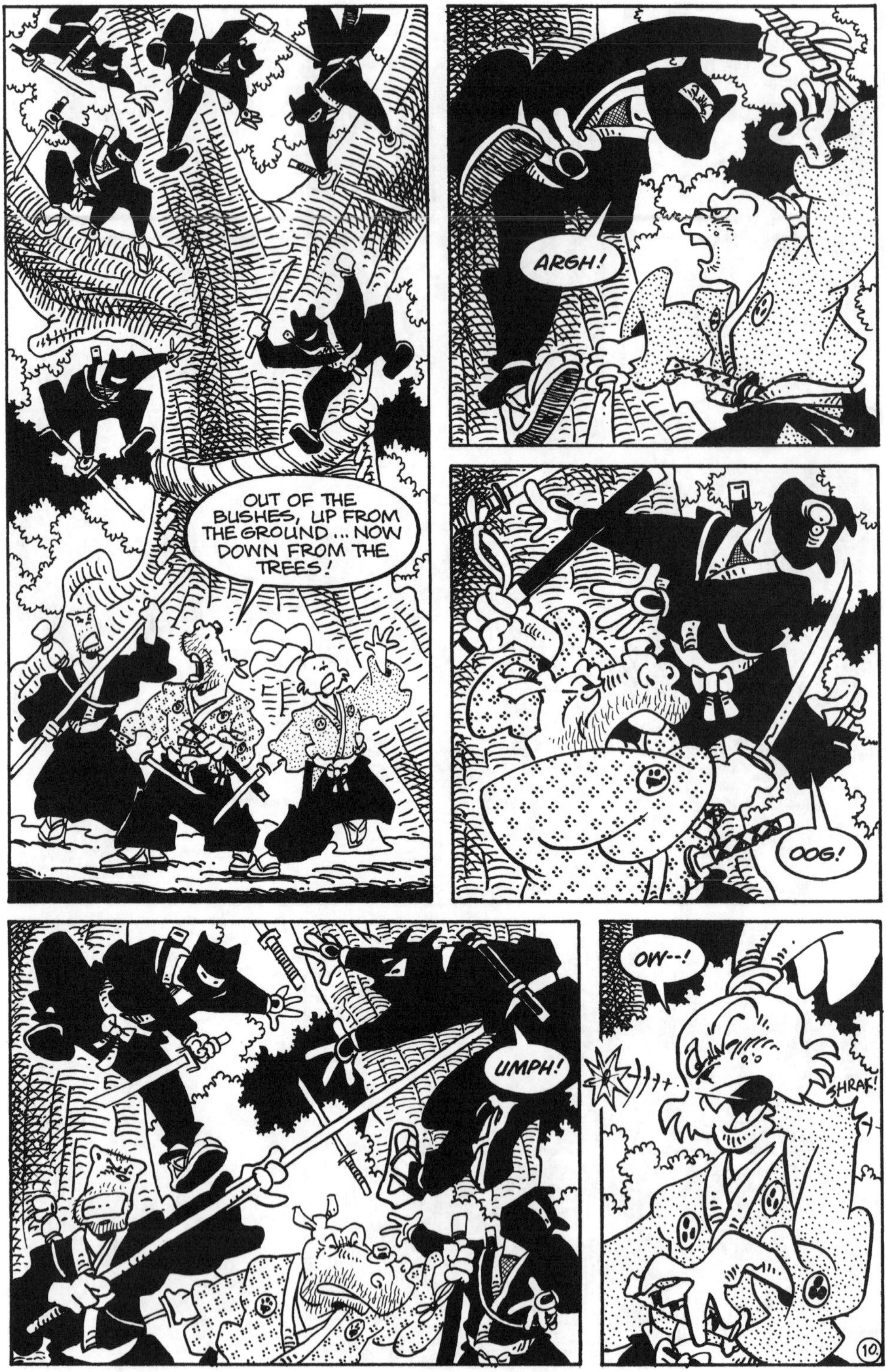
OUT OF THE BUSHES, UP FROM THE GROUND ... NOW DOWN FROM THE TREES!
ARGH!
OOG!
UMPH!
OW--!
SHRAK!
10.

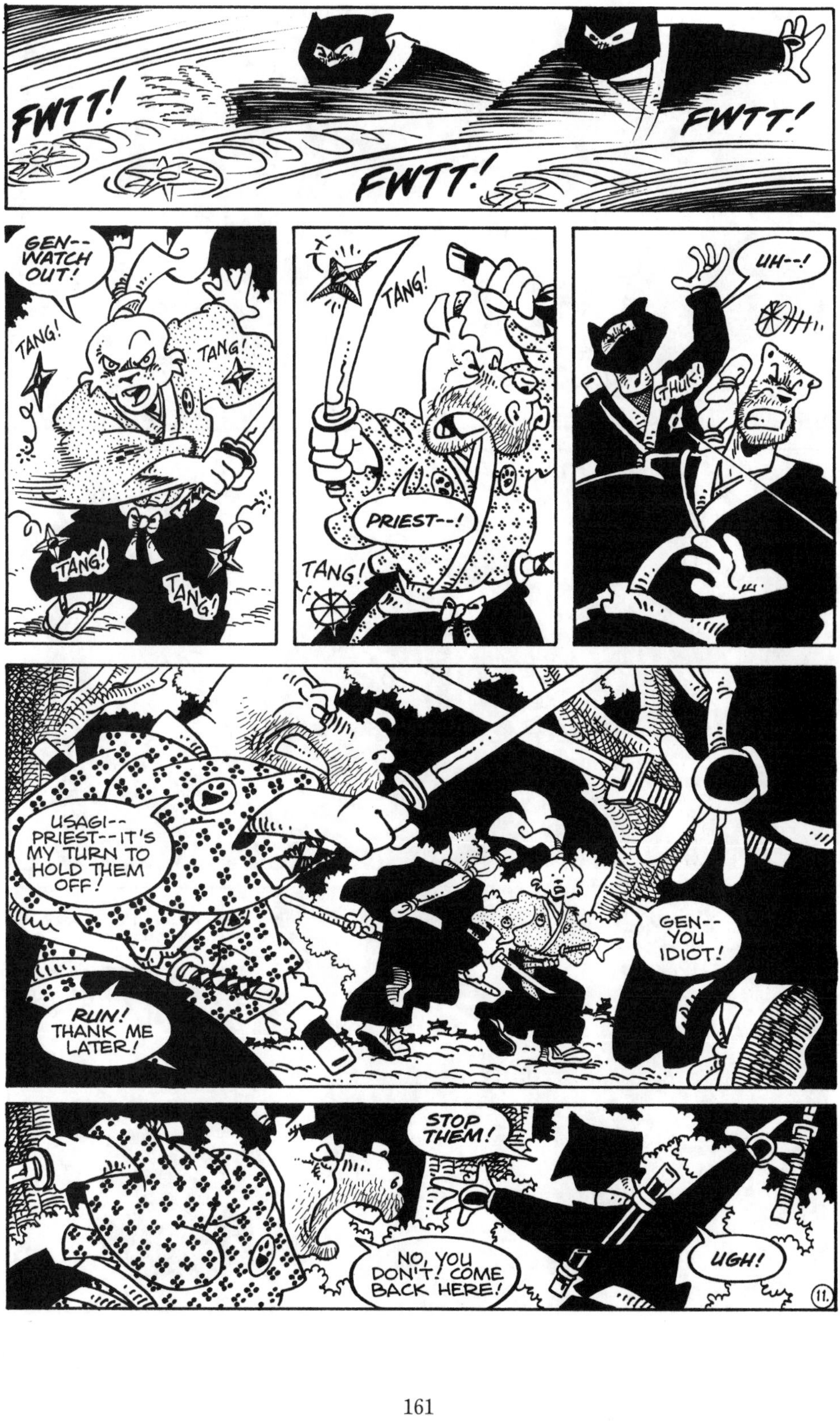
FWTT!
FWTT!
FWTT!
GEN--
WATCH
OUT!
TANG!
TANG!
TANG!
TANG!
TANG!
TANG!
PRIEST--!
TANG!
UH--!
THUK!
USAGI--
PRIEST--IT'S
MY TURN TO
HOLD THEM
OFF!
RUN!
THANK ME
LATER!
GEN--
YOU
IDIOT!
STOP
THEM!
NO, YOU
DON'T! COME
BACK HERE!
UGH!
11.

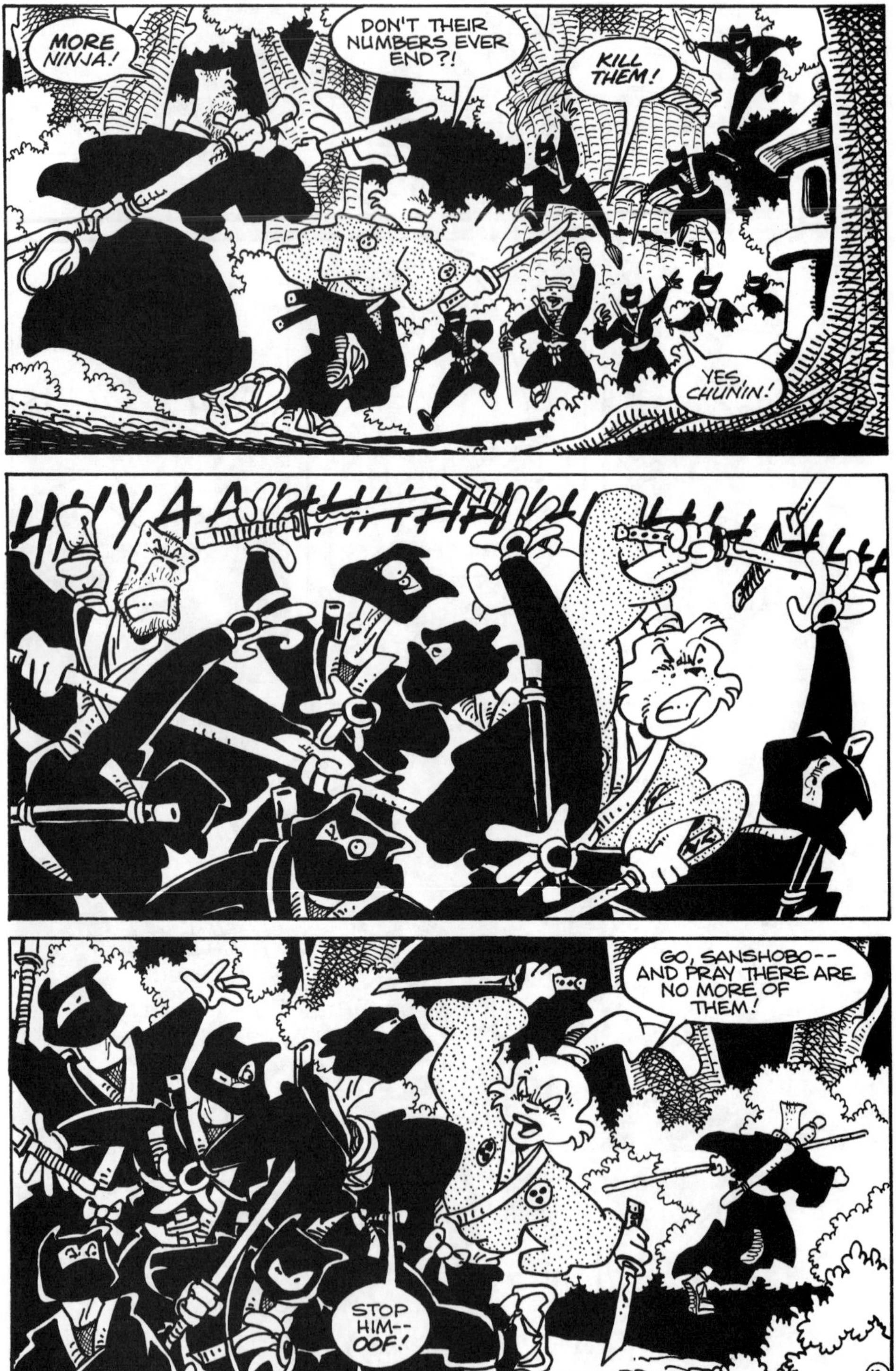
MORE NINJA!
DON'T THEIR NUMBERS EVER END?!
KILL THEM!
YES CHUNIN!
HIIYAAAHHHHHHHHHHHHHHHHHHHHA
GO, SANSHOBO-- AND PRAY THERE ARE NO MORE OF THEM!
STOP HIM-- OOF!
12.

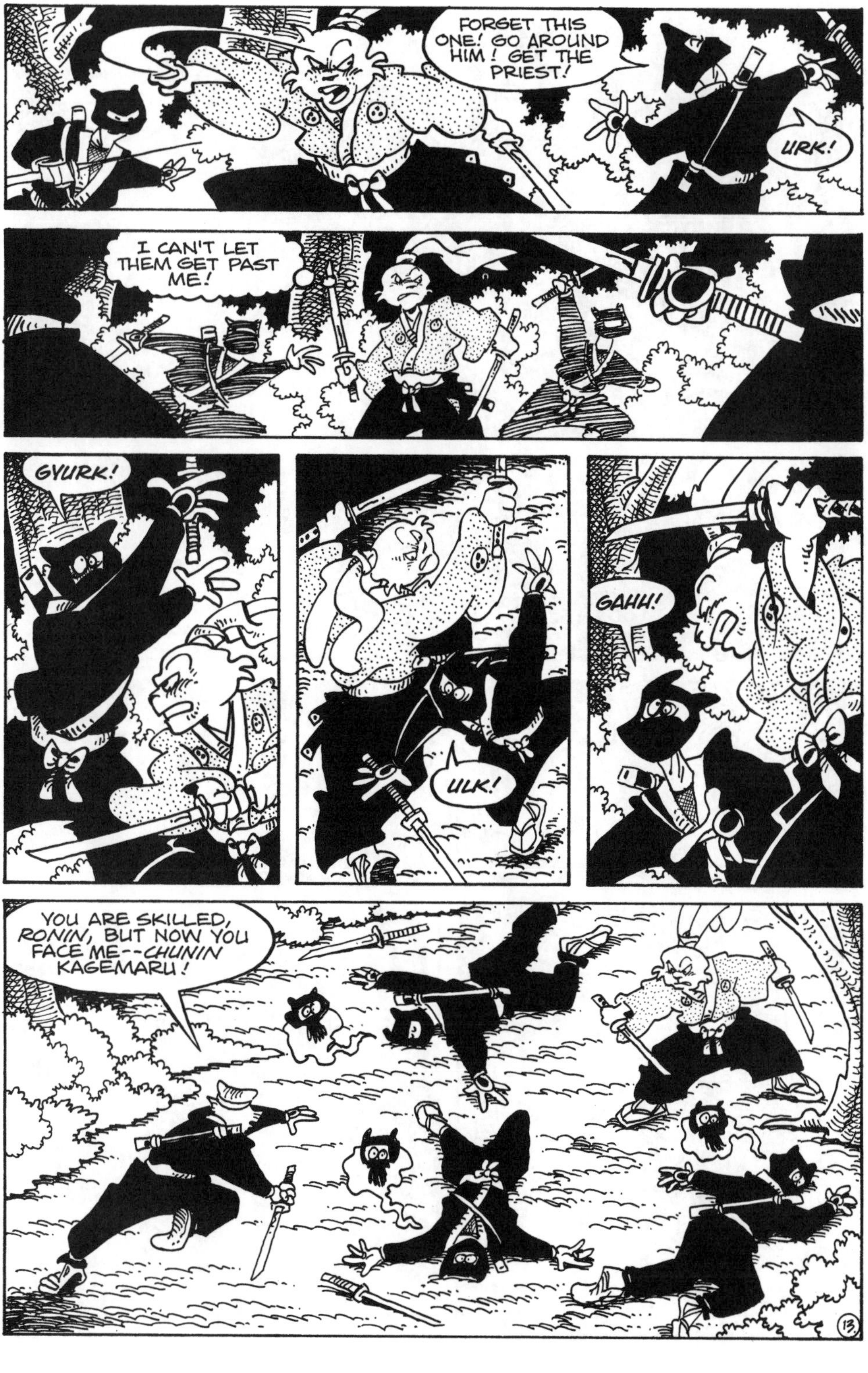
FORGET THIS ONE! GO AROUND HIM! GET THE PRIEST!
URK!
I CAN'T LET THEM GET PAST ME!
GYURK!
ULK!
GAHH!
YOU ARE SKILLED, RONIN, BUT NOW YOU FACE ME--CHUNIN KAGEMARU!
13

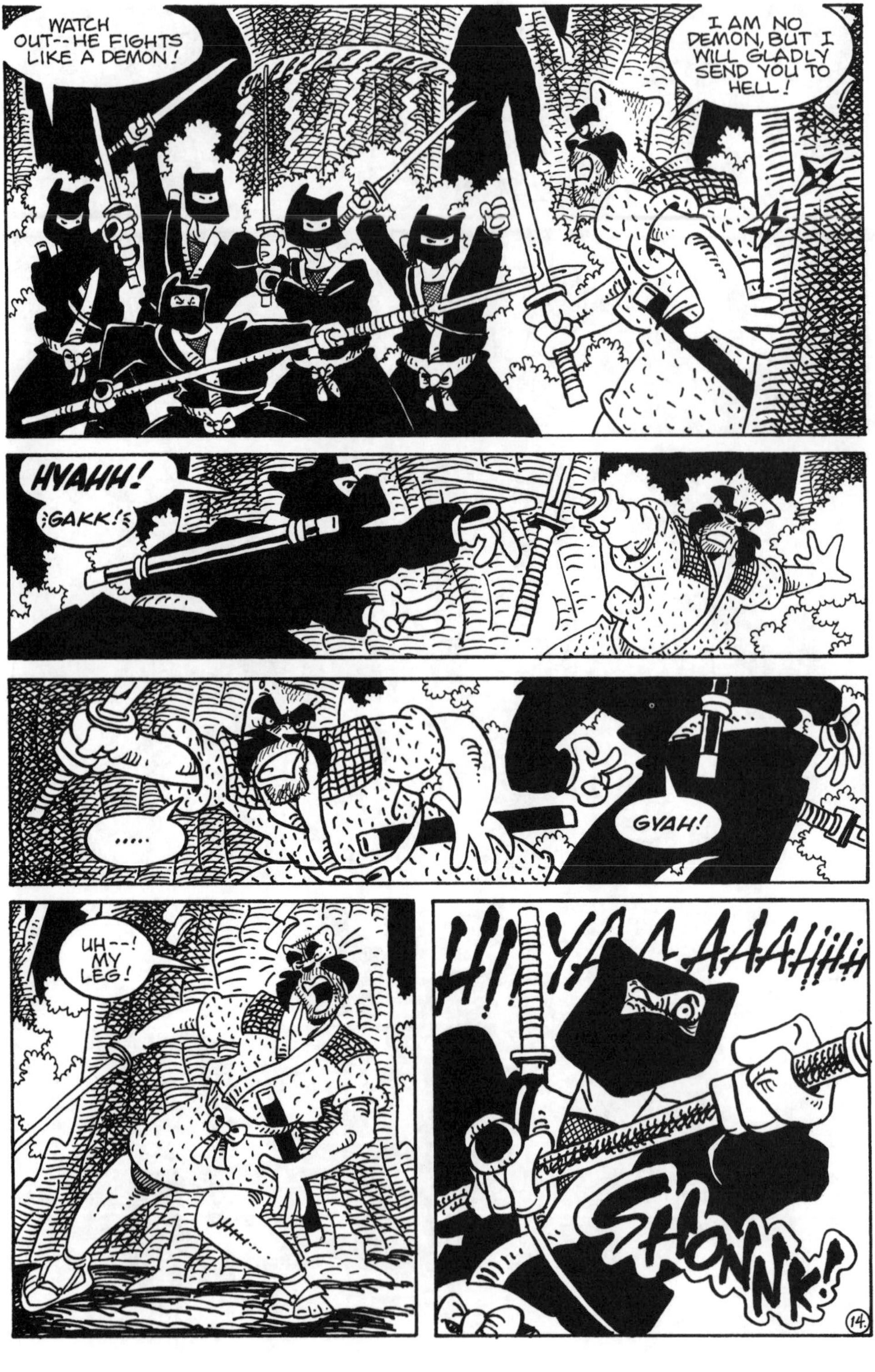

WATCH OUT--HE FIGHTS LIKE A DEMON!
I AM NO DEMON, BUT I WILL GLADLY SEND YOU TO HELL!
HYAHH!
¡GAKK!¡
.....
GYAH!
UH--! MY LEG!
HIIYAAAAAHHH!!
SHONNK!
14.

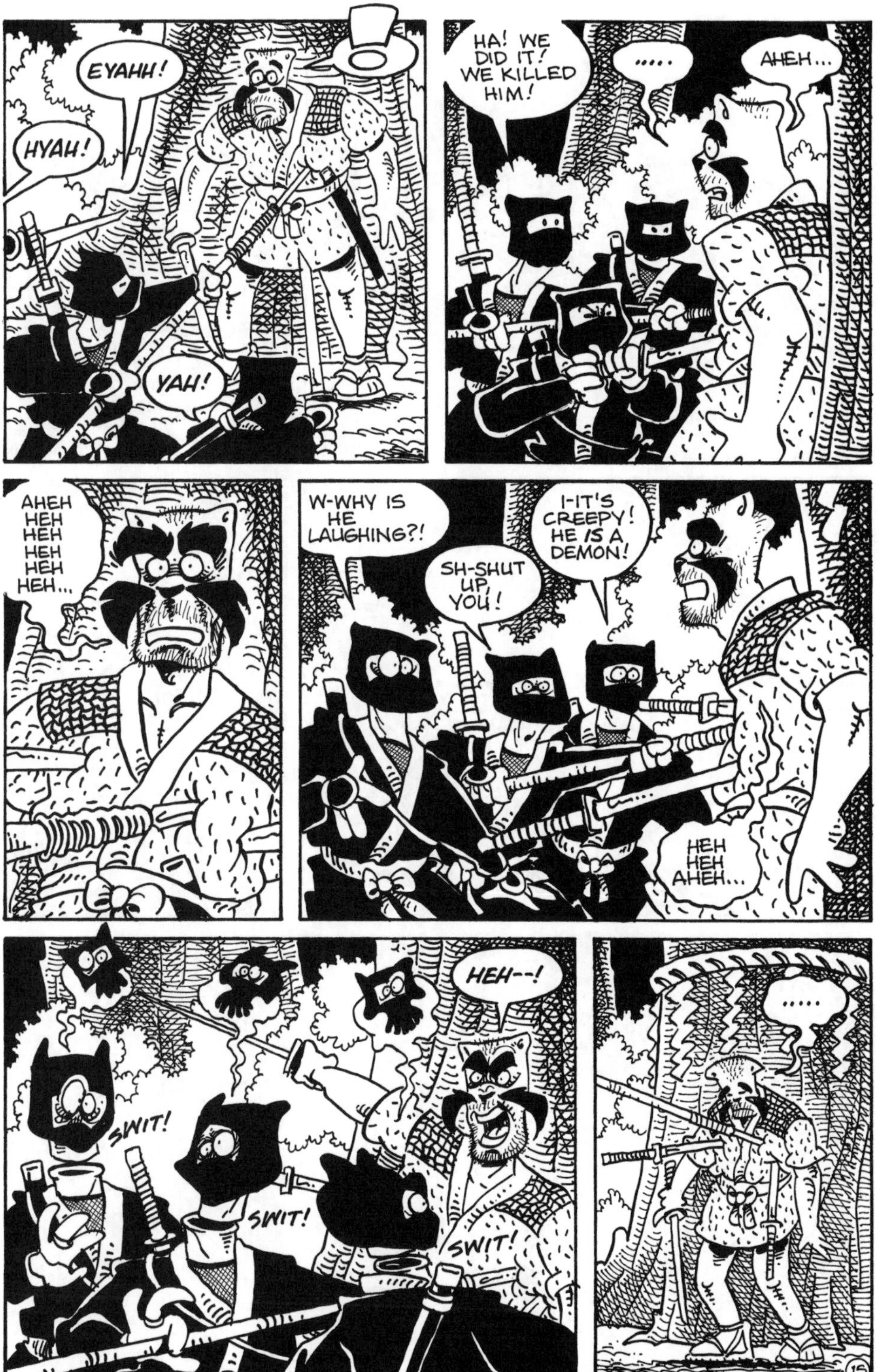
EYAHH!
HYAH!
YAH!
HA! WE DID IT! WE KILLED HIM!
.....
AHEH...
AHEH HEH HEH HEH HEH HEH...
W-WHY IS HE LAUGHING?!
I-IT'S CREEPY! HE IS A DEMON!
SH-SHUT UP YOU!
HEH HEH AHEH...
HEH--!
SWIT!
SWIT!
SWIT!
.....
15

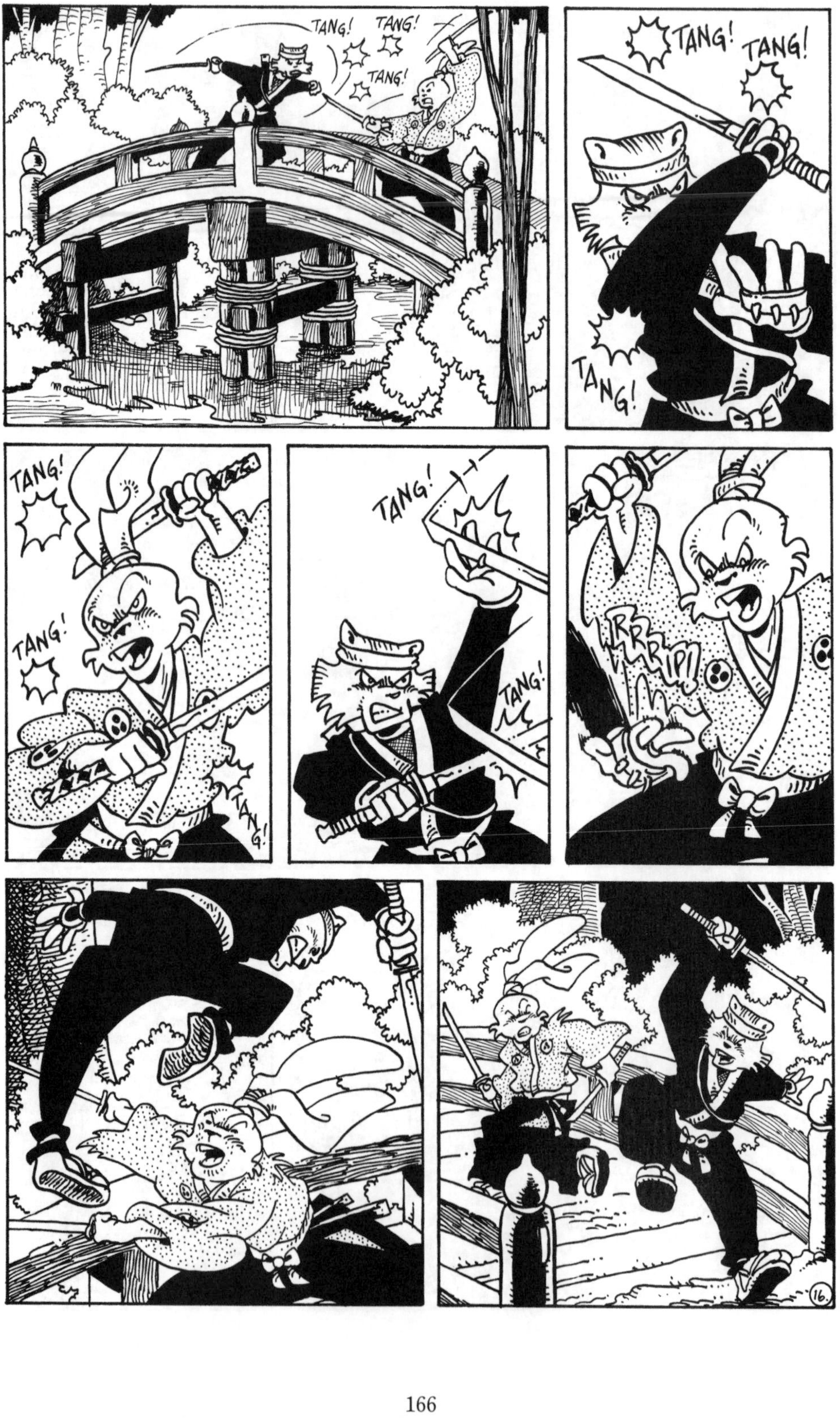
TANG!
TANG!
TANG!
TANG!
TANG!
TANG!
TANG!
TANG!
TANG!
TANG!
TANG!
TANG!
RRRRIP!
16.

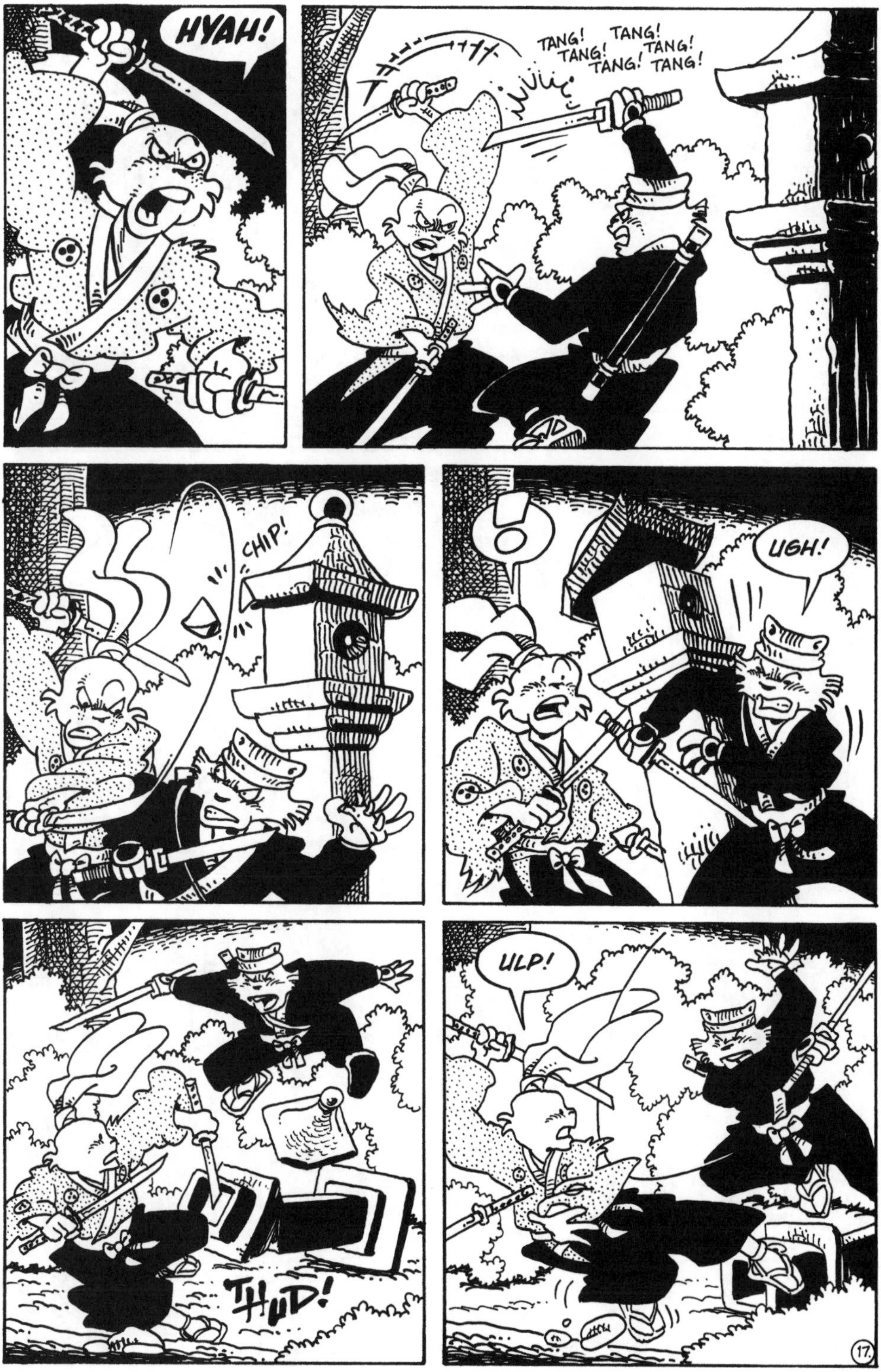
HYAH!
TANG! TANG! TANG! TANG! TANG! TANG!
CHIP!
!
UGH!
THUD!
ULP!
17

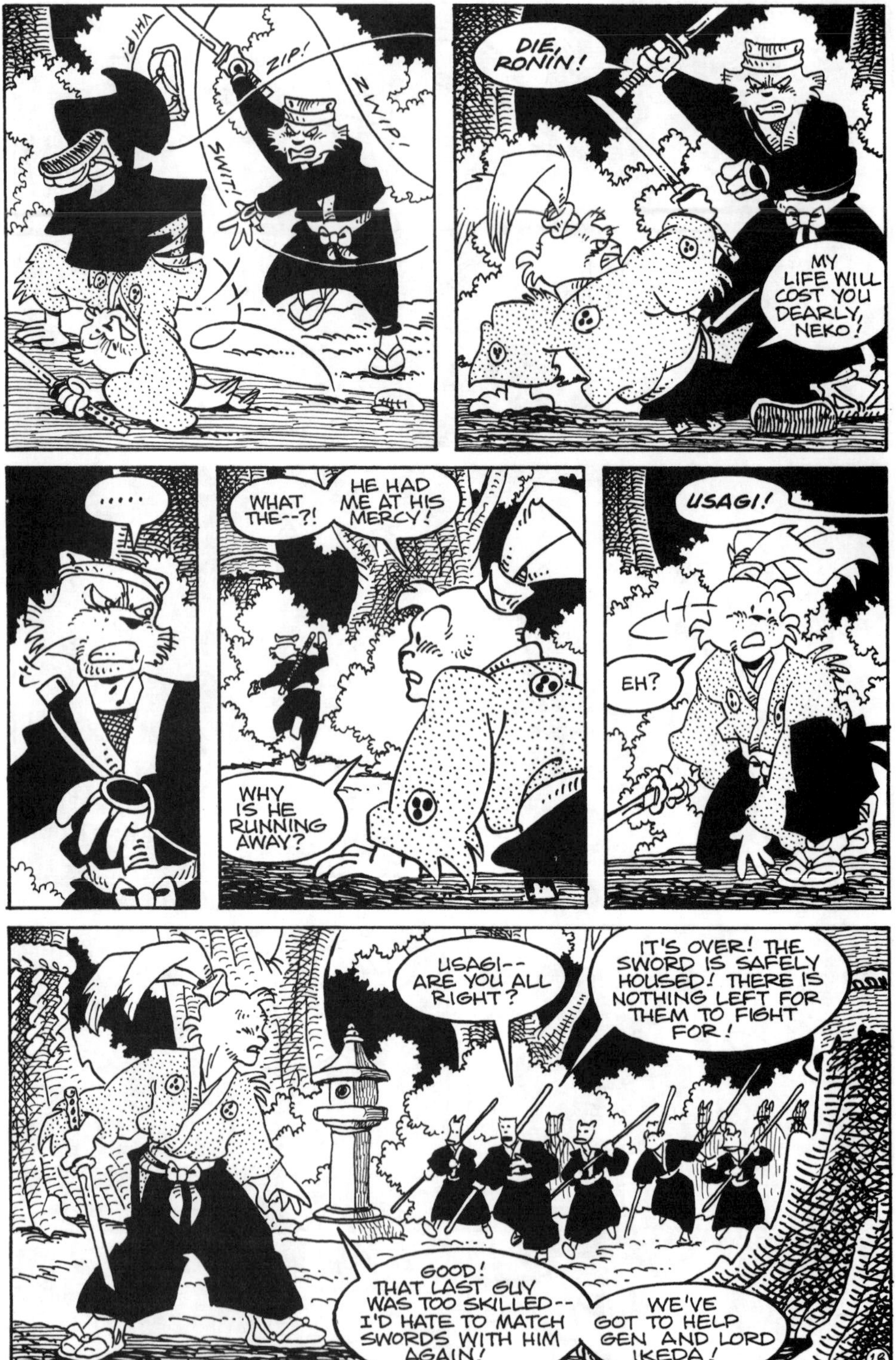
WHIP!
ZIP!
ZWIP!
SWIT!
DIE, RONIN!
MY LIFE WILL COST YOU DEARLY, NEKO!
.....
WHAT THE--?!
HE HAD ME AT HIS MERCY!
WHY IS HE RUNNING AWAY?
USAGI!
EH?
USAGI-- ARE YOU ALL RIGHT?
IT'S OVER! THE SWORD IS SAFELY HOUSED! THERE IS NOTHING LEFT FOR THEM TO FIGHT FOR!
GOOD! THAT LAST GUY WAS TOO SKILLED-- I'D HATE TO MATCH SWORDS WITH HIM AGAIN!
WE'VE GOT TO HELP GEN AND LORD IKEDA!
18

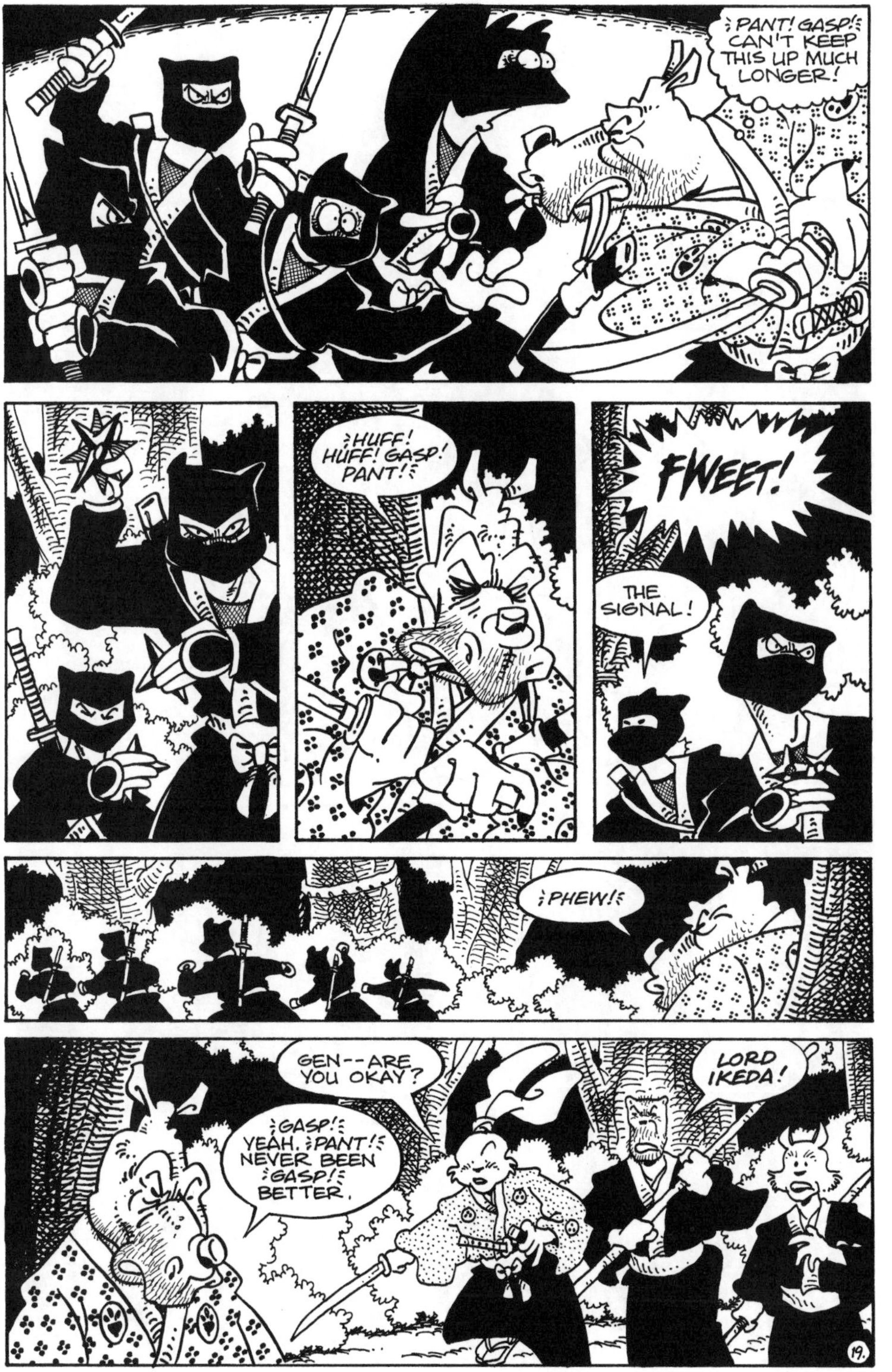
PANT! GASP! CAN'T KEEP THIS UP MUCH LONGER!
HUFF! HUFF! GASP! PANT!
FWEET!
THE SIGNAL!
PHEW!
GEN--ARE YOU OKAY?
LORD IKEDA!
GASP! YEAH. PANT! NEVER BEEN GASP! BETTER.
19.

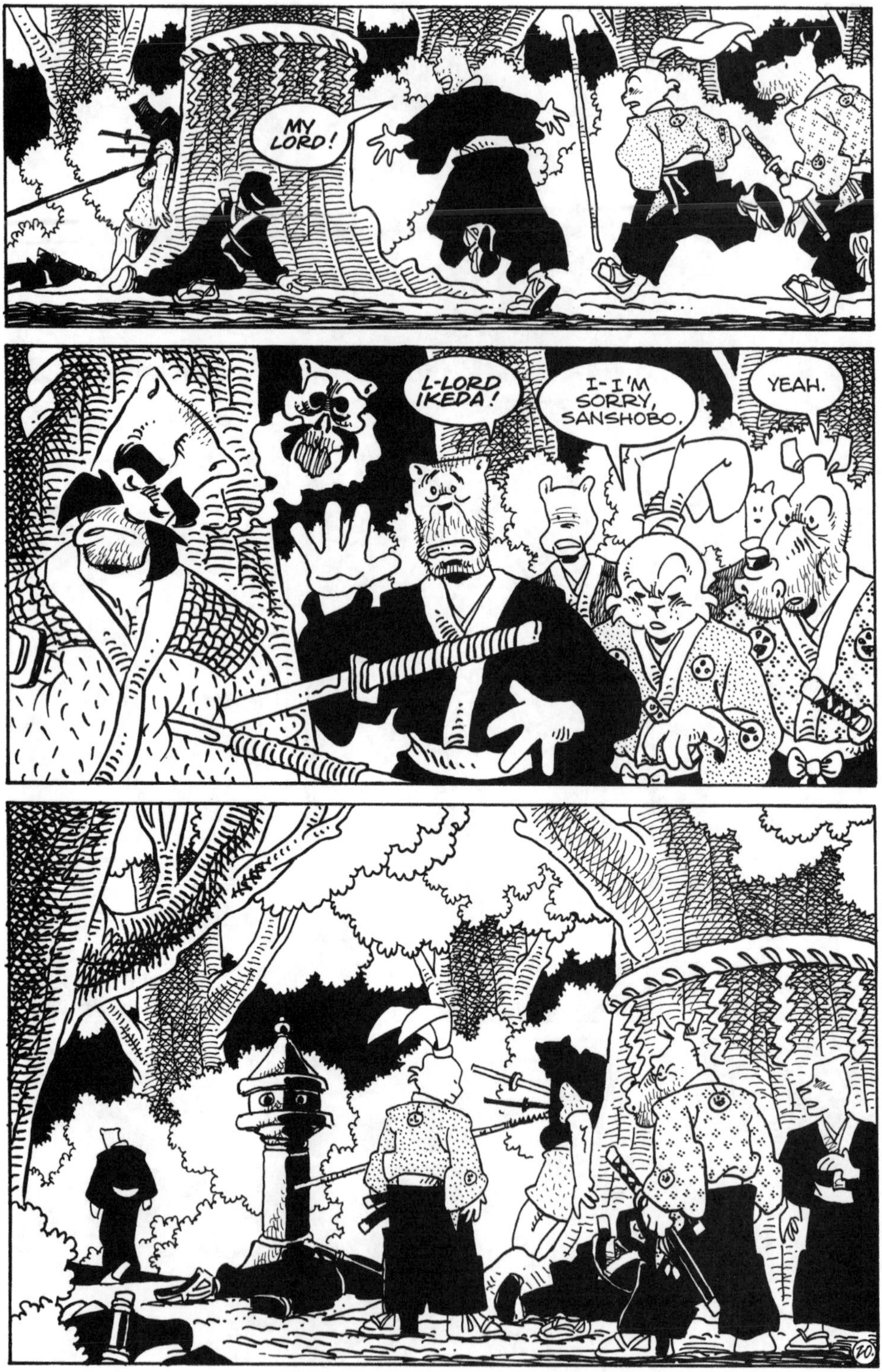
MY LORD!
L-LORD IKEDA!
I-I'M SORRY, SANSHOBO.
YEAH.
20.

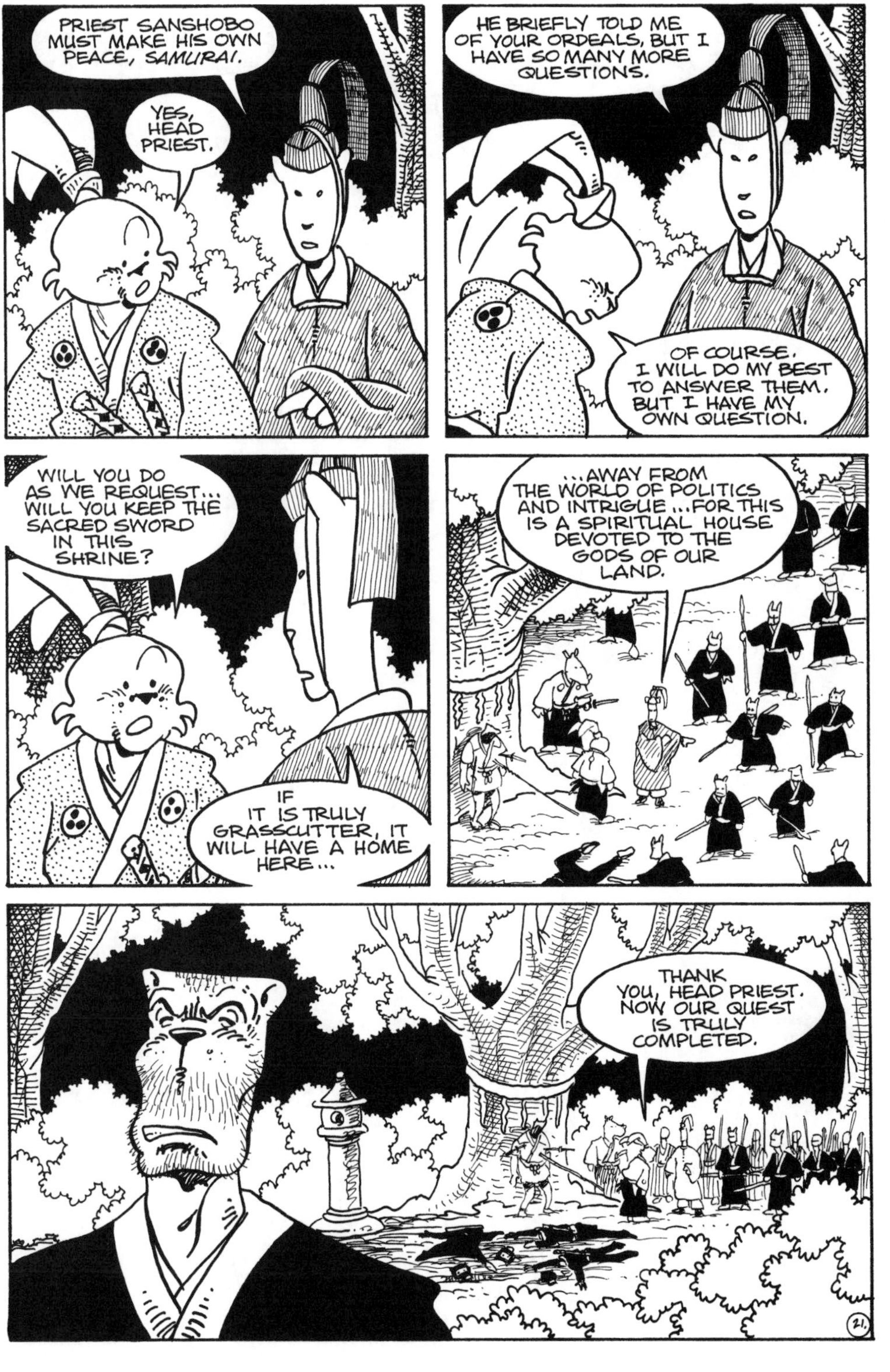
PRIEST SANSHOBO MUST MAKE HIS OWN PEACE, SAMURAI.
YES, HEAD PRIEST.
HE BRIEFLY TOLD ME OF YOUR ORDEALS, BUT I HAVE SO MANY MORE QUESTIONS.
OF COURSE. I WILL DO MY BEST TO ANSWER THEM. BUT I HAVE MY OWN QUESTION.
WILL YOU DO AS WE REQUEST... WILL YOU KEEP THE SACRED SWORD IN THIS SHRINE?
IF IT IS TRULY GRASSCUTTER, IT WILL HAVE A HOME HERE...
...AWAY FROM THE WORLD OF POLITICS AND INTRIGUE...FOR THIS IS A SPIRITUAL HOUSE DEVOTED TO THE GODS OF OUR LAND.
THANK YOU, HEAD PRIEST. NOW OUR QUEST IS TRULY COMPLETED.
21.

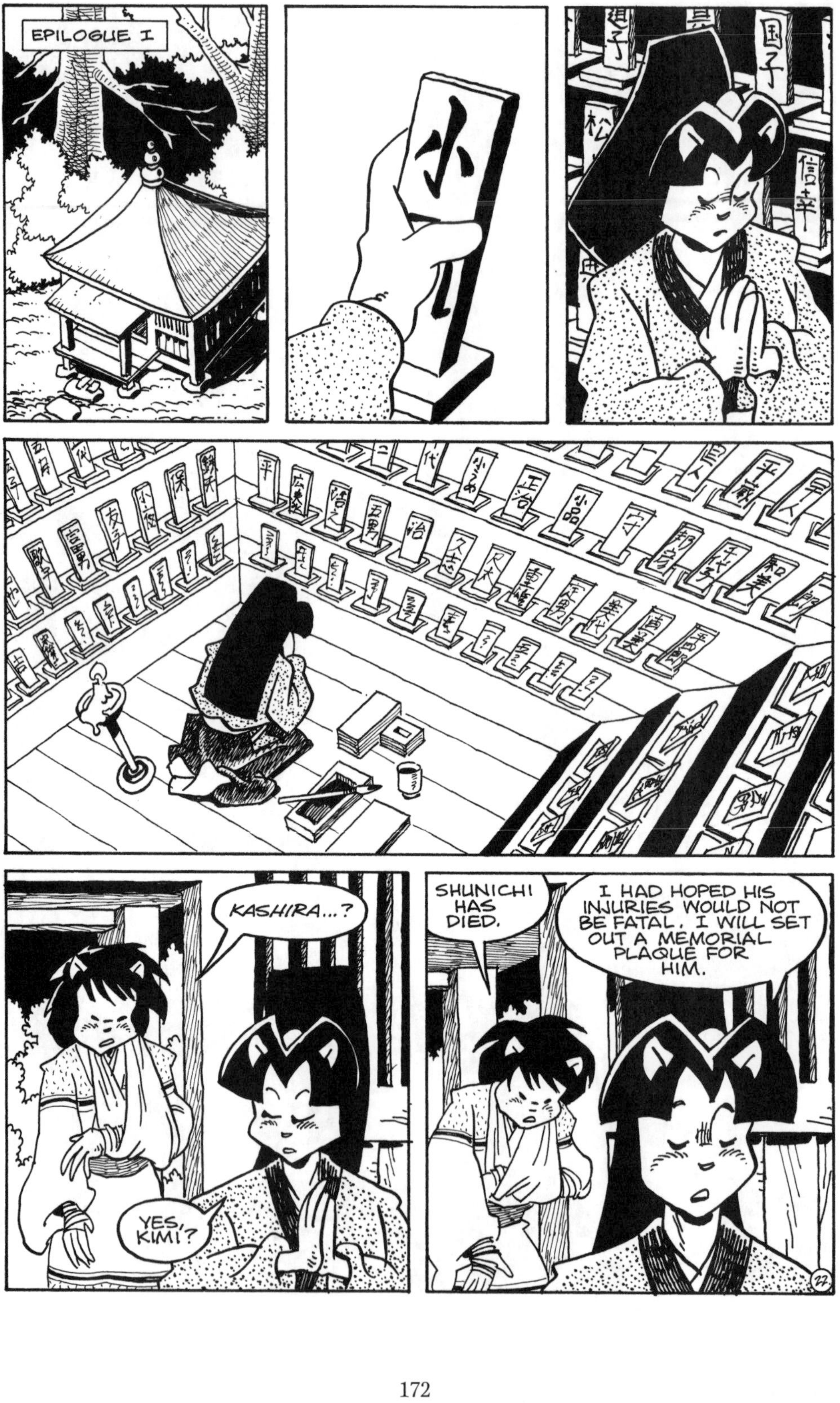
EPILOGUE I
KASHIRA...?
YES, KIMI?
SHUNICHI HAS DIED.
I HAD HOPED HIS INJURIES WOULD NOT BE FATAL. I WILL SET OUT A MEMORIAL PLAQUE FOR HIM.

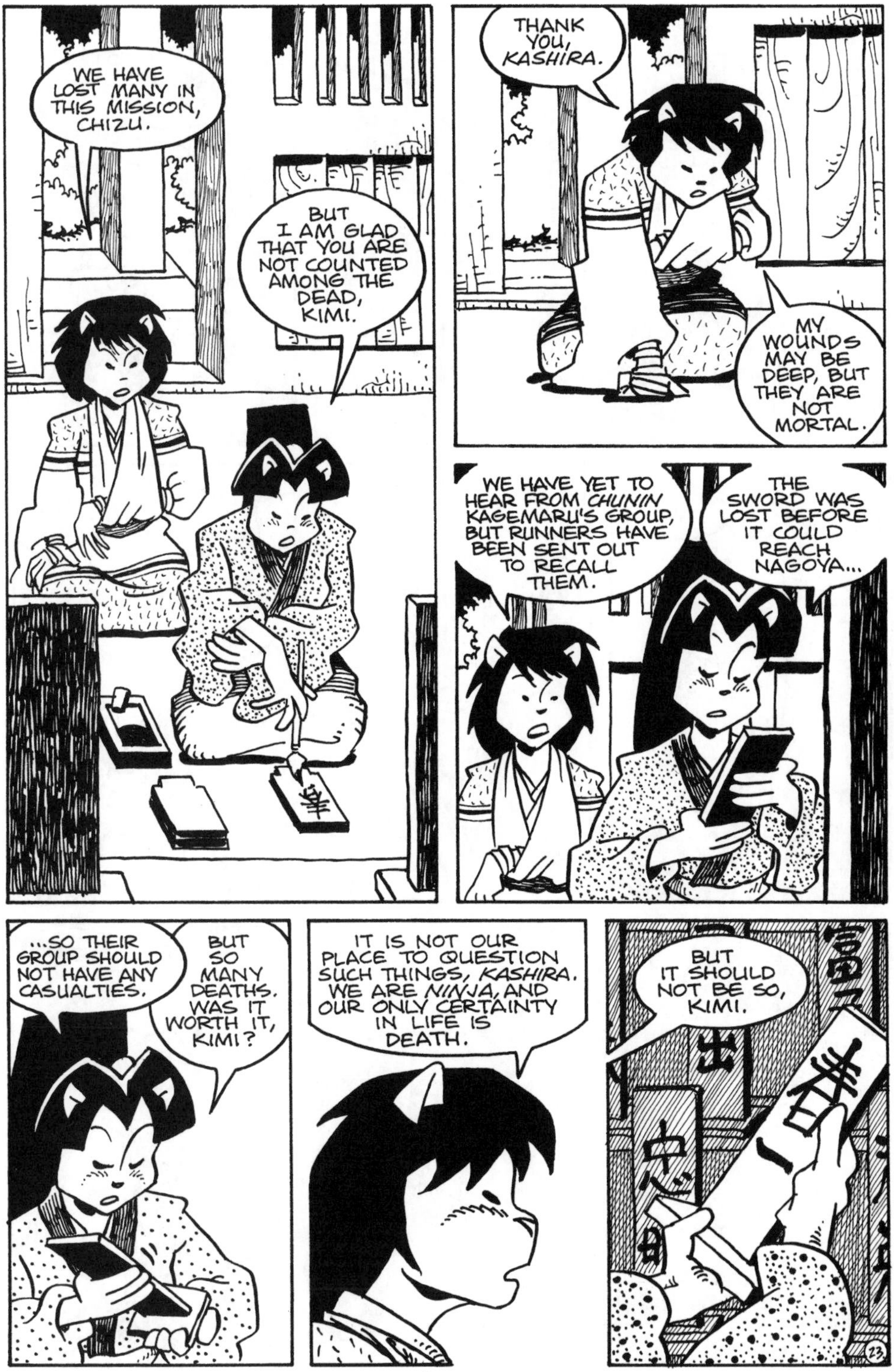
WE HAVE LOST MANY IN THIS MISSION, CHIZU.
BUT I AM GLAD THAT YOU ARE NOT COUNTED AMONG THE DEAD, KIMI.
THANK YOU, KASHIRA.
MY WOUNDS MAY BE DEEP, BUT THEY ARE NOT MORTAL.
WE HAVE YET TO HEAR FROM CHUNIN KAGEMARU'S GROUP, BUT RUNNERS HAVE BEEN SENT OUT TO RECALL THEM.
THE SWORD WAS LOST BEFORE IT COULD REACH NAGOYA...
...SO THEIR GROUP SHOULD NOT HAVE ANY CASUALTIES.
BUT SO MANY DEATHS. WAS IT WORTH IT, KIMI?
IT IS NOT OUR PLACE TO QUESTION SUCH THINGS, KASHIRA. WE ARE NINJA, AND OUR ONLY CERTAINTY IN LIFE IS DEATH.
BUT IT SHOULD NOT BE SO, KIMI.
23

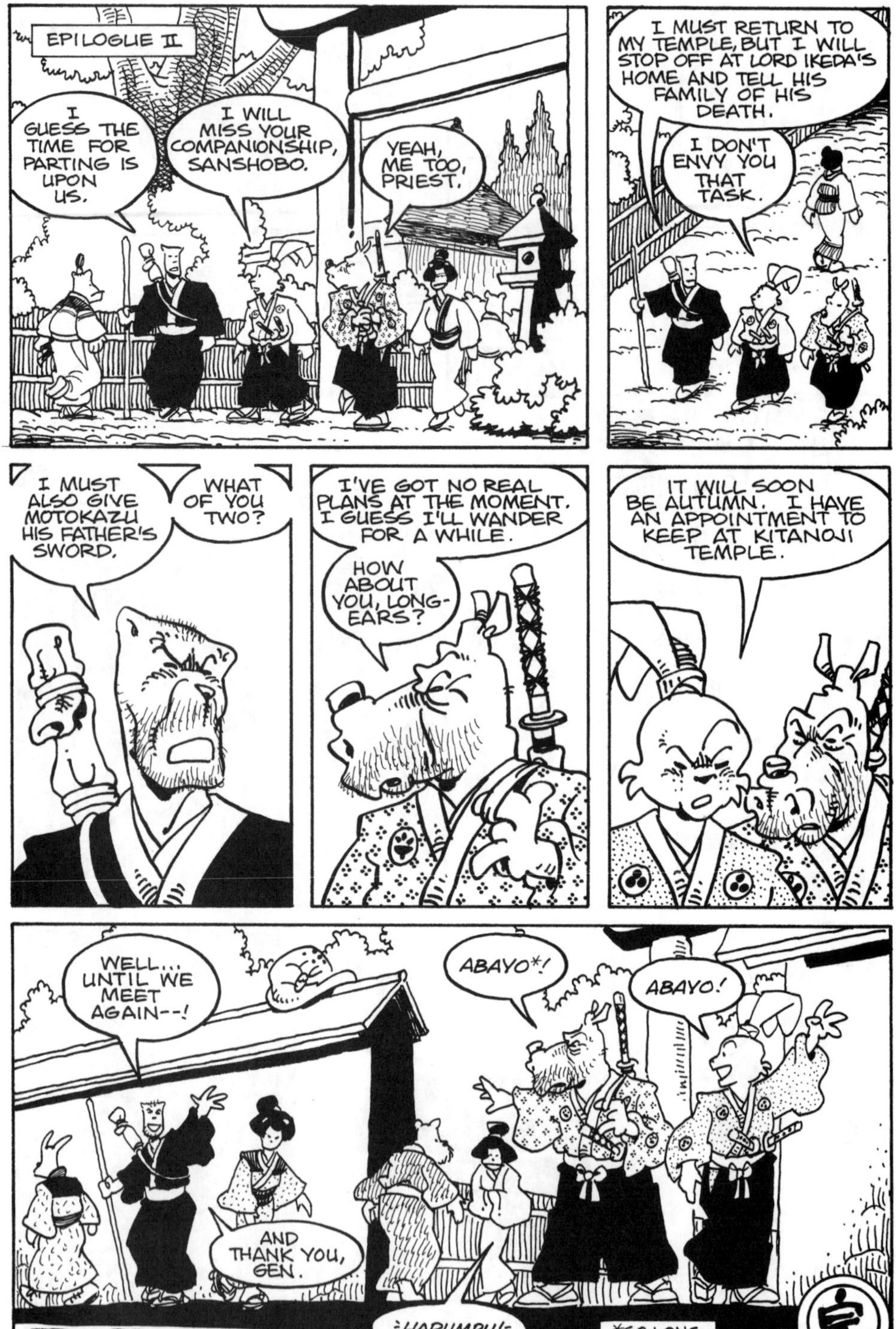
EPILOGUE II
I GUESS THE TIME FOR PARTING IS UPON US.
I WILL MISS YOUR COMPANIONSHIP, SANSHOBO.
YEAH, ME TOO, PRIEST.
I MUST RETURN TO MY TEMPLE, BUT I WILL STOP OFF AT LORD IKEDA'S HOME AND TELL HIS FAMILY OF HIS DEATH.
I DON'T ENVY YOU THAT TASK.
I MUST ALSO GIVE MOTOKAZU HIS FATHER'S SWORD.
WHAT OF YOU TWO?
I'VE GOT NO REAL PLANS AT THE MOMENT. I GUESS I'LL WANDER FOR A WHILE.
HOW ABOUT YOU, LONG-EARS?
IT WILL SOON BE AUTUMN. I HAVE AN APPOINTMENT TO KEEP AT KITANOJI TEMPLE.
WELL... UNTIL WE MEET AGAIN--!
ABAYO*!
ABAYO!
AND THANK YOU, GEN.
HARUMPH!
*SO LONG
完

USAGI YOJIMBO

Grasscutter II Story Notes

The tenth emperor, Sujin, ascended to the throne in the first century B.C. By this time, society had developed to the point where a clear distinction had to be made between worldly and spiritual affairs. Sujin established a shrine at Kasanui Village in Yamato Province dedicated to Amaterasu, the Sun Goddess, and installed there the sacred mirror and sword. The emperor ordered replicas of them made, which he kept in the Imperial Palace.

His successor, Suinin, established a new shrine in Ise Province and transferred the mirror and sword and a third treasure, a jewel, to be housed there. His daughter was given charge of Ise Shrine.

Yamato-Dake is the most famous hero of legendary times. He was the third son of Emperor Keiko. He was initially named Wousu (Little Mortar) and had an elder twin named Oouso (Big Mortar), whom he killed before being sent to quell the Kumaso rebels at the age of sixteen.

Before the start of a later campaign, Yamato-Dake paid his respects to the Grand Shrine at Ise and was given the sword Ame no Murakumo no Tsurugi by his aunt. He renamed it Kusanagi no Tsurugi (The Grass-Cutting Sword) after it saved his life in an open field.

There are many variations of the story of Yamato-Dake and the Kami of Mt. Ibuki. In one, the hero is unable to slay either the boar or the snake but is repulsed from the mountain by a violent ice-rain, and later dies, seemingly from fatigue. In another, he goes to a hot spring after the killing of the serpent and regains his health and strength. The events I've recounted are probably the most familiar and are found

in *The Kojiki: Records of Ancient Matters*, the oldest history of the Japanese people, written in 712 A.D. by Yasumaro as dictated by Hiyeda no Are by order of Emperor Temmu.

The hot spring Yamato-Dake came to after meeting the *kami* is now called Isame no Shimizu, "Clear Water Where He Came to His Senses." The area where he could hardly stand is Tagino, or "Totter." And when exhaustion finally took him, he walked with a stick at Tsuetsuki-zake, or "Slope with a Walking Stick."

His consorts sang four songs at the prince's funeral. These four were sung at every emperor's death since, until the funeral of Emperor Meiji in 1912 A.D.

Atsuta Jingu is one of the three major shrines in Japan, along with the Meiji Shrine and the Grand Shrines at Ise. Atsuta is said to be the repository of Kusanagi no Tsurugi, the Grass-Cutting Sword, though some believe the original sword was lost in the Battle of Dan-No-Ura Strait during the Gempei War, in the 12th century.

The shrine grounds cover 190,000 square meters of thickly wooded area in the middle of Nagoya. Some of the trees there are over a thousand years old. The shrine is also home to sixty annual festivals and ten religious events, including the Atsuta Jingu Hono Tanren, a festival for swordsmiths.

Kusanagi is actually housed in the Honden, or main inner shrine, along with many other treasures. Only priests and *miko* (shrine maidens) are allowed to approach the Honden. A few historians believe that the sword kept at the shrine no longer exists, that it was destroyed in an Allied bombing raid in WWII. The present shrine was built on the old site in 1955.

References for Yamato-Dake came from: *The Kojiki*, translated by Basil Hall Chamberlain, published in 1981 by Charles E. Tuttle Co. of Rutland, VT, and Tokyo, Japan; *Legends of the Samurai* by Hiroyuki Sato, 1995, Overlook Press of Woodstock, NY; *Myths and Legends of Japan* by F. Hadland Davis, 1992, Dover Publications of Mineola, NY; *The Japanese Fairy Book*, compiled by Yei Theodora Ozaki, 1970, Charles E. Tuttle Co.; *Myths and Legends Series: China and Japan* by Donald A. Mackenzie, 1985, Bracken Books of London; *History of the Japanese from the Earliest Times to the End of the Meiji Era* by Capt. F. Brinkley, 1915, Encyclopedia Britannica Co. of NY; and *Japan, a Country Founded by "Mother": An Outline History* by Hajime Hoshi, 1937, Columbia University Club in Tokyo, Japan.

References for the Japanese culture during that era came from: *Early Samurai: 200-1500 A.D.* by Anthony Bryant and Angus McBride, 1991, Osprey Press of Great Britain; *The Atlas of Japanese Culture* by Martin Collcutt, Marius Jansen, and Isao Kumakura, 1988, Facts on File Inc., of NY; and *Step*

into Ancient Japan by Fiona MacDonald, 1999, Anness Publishing Ltd. of NY.

References for Chapter 6, "In the Realm of Senses," came from: *Japan: A Country Founded by "Mother"* by Hajime Hoshi, 1937, published by the Columbia University Club in Tokyo; *The Japan Handbook* by J.D. Bisignani, 1983, Moon Publications of Chico, CA; reference for the *kannushi* was found in *A Look into Japan*, published in 1985 by the Japan Travel Bureau, Inc.; and additional reference came from the Nagoya Visitors Guide, the Live Map of Nagoya, and the Sightseeing Spot Guide to Nagoya and Inuyama, published by the Nagoya Convention and Visitors Bureau. I would also like to acknowledge the help of the Usagi Yojimbo Dojo web site members, who scoured the Internet for visuals and information on Atsuta Shrine.

Gallery

Stan Sakai's cover art from issues thirty-nine through forty-five of Dark Horse's Usagi Yojimbo Volume Three *series.*

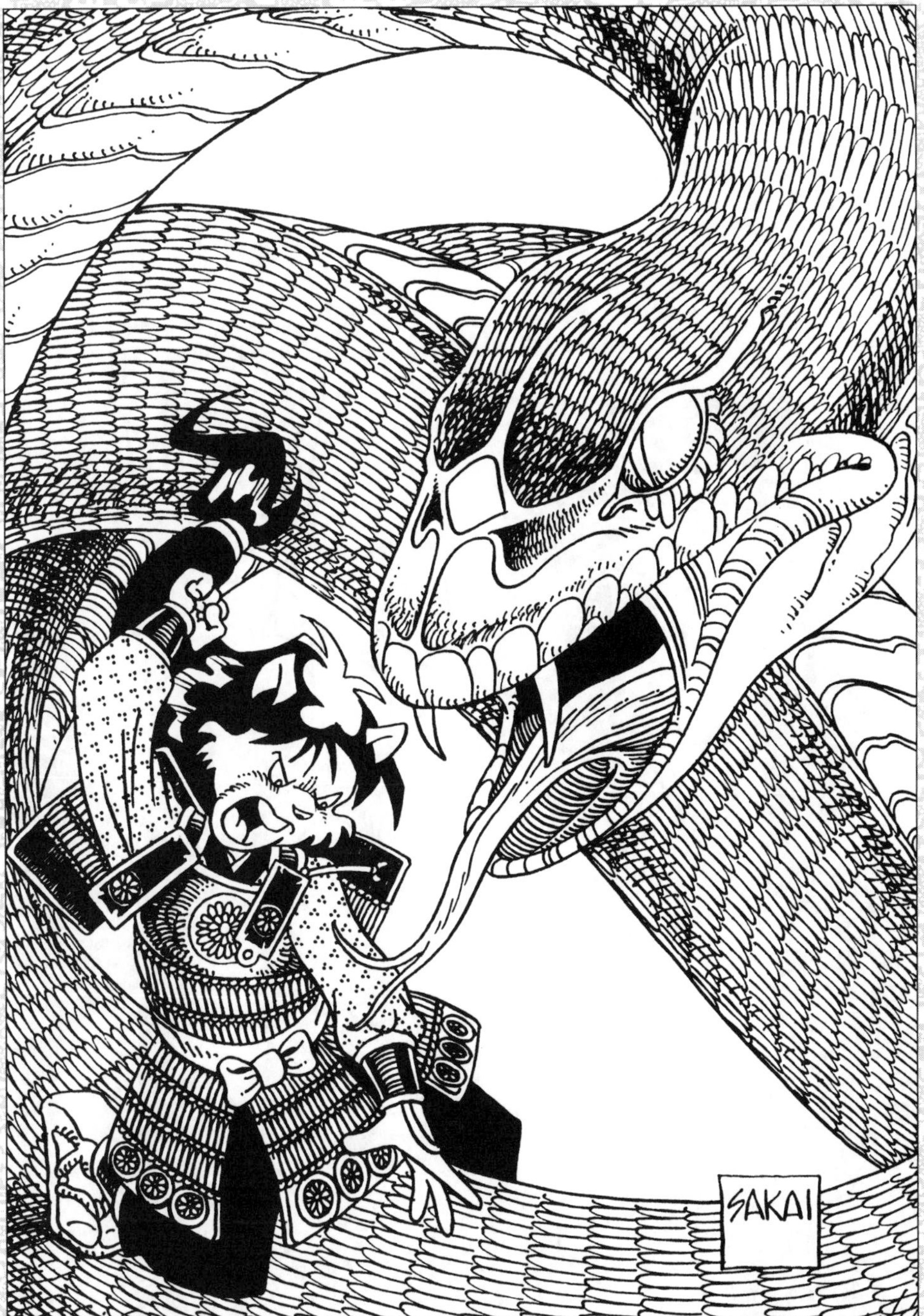
SAKAI

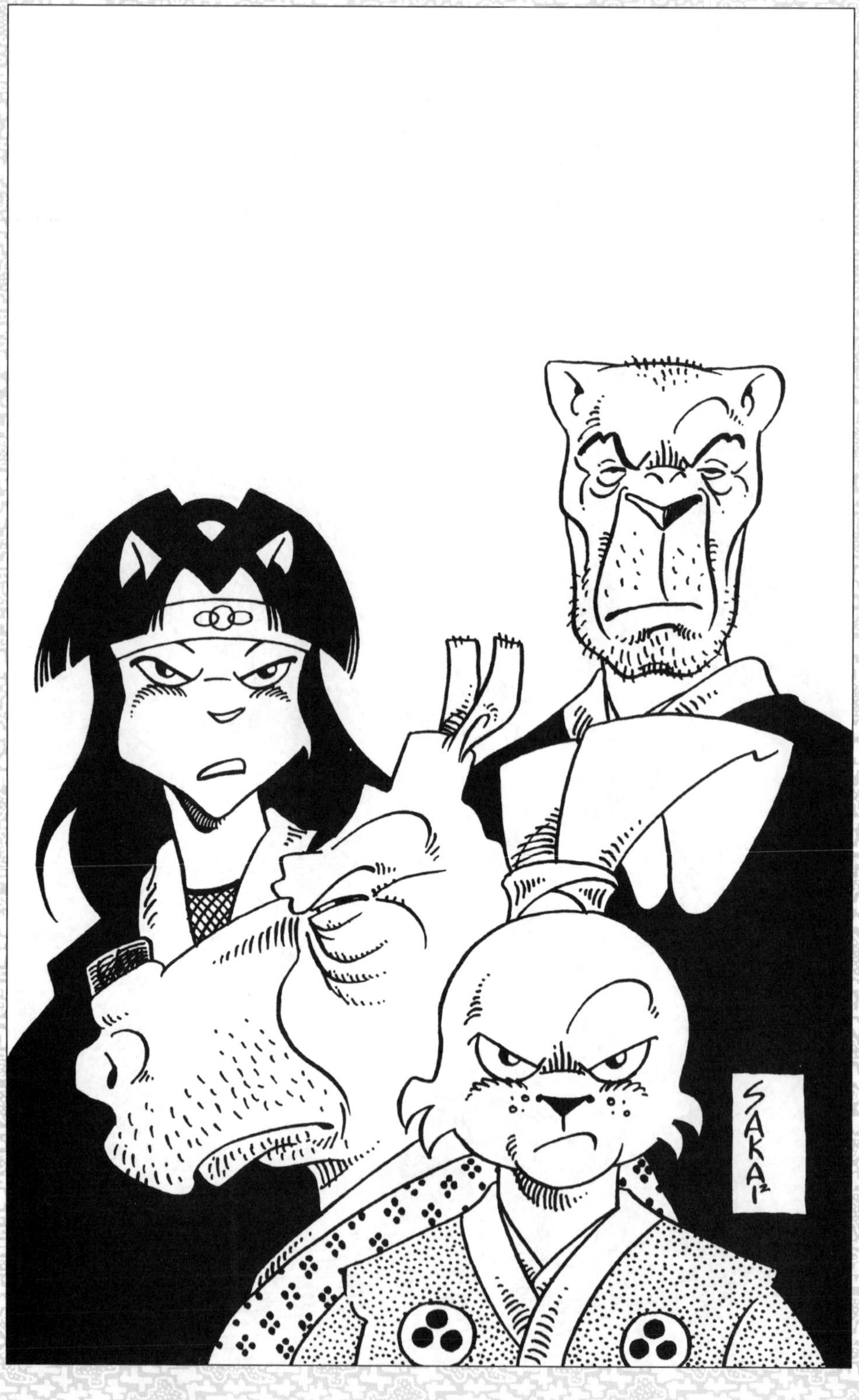
SAKAI

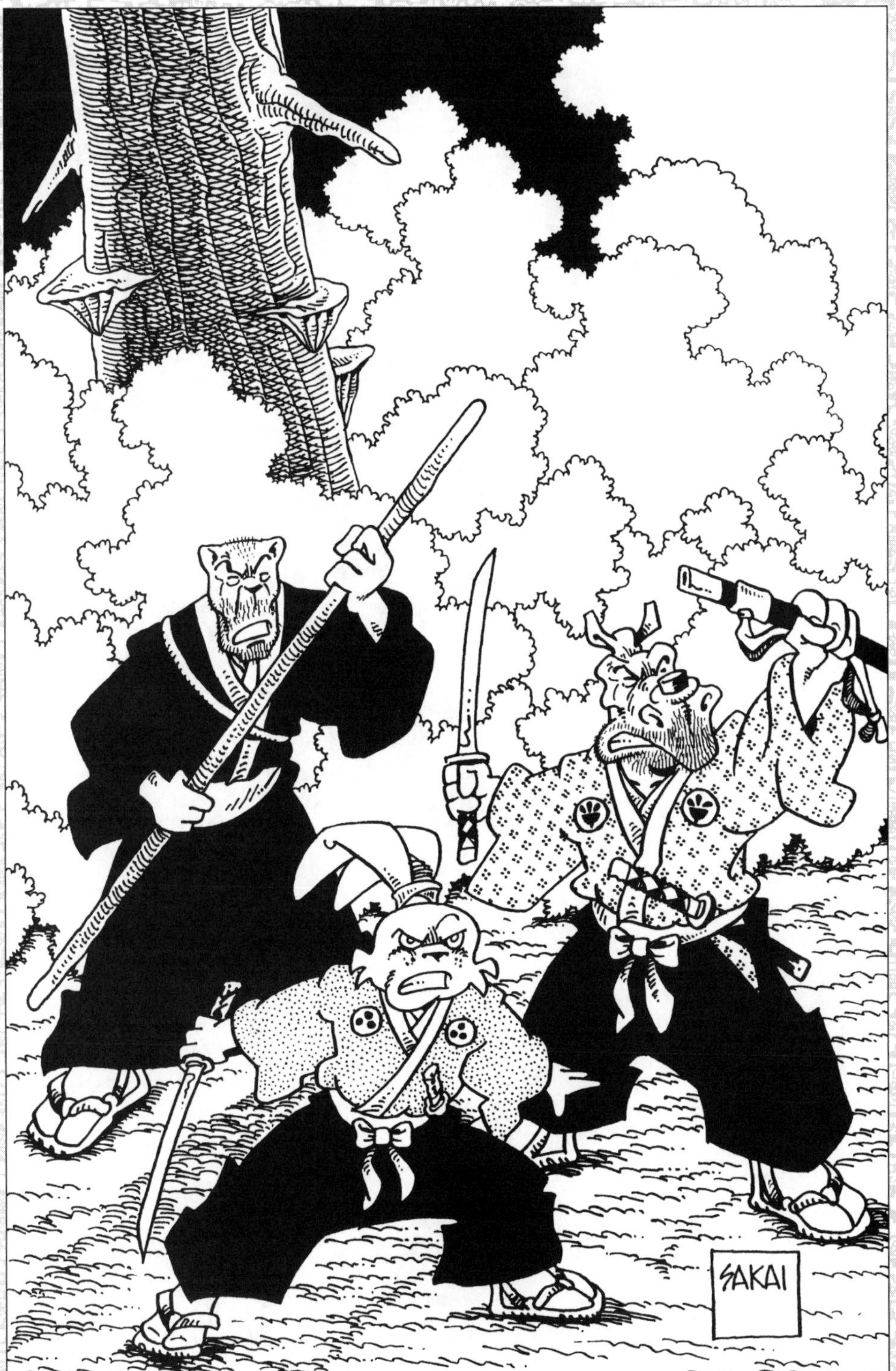
SAKAI

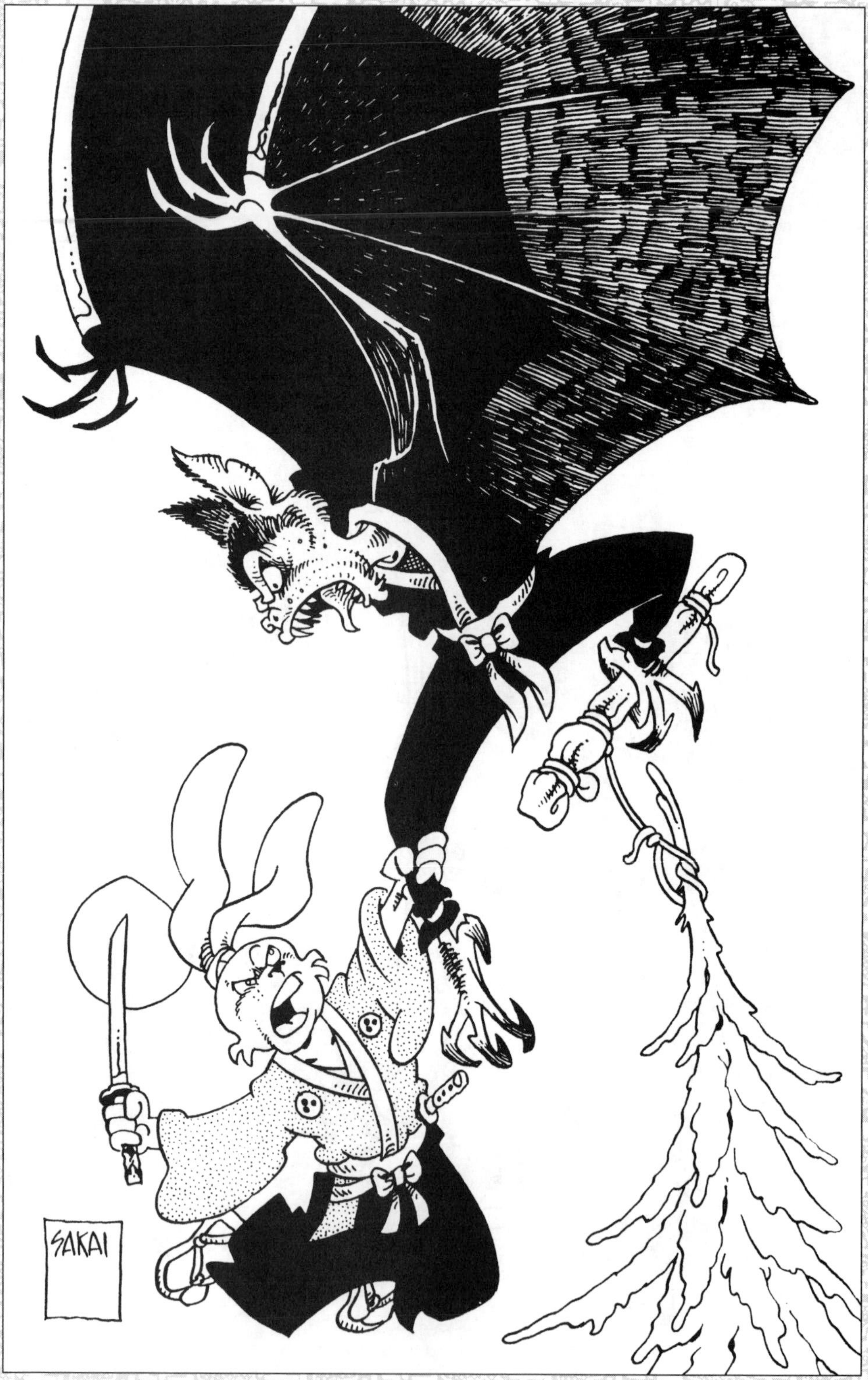
SAKAI

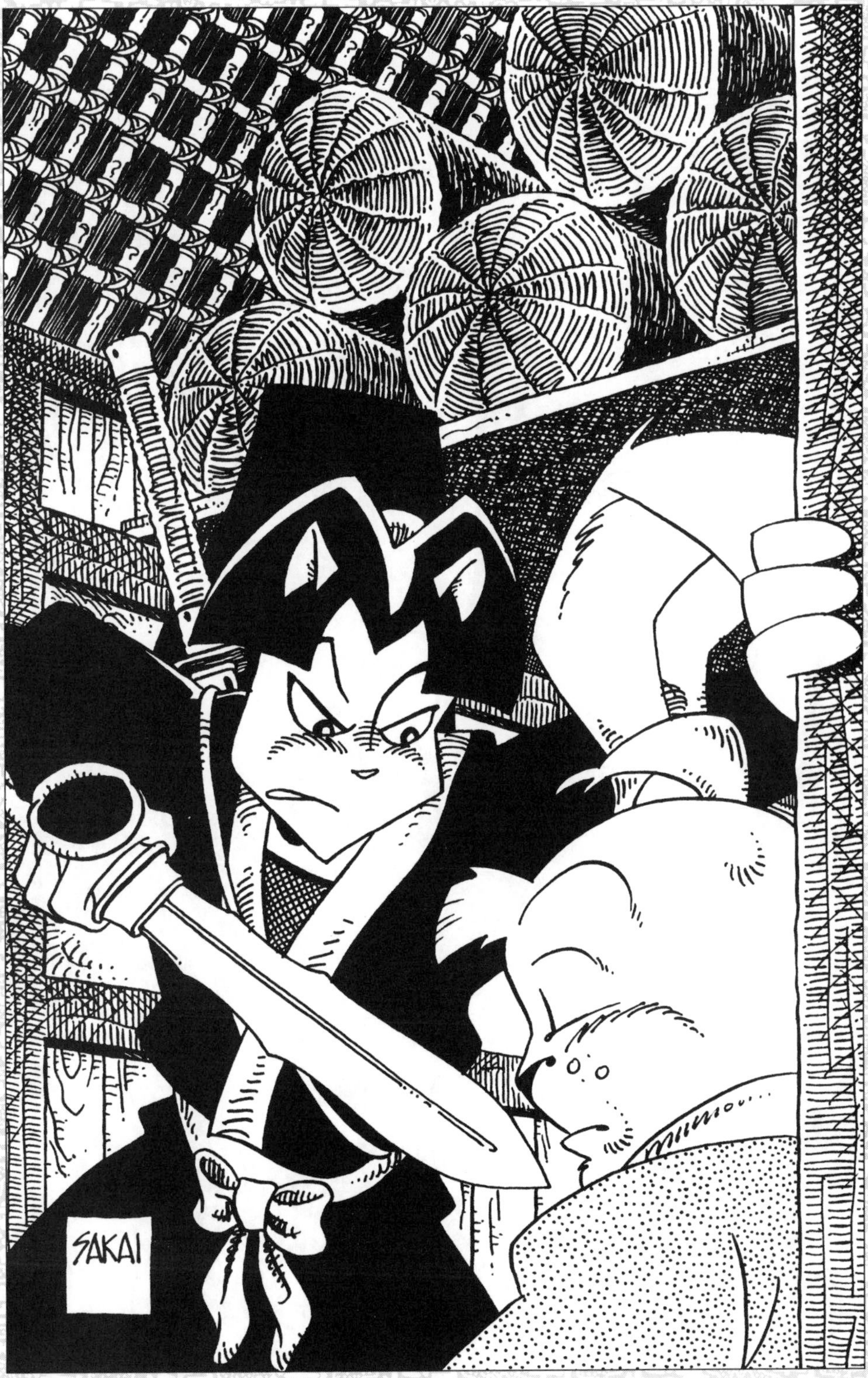
SAKAI

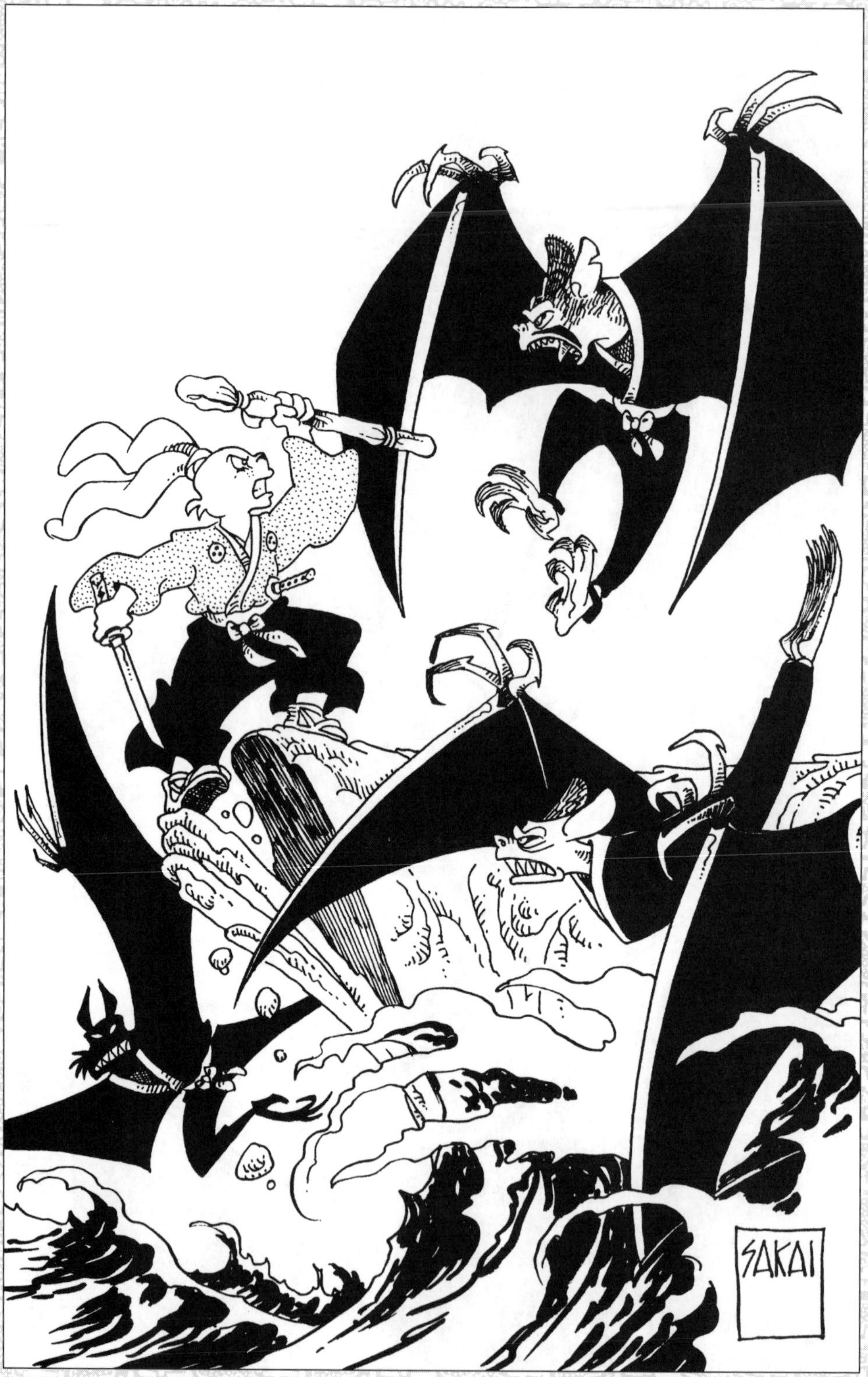
SAKAI

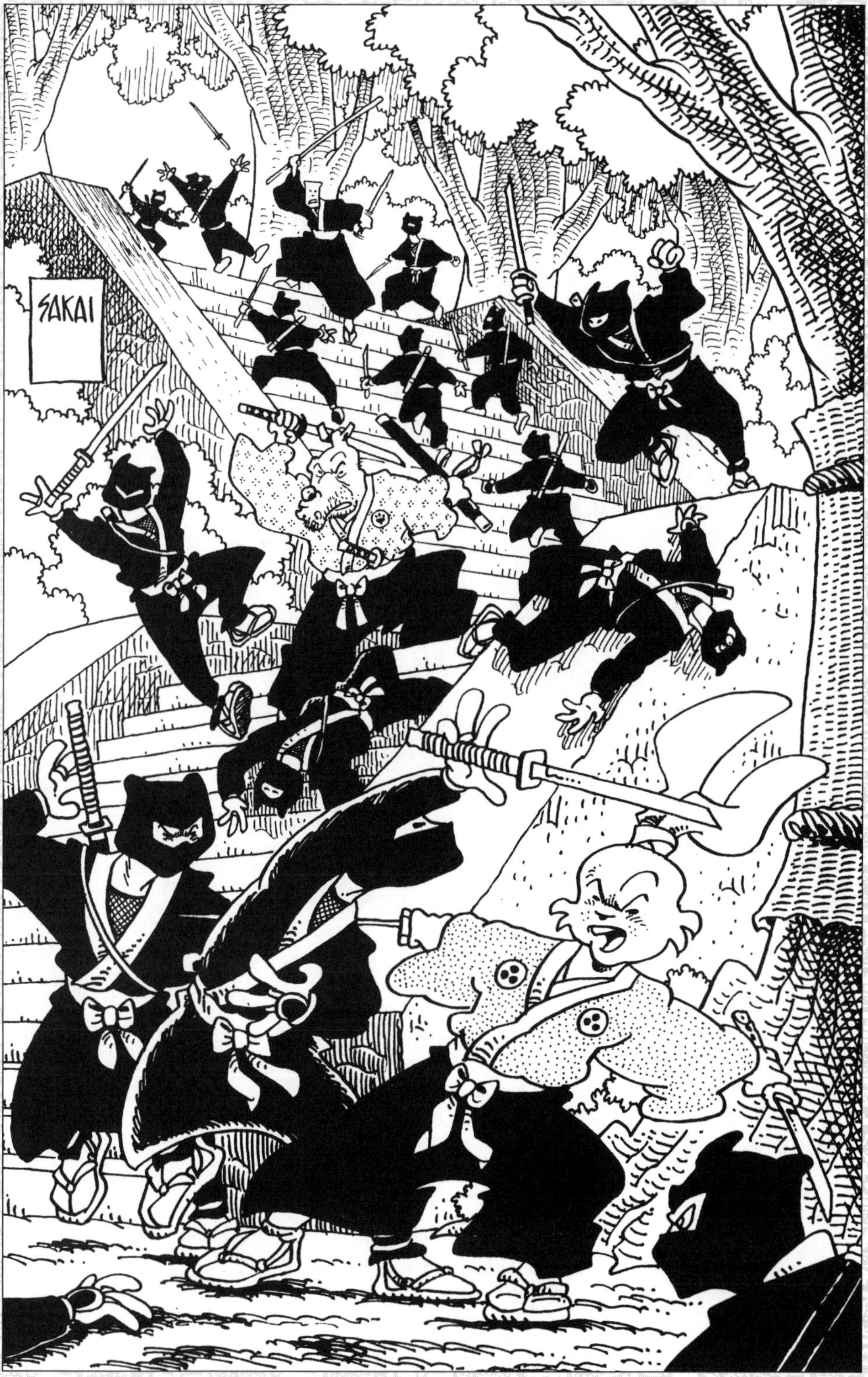
SAKAI

BIOGRAPHY

Stan Sakai

Stan Sakai in Gijon, Spain

Photo by Sharon Sakai

STAN SAKAI WAS BORN in Kyoto, Japan, grew up in Hawaii, and now lives in California with his wife, Sharon, and children, Hannah and Matthew. He received a Fine Arts degree from the University of Hawaii and furthered his studies at Art Center College of Design in Pasadena, California.

His creation, Usagi Yojimbo, first appeared in comics in 1984. Since then, Usagi has been on television as a guest of the Teenage Mutant Ninja Turtles and has been made into toys, seen on clothing, and featured in a series of trade-paperback collections.

In 1991, Stan created *Space Usagi*, a series about the adventures of a descendant of the original Usagi that dealt with samurai in a futuristic setting.

Stan is also an award-winning letterer for his work on Sergio Aragonés' *Groo*, the "Spider-Man" Sunday newspaper strips, and *Usagi Yojimbo*.

Stan is a recipient of a Parents' Choice Award, an Inkpot Award, two Haxtur Awards, and multiple Eisner Awards.